EVERYDAY LIFE
IN EGYPT

Plate I   Ramesses the Great

EVERYDAY LIFE
IN EGYPT

in the days of Ramesses the Great

By
PIERRE MONTET

Translated by
A. R. MAXWELL-HYSLOP
and
MARGARET S. DROWER
Senior Lecturer in Ancient History
University College, University of London

GREENWOOD PRESS, PUBLISHERS
WESTPORT, CONNECTICUT

Library of Congress Cataloging in Publication Data

Montet, Pierre, 1885-1966.
    Everyday life in Egypt in the days of Ramesses the
Great.

    Translation of La vie quotidienne en Egypt au temps
des Ramses.
    Reprint of the ed. published by E. Arnold, London.
    Bibliography: p.
    1. Egypt--Social life and customs. I. Title.
DT61.M6313 1974   913.32'031   74-3625
ISBN 0-8371-7446-5

First published 1958 by Edward Arnold (Publishers) Ltd.,
London

Reprinted with the permission of St. Martin's Press, Inc.

Reprinted in 1974 by Greenwood Press,
a division of Williamhouse-Regency Inc.

Library of Congress Catalog Card Number 74-3625

ISBN 0-8371-7446-5

Printed in the United States of America

TRANSLATORS' FOREWORD

ANY description of even a comparatively limited period in the history of a country so well documented and so carefully studied as Egypt, and especially one in which future excavation is constantly yielding fresh evidence, is bound to contain room for some differences of emphasis and for the periodical revaluation of previously accepted views. In our translation we have followed strictly the French text of Professor Montet, the *doyen* of modern Egyptologists, adding only such footnotes as seemed likely to be helpful to English readers.

The transliteration of Egyptian proper names is always a source of difficulty and admits of no absolute consistency. The reader must realize that we do not know how ancient Egyptian was vocalized or pronounced; and any attempt at transliteration can therefore be no more than guesswork. Some proper names have been altered so as to make them conform to the common practice of English Egyptologists or render them more easily pronounceable by English readers. In general we have followed the principle of giving Greek forms of names to the better-known Pharaohs (e.g. Amenophis, Tuthmosis, Sesostris), and leaving the rest in a form representing a possible transliteration.

We have made a number of additions to the French edition, namely a chronological table based upon the Egyptian chronology of M. M. Drioton and Vandier, a map, a glossary of Egyptological terms which are likely to be unfamiliar to the general reader, a short selection of general works and an index. We have also added to or altered the list of references either in order to supplement or to supersede what has been written before or where an English translation exists of a book cited in the French version.

Finally we should like to thank Sir Gavin de Beer, F.R.S., F.S.A., Director of the British Museum of Natural History, for his help in identifying various Egyptian fishes, and Mrs. Maxwell-Hyslop, Lecturer in the Department of Western Asiatic Archaeology in the Institute of Archaeology, for her advice on references to Egyptian weapons.

A. R. MAXWELL-HYSLOP
MARGARET S. DROWER

v

ἔρχομαι δὲ περὶ Αἰγύπτου μηκυνέων τὸν λόγον, ὅτι πλεῖστα θωμάτια ἔχει ἤ ἡ ἄλλη πᾶσα χώρη καὶ ἔργα λόγου μέζω παρέχεται πρὸς πᾶσαν χώρην. τούτων εἵνεκα πλέω περὶ αυτῆς εἰρήσεται.

"Concerning Egypt itself I shall extend my remarks to a great length, because there is no country that possesses so many wonders, nor any that has such a number of works which defy description."

Herodotus, II, 35 : tr. G. Rawlinson.

CONTENTS

ACKNOWLEDGMENT

Grateful acknowledgment is made to the Egypt Exploration Society for permission to reproduce many of the illustrations in this book.

PLATES

DRAWINGS IN THE TEXT

CHRONOLOGICAL TABLE

(The dates given here must be regarded as approximate only)

ARCHAIC PERIOD	1st Dynasty } 2nd Dynasty }	3000–2780 B.C.
OLD KINGDOM	3rd Dynasty 4th Dynasty 5th Dynasty 6th Dynasty	2780–2720 B.C. 2720–2560 B.C. 2560–2420 B.C. 2420–2260 B.C.
FIRST INTERMEDIATE PERIOD	7th to 10th Dynasties	2260–2040 B.C.
MIDDLE KINGDOM	11th Dynasty 12th Dynasty	2160–2000 B.C. 2000–1785 B.C.
SECOND INTERMEDIATE PERIOD	13th, 14th and 17th Dynasties [Hyksos 15th and 16th Dynasties	1785–1580 B.C. 1730–1580 B.C.]
NEW KINGDOM (see below)	18th, 19th and 20th Dynasties	1580–1085 B.C.
DIVIDED KINGDOM AND LIBYAN EPOCH	21st to 24th Dynasties	1085– 715 B.C.
LATE PERIOD	25th Dynasty (Ethiopian) [Assyrian domination 671–669, 666–?660 B.C.] 26th Dynasty (Saite) Persian Domination [28th to 30th Dynasties	730– 656 B.C. 666–?660 B.C.] 663– 525 B.C. 525– 333 B.C. 404– 341 B.C.]

THE NEW KINGDOM OR NEW EMPIRE

Eighteenth Dynasty		*The Ramessids**	
Ahmosé I	1580–1558 B.C.	*Nineteenth Dynasty*	
Amenophis I	1558–1530 B.C.	Ramesses I	1314–1312 B.C.
Tuthmosis I	1530–1520 B.C.	Sety I	1312–1298 B.C.
Tuthmosis II } Hatshepsut }	1520–1484 B.C.	Ramesses II	1298–1235 B.C.
Tuthmosis III	1504–1450 B.C.	Merenptah	1235–1224 B.C.
Amenophis II	1450–1425 B.C.	(5 more)	1224–1200 B.C.
Tuthmosis IV	1425–1408 B.C.		
Amenophis III	1408–1372 B.C.	*Twentieth Dynasty*	
Amenophis IV (Akhnaton)	1372–1354 B.C.	Set-nakht	1200–1198 B.C.
Tutankhamūn } Ay } Horonemheb }	1354–1314 B.C.	Ramesses III Ramesses IV Ramesses V to XI	1198–1166 B.C. 1166–1160 B.C. 1160–1090 B.C.

*Some scholars reduce Ramesside dates by about twenty years.

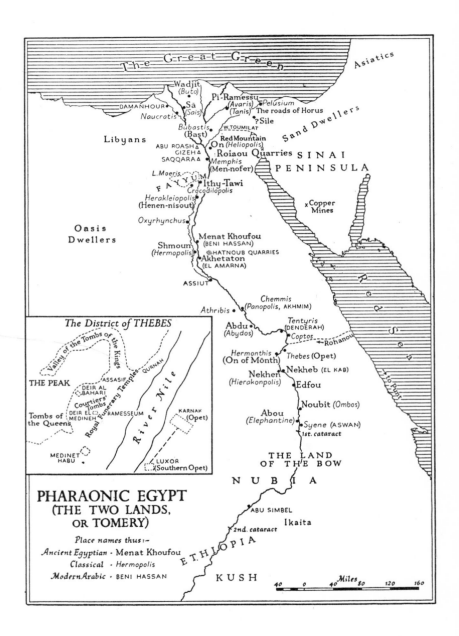

The District of THEBES

Valley of the Tombs of the Kings

THE PEAK

ASSASIFS
DEIR AL BAHARI
QURNAH

Courtiers' Tombs

DEIR EL MEDINEH
RAMESSEUM

Royal Funerary Temples

Tombs of the Queens

MEDINET HABU

KARNAK
(Opet)

River Nile

LUXOR
(Southern Opet)

The Great Green

Asiatics

Wadjit (Buto)

Pi-Ramessu (Avaris) (Tanis)

Pelusium

The roads of Horus

?Sile

DAMANHOUR

Sā (Sais)

Naucratis

Bubastis (Bast)

W. TOUMILAT

Sand Dwellers

Libyans

ABU ROASH
GIZEH
SAQQARA

Red Mountain

On (Heliopolis)

Roiaou Quarries

Memphis (Men-nofer)

SINAI PENINSULA

L. Moeris

FAYYUM

Ithy-Tawi

Crocodilopolis

Herakleiopolis (Henen-nisout)

Oxyrhynchus

Oasis Dwellers

x Copper Mines

Menat Khoufou (BENI HASSAN)

Shmoun (Hermopolis)

HATNOUB QUARRIES

Akhetaton (EL AMARNA)

ASSIUT

Chemmis (Panopolis, AKHMIM)

Athribis

Abdu (Abydos)

Tentyris (DENDERAH)

Coptos

Rohanou

Hermonthis (On of Month)

Thebes (Opet)

Nekhen (Hierakonpolis)

Nekheb (EL KAB)

Edfou

Noubit (Ombos)

Abou (Elephantine)

Syene (ASWAN)

1st. cataract

THE LAND OF THE BOW

N U B I A

ABU SIMBEL

Ikaita

2nd. cataract

E T H I O P I A

KUSH

Red Sea

To Punt

PHARAONIC EGYPT
(THE TWO LANDS, OR TOMERY)

Place names thus:–
Ancient Egyptian · Menat Khoufou
Classical · Hermopolis
Modern Arabic · BENI HASSAN

Miles
40   0   40   80   120   160

INTRODUCTION

THE ancient Egyptians set themselves far higher standards of service for the gods and the dead than for their own benefit. When they came to build a new 'house of a million years'* or to construct, west of Thebes, 'their houses of eternity'† nothing could ever be too beautiful or too durable for their purpose, and they held distance and expense of no account in their search for stone, metal or wood of the finest quality. Yet in their own houses of unbaked brick painted imitations of stone and metal served for genuine materials. This is why their temples and tombs have outlasted their towns to such a degree that our museums contain more sarcophagi and stelae, more statues of gods and kings, than objects made for use by the living, and more rituals and 'books of the dead' than memoirs and works of fiction. In the face of such handicaps, our task in attempting to describe the everyday life of the common man under the Pharaohs might appear hopeless, and to leave us with no alternative but to make the best use we can of the superficial observation and puerile judgements[1] of Greek and Roman travellers. The modern world is inclined to believe that the Egyptians were born in mummy wrappings. Gaston Maspero, after translating the first love songs, could write that no ancient Egyptian would willingly assume the role of a lover kneeling before his mistress. In fact it was because life on the banks of the Nile was good that the hearts of the Egyptians overflowed with gratitude to the gods who were the lords of all creation, and it was this same sense of delight which led them to seek to prolong the good things of life even into the grave. They believed that the secret lay in covering the walls of their tombs with bas-reliefs and paintings. There we can see the occupant of the sarcophagus as he was in life on his estate, accompanied by wife and children, relations, servants and a host of craftsmen and peasants. Perhaps he is making his rounds on foot or perhaps riding in a litter, or a boat; he may be content to survey the busy scene from

*i.e. temple.
†i.e. tombs.

I

a comfortable arm-chair, or he may himself take an active part, boarding a skiff and hurling his wooden throwstick at the birds nesting in the clumps of papyrus, harpooning fish nearly as large as himself, stalking wild duck and signalling to the trappers,* or shooting with his bow and arrow at oryx or gazelle. All his personal servants attend him punctiliously when he rises in the morning. While the manicurist is treating his hands and the chiropodist his feet, an overseer is reporting to him and guards roughly thrust dishonest servants into his presence. Musicians and dancing girls stand ready to charm his ear and eye; while in the heat of the day he relaxes with his wife in pleasant board games not unlike modern chess or a kind of draughts.

An artist who wanted to afford his patron complete satisfaction must find room on the walls of the tomb to portray every form of activity. The main pursuits of the people who lived round the edges of the marshes were hunting and fishing. In papyrus they had an admirable material from which to make not only their huts but also the light stiffs so well designed for the pursuit of the crocodile and hippopotamus among the water plants, for reaching the heart of the bird-haunted thickets or for discovering where fish lurked. Before setting out on an expedition the hunters would have tried out their boats in a test of their strength and skill (p. 127). We see them, crowned with flowers and armed with long poles, upsetting each other into the water and exchanging insults. After their return to the village, their quarrels forgotten, we see them making and repairing their nets and snares, drying fish in the sun and fattening birds for the table. The farmer sows and tills, pulls the flax and reaps and binds the sheaves of corn, which are carried on donkeys to the village, and there spread for the grain to be todden out by oxen and donkeys or even, at a pinch, by sheep. While some build ricks of straw, others measure the grain and carry it to the barns. These tasks are scarcely completed ere the grapes have ripened and it is time to harvest and press them, and to fill and seal the huge wine jars, while all the year round millers are heaping up and grinding the grain and delivering the flour to baker or brewer.

The materials which we see the craftsmen using are mud, stone, wood and metal. Wood is scarce in Egypt and domestic utensils required by farmer and vine dresser, by brewer, baker and cook,

*i.e. to pull the cords of his bird trap (p. 129).

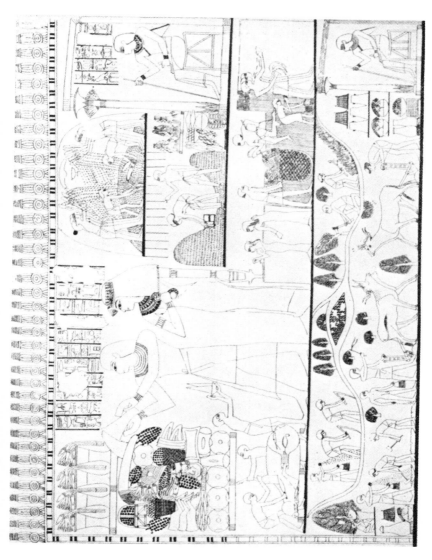

Plate II

Tomb owner watching activities on his estate

were all made of earthenware. Fine vessels were made of stone, notably granite, schist, alabaster and breccia; small bowls might be of crystal. The Egyptians loved pretty things, and from the jewellers' workshops there flowed a stream of necklaces and bracelets, rings and tiaras, pectorals and amulets; elegant baubles kept hidden away in jewel boxes, but sometimes borrowed by the daughters of the house for a moment's dressing-up. Sculptors were ready to portray in the round the master of the household in various poses, sitting, it might be, or standing, alone or surrounded by his family, in alabaster or granite, ebony or acacia wood. Joiners made cupboards and chests, beds, arm-chairs and walking sticks. Finally we can watch the carpenters felling and dressing trees and using the timber to build the barges and boats which were used indifferently for travelling throughout the country, gathering the harvest or joining in the pilgrimages to Abydos, Pé or Dep. In the words of the shipwrecked sailor, cast away on the island of the good serpent, 'there was nothing that was not there . . .'—nothing, that is, save any clue to how the occupant of the tomb had spent his life. Whether he was soldier or courtier, barber or doctor, architect or vizier, the same scenes, broadly speaking, meet our eyes, and differ only in scale. The hieroglyphic texts which frame the pictures, or fill in the blank spaces between the figures, describe the scenes in almost identical terms and repeat the same words, phrases and songs. Pictures and text alike derive from a common source. There must indeed have been a general pool of material on which the artists commissioned to decorate tombs could draw, and from which each could take what he would and dispose it as he chose. This common stock seems already to have been formed by the beginning of the fourth dynasty,* and throughout the Old Kingdom it was enriched by artists of striking humour and imagination. Here is a passer-by taking advantage of the herdsman's absence to milk his cow: here again, a nimble monkey grabs a servant with hand outstretched towards a basket of figs. A crocodile waits patiently for a she hippopotamus to give birth in order to gobble up the new-born calf. A little boy hands his father a rope's end only an inch or two long to tie up a canoe. The list could be extended. The artists have never forgotten their original purpose of depicting daily life on a great estate.[2]

*c. 2700 B.C.

This fund of illustrative material was never wholly discarded.
The main themes recur in tombs of the Middle Kingdom, at Beni-
Hasan, Meir, El-Bersheh, Thebes, and Aswan, and they were still
in regular use several centuries later, when the Pharaohs had their
seat at Thebes. They were employed at the beginning of the
Ptolemaic period in the decoration of the striking monument, in
the form of a temple, to Petosiris, a leading figure in the ancient
city of the Eight Gods, during his lifetime a 'Great One of the
Five'* priest of Thoth and of other divinities. Yet we should be
mistaken to imagine that the tombs merely repeated mechanically
and slavishly a form of decoration already invented and perfected
as early as the period of the great pyramids. At Beni-Hasan scenes
of games and wrestling, of fighting and the desert, and of warriors
of the province hastening to the siege of a fortress, figure far
more prominently than they had done previously. A new step
was taken, and side by side with the traditional scenes we find
pictures of important events in the dead man's life. In the tomb
of Khnoumhotep the arrival of Bedouin from Arabia on a visit
to the governor of the Oryx nome† in order to exchange a green
powder‡ for corn (p. 176), and in token of good faith offering a
gazelle and an ibex which they had captured in the desert, is inter-
posed between scenes of hunting and a procession of flocks.[3] The
governor of the Hare nome, on the other hand, might not have
received visitors from a far country: but he commissioned a statue
of himself, thirteen cubits high, from sculptors whose workshops§
lay close to the alabaster quarries of Hatnoub, not far from his own
home. When the finished statue was ready to leave the workshop
it was secured to a kind of sledge and slowly and painfully hauled
along a narrow rocky path to the temple by hundreds of men of all
ages, in four columns, between two lines of bystanders who
marked each stage of it progress with shouts and cheers.[4] True,
in tombs of the Old Kingdom we find scenes showing the transport of statues: but they are of a normal size, intended to stand in
tombs, and had not required the mobilization of every able-
bodied man in a province to get them there. This was a perfectly
normal feature of funerary rites. But Tahutihotep chose to astound
visitors to his tomb with this picture of an almost unparalleled

*A title of the high priest of Hermopolis.
†Province.
‡Malachite, for eye paint.
§Colossal statues were actually carved in the quarries.

undertaking, designed to leave them in no doubt as to his great wealth and the high favour he enjoyed in the king's palace.

Under the New Kingdom the themes used in the decoration of the tombs of private individuals fall into three main groups. The first comprises scenes drawn from the original repertoire but revised to please the taste of the day, which had changed considerably in a thousand years. Second come historical scenes. Men such as the vizier Rekhmarê, Menkheperrê, a high priest of Amūn, or Houy, a viceroy of Kush,* had played their part in affairs of state. They had introduced to their royal master foreign dignitaries from Crete, Syria or Nubia, who desired to be 'on the king's water'† or had come to beg the favour of the breath of life. They had levied taxes, dispensed justice, superintended building works and trained recruits. Whereas formerly an inscription in their tombs would have told their story, now it was told in pictures. Lastly, many paintings were inspired by a new sentiment—a sense of piety towards the gods. More space was given to the actual burial ceremony. No detail was omitted from the scenes which depicted the manufacture of the tomb furniture, sometimes bulky enough to stock a large warehouse, the marshalling of the funeral procession, the crossing of the Nile, the interment itself, the gestures of the mourners and the final leavetaking.

The temples, again, are so many vast books of stone, in which every flat surface has been employed by the sculptor. Architraves, shafts and bases of columns and doorposts are as densely covered with human figures and hieroglyphs as internal and external walls. Whereas in the best preserved temples, which are comparatively late in date, sculptured ornament and texts alike treat only of religious ceremonial, in an earlier age the temple might have been the house of god, but it was also a monument erected for the glory of the king. The achievements of Pharaoh had been accomplished by the permission, and frequently with the help, of his divine father, so that to rehearse the mighty deeds of a king's reign was a means of honouring the gods. That is why episodes in the king's life are interspersed with religious scenes, and why special care was taken to recall every royal action designed to beautify the shrine and to please the gods, whether it was an expedition to the land of spices or incidents from the wars in Syria, Libya or Nubia,

---

*The modern Sudan.
†i.e. to submit to his suzerainty, to be counted as a vassal.

with their spoil-laden homecomings, headed by prisoners destined for temple slavery. This series is rounded off by scenes of the king's hunting exploits and of the progress of the god through awestruck crowds: scenes whose interest for us is doubled by the descriptive text which quotes the very words of phrases, commands and songs.

An attempt to describe everyday life in ancient Egypt does not therefore present any insuperable obstacles, though some aspects must remain incomplete. The monuments were not merely repositories of bas-reliefs and painting, statues, stelae, sarcophagi and ritual objects, valuable though that material is, but they also housed an assemblage of very miscellaneous contents. We would admittedly rather possess the furniture from a palace of the Rammesside period than the tomb furniture of Tutankhamūn or Psousennes.[5] Yet fundamentally the needs of the dead were based upon those of the living: moreover, sometimes a pious hand has laid in the grave objects which the dead man had once worn or used, or some reminder of his family life.

Clearly we must exercise discrimination in drawing for information on documentary evidence covering more than three thousand years. Changes took place, though perhaps more gradually in Pharaonic Egypt than in other civilizations. The Nile, the focal point of life, was a master whose unchanging demands could not be gainsaid and did not vary. Nevertheless, customs and institutions, methods and beliefs did change. Although no Egyptologist would dissent from this conclusion, it is in practice widely disregarded. In certain recent works, texts of widely separated dates are quoted indiscriminately. Sometimes attempts are made to explain obscure features in an ancient text by quotations from Diodorus or Plutarch—if not Iamblichus; or the months are referred to by names which they only acquired late in history. This practice gives wider currency to the belief that Egypt remained almost unchanged throughout her interminable history.

If I was to avoid this error my first task was to select a single period. I began by discarding the two intermediate phases,* the long period of decline which followed the War of the Unclean† and the Saite revival when Egypt was devoted to mummifying

*See chronological table (p. xv).
†The civil war recorded by Manetho which may have put an end to the Ramesside twentieth dynasty, *c.* 1100 B.C. See Montet, *Le Drame d'Avaris*, 1940.

sacred animals and copying out gibberish; I also discarded the Ptolemaic period, which is a field no longer worked only by Egyptologists. I then considered in turn the periods of the great pyramids, the age of the Labyrinth,* the glorious epoch of the Pharaohs Tuthmosis and Amenophis,[6] the interlude of the solar disk of the Aton with its human-handed rays, and the nineteenth dynasty (the age of Ramesses the Great) with its natural extension, the twentieth. Each of them had its own attractions. The Old Kingdom, when Egypt was young, contained the visible beginnings of practically every great and original contribution which she made to civilization. Nevertheless my choice finally lighted upon the period of the Setys and the Ramesses, as best suited to my purpose. It was reasonably short; but its opening, in about 1320 B.C., was marked by a renaissance or 'renewal of births'—a phrase by which the Egyptians meant not only that a family with the certainty of numerous descendants had recently put an end to disputes over the succession, but also that it had introduced a number of changes. Before this date the Lords of the Two Lands† had either come from Memphis or Thebes, or they had grown up in the nomes of Middle Egypt between Coptos and the Fayyum. Now, for the first time, men of the Delta occupied the throne of Horus—men, moreover, whose ancestors, for at least four hundred years, had worshipped the ill-famed god Seth, murderer of his own brother. The period closed in about 1100 B.C., with another 'renewal of births', as a result of which Egypt rid herself decisively both of the Ramesside dynasty and of their god.[7] The two intervening centuries are brightly lit for us by the three glorious reigns of Sety I, Ramesses II and Ramesses III. A long past already lay behind Egypt: after a great convulsion her new rulers brought her for a time religious peace, destined to endure unbroken until nearly 1100 B.C. Not only did her armies gain a series of brilliant victories, but she played a far more active part in the affairs of other nations than she had in earlier periods. We find many Egyptians living abroad, and an even larger number of foreigners living in Egypt. Moreover, the Ramessids built on the grand scale. The Hyksos had laid everything waste as they swept through the country, and the Theban monarchs had not succeeded in repairing all the damage. At Thebes they had laboured greatly,

*The Twelfth Dynasty, *c.* 2000–1785 B.C.
†i.e. Upper and Lower Egypt, first united by Menes *c.* 3000 B.C.

but after the Aton heresy, their work had to be done all over again. The hypostyle* hall at Karnak, the pylon of the temple of Luxor, the Ramesseum at Medinet Habu and many other buildings both great and small—these, in the 'city with a hundred gates', are the splendid contribution of Ramesses I and his successors. No part of their great empire escaped their care. On all sides, from Nubia to Pi-Ramessu or to Pithom, we are greeted by newly founded cities, and by buildings restored, enlarged or first constructed by them.

The evidence of these monuments, and of the tombs of kings and queens, and especially of the noblemen of their day, has much to tell us, and we can fill in the gaps from the very large number of papyri dating from the thirteenth and twelfth centuries which include stories, polemical literature, collections of letters, lists of works and workmen, contracts, police reports and—greatest treasure of all—the political testament of Ramesses III. I have kept these sources constantly in mind while writing this book. This does not, of course, mean that we are debarred from using material earlier or later in date than our chosen period: for while I must register my protest against the tendency, visible in all too many books, to regard the three thousand years of Egyptian history as a single phase, and to attribute indiscriminately to the whole span of Pharaonic civilization characteristics which can be ascribed with certainty only to a limited period within it, I have not forgotten that many customs, institutions and beliefs did endure in Egypt for a very long time. When we find that a statement by a classical author agrees with the evidence of a bas-relief of the Old Kingdom from Memphis, we are fully entitled to suppose that at least in this respect Egyptians in Ramesside times behaved in the same way as both their predecessors and their successors. I have accordingly drawn on every source, whenever I have considered it possible to do so without painting in false colours my chosen picture of everyday life in Egypt at the time of Ramesses the Great and his successors.

*A hall supported on a number of pillars.

CHAPTER I

DWELLING PLACES

1. *The Towns*

IT is not surprising that the cities of Pharaonic Egypt are today mere heaps of dust, thickly strewn with sherds of pottery and rubble, since towns and palaces alike were constructed of unbaked bricks. None the less, some of them were more easily intelligible at the date when the scholars brought to Egypt by Napoleon compiled their accounts than they are today. The recent past has added a long tale of destruction to that of antiquity, for not only have the native inhabitants continued to dig for *sebakh** in the ruins and to remove blocks of stone, but they have also taken to the deplorable practice of searching for antiquities. There are virtually only two towns of which we can speak with any certainty, and that because they enjoyed but a brief existence. Both were founded on the monarch's personal decision and were no less arbitrarily abandoned. The more ancient of the two, Hetep Senousert, was built in the Fayyum by Sesostris II† and enjoyed less than a century of existence. The other, Akhetaton,‡ was the residence of Amenophis IV, after his break with Amūn, and of his successors until Tutankhamūn moved the court back to Thebes. We shall find it useful to examine them briefly before describing Ramesside cities.

Hetep Senousert lay within an enclosure measuring about 380 by 430 yards and was designed to accommodate a large number of people in a small area.[1] The temple lay outside the walls. The town was divided by a thick wall into two zones, for the rich and the poor respectively, through the latter of which an avenue about thirty feet wide ran at right angles to several narrower streets. In

---

*Decayed mud brick, valued as a fertilizer.
†*c*. 1900 B.C.
‡Tell el Amarna.

this area the houses stood back to back, with their front doors opening on to the street, and contained surprisingly small rooms and passages. The fashionable quarter on the other hand was traversed by wide streets leading to the palace and to the houses of the leading officials, which were almost fifty times as large as those of the poor. Although the Egyptians were traditionally garden-lovers, the whole area was taken up by houses and streets. Hark-huf, the explorer who brought back a dancing dwarf from Nubia as a present for his boy king (p. 65), tells us that he built a house, dug a pond and planted trees. The stele of a lady of the same period as Sesostris II describes her as a tree-lover, and Ramesses III planted on the grand scale. But in Hetep Senousert itself no concessions were made to the pleasure of taking a stroll through the town.

In complete contrast, Akhnaton's residence, Akhetaton, was wholly designed for luxurious living. The city, which lay in a huge semi-circular bay between the hills and the Nile, was traversed from end to end by an avenue running parallel to the river and intersected by other broad streets leading in one direction to the quays and in the other to the necropolis and the alabaster quarries.[2] The central area was occupied by the official palace, the temple, administrative buildings and warehouses. The streets contained unpretentious houses standing next door to the grander residences which excavators have assigned to various members of the royal family.

Huge areas were reserved for plantations of trees and gardens, both inside the town and on large estates outside. The workers employed in the necropolis and the quarries were segregated in a walled village. The city was so abruptly abandoned that there had been no time to modify the work of its original inhabitants.

Quite the reverse was true of those towns—the large majority —which had a long history. They displayed no coherent pattern at all. Men Nefer, transliterated by the Greeks into Memphis, meant 'The beauty [of the city or god] is enduring', but it was also known as Onkh Tawi ('the life of the two lands'), Hatka-Ptah ('the fortress of the double of Ptah') and Nehet ('the syca-more'). Each of these names could be used in reference to the whole city, but originally each had signified a particular feature: the royal palace and its related buildings, the temple of Ptah, the town's tutelary deity, or the temple of Hathor, who was known at

Memphis as the lady of the sycamore tree. The same was true of
Thebes, Homer's 'city of a hundred gates'. Its earliest name was
Iat, which it shared with the fourth nome of Upper Egypt of
which it was the capital. In the New Kingdom it came to be called
Opet, variously translated as 'harem', 'chapel' or 'castle'. The huge
group of monuments now called after the village of Karnak,
which was known from the time of Amenophis III onwards as
'Opet of Amūn',³ was linked with the temple of Luxor, Southern
Opet, by an avenue of sphinxes. Each Opet was enclosed in a
wall of unbaked brick, pierced by a number of monumental stone
gateways, their doors of Lebanon pine, reinforced with bronze
and inlaid with gold. When danger threatened the gates were
closed, as Piankhi (p. 237) tells us was done at his approach. But
the texts we possess never refer to their closure in time of peace,
and we are probably correct in thinking that traffic could pass
freely through them by night and by day.

Inside the walls, houses, shops and warehouses, which have
all completely disappeared, took up much of the area between the
temple and the walls. There were delightful vistas of gardens and
orchards, and the flocks of Amūn grazed in the parks. The walls
of the Hall of Annals, built by Tuthmosis III, preserve a picture of a
garden with plants and trees imported by him from Syria.⁴ Official
buildings and palaces extended along either side of the avenue of
sphinxes which linked the two enclosures and along the river
bank. Each king wanted a palace of his own, and the queens,
princes, viziers and high officials were content with little less. The
fact that the town grew steadily through three dynasties makes it
probable that the houses of the middle class, the dwellings of
the very poor and the residences of the rich stood side by side, and
did not, as at Hetep Senousert, occupy separate districts.

On the western bank, opposite Karnak and Luxor, a second
town, Tjame, grew up, perhaps more accurately described as a
series of enormous monuments in the midst of a huddle of houses
and shops, each surrounded by a wall of unbaked brick, and anything up to a quarter of a mile square,⁵ or even larger. Each side
of the encircling wall of Amenophis III is a good 550 yards in
length. These massive mud-brick structures may be as much as
50 feet wide at the base, and may have been 60 feet or even more
in height. They concealed practically everything which lay within
them, save for the pyramidal tops of the obelisks, the cornices of

the pylons, and the crowns surmounting the colossal statues. Nearly all these cities have suffered grievously from the ravages of time and mankind. The 'colossi of Memnon' now tower above the cornfields, but they were never designed to be seen in this splendid isolation. They graced the façade of a magnificent temple, hemmed in on every side by brick buildings which sheltered a swarming population and vast quantities of merchandise. The colossal figures themselves have withstood the assaults of the centuries, but of the rest only a few scanty remains survive. Elsewhere even these statues have shared the general fate, and such traces as come to light in a brief series of excavations are quickly lost beneath cultivation. The monument of Ramesses III at Medinet Habu known as the Ramesseum, which lies farther to the north, and in the extreme north the monument of Sety I—these alone, not forgetting the terraced, temple of Queen Hatshepsuf, still present impressive remains. It is especially from Medinet Habu that we can derive an impression of what these enclosed towns[6] must have looked like when they were newly built. Alighting from a boat at the foot of a double flight of steps the visitor would make his way past two guard rooms through a low crenellated stone enclosure wall running parallel with, but separated by a ring road from, the main walls of unbaked brick. These were pierced by a fortified gateway resembling a Syrian *migdol*,* and consisting of two lofty and symmetrical towers, about 20 feet apart, separated by a gatehouse and containing an opening just wide enough to allow the passage of a chariot. These walls were decorated with bas-reliefs extolling the power of Pharaoh. The corbels were in the shape of the heads of Egypt's traditional enemies, Libyans and Arabs, Negroes and Nubians. They must have made the visitor feel a trifle uncomfortable, but in the main rooms the atmosphere was less forbidding. There is a carving of Ramesses, attended by his favourties, chucking a charming Egyptian girl under the chin. This, however, was only a safe retreat in case of trouble, and was usually occupied by guards. Palace and harem stood a little farther on beside the temple.

On passing through the gateway, our visitor would find himself in a large courtyard across the far end of which ran yet a third encircling wall enclosing temple, palace and harem, and a complex of courtyards and buildings. Low buildings huddled round three

*Hebrew 'tower'.

sides of this third enclosure on both sides of a central road-
way. The residents of this little town, where the king lived
with his wives and numerous servants when he visited the left
bank of the river, comprised both the temple priests and a large
lay population.

This description is applicable not only to the fortress of Ramesses, ruler of On* in the domain of Amūn, but also to the Ramesseum, as well as to the twenty or thirty other royal towns on the
west bank of the Nile. Despite their extremely forbidding ex-
terior, within them wonderful examples of architecture, gilded
palaces and mud-coloured hovels stood in attractive confusion.
Sometimes the most splendid princes and the loveliest princesses
that Egypt could boast would pass by, bringing a transient
brilliance to the narrow alleys and courtyards, and the royal
apartments would echo with laughter and the strains of music and
song. But when the revels were at an end the traffic through the
fortified gateway would once again be but flocks and herds; or
files of slaves, their heads or shoulders laden with bales; or

*Heliopolis.

soldiers, it might be, or accountants or masons and workmen bound, amid the clamour and the dust, for workshop, stable or slaughter-house, while schoolboys and apprentices went off to receive their meed of learning and blows.[7]

The cities of the Delta were no whit less ancient than those of Upper Egypt nor were their monuments any less splendid, for though they had been sacked by the Hyksos and left neglected by the kings of the eighteenth dynasty, they were not only restored but enlarged and embellished by the Ramesside monarchs. Ramesses II was particularly fond of the eastern Delta, whence his family had originally sprung. He liked its temperate climate, its pastures, its wide expanses of water and its vines, which produced a wine sweeter than honey. In the open windswept meadows by the Tanite branch of the Nile stood the ancient city of Hat Wâret or Avaris, ancient centre of the cult of the god Seth, and since time immemorial the home of an original school of art. The Hyksos had made it their capital, but after their explusion by Ahmosé the town fell into neglect. Ramesses II, who took up his residence there as soon as he had paid his last respects to his dead father, forthwith began the great buildings which were to restore life and prosperity to the area and to turn the ancient city into an incomparable royal residence.[8] Here, as in Thebes, temple and other buildings were encircled by a great wall of brick from which, through four gates, roads and canals led north and south, east and west. Blocks of stone of unprecedented size had been brought from Aswan, regardless of distance and difficulty, in order to build the holy of holies, and to erect more and ever more stelae and obelisks, all dressed and polished to perfection. Snarling human-headed lions of black granite and sphinxes in roseate granite confronted each other all along the narrow basalt-paved alleys, while crouching lions kept watch in front of the gates. Before the pylons stood line upon line of dyads and triads, colossal figures both standing and seated, several of which rivalled those of Thebes and surpassed those of Memphis.

The palace blazed with gold, lapis lazuli and turquoise, and the whole scene was gay with flowers. The well-shaded roads ran through an admirably farmed countryside. The warehouses were crammed with merchandise shipped from Syria and the isles, and from the land of Punt.* Near the palace lay the quarters of the

*At the foot of the Red Sea (p. 183 ff).

detachments of infantry, companies of archers, chariots and the crews who manned the fleet. Many Egyptians had come to reside near the 'Sun'. 'Oh, the joy of dwelling there!' to quote the scribe Pabasa. 'No wish is unfulfilled: the humble man and the mighty are as one . . . all men equally can lay their requests before him.' Here, too, as in the other great cities, Libyans and Negroes would be found among the Egyptians. But of all foreigners it was the Asiatics who swarmed there most thickly before and even after the Exodus. There were the descendants of the sons of Jacob, as well as other nomad peoples who had been granted permission to dwell in Egypt, and were reluctant to leave it, together with captives from the countries of Canaan, Amor and Naharina,* whose descendants in the course of time would often settle down and become agricultural labourers or free craftsmen. Quite soon the royal city was enclosed by one far larger, comprising both warehouses and dwelling-houses, and it was not long before these new districts in their turn had their own temples within their encircling walls of brick. Space had also to be left for a cemetery,[9] for in the Delta, unlike the south, there was no desert near at hand in which to bury the dead. Tombs for human beings and sacred animals alike were built on the spot, either just outside or even inside the walls, almost touching the temple. Limitations of space made it impossible to construct monuments on the scale of those at Memphis, and in fact all the tombs at both Tanis and Athribis, irrespective of the rank of their occupant, were very small.

Ramesses II left few unfinished buildings for completion by his successors and Ramesses III was mainly preoccupied in maintaining and enlarging the gardens and the orchards: in his own words 'I made the whole land fruitful with trees and plants, so that men could sit beneath their shade.'[10] In the Residence city of his famous ancestor he created vast gardens, laid out country walks, planted vines and olives and beautified the verges of the sacred way with brilliant flowers.[11] At On (Heliopolis) the monarch had the sacred temple lakes cleaned out, again in his own words, 'removing all the filth which had accumulated there since the beginning of time', and planted new trees and shrubs everywhere. In order to be able to offer the god Atum wine and choice liquor he planted orchards and an olive grove from which came 'the finest oil in Egypt for burning in thy sacred palace'. The temple of

*Palestine, Syria and the Upper Euphrates region.

Horus, which had fallen into complete decay, deserved to enjoy pride of place above the other shrines. 'I caused the sacred grove which grew within its walls to flourish. I may papyrus sprout there as it does in the marshes of Akh Bit [where the infant Horus had lived]. It had long been abandoned to neglect. I caused the sacred grove of thy temple to flourish. I restored to its proper place that which had been laid low. I appointed gardeners to tend it, that it might produce libations of choice wine for offerings.'[12]

The whole operation was a nice blend of pleasure and utility. Herodotus* observed that the temple of Bubastis in its setting of great trees was one of the most delightful spectacles in the whole of Egypt, and a traveller of the twelfth century B.C. would certainly have gained the same refreshing impression in any of the main Egyptian towns, the austerity of whose massive brick walls was relieved by splashes of greenery. Their inhabitants could enjoy the cool shade of the great trees by the banks of the branches of the Nile, while in the temple courtyards flowers heightened the effect of the sculpture.

Men, animals and plants alike all needed an abundant supply of water. It would have been considered shocking to have to fetch it from a canal outside the walls, even when, as at Medinet Habu or Pi-Ramessu, this ran close to the monumental gate, and most walled cities contained a stone pool.[13] A flight of steps ensured access to the water level throughout the year. There is evidence of the existence of wells on private estates as well as in urban districts[14] from anyway the period of the New Kingdom onwards. The walls of Pi-Ramessu enclosed at least four, carefully constructed of stone,[15] the smallest of which, lying on the west side of the temple, has a diameter of about 10 feet. A rectangular staircase of twenty-three covered steps led down into it, followed, inside the well itself, by a spiral staircase of a dozen steps. The largest of the four wells lay to the south of the temple. It was about 16 feet in diameter, access being gained by a covered stairway of forty-four steps arranged in two flights with a level platform half-way down. Even when the water level was at its lowest, it was still possible to fill water jars by decending the actual shaft of this well by means of a spiral stairway ending in circular steps. At other times it was easier to raise the water to the

*II, 137–8.

pool by means of a *shadūf*,* and thence by a stone culvert to a second pool inside the actual temple. In the eastern quarter of the town we found several deeply buried systems of pottery pipes of different types, the largest of which consisted of pots without bottoms fitted into each other and carefully cemented together. Up to the present time it has not been possible to follow these water systems for their entire length so as to ascertain their starting and finishing points. Not only can we not date them, but we do not even know whether they were used to bring drinking water or as drains for waste. None the less they are worth mentioning as evidence of the concern of the government of the day for the welfare of the population and for public health.

The royal and divine precincts exercised a potent attraction on the surrounding districts. In unsettled periods the frightened populace would force their way inside the walls and refuse to leave, building their houses in the parks and orchards, and thus ruining the splendid vistas planned by the original builders. They would even penetrate the outer sanctuary of the temple and ensconce themselves on its walls, ignoring the daily ritual of the cult and defying the vigilance of the guards. A doctor named Udjahor-resenit, who was in practice during the reign of King Cambyses,† ruefully records that strangers had established themselves in the temple of Neith, the goddess of Sais.[16] Since he had access to the great king, he persuaded the monarch to order the expulsion of these undesirable intruders and the destruction of their houses, so that, cleansed of pollution,‡ the temple priests could celebrate the proper festivals and processions in the traditional manner. A sorcerer of Athribis, named Djedhor, tells us that some credulous individuals had built their mud huts on top of the burial places of the sacred falcons.[17] Not moving in such exalted circles as the doctor from Sais, he had to rely upon his powers of persuasion, by means of which he succeeded in inducing the trespassers to remove themselves to a highly salubrious spot which he had found for them. The fact that this happened to be a swamp was neither here nor there, since the offending structures had only to be pulled down and there, ready to hand, was the necessary rubble to fill it in. By this means the worthy inhabitants of Athribis

*A bucket on the end of a pole or rope which could be raised and lowered on a pivot (p. 104).
†525–522 B.C.
‡Because the intruders were Asiatics.

E.L.E.—C

acquired a convenient, clean and commodious site, albeit a little
damp when the water level rose. Our own excavations at Tanis
showed how the courtyards and enclosures of the temple precinct had been invaded by private dwellings. A certain Panemerit,
who seems to have been a person of some standing, had his house
built in the first temple courtyard up against the pylon, so that
his statues should derive virtue from the sacred rites.[18] Panemerit
lived at a later period than the doctor from Sais or the sorcerer of
Athribis, but as we shall see tradition dies hard in Egypt. I am
inclined to think that this kind of episode, though admittedly
known to us from late documents, must have been a recurrent
phenomenon. The inhabitants would have taken advantage of the
slackness or incompetence of the authorities to leave the comparatively less favoured districts in which they lived, in order to
settle under the shelter of the great walls—and also, it may be,
within easy range of something that could be robbed. Then, when
authority awoke to its responsibilities, out the intruders would go,
and temple and royal town would regain their dignity—until the
next time. When Sety I, or the great Sesostris, or Ramesses III
was on the throne, no one would have ventured to occupy a piece
of land where he had no business to be: but it might well have
happened between the reigns of Merenptah and Set-nakht: and we
find far worse things occurring under the last of the Ramesside
monarchs.

2. *The Palaces*

Although the royal palace of Pi-Ramessu was much admired
by contemporary taste, our descriptions of it are, unfortunately,
vague and excavation has not yet identified its precise site. Other
royal residences are known in the Delta: for example some remains of a palace have been found at the village of Qantir, which
lies in the shade of lofty palm-trees about 17 miles south of Pi-
Ramessu.[19] While Pharaoh's bride-to-be, the daughter of the
Hittite monarch, was travelling across Asia Minor and Syria in
mid-winter to join him, he showed his chivalry and devotion by
ordering a strong castle to be built in the desert between Egypt
and Phoenicia, where he went to await her. For all its remoteness,
the castle lacked nothing that imagination could supply. Each of
its sides was placed beneath the protection of a god: Amūn
guarded the west, Sutekh the south, Astarte the east and Wadjit

the north. In honour of the king of Egypt and his Asiatic bride two of these deities were Egyptian and two Asiatic, for by this date Seth had assumed the headdress and loincloth of a Baal and had lost practically all resemblance to an Egyptian god. Four statues with names like those of living persons: 'Ramesses Miamūn (Life, Health, Strength!)', 'Montou in the Two Lands', 'Sun of Princes', 'Charm of Egypt', here took the places of god, herald, vizier and pasha.[20] Within his city in western Thebes, Ramesses III had a palace facing the first courtyard of the temple, which he called his house of joy. Its remains have been preserved and studied by scholars from the Oriental Institute of Chicago.[21] The bas-reliefs, which were set between the pillars of the peristyle and served to decorate its façade, were admirably chosen to extol the monarch's might. One scene showed him crushing his foes with blows of his club; the next, inspecting his stables with a brilliant entourage; in a third, he was on his way to assume command of his army, mounted in his chariot and fully accoutred for battle; in the last, accompanied by all his courtiers, he was watching his picked troops wrestling and drilling. The richly decorated balcony on which the king made his public appearances occupied the centre of the façade, behind four small and most graceful papyriform columns supporting a triple cornice. On the lowest level hovered the winged disk: above it was a row of palm-leaf ornament, while the top cornice was decorated with a row of uraeus heads each crowned with the solar disk. This was the balcony on which the king appeared when the populace was permitted to gather in the courtyard for the festival of Amūn, and from which he distributed his bounty. The balcony opened from the royal apartments, the centre of which consisted of a suite of pillared rooms, including the throne room and the monarch's bedroom and bathroom. A lobby separated these rooms from the apartments of the queen, which comprised a number of rooms and bathrooms. Long straight corridors ensured not only easy access but easy surveillance, for Ramesses III, tutored by experience, trusted no one.

The interior of the throne room seems to have been plainly decorated, to judge by the small enamelled panels which were found over thirty years ago, and the fragmentary bas-reliefs discovered recently by the American expedition. On these the king is always shown as a rampant sphinx and is described by his names

in hieroglyphics. The enemies of Egypt are paraded in fetters before him, their rich robes embroidered with barbaric ornament, and
the artist has been at pains to reproduce faithfully their features,
hair and jewellery—tattooed Libyans, Negroes wearing ear-rings
and Syrians with medallions hung round their necks, while the
long flowing hair of the nomadic *Shasou* bedouin is kept in place
with a comb.[22] But the king's and queen's private apartments may
have been decorated with somewhat less aggressive themes.

This royal dwelling covered a fairly small area, with sides of
less than 120 feet in length. The king no doubt never stayed there
for very long at a time, for he could reside on the other bank of
the Nile. He had indeed plenty of choice in the delta, where
Memphis, On, and Pi-Ramessu stood waiting to receive him, while
between On and Bubastis, at the place later known to the Arabs
as Tel-l el Yahudieh, he had begun to erect yet another building,
which has yielded glazed plaques similar to those found at Medinet
Habu.[23] So harshly have the ravages of time treated the palaces of
the Ramessids that, if we want to gain a rather fuller idea of the
palace of a Pharaoh in the New Kingdom, we must imagine ourselves in the palace of Akhnaton, built not very much earlier. The
floors of the colonnaded apartments represent a lagoon full of
fish and carpeted with water lilies. Above the banks, fringed with
reed and papyrus, water birds fly, while calves at play in the thick
undergrowth have flushed some wild duck. Vines and convol-
vulus wreathe the shafts of the columns and capitals and cornices
are enriched with glittering inlay. The walls are painted with
scenes from the life of the royal family, showing the king sitting
in an arm-chair opposite Nefertiti, his queen, who reposes on a
cushion with a baby on her knee. The eldest of the princesses has
her arm round the neck of her younger sister, while two more
little princesses play on the ground.[24] This can be described without exaggeration as the most delightful scene in the whole of
Egyptian painting. In fact lagoons, papyrus plants, birds, and
animals at play or at the gallop were normal features of the art of
the period. We have already seen the king at Medinet Habu in the
midst of his charming favourites. We need have no doubt that the
palaces of the Pharaohs of the nineteenth and twentieth dynasties were always decorated with an equal measure of opulence,
and that, as in the time of Akhnaton, the painted walls and ceilings,
floors, columns and cornices gladdened both the eye and the

heart with the freshness of their colour. The rich furnishings and the luxurious ornaments and draperies combined to produce an effect of exquisite taste.

3. *The Houses*

The nobility spared no effort to emulate the comfort and luxury of the royal dwellings. Their town or country residences, anything up to 2½ acres in area, or even more, were surrounded, like those of god or king, by a wall both lofty and thick, through which a stone gateway gave access to the owner's private residence, while secondary entrances—mere openings in the walls— led to the outbuildings and gardens. It was to such a house that the treacherous Tbouboui brought her lover. The house of Apouy was like a small temple. A portico with papyriform

The house and garden of Apouy

columns projected from the façade and the architrave was surmounted by a palmetto cornice,[25] while the principal entrance was framed with dressed stone and a lintel with palmetto decoration. The house in which King Aÿ received and bestowed gifts upon the wife of Neferhotep (p. 205) had a colonnaded terrace, carrying a light roof which projected on each side and rested at its outer edge on long columns, tall and slender, which formed a peristyle running all round the house.[26] We can form some idea of the external appearance of these two houses from the reliefs which Apouy and Neferhotep had carved in their tombs, but if we wish to learn about their internal arrangements we must again visit the excavations at el Amarna. The entrance-porch led, through a lobby, into the reception rooms, whose roofs were supported on columns. At the farther end of these public apartments were dressing-rooms which were found to contain brick chests, possibly used as cupboards for linen and other clothes, and pantries where food and refreshments must have been kept. The remainder of the building was taken up with the owner's private apartments, including the bathrooms and lavatories. The bathroom walls were faced with stone; in one corner a stone slab was found, surrounded by a brick screen from behind which a servant could sluice the bather with water, after which he would go to an adjacent seat for his massage. The whitewashed lavatory lay behind the bathroom. It was fitted with a limestone seat with a hole in it, which rested on brick containers filled with sand.[27]

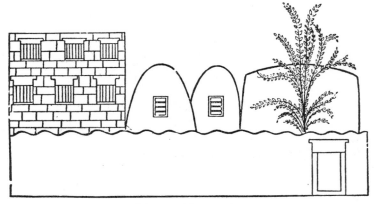

A house with granaries

Even less pretentious houses were surrounded by several courtyards, in one of which stood the beehive-shaped corn bins. The stables and kennels were on the north side, while the kitchen, bakehouse and brick-built servants' quarters usually lay to the east, which meant that they had a long way to carry dishes when waiting on their masters. A service door gave access to the main reception rooms. The servants' quarters generally consisted of four rooms—an entrance, a central room with a roof supported on a column, and a kitchen and a bedroom beyond. The family shared these extremely cramped quarters with the livestock. A staircase gave access to the roof. At one end of this area the stewards lived in large and comfortable houses.[28] Drinking water was generally supplied by a stone well.

Plate IIIa   Audience hall in the palace of Ramesses (restored)

Plate IIIb   Garden and pool of a nobleman's house

The carefully tended gardens belonging to the houses, shaded by climbing vines and edged with flowers, were divided into square or rectangular plots by straight tree-lined paths intersecting at right angles. Anni had formed a collection of practically every species of tree which grew in the Nile valley, including the date palm, the dōm palm, the coconut palm (known as the kuku palm), sycamore, fig, balanos,* sidder,† persea, pomegranate, acacia, yew, tamarisk, willow, and several other unidentified varieties—a total of eighteen:[29] while behind the stout walls of his garden Rekhmarê grew every species of tree and plant then known. Frequently a lightly built but elegant pavilion would be constructed beneath the trees, where the owner could eat during the summer. A number of wooden shelters were dotted around, where drinks were kept cool in great *zirs*‡ under a covering of leaves, beside the tables and stands on which servants had invitingly arranged the finest products of the Egyptian cuisine.[30]

No garden of any size was without its pool, usually square or rectangular and lined with masonry, and with floating water lilies and ducks swimming on the surface. It was reached by a flight of steps and a boat nearly always lay ready for use if wanted.[31]

The middle classes generally lived in houses of several stories in height, while sometimes corn bins were stored on the roof as well. The façade was completely plain. The door, framed between two uprights and a lintel, stood near one of the angles of the walls, and was the only source of light for the ground floor. Each upper story might have two, four or even as many as eight small square windows, fitted with blinds for protection against the dust and the heat.

Sometimes a stone grille did duty for a blind. At Tanis we found the framework of a stone window barely 15 inches high, and another whose square frame was filled by two fretted cartouches of King Merenptah. In a number of tomb paintings at Thebes the walls of houses are streaked with horizontal lines, which gives them the effect of being built of wooden beams or weatherboarded. We found the explanation for this at Tanis,

---

Balanites aegyptiaca, now rare in Egypt though plentiful in the Sudan. The acorn-shaped fruit yields an oil which was used in perfumery. See A. Lucas, *Ancient Egyptian Materials and Industries,* 3rd ed., 1945, p. 383.

†Or zisyphus (Arabic *nebk*).

‡Porous water jars which cool their contents by evaporation.

where we discovered that while the masons mortared the horizontal courses, the vertical joints were only treated with mud, so that the wall, when completed, showed a pattern of horizontal white stripes.

Ground-floor rooms were if possible reserved for domestic work. For example, in the house of a certain Thouty-nefer at Thebes we can see women spinning and men weaving, while in the next room corn is being ground and bread prepared. The owners of the house have withdrawn to a fairly large room on the first floor, lit by little windows high in the walls, with a roof supported on pillars with lotus-shaped capitals. The door appears to be decorated with inlaid plaques, unless indeed the wood itself was carved. There is no sign of any wall decoration, though the Egyptians normally painted every square inch of available surface. In a house of a late period at Tanis, with plastered interior walls, I discovered panels bearing drawings of dancers and of boats. There is no doubt whatever that this was an ancient practice, and we have every reason for thinking that rooms in houses resembled the chambers in Theban tombs whose ceilings are painted with vines, and whose walls bear hunting scenes, a journey to the sacred city of Osiris, or other conventional themes.

The ceilings of the second-floor rooms were so low that their occupants could touch them with their finger-tips without standing on tiptoe. The owner's dressing-room was on this floor. While he sat in his arm-chair servants would bring him ewer and basin, fan and fly whisk, and scribes would kneel before him to read him his correspondence and take down his orders. On the staircase and in the passages there was much coming and going of servants, carrying bundles on their heads and jars of water slung from a yoke across their shoulders.[32]

The same arrangement of rooms can be seen in the house of a certain Mahu. The ground floor was given over to storage jars, the dining-room was on the first floor and the second floor was stacked with shields, weapons and all manner of implements. Mahu was the chief of police, and it is tempting to think that he slept on the second floor so that, if he were suddenly roused during the night, he could grab his weapons and fall upon the criminals.[32a]

The roof was usually flat, and was reached by staircase or by ladder. Some house-owners, like Thouty-hotep, built corn bins there for grain storage, while others would erect a lattice work parapet round the edge to keep children from falling over or to conceal the family from prying eyes when they chose to sleep beneath the stars. Nebamūn and Nakhti built curious pyramidal structures on their roofs. These have been explained as airshafts, although examples of Egyptian houses with pointed roofs are known. I myself found two ivory gaming pieces in the shape of houses with sloping roofs, two of the surfaces being triangular and two trapezoidal.[33] These were in a tomb at Abu Roash near Cairo, dating from the time of King Den, who lived nearly two thousand years before the Ramesside period.* This is a surprisingly advanced type of roof for such an early date, and could only have been invented in a countryside with a significant rainfall and plenty of wood. In Egypt, however, the only considerable rainfall is found in the coastal strip, where all modern houses end in a projecting roof. This all suggests that the objects found at Abu Roash do not represent a native Egyptian type of house. There is at all events no proof that it survived anywhere in the country in the Ramesside period.

Even in Thebes, land was not so valuable nor the houses so congested that some trees could not be grown either in front of the house or within the courtyard. In Nebamūn's house two palm-trees seem to be growing out of the roof (though they bear a heavy crop of dates), while Nakhti's door was shaded by a sycamore and a palm tree. Tomb No. 23 at Thebes contains a painting of a house much taller than it is wide, standing between two rows of trees, while tomb No. 254, in the same city, shows another house with three pomegranate trees in brightly painted earthenware tubs, and two dōm palms growing in front.[34]

Even the comparatively poor took a lot of trouble both to make their houses comfortable and pleasant to live in, and also to protect themselves against the numerous impediments to a peacefu home life which are so common in Egypt—insects, rats, lizards, snakes and birds of prey. Several useful recipes are preserved in the Ebers medical papyrus.[35] For example in order to keep down insect pests, the house must be washed with a solution of natron, or daubed with a substance called *bebit*, crushed on

---

*King Den, or Udimu, was the fourth Pharaoh of the First Dynasty, and reigned *c.* 2950 B.C.

some charcoal. Again, to put natron or a dried fish, *tilapia niloticus*, or even some onion seeds at the mouth of a snake's hole ensures that the snake will stay inside. Oriole fat is an excellent specific against flies, and fish spawn against fleas. A little cat's fat smeared on sacks or bales is guaranteed to keep off rats, and rodents can be prevented from eating corn by burning gazelles' dung in the barn or by coating the walls and floor with a solution of the same substance. We are told that an infallible guarantee against thefts by kites is to stick a branch of acacia wood in the ground with a cake beside it and to recite over it the following formula, 'A kite has been raiding in town and country. . . . Fly, cook it, eat it.'

An effective method was known of fumigating and removing the smell from dressing-rooms in which clothes had been kept, though it was not within everyone's reach, since it involved making a mixture of incense, terebinth resin, and a number of other products not all of which were native to Egypt. This recipe, like the others I have quoted, is evidence of a wish to keep houses clean and fresh—a very natural sentiment which must have induced the authorities to make some general arrangements for the disposal of dirty water and household refuse, though we have no documentary evidence about it.

4. *Furniture*

In both the reception apartments of the palace and the houses of the rich, the main articles of furniture were a variety of seats. Some were little more than square boxes with backs only a few inches high and sides decorated with mother-of-pearl inlay framed by the wand of Egypt. In these examples the simplicity of the design might be more than compensated by the richness of the materials employed and the excellent workmanship. A far higher degree of elegance and comfort was represented by the high-backed fretted arm-chairs with legs ending in four lion's paws. The king and the queen required something more magnificent still and on their chairs both surfaces of the back and the arm-rests were decorated with themes borrowed from large-scale sculpture, engraved on wood or worked in leather or in repoussé gold, silver or copper and inlaid with precious stones. In this setting the monarch, represented as a griffin or a sphinx under the protection of uraeus, vulture or falcon, is shown tearing an Asiatic or a Negro with his talons, while grotesque dwarfs, like those brought at great expense from the land of Punt or the Upper Nile, are dancing and playing the tambourine. The king receives from the queen's hands the flower which brings desire, while she clasps a necklet round her husband's neck. The edge of the seat and the fronts of the arm-rests carry the heads of lions, of falcons or of women, while between the chair legs the emblematic plants of Upper and Lower Egypt spring from one base and twine round a great hieroglyph signifying their union.[36]

There were two types of stool. The simpler had straight feet; the more elaborate had crossed legs and feet in the form of duck's heads, while the cross-bars also ended in animals' heads. The floor was spread with rush mats and plenty of cushions,[37] which were also used to support the backs and feet of those who sat in the arm-chairs. When the company outnumbered the seats the last-comers or the youngest of those present sat either on cushions or else directly on the matting.

When a separate dining-room, as distinct from the reception room, existed, it was furnished with seats and occasional tables for the use of the guests, and with larger tables and stands set with baskets of fruit, dishes of meat and vegetables, jars and vases. None of the numerous pieces of furniture was large, for it never occurred to the Egyptians to make large tables at which a number of guests could eat together: instead they ate singly or in pairs.

In the very early periods two kinds of dinnerware were in use, that for everyday being made of pottery, while the best was of stone—generally black or blue schist or alabaster, or more rarely red breccia. Large vessels were made of granite, and miniature goblets of rock crystal. This wide range of materials was matched by an equally wide range of sizes and shapes—cylindrical or ovoid vases, goblets, bowls and cups, plates, spouted pots, large jugs, tureens and pedestal vases. Craftsmen of more imaginative skill might carve the surface of a jar with the net in which it was carried, or model a vessel after a boat or an animal.[38]

Although the tradition of manufacturing stone vases persisted, and many important examples have been found in the tombs of the New Kingdom, gold or silver plate gradually grew more popular and was used for ewers for ritual use and for large numbers of secular objects.[39] Kettle-like vessels, resembling modern teapots and with strainers fitted inside the spouts, were used for brewing hot drinks: alternatively the hot liquid might be poured through a strainer into a cup held by the drinker. The well-known 'kid vase'* from the treasure of Bubastis was admirably designed to hold milk, and for pouring other liquids there were vessels of various shapes—round-bottomed goblets with lips, hemispherical vessels with handle and spout, and bowls welded to the end of a long handle like modern milk ladles. Stemmed cups and fluted dishes were very suitable for sweetmeats and cakes. When Ramesses III went campaigning, he firmly insisted that his orderly officer should take with him his golden cup with handles, which held slightly over five pints, and his water bottle.[40] Those who could not afford this degree of luxury made do with pottery tableware. For some time potters had been engaged on the manufacture of various designs of fine quality painted with either geometric or floral patterns, or with lively scenes like those engraved on metal vases, a bird eating a fish, or animals at full gallop.

Ever since the beginning of the New Kingdom a stream of such purely luxury goods as mixing-bowls, wine jars and pot stands of metal or precious stones had been entering Egypt from foreign countries, from the isles or from Syria and Nubia. They were of no conceivable practical use, but they were an excuse for forming collections of every kind of animal and plant, real or imaginary. Most of these valuables found their way into temples, but Pharaoh kept some of the choicest for himself.[40a] A taste for this exotic bric-à-brac gradually spread through the population, and Egyptian goldsmiths began to manufacture them. The duties of Prince Qenamūn, the chamberlain responsible for great occasions, included that of presenting the king with his New Year gifts, and he had reproduced in his tomb all the whole series of objects which the royal craftsmen had manufactured for these occasions.[41] A particularly striking ornamental piece is that representing a grove of *dōm* palms and Syrian palmettoes mingled with water lilies and daisies, with monkeys climbing the branches to pluck the palm-kernels. The other pieces are more familiar: statues of ebony, some plain, others picked out in gold, representing the king and queen with various attributes, standing on

*The handle is modelled in the shape of a young goat.

pedestals or carved on the panels of a cupboard: sphinxes, human-headed or falcon-headed figures, goats or gazelles lying on plinths, and coffers. I imagine that they were all destined to form part of the palace furnishings and that many of them must have been displayed in the state apartments.

The central feature of the bedroom was, naturally enough, the bed. Some surviving examples are of extremely simple design, consisting mainly of wickerwork on a wooden frame resting on four feet, which are frequently carved as bulls' hoofs or lions' claws. Three magnificent examples were recovered from the tomb of Tutankhamūn: in all three, each side was carved in the form of a complete animal—cow, panther or hippopotamus—with elongated body. The room also contained cupboards of inlaid wood for holding linen and clothes. Toilet articles such as mirrors, combs, hair-pins and wigs were kept in a variety of boxes and caskets, while little jars of obsidian or ivory held beauty preparations, ointment, and scented unguents. In the private apartments belonging to members of the family—those of the children and girls in particular—musical instruments and boxes of toys lay about.

Ewer and basin on stand

Offices were fitted with a special type of cupboard, holding manuscripts, rolls of parchment and papyrus, and all the materials which the scribe used in his work. When a sheet of papyrus was completely covered with writing it was rolled up, tied and sealed. The rolls were then made into bundles, which were put into leather document cases, and the latter were stored in the cup-boards.[42] Scribes did not need tables; they would either spread the sheet of papyrus on their knee or, if necessary, they held it un-rolled in their left hand and wrote standing. When a scribe had to go out, he put all his writing materials in a kind of stiff flat-bottomed bag closed by a sliding catch and carried by a strap.

Kitchens were furnished with four-legged tables and bowls and dishes of every shape and size, all of thick earthenware. Ovens were made of heat-resisting clay. I think that the metal chafing dishes on a high pedestal foot on which we see geese being roasted were probably not used outside the temples and would never have been employed by an ordinary cook.

Among the very poor, where whole families were huddled into a space of perhaps 15 feet square, or even less, 'furniture' meant merely rush mats and a few pots. In such circles a pot-stand or two and a few wooden boxes represented comparative affluence.

CHAPTER II

TIME

1. *The Seasons of the Year*

THE Egyptians did not regard a year as the time required for the sun to complete a revolution, but as the period necessary to produce a harvest. The word for year, *renpit*, was represented by a hieroglyph depicting a young shoot in bud, and the same sign reappears in related words like *renpy* (to be fresh or vigorous) and *renpout* (yearly produce).

Harvests in Egypt are wholly dependent on the annual inundation of the Nile. At the beginning of June in each year the river shrinks to a mere trickle through the parched countryside, and the desert threatens to engulf the valley. It was a season of universal anxiety, for before the bountiful gifts of nature the Egyptians felt mingled thankfulness and fear—fear, for example, of injuring the god when stone was being hewn from the quarry, or of smothering him when the grain was buried in the furrow: fear of crushing him to death when the corn was trodden out or of beheading him when it was cut. Although within the most distant human memory the flooding—sometimes too violent, sometimes scarcely sufficient, yet nearly always a benison to the thirsty land—had never failed to follow its expected pattern, the dwellers by the banks of the Nile were never wholly reassured. 'Strong and weak unite to beg thee each year to grant thy water. Every man is summoned with his tools, and none tarries behind his neighbour. No man dons his raiment. The children of the great are not arrayed in finery, and songs are no more heard in the night.'[1] The Nile, Hâpi, had found a place in the Egyptian pantheon at a very early date, in the shape of a well-nourished man with pendulous breasts, the fat folds of his belly girt with a belt, and wearing sandals on his feet—a sign, this last, of wealth. He was crowned with a chaplet of water plants and his hands either

Hâpi, the Nile God

scattered symbols of life or held a table almost invisible beneath piles of fish and ducks, bunches of flowers and sheaves of corn. Several cities bore his name: he was sometimes referred to as King of the Gods, and he expected offerings on at least as generous a scale as did the rest of the pantheon. Ramesses III paid him lavish honours. Throughout the whole of his reign at On, and for three years at Memphis, he instituted or restored certain 'books of Hâpi', which listed huge quantities of provisions and crops. Thousands of miniature figures of Hâpi were manufactured in every sort of material, among them gold and silver, copper, lead, turquoise, lapis lazuli and faience, besides seals, pendants and statuettes of his consort Repît.[2] When the floods were due to rise, these were offered to the god in large numbers of temples and the books of the Nile, together, possibly, with the statuettes,[3] were cast into the lake of the temple of Rê Harakhté at On. This lake, like the Nile in the cataract reaches, was called Qebehou. The ceremonies were resumed two months later, when the floods had reached their peak. The whole valley between the two deserts was a lake, in which cities were islands, towns were islets and dykes formed the roads. Then, as if in obedience, the level of the waters began to subside until, four months after the floods had begun, the Nile flowed again within its own channel. These four months comprised *akhit* ('inundation'), the first season of the year.

As soon as the waters had receded, the peasants would scatter through the fields and set about ploughing and sowing, before the earth had time to harden. For about the next four or five months they had virtually nothing to do beyond keeping the ground irrigated. This phase was followed successively by harvest, gathering in the crops, treading out the corn and other jobs. Thus the season of flood was followed by going out (*perit*) and harvest (*shemou*), making in all three seasons, as against the four recognized by the Hebrews and the Greeks.

No matter how regular the flooding might be, it could hardly in itself have been a sufficiently precise phenomenon to mark the beginning of the year. However, the start of the rise of the waters coincided annually with an event which could be used to help to fix the calendar, when the dog-star Sirius (known to the Egyptians as Sôpdit), which had been invisible for a considerable period, made a brief appearance in the eastern sky immediately before sunrise. The Egyptians were quick to relate the two phenomena: they identified the star with the goddess Isis, whose tears, they said, caused the flooding, and they made her the patron deity of the year, which was regarded as beginning on the day when the star first rose. This identification of star and goddess was recorded in the books of the House of Life (p. 297 f), which was a kind of repository of tradition and knowledge maintained from the Old Kingdom right down to the late period.[4] In the calendar which was cut by command of Ramesses III on one of the external walls of his temple at Medinet Habu, the king explicitly states that the festival of the goddess Sôpdit, which was celebrated on the date on which the star rose, coincided with that of the New Year.[5] We possess a love song in which the lover compares his mistress to the star which shines at the beginning of the perfect year (*renpit nefert*)[6]—as contrasted with the 'lame' or 'wandering' year (*renpit gab*), when the god Shou rose no more, when winter came in summer's season and when the months strayed from their true sequence. But the public would have none of it. 'Deliver me', writes the scribe, 'from the lame year.'[7] Farmers and hunters, fishermen and explorers, doctors and priests, who were obliged to celebrate the great majority of festivals on fixed dates—everyone, in short, whose professions depended upon natural phenomena, used the perfect year, the year in which months and seasons followed their appointed cycle, when *akhit* could mean nothing but the four months when the Nile had overflowed its banks, *perit* the cool season when the seed was sown, and *shemou* the time of harvest and heat. This was why Pharaoh was spoken of both as a source of refreshment during *shemou* and as a corner warmed by the sun during *perit*.[8] The miners who went to mine turquoise in Sinai (p. 142) knew that they must not wait for the months of *shemou*, that evil season when the mountains became practically red hot, so that the precious stones changed colour.[9] It was common medical and veterinary knowledge that there were certain diseases and complaints which recurred in *perit* and others in *shemou* and physicians were prepared to go so far as to prescribe one form of treatment for use only during the first and second months of *perit* and another only during the third and fourth. Conversely some prescriptions could be used effectively in *akhit*, *perit* and *shemou*—i.e. all the year round.[10]

As a matter of convenience the three seasons were all assigned the same duration and were divided into twelve months each of thirty days. In the reign of King Ramesses III these were still known, as they had been since the earliest period, by their place in the cycle of the season, i.e. as the first, second, third or fourth months of *akhit, perit* or *shemou* respectively. It was not until the Saite period that they were called after the monthly festivals. Five extra or epagomenal days were added at the end of the fourth month of *shemou* to bring the annual total to 365. There is no documentary evidence from the Pharaonic period to show how the Egyptians succeeded in maintaining the accuracy of the calendar and in preventing New Year's Day from falling one day later every four years. Strabo leaves us little the wiser when he tells us that a day was added at certain intervals when the excess fractions of a day left each year made up a complete day.[11] It would have been better simply to add one day every fourth year, and this is no doubt what actually happened when Egypt had the good fortune to be governed by monarchs like Sety I or his son. In periods of disturbance the extra day could easily have been forgotten and in that case the calendar must have got progressively more inaccurate until the matter was brought by the wise men of the House of Life to the notice of a Pharaoh who could reconcile the calendar with observed natural phenomena and once again fix the festival of Sôpdit as New Year's Day.[11a]

2. *Festivals and Holidays*

New Year's Day was not merely the festival of the goddess Sôpdit: it was kept as a holiday throughout the whole country. On that day in the temple of Wepwawit 'the house gave presents to its Lord',[12] which means, I think, that the temple staff offered to the god the gifts which the villagers had brought on the preceding days. Prince Qenamūn had a picture painted in his tomb of the magnificent gifts which he had been punctilious in offering to the king on New Year's Day;[13] it makes one wonder whether people in Egypt used to exchange presents and good wishes on that date. An endless sequence of festivals extended throughout the year, but they were especially numerous during *akhit*, when agricultural work was at a standstill. The great festival of Opet,. which fell in the middle of this season, lasted for nearly a month, and while I would not go so far as to say that the entire population took a month's holiday, there is no doubt that the great sacred barque of Amūn was greeted and accompanied along the banks by an immense concourse on its return again towards Southern Opet (p. 290). In order to take part in the festivals of Bubastis the people of Egypt cheerfully abandoned their daily tasks and went aboard boats, the women carrying sistra and the men flutes. Throughout the entire journey the company sang, danced and exchanged badinage with everyone they met, while it was commonly said that more wine was drunk during this festival than in the whole of the rest of the year. Another festival that was always well attended was that of *tekhi* ('drunkenness'), which fell on the first day of the second month. The first day of the first month in the sowing season was kept as a general holiday throughout Egypt. Further, every district and every city regarded it as a matter of duty to celebrate at least once a year the festival of the particular local deity who was their lord and protector. All Egyptian gods were not only great travellers but also extremely hospitable, and consequently every temple of any importance at all was the seat of several gods. Ptah, god of Memphis, had his own enclave within the city walls of Karnak, as did Wadjit, Lady of Imit, at Tanis. The inhabitants, who were obliged as a matter of duty to celebrate the festival of their own local god, could not disregard his divine friends who shared his abode. They would assemble at the temple, glistening with oil and dressed in new clothes, and there present some offering, in return for which they were free to eat, drink and shout with even more than their usual gusto. Certain festivals were of such antiquity that even if the god concerned had no shrine in the neighbouring temple, his festival must be observed at home, during which no new task might be undertaken, and even sometimes no work done at all. The 'fellah' and the labourer might well have complained, like the cobbler in the fable, that the parson in his sermons was always announcing some new saint's day.*

*La Fontaine, *Fables*, Bk. VIII, No. 2.

Moreover, every tenth day seems to have been kept as a kind of Sunday.* On the stele erected in the temple of Hathor at On in the eighth year of his reign, King Ramesses II addresses all the workmen engaged in decorating his temples and palaces in the following terms: 'For you I have filled the storehouses with all manner of things: with cakes and meat and pastries: with sandals and garments and perfumes to anoint your hands every tenth day, your garments for all the year, and sandals for your feet each day.'[14] People who had dressed with greater care and eaten a more substantial meal than usual could not reasonably have been required to work.

3. *Auspicious and Inauspicious Days*

Even after fulfilling his obligations to the gods and observing the periods of inaction which they enjoined, an Egyptian could not always give himself with an easy mind to recreation or to useful work. Days fell into three categories—good, menacing and hostile—according to the nature of the events which had taken place on the corresponding days when the gods had dwelt on earth. At the end of the third month of the season of flooding, Horus and Seth had called a halt to their titanic struggle, and peace had been granted to the world. Horus had received as his personal possession the whole of Egypt, and Seth, the whole expanse of the desert. There was mirth then in heaven: the quarrels which had spread among all the other gods were made up and peace reigned: in their presence Horus assumed the white crown and Seth the red. These three days were good, like the first day of the second month of *perit*, on which Rê had raised up the sky with his two mighty arms, and the twelfth day of the third, when Thoth had replaced the majesty of At-u-m in the Pool of the Two Truths in the temple.

But Seth soon reverted to his old ways, and on the third day of the second month of *perit* he and his companions opposed the sailing of the sky god Shou in his barque. This made it a menacing day, like the thirteenth of the same month on which the eye of Sekhmet, the goddess who unleashed pestilence on mankind, had become an object of terror. The twenty-sixth day of the first month of *akhit* was not merely menacing but downright hostile,

*In some calendars, the year was divided into 36 decans.

marking as it did the anniversary of the great struggle between Seth and Horus. At the outset the two gods, who had begun by assuming human form, belaboured each other furiously: each then changed into a hippopotamus, and in this guise passed three days and nights, until Isis, mother of Horus and sister of Seth, threw her harpoon at them and forced them to resume their original shape. The birthday of Seth, which fell on the third of the five epagomenal days, was hostile, and the whole day was spent by the kings in complete idleness and neglect even of their own persons. Private individuals also adjusted their behaviour to the character of the days. On hostile days it was regarded as safer not to go out of doors either at sundown or during the night or—in extreme instances—at all. Prohibited activities might include bathing, embarking in a boat, making a journey, eating fish or anything which lived in water, or killing a goat, an ox or a duck. On the nineteenth day of the first month of *perit*—and indeed on a number of others as well—intercourse with a woman involved the risk of contracting a severe infection. On some days no fire might be lit in the house, on others it was unwise to listen to cheerful songs or to utter the name of Seth, the divine embodiment of strife, cruelty and lechery; should anyone do so, except by night, his house would never be free from quarrels.

No doubt the Egyptians relied upon tradition for their knowledge of what they were free to do, might do at a pinch, or must not do on any account whatsoever; but to refresh their memory and to resolve any doubts there were calendars which listed auspicious and inauspicious days. We possess some long extracts from one of these calendars, and fragments of two others.[15] I imagine that, if we were fortunate enough to possess one in its entirety, we should find a statement of the authority on which its injunctions and prohibitions were based. There were plenty of oracles in Egypt, and the calendars of auspicious and inauspicious days no doubt emanated from the temples where the oracles were delivered: they were also, no doubt, mutually contradictory, so that an Egyptian who was absolutely obliged to go out or travel or work on a day regarded as inauspicious for this purpose could always consult some other oracle which would declare auspicious the days which the first had asserted to be the opposite. In centres of the worship of Osiris, Horus or Amūn, the deeds of Seth were remembered with detestation; but at Papremis[16] and in the eastern part of the Nile Delta, in the central Delta, in the eleventh nome, and in Upper Egypt at Noubit and Oxyrhynchus—in fact in all the centres of the cult of Seth—they were much admired and in consequence their anniversary was necessarily regarded as auspicious. But what if our imaginary Egyptian was unable to consult another oracle, or believed only in his own? Then in all probability at the end of the calendar there was some rubric telling him how to make love without coming to any harm, how to bathe without being eaten by a crocodile and how to brand a bull without meeting instant death. All that was required was to recite the appropriate formula, to finger an amulet or—most effective of all—to repair to the temple and there make some small offering.

4. *The Hours*

The Egyptians divided day and night into twelve hours each, just as they divided the year into twelve months, but they do not seem to have sub-divided the hour. The word *at* which we translate as 'moment' had no recognized duration. Each hour had its own name: for example the first hour of the day was 'the brilliant', the sixth was 'the straight' and the twelfth 'Rê restores himself to life'. The first hour of the night was 'the discomfiture of the enemies of Rê' and the twelfth 'witness of the beauty of Rê'.[17] We might perhaps be tempted to think that with names like these the duration of the hours altered from day to day, but this was not so. At the equinoxes day and night were of equal length, while for the rest of the time the Egyptians were no more put out by the fact—which they knew—that the sun might sometimes be ahead of or sometimes behind the mean, than we are by the fact that six in the morning or eight at night are very different matters in winter and summer.

The names of the hours quoted in the preceding paragraph were used only by priests and men of learning. We find them listed in tombs because the passage of the sun through the twelve regions of the underworld is a recurrent theme of tomb decoration. Laymen simply called the hours by their numbers, a fact which raises the question whether the Egyptians wanted to tell the time and if so, whether they could. There was a particular class of priests known as *ounuît,* derived from *ounut* (hour), which suggests that they must have relieved each other hourly in order to perform ceaseless adoration. An official of King Pepy I* claims that he reckoned all the hours of work which the State required, exactly as he counted provisions, cattle or supplies paid in by way of taxation.[18] In his letter to Harkhuf, who was bringing the dancing dwarf to the court (p. 65), King Neferkarê advises the explorer to surround this precious being with men of discretion who should be counted hourly.[19]† It would perhaps be too much to conclude from the evidence of these texts that devices for measuring time were very widely known. King Neferkarê was only a child when he wrote to Harkhuf, and he may innocently have imagined that the instruments which he had seen in his palace were available to everyone. Be that as it may, such instruments were known by this period: and our museums contain specimens varying in date from the eighteenth dynasty to the late period.

During the night the hour could be ascertained by observation of the stars and by the employment of a slit ruler and of two set-squares fitted with a plumb-line. Two observers were required, one to take the observation and the other as assistant. They had to take up their position exactly facing the pole star. The observer used a previously compiled list, only valid for a fortnight, from which he could read that at the first hour some particular star would be observed over the exact centre of the assistant's head, and that at some other hour another star would occupy a position above his right or his left eye.[20]

When observation of the stars was impossible, conical vessels were employed, about eighteen inches in height and pierced with a hole near the bottom,[21] their capacity and the size of the hole being so calculated that the water took exactly twelve hours to drain out. The outside of these vessels was often ornamented with astronomical figures or with horizontal lines of inscription: at the top might be the gods of the twelve months, below them symbols of the thirty-six decans, below them again the dedicatory inscription of the object and, finally, in a little niche, a cynocephalus or baboon, the sacred animal of Thoth, god of sages and scribes. The hole through which the water ran was pierced between his legs. On the inside there were twelve vertical bands divided by equal panels containing the hieroglyphic signs of life, duration, or stability and shallow holes at almost equal intervals. In theory

*Of the Sixth Dynasty.
†Literally 'ten times in the night'.

each band corresponded with a certain month, but in practice, since all the holes were identical, they could all be used at any time of the year.

The clepsydra or water clock could be used equally effectively by day and by night, but in a country like Egypt, where the sun is scarcely ever obscured, it was far better by day to use sundials

A water clock

or gnomon clocks, of which there were two kinds. On the first, the length of the shadow was measured; in the other what mattered was the angle at which the shadow fell.[22] These instruments were of little general interest, and we are very rarely told the actual time of any event, great or small. One girl, whose moving story can be read on a stele in the British Museum (p. 52), tells us that her baby was born in the fourth hour of the night: but then she was the wife of a priest.[23] Again we know that it was during the seventh hour of the day that King Tuthmosis III reached the shores of Lake Qina in Syria and pitched his camp, but the chronicler does not say whether a gnomon was used to fix the time so precisely.[24] A mere glance at the sun would have sufficed to show that it was slightly after midday. When he comes to describe the actual battle, he simply says that on the twenty-first day of the first month of summer, the day of the festival of Rê, and in the twenty-third year of his reign, the king arose early in the morning.[24a] The narrator of the story of the flight of Sinuhe says vaguely 'the earth grew light', or 'at the time of the evening meal' and 'at dusk'—quite appropriate expressions, since a poor fugitive would have had no use for unwieldy devices for telling the time.[25] But we find identical or almost identical phrases used in a description of the battle of Qadesh, in the record of an official investigation, in the Abbot papyrus, and in the written report of a commission of inquiry. Even these vague indications of time are completely lacking when we come to paintings depicting a vizier receiving tax collectors, interviewing high officials or introducing a foreign delegation to the royal presence. We often hear of Pharaoh summoning his council, but no one has thought fit to mention even the approximate time. Diodorus asserts that the king was an early riser and that his time was strictly divided between work, devotion and relaxation.[26] This is not necessarily inaccurate, but his fortunate subjects scarcely seem to have troubled to follow his example. In the last resort they relied on the pangs of hunger and on the height of the sun to tell them the time of day: while at night honest men were asleep and the rest had other preoccupations than the time. Neither water clocks nor sun clocks were instruments for the civilian or for the soldier. They belonged among the temple furnishings, where the priesthood could consult them in connexion with the meticulous observance of divine worship.

5. *Night*

At least among the upper classes husbands and wives generally slept in separate apartments. There was once a king who was greatly grieved by the fact that he had no male child. He begged the gods of his time to give him one, and they decided to grant his request. He spent the night with his wife, and she conceived a child.[27] The author of 'The Doomed Prince' would clearly not have expressed himself thus if the king and his wife had normally slept together. Scenes in the women's apartments are common themes of drawings on ostraka.[28] The husband is absent and the only occupants are women and young children. The wife may be lying on her bed, wearing a diaphanous garment, sitting at her toilet assisted by a servant, or sometimes feeding her baby. The bed is the main piece of furniture. Its feet are sometimes shaped to resemble the grimacing god Bes, who hailed from the south and gave protection against falls and other accidents in the home, and toilet articles and a stool are arranged underneath it. The canopy of the tester rests on small papyriform pillars, twined from bottom to top with climbing strands of real or imitation leaves.[28a] The furniture in the husband's bedroom resembled his wife's, and consisted of bed, stool and footstool, the clothes and toilet utensils being kept in chests.

All Egyptians were deeply impressed by their dreams, and none more than Pharaoh. Once Prince Tuthmosis had gone hunting. He was tired and fell asleep in the shadow of the Sphinx. In a dream he saw the god, who commanded the prince to clear away the sand which was choking him and in return offered Tuthmosis a prosperous reign—an order which the prince instantly obeyed.[29] Pharaoh took dreams seriously, even in a time of crisis. In the fifth year of the reign of Merenptah, the Delta was the object of an attack in force by Tyrseni, Shardana, Lycians, Achaeans and Libyans. The king was anxious to take the field against them, but Ptah appeared to him in a dream and commanded him to stay where he was and send troops into the areas occupied by the enemy.[30] When the meaning of a dream was not clear, Pharaoh would summon his interpreters. Joseph made his fortune by interpreting the dreams of the fat and the lean kine and of the ears of corn. An Ethiopian monarch—and the kingdom of Ethiopia* was a small-scale replica of Egypt—one night saw two serpents, one on either hand. He woke up, but they had vanished: he had dreamed them. The priests interpreted this to mean that a brilliant future awaited the dreamer, who already held Upper Egypt and was soon destined to conquer the northern areas and to wear on his forehead the vulture and the cobra, symbolizing south and north respectively.[31]

Private individuals who had no interpreters at their beck and call were obliged to consult some such work as that contained in the Chester Beatty papyrus No. III which dates from the Ramesside period.[32] The first part of this work contained the dreams of the followers of Horus, who were regarded as an *élite* among the Egyptians. Under the Ramesses there was no disguising the fact that the Sethians, or devotees of the god Seth, were both very numerous and very influential, since the royal family traced a direct descent from him and the founders of the dynasty had been

*Kush, the modern Sudan, not Abyssinia.

his high priests. A bold face could accordingly be put on their unpopularity. The Sethians were on terms of superficial politeness with the priests and worshippers of Amūn and Horus, but in reality the latter always hated the Sethians, whom they described as quarrelsome, spiteful and bloodthirsty and as making no distinction between the sexes—this last, no doubt, an allusion to an episode one night involving the depraved Seth and his nephew Horus.[33] A Sethian, though he might be of the rank of 'him whom the king knows', remained a man of the people. On his death he would not become an inhabitant of the west but would remain in the desert, a prey for wild beasts. Accordingly the dreams of the followers of Seth are described in the second part of the papyrus. Were the manuscript complete we might have several other sections. By the time of Herodotus there were seven oracles in Egypt, each with its own methods of divination.[34] But unfortunately we possess only the opening section of the second part, and so we have only the dreams of the followers of Horus, albeit with many gaps, from which to learn what the Egyptians dreamed about and how they interpreted their dreams.

Very commonly the interpreter proceeds by analogy, so that a good dream signifies something advantageous, a bad dream, disaster. If the dreamer had seen someone giving him white bread, it is a good sign and things will go well with him. If he dreams he has a leopard's face, he will become a leader; while if he dreams that he is in the company of someone greater than himself, that too is good—his tutelary deity will advance his fortunes. On the other hand to dream of drinking warm beer signifies a loss of property, while to dream of pricking oneself with a thorn signifies a lie. If the dreamer's nails are pulled out, he will be cheated of his handiwork: to dream of teeth falling out means the death of someone dear. Looking into a well means being put in prison. To climb to the top of a mast means that god will raise the dreamer. To receive temple provisions means that god will send a livelihood. To be submerged in the Nile means to be purged of one's sins.

But not all examples were equally straightforward: if they had been, anyone could have interpreted them, and the key to their understanding would have been valueless. Let us examine a few examples of dreams with unexpected consequences. It is a bad sign for a dreamer to see himself embracing his wife in the sunshine, for god will witness his wretchedness. If he is breaking stones, god is blind to him; while if he is looking out from a balcony, god will hear his prayer. Steering a boat is a pleasant occupation, and one of which Prince Amenophis was fond: yet in a dream it foretells the loss of a law suit. It would have been difficult to explain why love of a dead father should protect one who had dreamed of Asiatics. Sometimes the interpreter is content simply to make a pun. Eating donkey's meat signifies coming greatness, since in Egyptian the words 'donkey' and 'great' are homonyms. To receive a harp is bad since *boine* (harp) recalls *bin* (bad). We often hear of obscene dreams, and they generally augured ill. Anyone who dreamed that he had intercourse with a kite would be robbed, probably because the kite is a thief: and we actually possess a spell designed to prevent its thefts (p. 26). Dreaming of divine affairs was not an invariable ground for reassurance. In real life it was an act of piety to burn incense in honour of a god, but to perform the same act in a dream meant that god would make difficulties for the dreamer.

But a man who had an alarming dream need not despair. The lean kine and the parched ears of corn were rather in the nature of a warning to be heeded than an announcement of inescapable disaster. In circumstances like these the best course was to call on Isis for help. She would come to the dreamer's aid and would know how to protect him from the dire consequences that Seth, the son of Nout, was eager to visit upon him. Take loaves of bread, add a few green herbs, moisten them with beer, add incense and smear one's face with the resulting mixture—this was enough to efface bad dreams.

CHAPTER III

THE FAMILY

1. *Marriage*

THE head of every family had his own house, be it large or small, full of treasures or simply furnished with matting. Setting up house and taking a wife were synonymous. The sage Ptahhotep advises his pupils to take both steps in due time.[1] In the story of the Two Brothers the elder possessed both a wife and a house, while the penniless younger brother lived there as a servant, looking after the cattle and sleeping in the stable. Before winning fame at the siege of Avaris, Ahmosé had lived a rough seafaring life since early boyhood, and had slept in a hammock like a veteran. He took the opportunity of a temporary lull in the fighting to return to his town of Nekhabit where he set up house and took a wife. He was not long destined to remain quietly by his own fireside, for war broke out again. Pharaoh's recruiting officers had not forgotten Ahmosé's valour and told him that they could not go to war without him.[2]

An official in the queen's service tells us that his royal mistress had married him off, first to one member of her entourage and later, after his first wife had died, to a second. He makes no complaint about it, for the queen had been careful to give her servants a good dowry.[3] It is, however, in fact clear from the love songs preserved in papyri in London and Paris that, while a good many marriages were admittedly arranged by parents or superiors, young people enjoyed a good deal of freedom.[4]

In the following love song a boy describes a beautiful girl: 'Her hair is black, blacker than the night, blacker than sloes. Red are her lips, redder than beads of red jasper, redder than ripe dates. Lovely are her twin breasts.' There speaks the pen of a true lover. To gain the girl's attention he resorts to cunning. 'I will take to my bed and pretend to be ill. My neighbours will come in to visit me and my sister* will be among them. She who knows the cause of my suffering will laugh at the doctors.'⁵ The plot miscarried; the lover, like his counterpart in the well-known poem by André Chénier, was taken ill in earnest. 'Seven days are now past and I have not seen my sister, weakness has overcome me: my flesh is numbed and my body knows not itself. The most eminent doctors may visit me, but they will not bring me relief; and the magicians will be of no avail. None has diagnosed my illness. What I have done in truth is what keeps me alive. It is her name that sustains me, the coming and going of her messengers that revive me. My sister is of more avail to me than all remedies, of greater worth than all books. When she visits me, then I am cured. When I see her I am well again. When she opens her eyes, my body is young again. She speaks and I am strong: let me but kiss her and she cures my illness. But she has not been to see me for seven days.'⁶

The girl for her part is not unmoved by the sight of a handsome boy. 'The voice of my brother has stirred my heart.'⁷ But she plans for the future and relies on her mother to help her. 'Though he lives close by my mother's house yet I cannot go to him. It would be kind of my mother to undertake that for me.'⁸ She hopes that her lover will understand and will himself make the first move. 'If he would but send some message to my mother! My brother, I have vowed myself to thee, as thy bride to be, by the goddess, "the Golden One". Come to me that I may see thy beauty! My father and my mother will rejoice. All men will rejoice at thee together and acclaim thee, my brother.'⁹

Meantime her 'brother', for his part, is eager for love and in his turn invokes the goddess, 'the Golden One', the lady of joy and of music, of song and banquets and love. 'I adore Noubit, I exalt Her Majesty, I adore Hathor, and I exalt the Lady of Heaven. I address myself to her and she hears my complaint. She has decreed my mistress to me, and she came of her own accord to see me! How wonderful is my lot! I exult, I rejoice, I am exalted.'¹⁰

The lovers have seen each other and are pledged, but the decisive words are still unuttered. The girl is torn between hope and fear. 'I passed close by the open door of his house. My brother was standing beside his mother, with all his brothers and sisters.

*In Egypt, 'sister' and 'brother' were used as synonyms for 'loved one'. For the implications of this, see p. 48.

Love of him captured the hearts of all passers-by. There is none
like my splendid lover: he is a paragon among brothers. He
looked upon me as I passed, but I had none to share my joy. My
heart rejoices in full measure that my brother has seen me. God
grant that his mother may know my heart; then she would come
to visit me. Oh, Noubit, put this thought in her heart. I run to my
brother and I kiss him, nose to nose,* before his companions.'[11]
While waiting the girl confides her love to the birds and trees in
the garden, and dreams of herself as mistress of the household,
walking on her lover's arm.[12]

If matters hung fire for the lovers, or if difficulties were encountered, the young couple themselves must be held responsible.
Their parents raised no difficulties and seemed to approve of their
children's choice. Any opposition was purely formal. Pharaoh
had planned to marry his daughter Ahouri to one infantry
general and his son Nenoferkaptah to the daughter of another
general, but he married the boy and girl to each other when he
realized that the two young people were genuinely in love.[13] The
'Doomed Prince' in the tale arrives at a town of Naharina where
his young contemporaries have gathered in order to try their luck
in a contest of daring. The king of this country has decided to
grant the hand of his beautiful daughter to the intrepid climber
who can first reach the window of her room in a castle perched
on a crag. The prince enters the contest disguised as the son of an
Egyptian officer who has had to leave his father's house, since his
father has remarried and his stepmother, who hates him, is making
his life a misery. He duly wins the contest, but the king loses his
temper and declares that he will never allow his daughter to marry
an Egyptian exile. The princess, however, has other ideas, for no
sooner has she seen this Egyptian than her heart is melted, and if
she cannot have him for her husband, she will die then and there.
This threat is enough to dispel her father's opposition forthwith.
He warmly welcomes the young stranger, listens to his story with
keen interest and without even realizing he is in the presence of
Pharaoh's son, but, powerless before a supernatural charm, he embraces him affectionately, accepts him as his son-in-law and loads
him with gifts.[14]

In love songs the young man addresses his sweetheart as

*The Egyptians kissed with their noses and not with their lips like the Greeks.
But in later periods the Egyptians were to copy the Greek practice.

'my sister', while the girl calls her lover 'my brother'. It is nevertheless quite clear that the lovers do not live in the same house, nor are they children of the same parents. After marriage the husband continues to call his wife *sonit* (sister) instead of *himit* (wife),[15] a mode of address which was introduced towards the end of the eighteenth dynasty. We do not know when it was abandoned, but it certainly lasted all through the New Kingdom. In courts of law this practice was not followed and *son*, *hay* and *himit* were given their proper meanings of 'brother', 'husband' and 'wife'. Nevertheless the Greeks were the first to believe that marriage between brother and sister was normal in ancient Egypt[16] and they have been followed by a large number of modern historians. Certain of the Pharaohs did marry their sisters and even their daughters, but on this subject we might remind ourselves of the reply of the royal judges to King Cambyses when he asked whether the law permitted anyone to marry his sister who wished to do so. No law permitted it, they said, but there was a law which permitted the king to do as he pleased.[17] Hitherto no single instance has been found of an Egyptian at any level of society whatsoever marrying his full sister.[17a] Marriage between uncle and niece does seem to have been permitted, for in a tomb of a certain Amenemhat, we find a picture of his sister's daughter, Baketam-ū-n, sitting beside her uncle as though she were his wife.[18]

Marriage is very seldom mentioned in surviving literary and pictorial records. When the Pharaoh in the story of Setnakhamwese has decided to marry his son and daughter he says, 'Let Ahouri be brought to the house of Nenoferkaptah this very night, and bring with her all manner of rich gifts.' His command was obeyed and in the words of the young bride, 'They brought me as a bride to the house of Nenoferkaptah. Pharaoh commanded that I should have a great dowry of gold and silver, and all the members of the royal household gave it to me.'[19] It is clear that the essence of the ceremony was the girl's removal with her dowry from her father's house to that of her future husband. I imagine that this procession was as picturesque and noisy a scene as those of offerings being brought to the temples, or of streams of suppliant foreigners begging to be allowed to be 'on the king's water': or, indeed, funerals, which were regarded by the Egyptians as essentially a change of residence. The bridegroom very likely went to meet his bride's procession, for we know that King Ramesses II went to one of his border castles lying between Egypt and Syria, there to await the daughter of King Hattusil, who had travelled in midwinter through part of Asia Minor and across the whole of Syria in order to become the great royal bride (p. 216). The Egyptians had a passion for putting everything into writing, and it is quite likely that, on marriage, husband and wife had to

A married couple

appear before an official who took their names and registered the details of the marriage settlement. When a married woman had to go to law, she was referred to by her own name followed by her husband's, e.g. Moutemouia, wife of Nesiamūn, the scribe of the sacred books. From an ostrakon found in Thebes we learn that the husband contributed two-thirds of this settlement and the wife one-third. If either part died, the survivor enjoyed the income of the whole, but could only dispose of the proportion which he or she had contributed.[20] Thus, a barber made over the proceeds of his business to a slave and gave him to his orphan niece in marriage. She received a dowry proportionate to the barber's private means, the latter having previously made a registered division of his possessions with his wife and sister.[21]

It would be difficult to believe that religion played no part in a matter as important as marriage. When a married man made his pilgrimage to Abydos his wife always accompanied him, and very frequently they went to the temple together. Neferhotep, Head Keeper of the flocks of Amūn, was attended by his wife, the Mistress of the House, praised of Hathor, Lady of Cusae, and singer of Amūn, when he celebrated the adoration of Rê as he rose above the eastern horizon and the adoration of Harakhté as he sank in the west. It therefore seems to me likely, though there is no documentary evidence for it, that newly wed husbands and wives, and possibly all their relatives, would together enter the temple of the god of the city and there offer a sacrifice and receive a blessing.

When scribes and priests had done their part and the newly wed couple had entered their house, it was time for the guests to take their leave. Since we know that the Egyptians liked family gatherings for meals, I venture to suggest that before leaving the couple alone together there was a special celebration with eating and drinking on whatever scale the family means or pride suggested.

2.   *The Wife*

Painters and sculptors have left us an attractive picture of the Egyptian family. Father and mother hold each other by the hand, or clasp each other's waists, while even the very youngest and smallest of the children gather close round their parents.[22] In the reign of Akhnaton the demonstrative affection of the royal couple was conventionally represented by showing the queen seated on the king's knee. Both parents are tenderly kissing their children, who, in return, are patting their father and mother on the chin with their tiny hands. This particular fashion lasted only as long as the heresy of which it was both manifestation and effect, and by the beginning of the nineteenth dynasty Egyptian art had resumed its habitual severity. But tomb paintings always show us husband and wife close together, as united in the hereafter as it is pleasant to imagine they had been in life.

Literature however draws an unflattering picture of Egyptian womanhood. She is frivolous, flirtatious and unreliable, incapable of keeping a secret, untruthful and spiteful as well as naturally unfaithful. To the story-tellers and moralists she was the epitome of all sin and an endless source of mischief.[23] One day when King Snefrou was bored to distraction someone tried to amuse him by arranging for twenty girls wearing only snoods to sail on his lake in his royal part. One of them lost her new turquoise and stopped rowing. The king told her to row on, saying that he would replace it. 'I prefer my own pot to a copy'* answered the beauty. The king humoured her and summoned his magician, who succeeded in finding the lost jewel by the novel device of piling one half of the water upon the other.[24] In another story of the Nine Gods, seeing Bata alone in the Valley of Pines, take pity on his loneliness and give him the gift of a peerless wife in whom the essence of each god was combined. She begins by deceiving him and then betrays him. Bata recovers and changes into a bull. His former wife, who has become Pharaoh's favourite, cajoles her lord and master into ordering the bull to be slaughtered, and when Bata changes himself into a persea-tree, she wants him to have it cut down. Bata had already first experienced female perfidy when he was working as a farm hand in his old home.

One year at sowing ti[me ...]
earth was ready for th[...]
into the fields. They ha[...]
the house alone to fetc[...]
light of the heavy load [...]
saw him. She instantly [...]
hour in each other's arm[s ...]
fierce as the panther of [...]
mother and your husban[d ...]
words again, and I will [...]
his guilty sister-in-law [...]
venge. Her husband, A[...]
hasty judgement, so that [...]
persuade him that his br[other ...]
tend that she had virtuo[us ...]
satisfied and would be co[...]
her alleged seducer.[25]

*Literally 'to its bottom', i.e. 'I want mine and no other.'

At a very early date, the wife of a master of ceremonies deceived her husband with a young man to whom she gave many presents. Roudidit, the wife of a priest of Rê, also deceived her husband and gave birth to three illegitimate children, whom she explained away by saying that they were the offspring of the god Rê himself, who had chosen this way of giving Egypt three pious and liberal monarchs.[26] One day Roudidit lost her temper with a servant and dismissed her. The servant, who knew the true state of affairs, meant to report this matter to the proper quarters, but most unfortunately she first mentioned it to her brother, who repaid her confidences by beating her soundly (p. 62).[27] Another noble lady, Tbouboui, who was no common whore but a temple prostitute, demanded that her lover should first of all disinherit and then kill his children.[28] Yet another lady of noble birth, having caught sight of Truth disguised as a handsome young man, became his mistress. When she had satisfied her desire she was so uninterested in her casual lover that she left him to beg at the door of her house and only long afterwards let her small son know that the beggar was his father.[29]

No, Egyptian literature has little use for women, and it is men whom it depicts as faithful and affectionate, devoted and reasonable. Yet the same literature, in deference to convention, represents Pharaoh as a wilful and fantastical figure driven at every turn to seek the advice of his scribes and magicians. The truth of course was that plenty of Egyptian kings were brave soldiers and skilled statesmen, and plenty of Egyptian women were model wives and devoted mothers, like the young wife whose story can be read on a stele in the British Museum:

'Oh ye wise men and priests, princes, nobles and all mankind, all ye who enter this tomb, come, hear my tale. I was born on the ninth day of the fourth month of the season of flood in the ninth year of the reign of King Ptolemy XIII. On the first day of the third month of summer in the twenty-third year of his reign, my father gave me as wife to the high priest Pekherenptah, the son of Petoubasti. It was a great grief to him that thrice I conceived daughters but no son. But with my husband I prayed to the Lord God Imhotep, son of Ptah, the giver of favours, who grants sons to those who have none and he answered our prayer, as he does for those who pray to him. . . . [In recompense for the works of piety performed by her husband] I conceived a son and I gave

birth to him at the first hour of the day on the fifth day of the third month of summer in the sixth year of the reign of Queen Cleopatra: the day of the festival when offerings are laid on the altar of this great and mighty god, Imhotep, called Petoubasti, and everyone rejoiced. On the sixth day of the second month of winter in the sixth year, I died. My husband, the high priest, Pekherenptah, laid me in my grave, granting me all the rites proper to perfect beings. He left nothing undone in my embalming, and laid me in my grave behind Rakoti.'[30] Victim alike of her father's choice and ultimately, even unto death, of her husband's ambitions, the hapless Ta-Imhotep died in the prime of life, bitterly mourned by her husband, who spared no expense over her funeral.

With this touching story fresh in our minds, we shall find it instructive to read the complaint of a widower to his dead wife recorded in a papyrus now in the Leiden Museum (p. 327).

'I was a young man when I married you, and I spent my life with you. I rose to the highest rank but I never deserted you. I never caused you unhappiness. I never deserted you from my youth to the time when I was holding all manner of important posts for Pharaoh (Life, Health, Strength!): nay rather I always said to myself "She has always been my companion." When anyone came to talk to me of you I would not heed the advice he gave me about you, saying instead, "I will do your pleasure." Moreover, when I was responsible for training the officers of Pharaoh's infantry and cavalry, I caused them to come and prostrate themselves before you, bearing rich offerings of every kind to lay at your feet. Never have I concealed from you anything I have gained until this very day. . . . No man has ever seen me playing you false, like the peasant who sneaks into another's house. I never had my scents, cakes and garments taken to the house of another, saying instead, "My wife is there", for I would do nothing to distress you. When you fell sick and suffered your illness, I summoned a master physician who gave you treatment and did everything at your behest. When I accompanied Pharaoh on his journey to the south, see how I behaved towards you—for eight months I neither ate nor drank as befitted a man of my rank. When I returned to Memphis I begged leave of Pharaoh and I went to your dwelling place,* and there I wept much before you

*i.e. your tomb.

with my kinsfolk. And now behold I have spent three years alone and yet I frequent no other house, though such a man as I could do so if he would. . . . Nay, I never go to any of the sisters that are in the house. . . .'[31]

This very pattern of the inconsolable widower makes it perfectly clear that many men in his position would have behaved differently. They would, that is, on obtaining high official position, have discarded the low-born wife whom they had married before they began to rise in the world: they would have behaved with far less restraint and finally, when their wives died, they would not have continued to weep and mourn for three years. A lifetime of such virtue and patience justifies a little expatiation on one's qualities.

Literature tells us that an unfaithful wife was punished by death. When Anpou, the elder of the two brothers in the story (p. 51), had learned, just too late, what had really happened he first sat down and wept for his younger brother and then returned home and killed his wife and cast her to the dogs.[32] At the end of Bata's story we know that he was planning to bring his wife to court before the great magistrates of His Majesty (Life, Health, Strength!) and though we have no record of the judgement, the Hathors (p. 57) had foretold that she would perish by the knife.[33] The wife of Oubainer, who deceived her husband and devoured his substance, was burnt alive with her paramour and her ashes were thrown into the Nile; this was the penalty prescribed by law.[34] In the words of the scribe Any, 'Be on your guard against the woman who walks abroad stealthily and do not follow her or any like her. A woman whose husband is safely out of the way, as soon as she is free from observation, sends you notes and calls you to visit her each day. If she can entangle you in her snares it is a crime which, once discovered, means death, even though her design is not fully accomplished.'[35] On the other hand we know of nothing to suggest that a husband's adultery was liable to punishment. A man could, if he wished, import concubines into his household. A chapter of a Book of the Dead intended to unite relatives in the grave suggests that a family included father, mother, friends, colleagues, children, wives, a personage called *int-hnt*, the meaning of which I do not know, concubines and servants.[36] There are occasional cases of polygamy. We know of a tomb robber who had four wives, on perfectly friendly terms, two of whom were still living when he was tried.[37] In a country in which the stick played so large a part, a husband had the right to beat his wife and a brother to beat his sister, provided that they did not go too far: anyone who inflicted injury was punished by having to undertake before the judges not to injure his wife in future on pain of receiving a hundred lashes and of forfeiting everything that she had contributed to their joint estate. In one case it was the wife's father who had demanded the protection of the authorities on her behalf.[38] He was right to do so, but we must remember that Mârouf was an Egyptian and that there may have been more than one shrewd woman who, with the backing of the authorities, caused her husband a good deal of trouble.

3. *Children*

The scribe Any advises his readers to marry young and have plenty of children. He might have saved his breath, for the Egyptians were great child-lovers. In the words of the Good Serpent to the shipwrecked sailor in the story, 'In two months you will reach your homeland. You will have an abundance of children and will enter on a happier life in the bosom of your family.'[39] Anyone who visits the tombs of Memphis, Amarna or Thebes, or studies in museums the steles of Abydos and the sculptured groups, will see plenty of pictures of children. When a great landowner like Ti visited his estates and reached a point from which he could see the harvesters, or watch the work on the threshing floor, a mat would quickly be spread on the ground and seats brought, and his family would gather round him, the children clutching their father's stick. However he chose to occupy himself—following the fishermen in a boat, throwing his stick at the birds roosting high in the trees, or in due season paying honour among the papyrus clumps to the beautiful goddess Hathor, the Lady of Imaou and of the Sycamore—his pleasure would be incomplete without the company of his wife and children. The younger members of the party would practise competently with their throwing sticks and harpoons. While Prince Amenophis was still a small child he liked attempting feats of strength (p. 211), and his father would proudly test his prowess.[40] We see a shepherd in the fields, accompanied by his children standing on tip-toe to raise their father's jug to his mouth when he was thirsty. The crafts-man's sons would wander round his workshop looking for ways of making themselves useful. Akhnaton and his queen, Nefertiti, were accompanied by their daughters when they drove abroad, while in the palace the princesses were always with their parents both while they were attending to public business and during their hours of leisure. We can see them climbing on their parents' knees

Amenophis IV with his wife and children

and fearlessly stroking their faces. The older ones would even take part in investiture ceremonies, while their fond parents would embrace and kiss them in an access of affection. King Ramesses II was exceedingly proud of his one hundred and sixty-odd children. Strabo reports with astonishment that the Egyptians made a point of bringing up all the children who might be born to them.[41] The size of Egyptian families, in marked contrast with Greek experience, is the result of the fertile soil and mild climate of the country. In the words of Diodorus, Egyptian children cost their parents virtually nothing, for while they were still small they went naked and barefoot, the boys wearing a necklace and the girls a comb and a girdle, and they could all feed for practically nothing on papyrus shoots and raw or boiled roots.[42]

Though all children were welcome, everyone wanted a son. We may recall what the great priest of Ptah, Pekherenptah, thought on the subject (p. 52). 'Once upon a time,' in the opening words of the story of the 'Doomed Prince', 'there lived a king who was much grieved that he had no male child. He begged the gods of his country for a son and they decided to grant this prayer.' It was a son's part to keep his father's name alive, and his filial duty, as a hundred inscriptions remind us, to bury him and to see that his tomb was properly cared for [43] (p. 314).

The Egyptians were always anxious to know the future and in order to ascertain the destiny of new-born children they relied upon a group of seven divinities collectively known as the Hathors, who hovered invisible over a child's cradle and pronounced the ineluctable manner of his death. Of the girl whom the gods wished to give as companion for Bata[44] they said, 'She will die by the knife', while their verdict on the male child so long desired by [...] y a serpent or hap[...] he fatal accident w[...] prince's life was rig[...] od and declared th[...] y as he might, he [...] left in freedom to [...] rs were equally inte[...] s to fix his child's [...] odotus, 'the Egypti[...] th and day is sacre[...] date of a child's bi[...] nd his days and w[...] ample, according to [...] days, someone born [...] of *perit* was destined to [...] to be older than his fath[...] of the second month of a[...] was lucky, since he would die of old age, while those born on the twenty-ninth day of the same month were luckier still, since they would die widely respected. On the other hand the fourth, fifth and sixth days of this month were most unfortunate, involving death respectively from fever, from love and from drink. Anyone born on the twenty-third must beware of crocodiles; on the twenty-seventh, of snakes.[47] The most apparently trivial circumstances might be pregnant with the gravest consequences. The medical treatise known as the Ebers Papyrus gives some examples. A child that cries 'Hii' will live, but one that says 'Mbi' will die. For a child to make a noise like a pine-tree or turn his face to the ground were fatal signs.[48] Those who were well up in religious mythology knew that Osiris, cast up on the Byblos coast, had been absorbed by a miraculous pine-tree. For a child whose cry resembled the creaking of the pines—a sound familiar to anyone who had travelled in Syria—the future could hold nothing but evil.

Whether the prospects were good or bad, the parents would lose no time in giving the child a name, which was all the more necessary since there were no family names in Egypt. As soon as Pharaoh's daughter found Moses in his basket, she gave him the name that was destined to be world famous. Many people both in antiquity and at the present day have supposed that the name Moses must be connected with the circumstances of his discovery and have struggled to explain its etymology in these terms. *Moshe* however does not mean 'rescued from the water'; it is simply a transcription of the Egyptian *mosé*, i.e. the ending of Thutmosé, Ahmosé and a number of similar names, and all that happened was that the princess found a child whom she took to be an orphan and acted for his parents in giving him a name.

Some Egyptians had very short names like Ti, Abi, Toui and Tō, while others have a complete phrase like Djedptahioufânkh ('Ptah says that he will live'.) In the course of time some common nouns, adjectives and participles came to be used as proper names, e.g. Djaou (stick), Shedou (leather bottle), Nekhti (strong), Shery (little one), or Tamit (she-cat). Most parents liked to put their children under the sponsorship of some divinity, and so the god-children of Horus were called Hori, those of Seth, Seti, and those of Amūn, Ameni. The historian Manetho was under the protection of Montou or Mōnth, a god worshipped at Thebes. Names could signify the god's pleasure, which accounts for the innumerable Amenhoteps, Khnoumhoteps, and Ptahhoteps, that 'god is before' (the child)—hence, Amenemhat—or that 'the god protects', or 'is the father of', the child. People with the name of Senousert (in Greek Sesostris), were 'sons' of the goddess Ousert, just as those called Siamūn were 'sons' of Amūn. Moutnedjem means that the goddess Mout is gentle. We can thus judge the comparative popularity of various divinities at different periods of history. During the Middle Kingdom the Lady of Byblos was invoked as the 'godmother' of a very large number of Egyptian women. From the time of the accession of King Ramesses I until the period of the War of the Unclean we hear of the names Sethnekhti, and Sethemouia ('Seth in the Barque [of Rê]') for the reigning dynasty boasted of its direct descent from the slayer of Osiris. But after these wars Seth became an object of detestation and no child would be named after him. The king himself was also a divinity whose protection was as effective as that of a god. During the eighteenth dynasty we meet people with the royal names Djeserkarê-senb, Menkheperrê-senb, and Nimârênekht. In the succeeding two dynasties there was a crop of Rammesses-nekhts ('Ramesses is mighty').

The field of choice was clearly enormous,[48a] and parents might often be guided by some quite extraneous circumstance such as a dream. The wife of Setnakhaemwēse, who had no male child, spent the night in the temple of Ptah. The god, appearing to her in a dream, gave her certain advice which she hastened to obey and she conceived a child. Her husband in turn dreamed that his son should be called Senosiris.[49]

After choosing a name for their child all the parents had to do was to register it with the proper authorities. We find the Princess Ahouri, wife of Nenoferkaptah, declaring 'I gave birth to this baby that you see, who was named Merab and whose name was entered in the registers of the House of Life.'[50] This last, to which we shall have occasion to refer frequently, was a kind of Egyptian Academy, where the sum of historical astronomical and abstract thought, which scholars were perpetually trying to use as the basis for extending their knowledge,[50a] was preserved. Perhaps it also performed more mundane functions, and, besides scholars, housed some ordinary scribes who acted as registrars of births, deaths and marriages. But there is nothing to support this conjecture, and it may be more prudent to follow Maspero in supposing that children were brought to the House of Life to have their horoscopes cast and to learn of the proper precautions in order to postpone as long as possible the ills which destiny had in store for them. Merab, son of Nenoferkaptah and Ahouri, was, after all, no ordinary child. In any event, the civil authorities certainly kept a record of births, deaths and marriages. In documents relating to legal proceedings accused and witnesses are called by their names, followed by those of their parents and by their occupation. Despite the enormous number of possible names for a child, we find plenty of homonyms. Amenhotep, the favourite minister of King Amenophis III, had the surname of Houy—and Amenhotep was so common a name that this was fairly usual. He had moreover the admirable habit of adding to his name and surname the epithet 'son of Hâpi'. Additional names of this kind were not merely a whim of the user, but had some official significance, and afford further proof of the care which the authorities devoted to public administration.

A baby stayed with its mother, who generally carried it against her breast in a kind of pouch slung round her neck, which left her arms free.[51] The scribe Any paid a tribute in the following terms to the devotion of Egyptian mothers, 'Repay thy mother for all her care for thee. Give her as much bread as she needs, and carry her as she has carried you, for you were a heavy burden to her. When in due time you were born she still carried you on her neck and for three years she suckled you, nor did she shrink from your dirt.'[52] Queens and perhaps some other mothers did not take their duties quite so seriously. The mother of Qenamūn had the title of 'Great Nurse, she who brought up the God'. In actual fact the 'God' was Pharaoh Amenophis II, who always felt a debt of gratitude to his nurse; he used to visit her and sit on her knee, as he had done when a baby.[53] Young princes were often entrusted to persons of high rank who had grown old in the royal service. Paheri, prince of Tjeni and governor of Nekhabit, is shown in his tomb holding on his knee a tiny naked child, whose right cheek is masked by a lock of hair: it is the royal child, Wajmosé. This senior official included among his titles that of tutor to the prince.[54] Ahmosé of Nekhabit, a veteran of the wars of liberation, tells us 'My old age was very happily passed among those who dwelt near the king . . . the divine consort, the great royal consort Makârê (Hatshepsut) renewed her favours towards me . . . it is I who brought up her elder daughter, the royal infant Nefe-rurê, when she was a tiny child at the breast.'[55] The old campaigner could not have devoted much time to the child, for we know of another foster father, namely the chief architect Senmout, to whom we owe Deir el Bahari, one of the finest of the Egyptian temples, and the erection of the obelisks of Karnak. The great artist and the baby got on splendidly together, and sculptured groups express vividly their undisguised affection for each other. One statue of Senmout appears as little more than a cube covered with hieroglyphs, the only recognizable feature being his head and, in front, the head of the little princess.

Sooner or later a child had to wear something more than just a necklace, and when the time came boys were given a loincloth and belt, and girls a dress. The day when a child received these objects marked a turning point in his life, and aged courtiers like Ouni and Ptahshepses never forgot it was in the reign of such and such a king that they first put on the belt. This may also, of course, have been the day that they first went to school. Children of the lower classes, peasants or artisans, lived at home and learned to tend the herds or handle tools in order, in due course, to ply the trade to which they were born.

4. *Servants and Slaves*

Among the entourage of an important dignitary, it is sometimes difficult to tell his staff of officials from his personal servants and those of his family. In Egypt the two were however sharply distinguished. Hâpidjefai, the governor of the district of Siout, sometimes had to deal with the possessions of his father's house, which might be described as his private fortune, and sometimes with those belonging to the prince's household, i.e. the property which he administered on behalf of the State. It is out of the funds of his parental estate that we find him paying those employed in maintaining his father's funerary cult. Since this last represented only a continuation of life on earth, we can conclude that personal servants were paid and maintained out of their master's personal estate.

Several Egyptian words are more or less equivalent in meaning to the modern 'servant'; 'listeners' (i.e. those who listened for their master's call), cupbearers, *wedpou*, a word written with the determinative of a vase, or by the vase-sign alone, and *shemsou* or 'follower', the ideogram of which was a complex sign comprising a long curved stick, some rolled-up matting or covering tied with a strap, and a small whisk. A *shemsou* accompanied his master when he left his house, and when he stopped would unroll the matting and spread it on the ground, place the long cane in his master's hand and from time to time ply his whisk. His master was then ready to receive his bailiffs or listen to a report. Another *shemsou* would carry his master's sandals when he walked abroad and when he stopped would wipe his feet[56] and put on his shoes. Cup-bearers or *wedpou* supervised the meals and waited at table. Their position was one of importance, giving as it did the opportunity of picking up confidential information and choosing the right moment to whisper a reminder. All important committees of inquiry included Pharaoh's cupbearers.

All these categories were, as far as we know, free servants, at liberty to leave their master's service and set up in business or to inherit property and, if they could afford it, sample in their turn the pleasure of being waited upon. After the fatal wrong inflicted on him by his elder brother, Bata declares that he will serve him no longer and that Anpou must henceforward look after his cattle himself. Admittedly in this case master and servant are brothers, but there is no reason to doubt that even if they had not been related, Bata would have acted as he did. Roudidit, the mother of three kings, had her servant whipped after a quarrel (p. 52), whereupon the servant left without any further explanation. She was admittedly punished twice, first by her brother and then by the crocodile as the instrument of divine vengeance, but this was because she planned to reveal Roudidit's secret to the king, and not because she had left her job. Naturally therefore it was still easier for an employer to dismiss a servant.

By way of contrast, as least under the New Kingdom, those called *hemou* or *bekou* are properly regarded as slaves in the full sense of this word.[56a] Not only were they harshly treated but if they ran away they were pursued. We have a letter in which a scribe reports to his superior, 'Two men have run away from Neferhotep, the master of the horse, who had had them beaten, and since they went there is no one left to do their work. This is for my master's information.'[57] One day, either because they had been beaten or because they yearned for freedom, two workmen ran away from Ramesses' residence. Kakemour of Tjekou,* captain of archers, was sent to recapture them. He arrived at the walled city of Tjekou the day after leaving Pi-Ramessu. Here the fugi-

*A fortress on the north-east frontier of Egypt, perhaps the modern Tel el Maskhuta.

tives had been seen heading south. Kakemour made his way to the fortress only to learn that they had passed the frontier wall to the north of the *migdol* of Sety Merenptah. At this point pursuit was abandoned and it only remained to close the file on the subject.[58] Not all runaway slaves were so lucky. In the tomb of Neferhotep we can see a scribe calling over a list of slaves in his master's presence. One slave has his hands bound and is being dragged along by a rope, while two others have been punished and the guard is about to fetter them. The scene might be entitled 'The recapture of the runaways'.[59]

Usually, if not invariably, slaves were foreigners captured during some successful campaign in Nubia or Libya, in the desert east of Egypt or in Syria, and handed over by Pharaoh or his herald either to their captor, if he had taken them prisoner single-handed, or to be shared out among the army if a large number had been taken in one action. By these means during his long career the brave Ahmosé had acquired nineteen slaves, ten women and nine men, some with foreign names such as Pamedjaiou, Paamou, Istaroummi and Heditkush. The remainder have Egyptian names and may have been handed over to Ahmosé during the campaign in the Delta—unless, as happened to Joseph,[60] their master changed their Canaanite or Nubian names for a native one.

An owner could hire out or sell his slaves. A man who needed clothes hired out the services of a Syrian slave woman for two or three days. The work which she was intended for is not specified, but the price demanded for her services was extraordinarily high.[61] A citizen of Thebes was under suspicion of having taken part in tomb robbery because his standard of living had risen noticeably sharply. When the judge asked his wife, 'How did you get the slaves that were with him?' she replied, 'I never saw the money he paid for them with; he was away travelling when he was with them'.[62] A recently published papyurs from Cairo throws some light on how slaves were bought. A merchant called Raia offers a client the chance of buying a young female slave from Syria and the deal is concluded. The price is not paid in gold or silver but in quantities of different goods calculated in terms of a weight of silver. Oaths are exchanged in the hearing of witnesses and registered with the tribunal, and the slave becomes forthwith the property of the buyer, who immediately gives her an Egyptian name.[63]

When the government began seriously to suppress tomb robbery a large number of slaves were found to be involved (p. 261). The court treated them with the utmost severity, administering the bastinado two or three times, but not more severely than the freemen who were also accused. A master would beat his slave, but then he would also beat his shepherds, his servants, or recalcitrant taxpayers. There were not many who could say, like a certain Nedjemab under the Old Kingdom, that they had never been beaten in the presence of the great since the day they were born;[64] and indeed this most fortunate of men may, for all we know, have taken a blow or two in secret and without witnesses, and kept quiet about it. Generally speaking, if we consider how hard it was for those from the lower ranks of society to rise in the social scale, we may well reflect that the difference between free men and those whom we call slaves was small enough. We have already (p. 49 f) quoted a document which shows that a former slave belonging to a barber was granted his freedom by his master, succeeded to his business and married his niece. An enterprising and intelligent slave could succeed in escaping from his servile status and in becoming assimilated in the mass of the population.

5. *Domestic Pets*

The dog, man's friend and hunting companion, was allowed to enter the house, and there curl up quietly beneath his master's chair and sleep, as dogs do, with one eye open.[65] The sheepdog

likewise stayed at his master's heel, waiting for his command by voice or sign to collect the stragglers or to guide the flock in the right direction.[66]

The breeds most commonly employed in Egypt as sheepdogs or watchdogs were greyhounds, long of leg, tail and muzzle, with ears which were generally large and floppy, more rarely pricked. By the New Kingdom the old breed of curly-tailed salukis and the medium-sized and straight-eared watch dogs had both disappeared along with the basset hounds which had been fashionable under the Middle Kingdom.[66a] But besides the greyhounds there was a small breed called *ketket*, and this is the breed that is presented in the story to the 'Doomed Prince' who had demanded a 'real dog' and angrily rejected the miniature species.

Pictures show greyhounds as generally kept on a leash, though they were sometimes allowed to run free. It was the monkey, another household pet, which often made itself responsible for looking after them, as we can see on the relief of Montouhirkhopshef,[67] where the monkey is holding the dog on an extremely short leash. The dog is evidently most uncomfortable, and is twisting back to bark and perhaps also to bite.

Dogs had their own names. Under the first dynasty we find a dog with the name of *Neb* (lord) buried near his master under a tombstone with his name and picture carved on it. King Antef was so proud of his four dogs, to which he gave Berber names, that he not only had them all carved in relief on a stele now in the Cairo museum, but he also had a statue-group, now lost, erected in front of his own tomb. As we know from a description in the report of the magistrates on thefts from royal tombs, it portrayed the dog called *Bahika* (a Berber word meaning oryx) standing between the king's legs. Dogs have been found buried at Abydos, among the tombs of women, archers and dwarfs, and there were dog burials at Siout, the source of the well-known limestone dog in the Louvre. Despite the bell on its collar, it does not look like a very effective watchdog. Although dogs in Egypt could be granted funerary or divine honours, it is noteworthy that there are no representations of men patting or playing with their dogs. They always kept their distance.

Monkeys may have inspired more affection. As early as the Old Kingdom they were allowed indoors. No one could help laughing at their funny faces and antics, as well as the practical jokes which they played with the aid, or at the expense, of the dwarfs and hunchbacks who were normally attached to a large household. The most valuable dwarfs were those who came from the most distant lands. Harkhuf gained the royal favour, and has become famous among Egyptologists, by bringing back a dancing dwarf from one of his missions to the far south; such a thing, we are told, had not happened since the reign of King Isesi, a century earlier. One of the richest tombs round the pyramid of Chephren belonged to the dwarf Senb. We know that the monarchs of Menat Khoufou still numbered dwarfs and hunchbacks among their households, but by the time of the New Kingdom this practice had died out in both royal and private circles. Monkeys, on the other hand, had never lost their popularity. In the tomb of King Tuthmosis III, Loret found a mummified baboon. Its presence was due less to the fact that it was the symbol of the god of writing and learning than to its having amused the king during his life and to the hope that it would do the same in the next world; and the same motive accounts for the presence of a dog in the entrance of the tomb of Psousennes. Monkeys had a particular liking for their masters' chairs.[68] In the absence of dwarfs and hunchbacks, their inseparable companions—and sometimes their victims—were the piccaninnies of the household.[69] When the fruit ripens we see monkeys clambering in the trees.[70] No doubt they eat more dates and figs than they actually pick, but the gardener takes it all quite calmly. Is not Egypt fertile, and has not everything a right to live? All life was created by Amūn, and Hâpi's waters flow for the benefit of all living creatures. The monkeys got on well enough with dogs and cats, but not so well with the Nile goose (*smon*), an ill-natured creature which they chastised when necessary.[71]

Until the Middle Kingdom the cat seems not to have been allowed indoors. It lived in the marshes, where it raided birds' nests, like the genet and the other small bird-eating carnivores.[72] It was indifferent to the rival efforts of human hunters: for while the latter are stealing silently between the papyrus reeds, their boomerangs still unthrown, the cat must have already sprung twice on its prey, for it holds a duck in its mouth and has just caught a brace of orioles.[73] It was eventually allowed to live indoors, but it never lost its independence of character, nor forgot its hunting instincts. It would sometimes condescend to sit under its master's chair, but, bolder than the dog, it would often jump unbidden on his knee and sharpen its claws on his robe of fine linen.[74] It would condescend to wear a collar. As long as this was only an ornament, all well and good: but when the cat was tied to the leg of a chair, with a bowl of milk placed just out of its reach, it would realize that it was being laughed at. Its hair would rise, it would bare its claws and strain against the leash.[75] It was generally on good terms with other domestic animals like the monkey and the goose. In one small group a female cat and a goose are confronting each other with a calmness which would be remarkable if we did not remember that they represent the god Amūn and his consort Mout, behaving as sacred animals should. But they were ready enough to peck and scratch, and in a real set-to the cat might get the worst of it.[76]

The Egyptians were well aware that a cat was the scourge of mice.[77] An even better way of ensuring that it would not run away

Queen Tiy's pets

than tying it up was for its master to give it a fat fish to eat beneath his chair.[78] On one occasion when Apouy went hunting water-birds in his duck-shaped boat with his wife and a servant, his cat—that same cat we have already seen sharpening his claws on his master's robe—was brought too. It raided the nest like its wild ancestors, but its master knew quite well how to call it to heel and take it back home whenever he wished.[79]

The Nile goose, known to natural historians as chenalopex, was soon singled out from the other farmyard fowls for special treatment.[80] Instead of being kept shut up with the other birds, it was allowed to wander through the courtyards and gardens and even into the house. This is why, when King Cheops wanted to test the skill of a magician who boasted that he could put a decapitated head back on its owner's shoulders, he immediately had a *smon* brought to him. This breed of goose, which shared with the cat the privilege of sitting beneath its master's chair, was of independent character, and did not presume on its position but would return from time to time to disport itself upon the banks of the Nile. It was constantly in mischief, destroying dates in the warm season and the fruits of the dōm palm in the cold, while during the rest of the year it would walk behind the man working on the land, gobbling the seed almost before it had reached the ground. Yet in spite of everything and although the Egyptians might curse it and had long ceased to trap it and lay it as an offering on the table of the gods, they still had a soft spot for its greed, its aggressiveness and its raucous squawk.[81] It may in a crisis have proved as tireless and staunch a protector as a watchdog, while, if it had to be punished, the monkey would cheerfully undertake the task at the risk of a peck or two.

CHAPTER IV

LIFE AT HOME

1. *Toilet*

THE Egyptians set much store by cleanliness and were as meticulous over their clothes and their houses as they were about their persons.[1] One of the things which Sinuhe most enjoyed on his return to Egypt after his pardon was discarding the clothes of coloured wool which he had worn while he was among the Bedouin.[2] Like Ulysses among the Phaeacians, he shook off the burden of his years; he plucked and combed his hair and he rubbed himself no longer with vegetable fats, but with the finest incense,* taken, likely enough, from a jar of obsidian and gold, like the one which King Abishemou of Byblos received from King Amenemmes III: and the clothes he put on were of linen.[3]

People generally washed several times a day, not only on first getting up but also before and after the main meals. The usual toilet articles comprised a basin and a spouted vessel, the latter generally kept under the table on which the food stood. The words for basin (*shaouty*) and jug (*hesmenyt*) seem to to be derived respectively from *sha* ('sand') and *hesmen* ('natron'), which suggests that the latter substance was added to the water in the jug and that some sand was put in the basin. Water used in finger bowls was sterilized by the addition of another kind of salt called *bed*. The name *souabou*, a derivative of *wâb* ('clean, pure') was given to a stiff paste which contained some cleansing and lathering ingredients, such as ash or fuller's earth.[4]

Directly after getting up and washing, gentlemen were taken in hand by the barber, chiropodist and manicurist, and ladies by the hairdresser. The king's levée was an important feature of court life, and the highest in the land boasted of being permitted to be present, and made a point of regular attendance.[5] Viziers, high

*Probably in the form of a powder or paste rather than a pomade.

officials and district governors also held similar levée ceremonies surrounded by their relatives and dependants, while scribes knelt before them with pens poised to take down their orders, or unrolled a long scroll of papyrus covered with names and figures and lists of tasks completed or work still to do. Meanwhile the chiropodist and manicurist had taken charge of their masters' feet and hands, and the barber would be shaving their beard and hair. The latter used a hooked razor with a curved blade, which was an improvement on the ancient type, shaped like a carpenter's knife, which had been employed during the Old and Middle Kingdoms. Razors were kept in leather cases with handles, and the cases themselves, together with tweezers, scrapers and knives for manicure and pedicure, were kept in pretty little ebony boxes.[6] After such treatment our imaginary friend would face the day clean and smart, with beard clipped square and hair cut short or trimmed. This was the signal for other experts to make their entry, the pharmacists with their sealed crystal, alabaster or obsidian vases of perfume and unguents and their little bags with a string at the neck containing green and black powders* which were used for making up the eyes.[7] Almond-shaped eyes were fashionable in Egypt; besides, these powders possessed prophylactic properties, saving delicate eyes from infection from the glare, dust, wind or insects.

Caricature of girl making up her face

The Egyptians possessed a wide range of make-up and toilet preparations. To ensure personal freshness during hot weather the body was rubbed for several successive days with an ointment of which the main ingredients were turpentine (*sonté*) and incense (*ânti*), compounded with some unidentified powder, and scented.[77] Other concoctions were intended for application at armpit and groin. They had beauty lotions for making the skin fresh and firm and others for removing spots and pimples from the face. For smoothing wrinkles, for example, a compound of powdered alabaster, powdered natron, salt from the north and honey was

*Malachite and galena, the ores of copper and lead respectively.

employed, and other recipes had a base of asses' milk. Endless trouble was taken over the scalp, whether it were to eliminate grey hair or to keep the eyebrows from going grey, to prevent baldness or to stimulate the growth of new hair. Castor oil was well known as a sovereign hair restorer. But ways and means were also known for getting rid of superfluous hair, as well as a recipe to enable women to make a rival's hair fall out.[8]

We possess the formula, recorded at the end of a treatise on surgery, of a most elaborate preparation with the somewhat ambitious title 'To change an old man into a young one'. Pods of fenugreek* had first to be dried and then stripped and the husks separated from the seeds. A paste was made by mixing the grains with an equal quantity of ground husks. Any surplus water was allowed to evaporate and the mixture was then moistened, dried and ground to powder. If a paste made from this powder was warmed, droplets of oil would be seen to form on the surface. This precious oil was then poured off, clarified and decanted into a vessel of some hard stone like obsidian. The oil was a perfect natural cosmetic, guaranteed to cure baldness, freckles, crows' feet and all skin blemishes.[9] This particular preparation was successfully used on innumerable occasions. Its only disadvantage was that it took a long time to prepare and that since only a minute quantity could be made at a time, it was extremely expensive.

Humbler folk would go and find a barber at work in the open air beneath the trees (p. 163). While they waited they would pass the time in gossip or dozing, sitting huddled up, their heads pillowed on their arms and their foreheads on their knees. Sometimes two people would share one seat. The person whose hair was actually being cut sat on a three-legged stool. When the barber had finished with him his head would be as bald and shiny as a pebble polished by the sea.[10]

The toilet of a lady of fashion, like her husband's, was an elaborate affair. We can watch it on a bas-relief of one of the royal favourites.[11] She is seated on a comfortable high-backed armchair, and holding her mirror, a disk of polished silver with a gold and ebony handle shaped like a papyrus stem. Meanwhile, though her hair has been cut a little short, the nimble and slender fingers of the hairdresser are busy gradually shaping it into many tiny

Helba in Arabic.

plaits, tying back the locks with an ivory pin until she is ready to deal with them. It is a lengthy process, and to while away the time a servant has brought her a cup into which he has poured the contents of a small bottle, saying 'To thy *ka*' as she raises it to her lips. The wife of Anpou, who was a peasant with a smallholding, was nothing like so grand. She did her own hair unaided while her husband and brother-in-law were working in the fields. She was anxious not to be interrupted, for if she got up her hair might get disarranged and she would have to begin all over again.[12]

2. · *Dress*

Until his morning toilet was complete, a man's head and feet were bare and he wore nothing but a loincloth and little or no jewellery. When it was finished he could, if he wished, still continue to wear the loincloth even if he intended to go out, but he would clasp one or more pairs of bracelets on his wrists, slip a ring on his finger, and hang round his neck a pectoral of five or six rows of beads suspended between two large terminal beads modelled as falcon-heads. With the addition of a pendant of

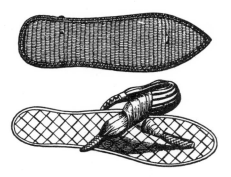

Palm-fibre sandals

jasper or cornelian on a long cord he would be fit to appear in any company, and could visit his estates, receive visitors on business or go to an office.

If he liked he could change his loincloth for a full skirt and put on sandals.[13] These last were a very early invention, but care was taken that they were not worn unnecessarily. The very early king

Plate IV   Two ancient Egyptian beauties

Narmer* used to walk barefoot with an escort of his personal servants, one of whom carried a pair of sandals. Ouni took care to see that soldiers on the look-out for plunder did not snatch the sandals from the hands—not the feet—of the passers-by.[14] A countryman on a journey carried his pair of sandals in his hand or tied to a stick over his shoulder, and put them on when he got to his destination. During the New Kingdom, and more particularly under the Ramessids, sandals of plaited papyrus, of leather and even occasionally of gold, were in more general use. A thong ran from the point of the sole between the first and second toes to the instep, where it joined other thongs to form a loop, the whole being knotted at the back of the heel. When the soles were of gold, so were the thongs, which must have been very painful for the unfortunate wearer, especially if the sandals did not fit him properly.[15] We know from medical papyri that foot complaints were very common in Egypt.[16]

Some Egyptians wore long plain robes held up by braces which feel straight from chest to ankle,[17] but most, instead of this rather severe attire, preferred a pleated linen robe, loose at the neck, which fitted closely to the upper part of the body and widened out towards the hem.[17a] The sleeves were fairly short and flared at the bottom. Over it was knotted a broad belt, made of a pleated scarf of the same material as the robe, the loose end being arranged to form a kind of triangular apron. Full ceremonial dress required a large curled wig, which completely hid the wearer's natural hair, and a dazzling display of jewellery, necklaces, a gorget, a pectoral on a double chain, bracelets at wrist and elbow and sandals on the feet.[18]

The clothes of a lady of fashion were not very different from those worn by her husband. They consisted of a very fine shift under a transparent white pleated robe like that worn by men, but gathered over the left breast and leaving the right uncovered, which opened below the belt and fell to the feet. The fringed sleeves left the forearms bare, thus showing off long and shapely hands and wrists heavily loaded with bracelets of varied design, sometimes in the shape of two engraved gold plaques mounted on a rigid hinged circlet. A lady might also wear rings of solid gold, strings of beads or twisted cords or ribbons of gold. A curled wig fell over her back and shoulders, and a handsome

*The first Pharaoh of United Egypt, *c.* 3000 B.C.

tiara of turquoise, lapis lazuli and gold, tied at the back by a cord with two tassels, might sparkle in her hair, while the whole elaborate coiffure was crowned by a conical object which stayed balanced miraculously upright—probably, though we do not know, made of some kind of scented pomade (p. 94). Men, as well as women, are very frequently portrayed wearing a similar ornament.[19]

Such clothes could only be worn by the idle rich, and ordinary workers were a good deal more practically dressed. Peasants and

craftsmen wore nothing beyond the traditional brief loincloth supported by a belt about four inches wide, unrelieved by ornament or embroidery and lacking the tassels which trimmed the loincloths worn by Asiatics. The poor were just as fond of ornament and jewellery as the rich, and since they could not afford gold they took to wearing trinkets of faience and bronze. Professional female musicians sometimes wore a long transparent robe like ladies of quality, but they often wore no clothes at all and only a little jewellery—belt and necklace, bracelets and earrings. The young servant-girls, who are often difficult to distinguish from the children, went about their work naked, especially when their master had guests, and displayed their lissom and graceful bodies to admiring eyes without embarrassment.

3. *Food*

The Egyptians, who were well aware of the value of their soil and were not in the least afraid of hard work, never lost their fear of famine. They knew that if the Nile floods were either too slight or too violent the resulting harvest would be poor. It was the government's responsibility, as Joseph warned Pharaoh through his interpretation of his dreams of the seven kine and the ears of corn, to see that large food reserves were built up, but there is no doubt that this primary duty was left undischarged in the years preceding the fall of the Ramesside dynasty. A woman under cross-examination about the source of gold found in her house replied: 'We got it selling barley during the year of the hyaenas (p. 267), when people went hungry.'[20] This was during the War of the Unclean. Bandits were killing, robbing and burning, in temples and palaces and on private estates, and the peasants would only sell their produce for gold. Similar horrors accompanied the invasion of the Hyksos. But for many generations between these two reigns of terror the Egyptians had lived well enough, while in the reign of King Sety, and notably under the great Ramesside Pharaohs, there had been enough food and to spare. Bas-reliefs in the temples and paintings in private tombs all tell the same story of mountainous offerings and of men bringing food or driving herds of cattle. The great Harris papyrus, which lists in detail all the offerings made by Ramesses III to the gods, records the presentation of foodstuffs at least as often as of precious metals, garments and perfumes. This is all evidence that the Egyptians liked good eating, and they displayed the same characteristics when they were abroad. In the land of Iaa, in Syria, Sinuhe found figs and grapes, wine flowing more freely than water, honey, oil, every kind of fruit, barley, wheat and flocks without number; practically everything, in short, that a good estate in Egypt could provide. As he says, 'Cakes were my daily bread, I drank wine with my meals every day. I ate meat and roast fowl as well as the wild animals which were trapped and laid before me for my pleasure, not to mention what my greyhounds caught.'[21] He could not have been better off in Egypt itself. The shipwrecked sailor, for his part, cast up on his island in the Red Sea, was also in luck. 'I found figs and grapes, every kind of vegetable, magnificent leeks, cucumbers and water melons, melons growing wild, fish and birds. Absolutely everything grew there.'[22]

When we turn to the list of the food that Egypt could supply from her own resources, we may as well begin with meat, of which the Egyptians ate a very great deal. The walls of private tombs are covered with long processions of animals being led to slaughter for human consumption. Cattle were the chief source of meat. The name *ioua* signified the African ox—a large, long-horned and swift-footed species. With careful fattening it grew very big and heavy and was regarded as ready for slaughter when it was practically incapable of walking, as we can see from the processions of Abydos and Medinet Habu.[23] A rope was passed through its nostrils and round its lower lip so that it was easily led. Prize beasts wore ostrich feathers fixed between their horns and a pair of streamers. When the procession reached the entrance of the temple it was greeted by a priest pointing a burning torch at arm's length towards the animal. In the words of the description: 'Consecration of the beast that is pure of mouth for the purified slaughter house of the Temple of Ramesses Miamūn adjoining Ta Our.' Those who were responsible for inspecting the victims would only accept healthy animals and they made a further examination after they had been slaughtered.

A much smaller breed of oxen, usually without horns or with only very short ones, was called *oundjou*, and there was another long-horned and large variety known as *nega*. This was, however, less tame than the *ioua*, and presumably harder to fatten, since in all the pictures it looks thin. A number of phrases of uncertain meaning designate different kinds of animals for slaughter, e.g. 'oxen of the flocks' mouth' and 'oxen of *qite*'.* The ox known as *herysa* was, I think, the finest in the stable. We find occasional references to draught oxen from Syria and to oxen from the land of Kush.[24]

Under the Old Kingdom, the fauna which were hunted in the desert, and included oryx, gazelle and antelope, were an important source of food. The Egyptians were particularly pleased if they succeeded in capturing live specimens, and tried to domesticate them in their parks, but this method of breeding had grown much less important by the period covered by this book. We know that Ramesses III sent huntsmen into the desert to bring back oryx. In the course of his reign he offered in the great temple of Amūn 54 oryx, 1 bubal† and 81 gazelles. A second list records 20,602 oxen as well as 367 oryx, ibex and gazelles.[25] In the Abydos procession we can see a fine oryx with straight horns, oddly described as 'bull-oryx', from Ramesses' stable. Every now and then the slaughter-house scenes show oryx instead of oxen, but I know of none showing oryx being slaughtered for a banquet. It is probably fair to conclude that the desert fauna were of no real significance as a source of food, but that the gods were believed to take pleasure in the sacrifice of an oryx or a gazelle in their honour as a reminder of the period when the population of Egypt lived

*A small unit of weight (p. 167).
†A species of antelope.

by hunting rather than by cattle breeding. I know of no documentary evidence for the eating of pork, goat or mutton, but this must remain an open question, for we know that pigs, goats and sheep were kept on farms, even in Upper Egypt.

When the ox entered the slaughter-house the butchers took over from the stockmen,[26] and without more ado four or five of them would set to and slaughter the beast in the traditional and indeed immemorial manner. Its left foreleg was caught in a slip knot and the other end of the rope was thrown over its back and pulled by a second man. This forced the roped leg off the ground and threw the animal off its balance. At once several men would seize it simultaneously, the toughest of them perched on its neck and

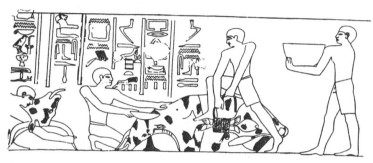

pulling its head backwards, another hanging on to its tail and a third trying to lift one of its hind legs. As soon as the animal was down on the ground the two hind legs and the roped foreleg were tied together so that it could not get up again. The other foreleg was left free, for it was useless to the helpless victim, which might yet delay its death for a moment by arching its back. Then some strapping fellow would twist its head back and hold it still with its horns thrust against the ground and its throat uppermost, whereupon the master butcher bled the animal to death, the blood being collected in a vessel. His only instruments were his long-handled knife, some nine inches in length and round-ended to prevent the hide being slit, and the whetstone that hung from the corner of his loincloth.

If this all took place in the slaughter-house attached to a temple, a priest would come forward and pour the contents of a ewer over the cut, doubling, perhaps, in this action, the duties of priest and sanitary inspector. The butcher would thrust his fist, reeking with gore, under the priest's nose with the words 'Behold this blood.' 'It is pure,' the latter would reply, leaning forward to examine it more closely.

The carcass was forthwith cut up with astonishing speed. The first piece to be dismembered was the right foreleg, which had been left untied when the animal was brought to the ground. One of the butcher's assistants held it up or moved it forwards or backwards to help the butcher while he severed the tendons and cut through the joints. The dismembered leg was handed straight over to the porters, whereupon the head was removed from the body and the latter itself opened up for skinning and for the removal of the heart. Next, the remaining three legs were untied and cut off. The hind legs each furnished three separate pieces, namely haunch (*sout*), shin (*ioua*) and foot (*inset*). The different cuts from the flank were then successively removed, first the fillet, which was the choicest piece, and then the chine. Of the offal, the spleen and liver were regarded as great delicacies. The butcher was careful to lift and empty the intestine as he removed it. The whole operation took place to the accompaniment of shouts and orders of 'Hurry up, man! Hurry up for goodness' sake! Finish with that leg! Out with the heart!' If the scene was a temple, the arrival of the master of the ceremonies—or perhaps the very mention of his name—was a great inducement to speed. 'Get up quickly, man, get those ribs out before the master of the ceremonies comes to set the table! Here, take the fillet—put it on the side table!' Meanwhile the recipient of these adjurations would reply placidly: 'Very good. I am doing what you want.' Sometimes the butcher would be left without any assistants and he would grumble to himself: 'This is a difficult job to do singlehanded.'

Cocks and hens were not known at this date:[26a] but birds were reared and eaten on a large scale. In the great Harris papyrus they are numbered in hundreds of thousands. One list of offerings comprises only 3,029 four-footed animals, but no less than 126,250 fowl, including 57,810 pigeons, 25,020 water birds captured alive in the marshes, 6,820 *ro*-geese, 1,534 *terp*-geese, 4,060 laying birds, 1,410 'big sticks' and 160 cranes; while quails (*part*) add a further 21,700 and 1,240 to the total. But even this list is only a fraction of the number one might reach by examining the scenes of hunting and breeding in Old and Middle Kingdom tombs. There were three distinct species of crane known as *djat*, *âiou* and *ga*, besides

demoiselle cranes (*oudja*). These reliefs record a score of varieties
of geese, ducks, pigeons and teal. No doubt they still survived in
our period, but breeders had come to concentrate on the limited
range which were regarded as best worth domesticating.[27]

Fattening ducks for the table

The stele of the Ethiopian King Piankhi records that after con-
quering Egypt* he refused to allow the princes of the south and
of the Delta to eat at his table, since they were lechers and fish
eaters—a thing not to be tolerated in a royal palace—with the
single exception of Nemarot, who did not eat fish, possibly because he was an inhabitant of the town of Shmoun,† an ancient
religious centre.[28] Neither during the New Kingdom nor earlier
was fish included in the food of the dead, while the eating of
particular varieties of fish was explicitly prohibited at various
times in certain villages and nomes. This is evidence that, unless
Piankhi was merely joking about purity and impurity, most
people, even in the temples, had no qualms about eating fish—
though presumably they avoided the unappetising varieties like
bou ('disgusting') or *shep* ('regret'). The inhabitants of the Delta
and the dwellers by the Fayyum lake made their living by fishing.
At Tanis, Mariette found a granite group of two plump individuals with beards and long hair walking in step, each carrying a
table with some fine grey mullet hanging from it.[28a] The Harris
papyrus records, among the foodstuffs distributed at the temples
at Thebes, On and Memphis, no less than 441,000 fish all
told—mainly mullet, mormyr‡, catfish§, middle-sized fish called

*In 730 B.C.
†Hermopolis, the city of the god Thoth.
‡*mormyrus caschive.*
§*clarias anguillaris.*

batensoda,* large *chromis*† and giant perch‡ so big that two men
were needed to carry them[29] on a long pole passed through the gills
and laid across their shoulders; they would then walk briskly with
the tail of the fish brushing the ground (p. 128). A fish like that
was food for several whole families.[29a]

Vegetables, which in the calendar of Medinet Habu are classi-
fied under the general heading of *renpout* or 'annual produce', were
either spread out on tables or tied in bunches. Onions and leeks,
which had been known since very early times, are explicitly mentioned. An Old Kingdom merchant says to a customer who comes
with a loaf in his hand: 'Put it down and I will give you some lovely
onions (*hedjou*).' The Ebers medical papyrus contains a reference
to leeks (*iaqet*); they feature in the story of Cheops and the
magicians, and the shipwrecked sailor picked some on his island
of plenty (p. 75).

The Egyptians liked garlic. Herodotus asserts that the workmen employed on building the pyramid of Cheops ate 1,600 silver
talents' worth of radishes, onions and garlic. They may have done
so, though it is quite certain that this information was not, as
Herodotus believed, inscribed on the pyramids themselves. At all
events packets of garlic have been found inside tombs at Thebes.
The word *khizan*, the hieroglyphic name for garlic, was identified
by Loret both in the great Harris papyrus and in the Coptic version of the Bible.[30] King Ramesses III had it distributed in large
quantities to the temples. On their wanderings towards the
Promised Land the Jews looked nostalgically back to the plentiful
cucumbers, water melons, leeks, onions and garlic of Egypt.[31] We
can often see water melons, ordinary melons and cucumbers lying
on offering tables beside bundles of papyrus stalks (wrongly
identified by some scholars as asparagus). The classical authors
claim that the eating of beans and chick peas was forbidden on
religious grounds—according to Diodorus, in order to teach men
self-denial:[32] but as a matter of fact both these vegetables as well as
ordinary peas have been found in tombs. We know that the priests
of On and Memphis ate beans during the reign of Ramesses III.[33]
It is perfectly true that the chick pea bears a remarkable resemblance to a falcon's head—particularly indeed to the falcon's head

---

synodontis batensoda, which swims upside down.
†*tilapia niloticus.*
‡*lates niloticus.*

surmounting the third of the Canopic jars known as *Qebehsenouf* (p. 311)—but this would have been no reason against eating them, except possibly on particular occasions or in particular places.

Lettuces were sacred to the ithyphallic deity Min, whose statue often stood in front of a lettuce bed. They were grown in gardens near houses but needed a great deal of water. Other gods enjoyed lettuces as well, and the author of the story of the quarrel between Horus and Seth tells how Isis made her way to the latter's garden and asked his gardener what vegetables the god was wont to eat. The gardener told her that he had seen Seth eat no vegetables but lettuces. The following day Seth returned to the garden and in

Offering table piled with food

accordance with his daily habit ate still more lettuces. Seth was generally regarded as lecherous but far less so than Min. The Egyptians, who had observed that lettuces made men amorous and women fertile, consequently ate them in large quantities. No doubt the fat green lettuces which are a common feature on offering tables were eaten in the modern Arab fashion, i.e. raw and dressed with oil and salt.[34]

The Egyptians of antiquity were less fortunate than their modern counterparts in not knowing oranges, lemons or bananas, while pears, peaches, almonds and cherries were not grown before the Roman period. None the less throughout the summer they had always had a regular supply of grapes, figs and dates besides the smaller and less appetizing sycamore figs. The only really good dates in Egypt grew near Thebes, and the fruit of the *dôm* palm, though edible, was more commonly employed for medicinal purposes. Coconuts were prized as rarities by their fortunate

E.L.E.–G

possessors. The pomegranate, the olive and the apple-tree were first introduced in the Hyksos period and were regularly and successfully cultivated thereafter. Olive oil was used for lighting as well as for cooking: before the introduction of the olive-tree other oil-yielding species, principally the moringa or *bak*,* were cultivated. Other species of fruit-trees included the mimusops,† the balanite and the jujube or zizyphus. We must always remember that several tree species and many plant varieties are still unidentified, so that we cannot compile a complete catalogue of the vegetables and fruits of ancient Egypt. The poor were reduced to chewing the pith of papyrus stalks, as their modern counterparts chew sugar cane, and the rhizomes of various water plants. Jars filled with the latter have been found in tombs.[35]

Milk, which was regarded as a great delicacy, was poured into ovoid pots which were then stoppered with a bunch of grass in order to keep out insects without making the jars airtight. Several words are known for milk products such as cream, butter and cheese, but their translation is not in all cases certain. Certain prescriptions and diets required the addition of salt, which may well have been used in large quantities. Food and drink were sweetened with honey and carob-seeds,[36] and the sign for *nodjem* ('sweet' or 'sweetness') is a carob pod. The collection of honey and wax from the wild bees deep in the desert was a highly skilled occupation; in their explorations of the desert wadis the honey gatherers were joined by the collectors of turpentine resin. The king provided them with an escort of archers in an effort to protect them from the dangers consequent on venturing far out of the Nile valley. Bees were also kept in private gardens with pottery jars for hives, and the bee-keeper would brush them boldly aside on his way to collect the combs, the honey from which was kept in large covered stone bowls.[37]

4. Cooking

What might be called cooking equipment consisted to all intents and purposes of movable cylindrical earthenware stoves about three feet in height, with a grill or bars inside to support the fire and an opening at the bottom to create a draught and en-

*moringa olifera or ben-nut tree.
†persea.

Bee-keeping

able the ashes to be removed. There must have been a vent for the smoke, but we possess no picture of a stove with a chimney. A two-handled saucepan, slightly wider than the top of the oven, and of varying depth, stood on top. At a pinch, cooks could dispense with stoves altogether by balancing their saucepan on three stones over a little pile of wood or charcoal. Metal stoves like low boxes without bottoms were also used, the fuel being spread on a surface in which holes were pierced. I myself found a little stove of this description in the tomb of Psousennes, dating from the reign of Ramesses II. The draught must have been very poor and the cook had continually to fan the charcoal fire while he was cooking.[38]

There is no coal in Egypt or in any of the neighbouring countries, and cooks, like potters, workers in ceramics, bronze founders and all other craftsmen whose work involved the use of furnaces, had to make do with charcoal or wood. Charcoal (*djâbet*), which was delivered in bags or baskets, is mentioned as a valuable commodity in contracts from Siout. The quantities recorded in the calendar of Medinet Habu and in the Harris papyrus are extremely small.

For making fire, the Egyptians possessed what they called 'fire-wood', but its scarcity is shown by the fact that a temple as important as that of Karnak used only sixty pieces a month, or two a day. It must have been a very early discovery, since one of the first lists of hieroglyphic signs contains a miniature picture of it. The device, which consisted of two pieces, a pointed stick swelling slightly at the base, and a kind of small saucer, was traditionally supposed to have been invented in the south. The shipwrecked sailor in the story very conveniently found a specimen on his Red Sea island and with its aid he quickly lit a fire and prepared a burnt offering for the gods and a meal for himself. Households which did not participate in the official distributions may have found themselves at a loss when it came to lighting a fire, and have been reduced to begging a few glowing embers from a prudent and kindly neighbour.

Apart from the stoves, chafing dishes, fuel and 'fire-wood' already described, kitchen equipment comprised saucepans, basins, pitchers and jars, all made of earthenware, as well as jugs, bundles and bags, buckets and shopping baskets for carrying provisions, three- or four-legged tables for carving and dressing meat and fish, or sorting vegetables, low tables at which scullions could squat and trestles for hanging meat and game.[38a]

We know two Egyptian words—*psy* and *asher*—which relate to the cooking of food. The former of these is applicable both to milk and to meat, and should therefore probably be translated as 'boil'. We occasionally find a picture of a deep saucepan standing over a fire with lumps of meat visible over the rim, which suggests that they are floating in some kind of liquid, but we do not know whether after boiling the meat was dished up forthwith or whether it was chopped up with vegetables and seasoning and served in the form of rissoles or meat cakes.[38b] No Egyptian cookery book has survived, but the medical papyri, with their recipes for illnesses and indigestion, give us some idea of their ingenuity in this field. The Egyptians were well aware of the value of butter, cream (*smy*) and goose and calves' fat as ingredients for sweets.[39] In the kitchen of the vizier Rekhmarê the saucepan on the stove is not deep enough to hold a pot roast. According to the text, at the moment when the cook puts in the fat an assistant stirs the contents of the saucepan with a long-handled implement. We cannot see whether it ends in a fork or a ladle, but the dish in question was probably a stew.[39a]

The word *asher* referred to grilling, which was the usual method

of cooking birds. After pluck-
ing and drawing a goose or a
duck and cutting off its head,
wing tips and feet, the cook
would spit it and hold it at
arm's length over a low stove.
It was not only birds which
were cooked like this, since a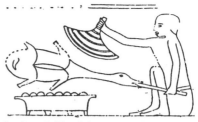
piece of meat—so far unidentified—in a bill of fare is called 'asher'
or 'grill'. Fillets, whose name meant 'choice meat', and the upper
cut (literally 'flesh') were also probably roasted on the spit.

Herodotus has the following remarks to make on the subject
of fish and game: '(The Egyptians) dry some kinds of fish in the
sun and eat them raw and others they eat as salt as when they leave
the brine. Quails too and ducks and small birds they eat uncooked, merely first salting them. All other kinds of birds and fishes
are eaten roasted or boiled.'[40] On the whole this evidence gains
support from contemporary texts and illustrations. We can see
grey mullet, *chromis* and mormyrs brought in small baskets and
spread out on the ground, where a man on a stool picks up a
knife and splits them to dry. The master of the household and his
wife watch this operation with keen interest, apparently without
finding the smell unpleasant. The mullet roe is put on one side to
be made later into botargo.*[41] Large quantities of split fish were
delivered to the temples together with other fish described as
'whole'—probably ungutted or 'fresh'. Temples also received
pots full of fish covered with 'wood of sail:'†[41a] this must refer
to some method of preserving of which we know nothing. We
occasionally find water birds being split open alongside the fish
salting, clearly so that they too should be dried and salted. Water
birds were sometimes sent alive to the temples, or else dead but
undressed and consequently needing to be eaten almost at once,
or split open and dried so that they would keep, at any rate for a
time.[42]

5. Baking

The culinary vocabulary of a nobleman of the Old Kingdom
included no less than fifteen words for bread or cakes, and others

---

*A caviar-like delicacy, made nowadays of mullet or tunny roes.
†Breasted (A.R. IV, §243,394) translates 'having wooden lids'.

can be unearthed from the texts. We are quite unable to distinguish them: they probably represented differences in the type of flour used, in shape, in the method of cooking and above all in the ingredients—honey, milk, fruit, eggs, fat or butter—which they contained. Barley (*iot*),* spelt (*bôti*)† and wheat (*sout*)[42a] were all used in the manufacture of flour. The rich kept their stocks of grain either beside their houses or on the roof. Flour was ground and bread was made both in private houses and in temples, but some millers and bakers may have set up in business on their own account and sold their wares to the poor. Grain was first thoroughly cleaned and then handed over to a group of people in which the women outnumbered the men.[43] The latter began by putting a small quantity of grain in a stone mortar, where two or three stalwarts pounded it rhythmically with heavy wooden pestles about three feet long. When it had been crushed the women took it over and sifted it, putting the bran aside for the animals, and giving the rest to be milled. Conical-shaped mills had not yet come into use and the apparatus consisted of a hollow container with two compartments and a large stone. The grain was put in the upper compartment and the women, bending double, rolled the stone backwards and forwards over it and forced the flour into the lower compartment. This flour was repeatedly sieved and ground until it reached the required fineness, to a perpetual chant of 'May all the gods of this land grant my lord strength and health.' No more flour was ground each day than was wanted for that day's bread. We possess pictures of bakers working side by side with millers and sometimes among them. A woman is busily arranging some pointed moulds over a hearth so that the flames can reach the inside, blowing up the fire with a fan and shielding her eyes with her free hand. When the moulds were hot enough they were placed on a plank with round holes drilled in it and filled with the dough,

Storing wine in jars

Hordeum vulgare.
†*Triticum dicoccum*, really emmer wheat.

freshly kneaded and mixed with leaven. They were then covered over and left until the bread was far enough baked to be removed from the moulds. The loaves were then counted—the Egyptians always counted everything—and carried in baskets to the expectant consumers.[43a]

This had been the normal method of breadmaking since the Old Kingdom, but it was slow and required a large number of workers, who must at least have been given something to eat even if they were paid no wages. One tomb painting shows a hungry child coming up to its mother, porringer in hand, just as she is patting out the dough with the palms of her hands, and begging for a cake. He gets a scolding for having such a big appetite and eating more than one of the king's slaves.[44] Bread was still made by this method during the New Kingdom, but by then ovens were in use in which several loaves could be baked simultaneously.[45] Besides this there was the immemorial art of making loaves in hot sand, as the modern Bedouin do.

6. *Drink*

The Egyptian national drink was beer,[46] which was drunk everywhere—in private houses, in the open air and on board ship as well as in taverns. When Sinuhe had been pardoned and returned by boat from the Roads of Horus to Ithy-Tawi,* he celebrated his resumption of the Egyptian way of life by drinking the beer that he had been so long without. Beer was made from barley or wheat and dates, with apparatus consisting of moulds similar to, though larger than, those used by bakers, a basket, and a variety of pottery jars and bowls. The first step was to make some loaves. As when bread was being baked, a pyramid of moulds was built up round an open fire. Simultaneously a paste (*wadjit*, the fresh) was compounded and packed into the hot moulds for just the time needed to brown the outsides lightly, for the inside had to remain uncooked. The half-cooked loaves were then crumbled into a large vat and mixed with a sweet liquid derived from dates. The mixture was stirred and strained, and soon began to ferment, after which it only remained to pour it off into

*i.e. from the foreign country of his exile, past the frontier post to the capital.

jars and stopper it with a small flat disk and lump of mud plaster. Once the jars had been sealed in this way, they could travel safely. When the time came to drink the beer, it was poured off into jugs holding about three or four pints and drunk from goblets of stone, faience or metal. The bitter beer from Nubia, which was made in an almost identical manner, only kept for a very short time. A dead king was promised loaves which would not crumble and beer that would not turn sour—evidence that in real life bread often went stale and beer went flat.

Since Egypt had had the good fortune to be governed by a family from the Delta, the devotees of the juice of the grape, that never-failing gift of Osiris, had been more numerous than ever. In consequence a large-scale wine trade had developed. An official responsible for the commissariat of the royal palace took three boats on a visit to the dependencies of Pi-Ramessu, one being his own and the others being lighters supplied by the 'House of a Million Years' of Ousirmarê. He embarked twenty-one passengers, fifteen hundred sealed jars of wine, fifty jars of a drink called *shedeh* and the same quantity of another drink called *paour*, as well as some baskets of grapes and pomegranates and other baskets of unspecified contents.[47] Presumably one of the drinks was pomegranate syrup and the other some derivative of wine: *shedeh* is anyway often mentioned in the same context as wine, and young students got equally drunk on both, much to the annoyance of the elderly scribes who taught them.

A large number of wine jars were found in the Ramesseum. Though they were naturally broken they still bore faint traces of ink dockets in the hieratic script, giving interesting information about the origin of their contents.[48] Almost all the vineyards were in the Delta, the great majority on the eastern side. There are also references to 'good eighth-time wine' or 'third-time wine or 'sweet wine', and I have little doubt that the latter was new wine and that the other labels refer to the third or eighth drawing off. Frequent drawings off are a recognized method of maintaining the quality of the wines: mulling is another, and I think that a picture from Beni-Hasan, though not in a very good state of preservation, depicts this process.[49] I do not know whether the Egyptians treated the inside of the wine jars with resin like the Greeks, though I doubt it, since the most popular wine was extremely sweet—sweeter, indeed, than honey.

7. *Meals*

We have now described the main foodstuffs which Egyptian families ate throughout the year. Although we have no detailed documentary evidence of how meals in private houses were served, we do know that Egyptians ate either singly or in pairs, seated at small tables piled with a mixture of meat, game, fruit and vegetables, or made a round pile of slices from a conical loaf rather like the Alsatian 'Kugelhopf'. Children sat on cushions or on the rush-covered floor.

Breakfast was not a family occasion. When the head of the household was dressed, he ate a meal consisting of bread, beer, a thick slice of meat cut from the joint and a cake (*shens*). His wife also ate as soon as her toilette was finished or while her hair was being done. A painting from Thebes[50] shows a servant offering a cup to her mistress who sits with a mirror in her hand. A box and two vases stand on a table beside her.

The two main meals in all probability comprised meat, game, vegetables, fruit in season, bread and cakes, all washed down with copious draughts of beer. It is by no means certain that even the wealthier Egyptians ate meat at every meal, for we must remember that Egypt is a hot country and that retain trade was virtually non-existent. The only people who could have an ox killed were those who could be sure of eating it inside three or four days, which meant big landowners with large establishments, temple staffs, and people who were giving a banquet; the common people could do so only on the occasions of feasts and pilgrimages. I only know of one relief, from a tomb at el Amarna, showing a meal in progress. It depicts Akhnaton and his family,[51] the monarch munching a rolled shoulder and his consort gnawing a whole bird. The queen mother is lifting food to her lips with one hand and with the other is passing a piece to one of the little princesses seated on a cushion beside her. The diners are surrounded with tables laden with food, but dishes, cups, plates and bowls are conspicuous by their absence, which is all the more surprising since archaeological collections contain so many different kinds of pottery vessels suitable for serving soups, sauces, dishes with vegetables and dressings, sweets, fruit and cream. I imagine therefor that at a certain point in the meal not only plates but also knives, spoons and forks were handed round to the guests, for examples of these objects, though not very common, can be found in our museums. The Louvre contains a fine set of wooden spoons with delicate and delightful decoration on the handles—never, perhaps, put to practical use. Above the tomb of King Osorkon II I found a spoon with a bowl held by a hand emerging from a metal tube. As against this we must remember that toilet utensils, a jug and a bowl, are often visible under the side tables piled with food[52]—further evidence that the Egyptians ate a great deal with their fingers.

Sometimes a meal was served in the middle of the afternoon—at about four or five o'clock—after which work or recreation was resumed.

8. *Dusk*

In autumn and winter the peasant worked out of doors until nightfall, but he expected to find his house lit when he returned. When Anpou entered his house and found it plunged in darkness, he had an immediate presentiment of disaster.[52a] Even peasants could afford light in their houses on dark evenings and while the days were short schoolchildren and craftsmen continued to work by the light of lamps burning either castor oil or olive oil.[53] Our museums contain few objects of this nature. I once found a handsome stone lamp shaped like a papyrus bud, with a horizontal groove for the wick,[54] in a first dynasty tomb, and we possess other examples in the shape of a lotus. The Louvre has some little shallow pottery bowls still containing blackened strands of wick, once no doubt saturated with oil. These were the common or garden lamps of the kind used by workmen attached to the cemetery for working in the tombs. Candles were also made for use in temples on the evening or night of the New Year or the night of the feast known as *Wâg*. They were evidently of considerable value, for the temple official responsible for them was paid a large sum to send them, after use, to the *ka* priest* of Hâpidjefai for use in illuminating the statue of his client.[55] Prayers for the departed included a wish that his lamp might ever be kept alight till dawn, and on the five perilous epagomenal days at the end of the year (p. 37) he was offered five conical vessels with handles, rather like Christmas trees in shape, the upper parts of which were covered with wax and were inflammable. These

*The priest responsible for the mortuary cult of a dead nobleman (p. 313ff).

lamps gave the dead man light in his solitude, but there is no evidence of their use by the living.[56]

This rather meagre information leaves us little the wiser about how houses were lit. The evenings did not last long, for, except for priests and guards on night duty, Egyptians rose with the sun and were early abed. In narrating the attempt at his assassination which taught him the ingratitude of mankind King Amenemmes I tells us that after eating *mesyt* or the evening meal he had relaxed for an hour after dark and had then gone to bed where, overcome by fatigue, he had quickly fallen asleep.[57] We may conclude that after supper Egyptians spent an hour or more chatting over a smoky lamp and that silence reigned thereafter.

9. *Banquets*

A wealthy Egyptian had plenty of spare time and plenty of ways of spending it. Hunting in the desert, walking, making pilgrimages to the temples, fishing or fowling in the marshes and the pleasures of the tavern might all in turn catch his fancy, or he could, if he chose, pass the time away agreeably at home. We will consider the latter first.

The Egyptians enjoyed few things more than gathering a large number of relations and friends for lunch or dinner, and the tombs present innumerable pictures of banquets in the Houses of Eternity or Everlasting Mansions in which the souls of the dead would dwell. The guests are indeed but ghosts, but the banquets are identical in every detail with those at which the occupant of the tomb had presided during his lifetime on earth, and with the help of these paintings and certain passages from maxims and stories we can describe a gathering of friends in a well-to-do household.

Before the meal took place there had—inevitably—been a mighty coming and going in the storerooms, the kitchens and indeed all through the house. An ox was slaughtered in the usual way, dismembered and jointed. Steaks, stews and sauces had to be prepared, geese spitted and roasted, beer, wine and liqueurs decanted and fruit piled high on dishes and in baskets, while everything had to be protected from flies and dust. Gold and silver cups and tableware of alabaster and of painted pottery were taken from the cupboards where they were kept. Water was put to cool in great jars. The house was washed and scrubbed and polished till it shone, and not a leaf allowed to remain on the carefully swept garden paths. Male and female musicians, singers and dancers stood ready to perform and the door-keepers waited at their post. Only the guests had yet to arrive.

If important guests were expected, the host would stand near his front door and escort them across the garden. This was the practice of the priests when the king visited a temple, and when the head of a family returned from the palace bearing evidence of the royal favour, he would find his household gathered before the front door to greet him. Sometimes, however, the host would wait in his reception-rooms like Pharaoh in his audience chamber, in which case guests would be received by the children and the servants.

The Egyptians were never tired of exchanging compliments. We know from the steles which they erected for the edification of posterity how ready they were to expatiate on their own virtues, and a guest must have addressed his host in very much the same eulogistic terms as those of a papyrus of the Ramesside period. 'May the grace of Amūn be in thy heart! May he grant thee a happy old age and let thee pass thy life in joy and attain to honour! Thy lips are healthy, thy limbs strong and thine eyes keen. Thy raiment is of linen, thou ridest in a chariot, a golden handled whip in thy hands, and thou holdest new reins. Thou art drawn by colts from Syria and negroes run before thee to clear the way. The boat thou boardest is of firwood, decorated from stem to stern. Thou comest to thy fine mansion which thou has built for thyself. Thy mouth is filled with wine and beer, with bread and meat and cakes. The oxen are dismembered and the wine unsealed. Sweet strains of song echo in thine ears. Thy scent-maker spreads over thee the odour of sweet resin, and the chief gardener comes to offer thee garlands. Thy chief hunter brings thee quails from the oases and thy chief fisherman presents thee with fish. From Syria hath thy vessel brought thee all manner of precious cargo. Thy stalls are full of calves and thy women spin to much profit. Thou art secure and thine enemies are brought low. The evil that men speak of thee doth not exist. Thou enterest into the presence of the Divine Ennead* and thou comest forth in triumph!'[58]

There were a number of replies which a host could properly

*The nine divinities who judged mankind.

Plate Va   Articles of toilet

Plate Vb   Orchestra playing at banquet

make. One was, with perhaps a faint tone of patronage, to murmur, 'Welcome, welcome', or 'Bread and beer'. Alternatively he could invoke the god's blessings on the newcomer. 'In life, health and strength. In the favour of Amonrâsonter. I pray Prâ-Harakhté, Seth and Nephthys, and all the gods and goddesses of the kindly region, to grant thee health and life, that it may be granted me to see thee in full vigour and to embrace thee.'[59] Good wishes for a courtier were couched in the following terms, 'I ask Prâ-Harakhté from his rising to his going to rest, I ask all the gods of Pi-Ramessu, the great *ka* of Prâ-Harakhté, to grant thee to be favoured by Amonrâsonter; the *ka* of King Ban-Rê Miamūn (Life, Health, Strength!) thy good lord (Life, Health, Strength!) each day.'[60]

When every conceivable compliment and good wish had at last been uttered and the embraces were finally over, it was time to sit down to eat. The host took his place on a high-backed seat, whose wooden surfaces were inlaid with gold and silver, turquoise, carnelian and lapis-lazuli. Privileged guests were seated no less luxuriously; the remainder had to make do with cross-legged or—at a pinch—straight-legged stools. In the houses of the poor the guests sat on mats on the floor. Young girls preferred to sit on finely worked leather cushions. Men and women sat on opposite sides of the room.[61] The wordly wise moralist Ptahhotep advises young and indeed older male guests at a friend's house not to stare at the ladies.[62] This was not the invariable seating arrangement, and when the men and women were not separated, husbands and wives were free, if they chose, to sit beside each other. Servants of both sexes moved among the guests and offered them flowers and perfumes. Female servants are always depicted as young and pretty. Transparent robes make the most of their charms—generally, indeed, they seem to have worn nothing beyond a necklace and a girdle. Pretty soon everyone, male and female, had a lotus flower in their hand and a white conical ornament on their head, made by the female servants from a sweet-scented pomade, which they took from a large bowl. The whole company—host, daughters of the house and serving-girls alike—wore this indispensable party ornament, which was the object of the allusion in the compliment quoted above in the phrase 'Thy scent-maker spreads over thee the odour of sweet resin'. No celebration was complete without scent—besides which it helped

to mask the smell of beer, wine and roast meat. The serving-girls do not seem to have been in the least incommoded in their work by wearing this conical ornament on their heads, while the artists of the tomb paintings, who missed no opportunity, even in a tomb, of depicting the laughable or the ridiculous, have left us no picture of the disaster of one of these ornaments falling off. From time to time the maidservants would pause for a moment to make a dexterous readjustment of a guest's neck ornament which looked as if it was disarranged.

At last it was time to serve the delicacies prepared by the cooks and pastrycooks. Even the most discriminating palates were satisfied, for old Ptahhotep balanced his warning to the guests to be discreet in their glances and words, by advice to the host to feed the company as well as he could afford, whereby he would gain the gods' praise as well as a good reputation among men. To that end the ear as well as the palate must be gratified, and the musicians would enter with their intruments while the guests were still taking their seats. Music had been a source of pleasure in Egypt from time immemorial; even before any musical instruments had been invented the Egyptians had loved to accompany song by clapping their hands. By the date of the building of the pyramids flute, oboe and harp were already known and played in duets or trios, while any one of the three instruments, or all of them together, might be used to accompany voice and hands. From the beginning of the New Kingdom, partly as a result of lessons learned from neighbouring countries, musical instruments developed considerably. Harps grew bulkier, their sound boxes doubled in size and they had more strings. Some of these instruments were small and portable, others were of medium size with a foot, and a third type were very large and elaborately decorated all over with geometric or floral ornament and enriched with a gilded wooden head projecting from the upper end or fitted to the base.[62a] The zither was an import from Asia: we can see it being played by the nomadic *Aamou* (Bedouin) when they came to Menat Khoufou* to see the governor of the Oryx nome.[62b] Elsewhere what are evidently foreign musicians are sometimes shown playing very large zithers on feet. The portable variety, often very elegantly designed, did not have more than five strings. The double flute had evolved from its original shape of two parallel reeds bound closely together into a pair of reeds diverging at an angle. The lute took the form of a small oblong box flat on both faces, with six or eight holes pierced in it and a long neck decorated with streamers, along which four strings were stretched. Both round and square tambourines were known, but they were used mainly in connexion with popular religious festivals, like most of the other percussion instruments such as castanets and sistra, though Hathor, to whom they were sacred, was the goddess of banquets as well as of music. Castanets or crotals (*menat*) consisted of a pair of small flat disks, probably of wood or ivory, hung on a necklace. The sistrum was more elaborate and took the form of a head of Hathor on the end of a handle, the horns being replaced by two much longer metal

*Near the modern Beni Hasan.

projections, crossed by a number of wires on which several small metal disks were threaded. The instrument could be shaken to produce sustained or staccato sounds as desired, which served very well to accompany a song or to emphasie a rhythm. Crotals were the equivalent of the modern castanets, and anyone who has admired the art of Antonio or other Spanish dancers will have no difficulty in visualizing the effects which the Egyptians could get from these two instruments. Singers could also accompany themselves by clapping their hands.

Other distractions for the amusement of the guests included dancing[62c] and occasionally a female acrobat, who would bend so far backwards that her hair touched the ground.[63]

When all had eaten their fill, the party would continue with music, songs and dancing. Fresh delicacies were eaten now, not from hunger but from sheer greed, and were enjoyed all the more because of it. Singers extemporized verses in honour of the gods' goodness or their host's generosity[63a]—'His perfection is in all men's hearts. . . . Ptah hath done this with his own hands for the soothing of his heart. The canals are freshly filled with water: the earth is bedewed with his love.' 'Happy is his day,' in the words of another, 'when man thinks of the beauty of Amūn! How sweet it is to make the vault of heaven ring with praise!' It was fitting that man should praise the gods, but all realized the brevity of our time on earth to enjoy their bounty. Man ought therefore wholeheartedly to enjoy this happy day when the divine mercy and a generous host are so perfectly united. The harpist of Neferhotep recalled these truths to mind during a banquet:

'Men's bodies have returned to the earth since the beginning of time and their place is taken by fresh generations. As long as Rê rises each morning and Toum sinks to rest at Manou, so long will men beget and women conceive and through their nostrils they will breathe; but one day each one that is born must go to his appointed place. Make a happy day, O priest. May you be granted the finest of essences and perfumes to delight your senses, may you have lilies and garlands to lay upon your shoulders and to wreath the neck of your beloved sister who sits at your side, may there be singing and the music of the harp in your presence. Put misfortune out of your mind and think only of pleasure until that day comes when you must travel to the land of Mertseger, the lover of silence. Pass your day in happiness, O Neferhotep of the true voice, excellent divine father whose hands are pure. I have heard of all that has befallen [our ancestors]. [Their walls] lie in ruins, their habitations are no more and they themselves are as though they had never existed since the beginning of time. The walls of thy house are secure. Thou hast planted sycamore trees on the margin of thy pool and thy soul rests beneath them and drinks of their moisture. Follow thy heart's bidding and falter

Mereruka listens to music

not while thou art on earth. Give bread to him that hath no possessions, that thy repute may stand high for ever. Pass thy day in happiness . . . think on the day when thou must fare to the land where all men are as one. Never a man hath taken his possessions with him to that land, and none can thence return.'[64]

Another harpist reminds us of the vanity of man's efforts to overcome death. Egypt was already an ancient country and by our period the fate of the pyramids was plain for men to see. 'The gods who were of olden time and who rest in their pyramids, likewise the mummies and the spirits buried deep in their pyramids which were built as strong places for them, their places are no more. What hath become of them? I have heard the words of Imhotep and of Hardidef in many a song. Their sanctuary is destroyed, their places are no more, as though they had never been, and none comes to tell what manner of men they were, or of their possessions.'

E.L.E.—H

'Whilst yet thou livest, follow they heart's desire. Sprinkle thy head with incense, clothe thyself in linen, anoint thyself with the rarest of all the perfumes of the god . . . follow thy heart and thy happiness as long as thou art on earth. Consume not they heart until there cometh for thee that day when man begs for mercy, unless the god whose heart beats no longer hears them who call upon him. . . .'[65]

By the late period it was no longer thought sufficient to point verbal contrasts between the misery of the kingdom of the dead and the joys of life on earth and to enjoin the guests at a banquet to make the most of the latter. According to Greek authors, whose information on this subject is apparently reliable, at the banquets of the rich, after the end of the meal, a little wooden figure lying in a coffin seems to have been shown to the guests. This was carved and painted with great care in imitation of a corpse—a mummified corpse, of course, and not, as modern readers might be inclined to imagine, a skeleton. In a private house at Tanis I have myself found mummy figurines which in their original condition may have been about eighteen inches in length and were perhaps used for this purpose. The host would show this figure to each of his guests with the words 'Look on this and then drink and take thy pleasure, for when thou art dead thus wilt thou be.' This was normal behaviour when friends met to drink, or so Herodotus and Plutarch tell us. Lucian, purporting to be writing as an eyewitness, alleges that the dead were literally present at the banquet. The story improves with the telling: but there is no evidence that Neferhotep invited the dead to join the living at his table or had a small mummy passed round, let alone a skeleton with silver joints like the plutocrat Trimalchio.[66]

In other respects the guests scrupulously obeyed the advice of the sweet-voiced harpist. The need to celebrate a day of rejoicing was used as an excuse for the family gathering to begin drinking. Let us consider for instance the reception given by Paheri and his wife.[67] The host and hostess sit side by side while a monkey, tied by the foot to Paheri's chair, is pulling figs out of a basket and nibbling them. The servants are standing in the background. Paheri's parents are comfortably seated facing their son, while though his uncles, cousins and friends are sitting on mats on the floor, they are being well looked after by servants, some of whom carry round fluted cups, while others are attending to the female guests. 'Health to thy *ka*,' cries one, holding out a cup full of wine, 'drink till thou art drunk! Spend thy day in happiness, listen to the words of thy companion!' The lady in question has just cried to the servant: 'Give me eighteen measures of wine! Look—I love it madly.' Another servant is equally friendly: 'Do not worry, for I am not going to leave it [the wine jar].' The woman next him, who is waiting her turn, cries: 'Drink up, no heel taps! Can the cup come round to me? This is the prince of drinks.' In one corner two of the women guests who have been left unattended by the servants are gesturing as if to repulse an imaginary advance. Paheri lived at Nekhabit, at the end of the war of liberation, and the festivities are slightly provincial and crude: but at Thebes the principle of Maneros,* the equivalent, according to Plutarch,[67a] of the Greek μηδὲν ἄγαν (moderation in all things) was no better observed, and guests who have eaten and drunk to excessive hilarity are by no means rare.[68] Both sexes are depicted as—not to put too fine a point upon it—disgustingly sick, while their neighbours, who find nothing particularly unusual about the episode, hold their heads and, if necessary, help them to lie down. The mess is soon cleared up and the feast continues.

10.   *Games*

Banquets did not happen every day, and when people were alone they liked to sit beneath an arbour in the garden and enjoy the freshness of the mild north wind or to take a boat round their lake and pass the time in fishing. Married couples were very fond of draughts,[68a] which was played on a rectangular board, divided into thirty or thirty-three squares, with black and white pieces very much like pawns in modern chess. The players sat on stools with their feet resting on cushions. Husbands and wives often played against each other, and sometimes a daughter stands beside her father with an arm round his neck. We see Petosiris playing with his friends after lunch until it is time to refresh himself with beer in his room, while an anonymous Theban, who cannot be bothered to wait, is drinking in the middle of his game.[69] We do not know the rules, but the moves seem to have been governed by throwing dice, unlike the free moves in modern draughts.

*Plutarch, *Isis and Osiris*, ch. 17. According to Herodotus (II, ch. 79) Maneros was a dirge.

During the earliest period games were both more numerous and more varied, the most popular being the snake game (*mehen*). This was played on a low table on the surface of which a coiled snake was engraved or inlaid, its head in the centre of the board and its body divided by transverse lines into 'squares'. The pieces, which were replaced in an ebony box after the game was over, consisted of three lions, three lionesses, and white and red balls. There is no evidence for or against the survival of this game after the end of the Old Kingdom.[70] From two first dynasty tombs which have yielded the finest sets of ivory lions and lionesses, there have also come some very remarkable ivory pieces, some in the form of a house consisting of three main blocks, with triple pointed roofs, while others resemble kings and castles in modern chess. The pawns are cylindrical with a rounded top ending in a knob.[70a] It seems unlikely that the various and ingenious games invented in earlier times should later have been generally abandoned and seldom played. The Egyptians were extremely fond of games. Husbands and wives and friends played them for amusement, and even enemies would sometimes play to settle some dispute.[71]

Children too played games which required no elaborate equipment. A large group of boys would make up two sides, each player in either team holding the boy in front of him round the waist. The two leaders would stand toe to toe, link arms, grasp each other's hands and each try to throw his opponent down. Meanwhile those behind would encourage their leaders with cries of 'Your arm is much stronger than his! Hold on!' while the others would answer 'Our team is stronger than you are. Get hold of them, comrade!'

(*above*) Boys' games. Picking, treading and pressing grapes (*below*)

The game of 'kid on the ground' was a kind of obstacle race.[72] Two boys sat on the ground facing each other, arms and legs stretched out and fingers extended, and with the left heel resting on the top of the right foot. These two boys were the obstacle which the other players had to jump without getting caught. The 'obstacle' would of course try to catch the legs of the jumpers and so 'bring the kid to the ground'. The jumper was not allowed to pretend to be going to jump and then not do so, but as he began his run he called out 'Look out, boys! Here I come!' Other children ran races, but to make it more difficult they ran not on their feet but on their knees, with legs crossed and holding their feet. A boy who was much bigger than the others might go down on all fours, and two smaller children might link hands and feet and balance on his back. Another game was to throw javelins at a target marked out on the ground. For some reason we do not know this target bore the name of Seshemou, the highly respected god of the wine press, though one might rather have expected it to be called after the salyer of Osiris. Other boys liked wrestling and if there were enough of them a group of the players made a kind of human tower, each player stretching out his arms and putting them on his neighbour's shoulders, while the others had to jump on the 'tower' without getting caught by the boy who was 'he'.

Sometimes these games led to trouble and a child who was clumsy or who tried to cheat was punched and kicked, or sometimes even bound like a real criminal and beaten by his tormentors with a stick ending in a little wooden hand.

Girls playing ball

Little girls preferred games that required some skill, like juggling or throwing balls to each other while riding on bigger girls' backs. They also caught each other by the waist and wrestled. But their favourite pastime was dancing, which was an essential accomplishment for every girl and not only for those who aspired to take it up professionally. They tied a heavy pompon to the end of their long pigtails and made their arms seem longer by holding a mirror or one of the carved sticks mentioned in the last paragraph, which they must have borrowed from neighbouring boys. Thus arrayed they twirled and jumped and postured while their companions stood round in a circle clapping their hands and singing a song which is not altogether clear to us, but in which they invoked Hathor, the goddess of all pleasures. There was one very curious kind of dance, in which two big girls stood back to back and stretched their arms out sideways. Four other little girls stood with their feet close to them and took their outstretched hands, holding themselves rigid as if they were hanging from them. When the word was given the whole group whirled round at least three times—unless they all fell down and brought the game to an end.

Harps, zithers, lutes and tambourines were practically always to be found in the harem,[73] no doubt because the family liked to pass the time after the evening meal in music, dance and song, as well as story-telling. The Westcar papyrus in the Berlin museum shows us Cheops passing from boredom to absorbed interest as he listened to the stories about magicians told by each of his sons in turn. No doubt this royal recreation was a pleasure which all who wanted to could share.

CHAPTER V

COUNTRY LIFE

1. *The Peasants*

THE scribe regarded all manual occupations as contemptible, but he reserved the lowest place of all for agriculture. Men and their tools wore out equally quickly. Beaten and exploited by his masters and the tax collectors, robbed by his neighbours as well as by thieves, caught unawares by the weather, ruined by locusts and rodents and all the natural enemies of man—such was the life of an agricultural labourer. With his wife in prison and his children seized as security for debt, he might serve as the very picture of misery.[1]

But to the eye of the Greeks, coming from a barren land where a meagre crop was the sole reward of harsh toil, the picture was very different. Herodotus says that when the fields were once sown, the peasant had only to sit back and wait for the harvest, and Diodorus goes even further and declares 'Whereas generally speaking among other peoples agriculture demands a heavy outlay and much anxiety, in Egypt alone it is carried on at little expense of money or labour.'[2] Among the young Egyptians who went to school in the towns there was, moreover, a party that advocated a return to the land. These were the fools for whose benefit the scribe had compiled his catalogue of woe. The peasant in the salt oasis is not presented to us as in need of our sympathy. Long is the list of the good produce of his land which he loaded on his donkeys to sell at Nen-Nisou, and with the proceeds of which he intended to bring home delicacies for his wife and children. No doubt some criminal who met the little expedition on the road might seize his pack animals and their load. But authority took him seriously and if we knew the whole story we should be sure to find that the king's justice was weighted in his favour.[2a] The elder of the two brothers in another well-known story (p. 51) is far from being an object of pity. He is the sole owner of a house, an estate, stock, farm equipment and corn. His wife can stay at home like a lady and can linger over her toilet while her husband and brother-in-law are working in the fields. She can spend the whole day in running the house, getting ready the evening meal, and lighting the lamps before her husband comes home, and when he does she will have jug and basin ready for him to wash with.

2.   *Watering the Garden*

Our description of Egyptian houses remarked upon the national love of gardens. Whether he lived in town or in country, it was every householder's ambition to possess a garden of his own and to grow his own fruit and vegetables. Of all the tasks that this involved, the most time-consuming, as well as the only one about which we have any information, was watering. The kitchen garden was divided into square plots by a criss-cross of intersecting trenches. The traditional method of watering, still employed during the Middle Kingdom, was for the gardeners to fill from the pool their round pottery jars that were slung in pairs on a yoke and to empty them into one of the trenches, so that eventually the whole garden was watered.

This was a long and laborious job[3] and the invention of the *shadūf* must have been hailed as a welcome advance.[4] It consisted of a stout upright post about twice the height of a man, driven into the ground at the water's edge. A tree with lopped branches would do equally well if it happened to be in the right place. A long pole was fixed to the top of the post so that it could swing freely in all directions and a heavy stone was attached to its thicker end. A bucket of pottery or canvas was slung from the thinner end by a rope about eight or nine feet long. This container was filled with water by pulling on the rope at one end and then letting the counterpoise raise it to the level of the trench. The water was then emptied out and the whole process repeated. Four *shadūfs* were in operation simultaneously in Apouy's garden;* we can still see the gardener's dog following the moving buckets with his eye. Their general use proves that these machines, crude as they were, worked satisfactorily. Nevertheless under the New Kingdom they seem only to have been used for watering gardens,

*See illustration, p. 21.

and we never find them in scenes of agricultural work. The water wheel or *saggieh*, whose creaking seems today an inseparable feature of the Egyptian countryside, never appears at all in documents of the Pharaonic age and we cannot say when it was introduced into the Nile valley. Fine wells of considerable diameter have been discovered in the necropolis of the priests of Thoth at On, near the tomb of Petosiris, at Antinoë and in the temple of Tanis. The first of these was certainly designed to take a *saggieh*, but it cannot antedate Petosiris' tomb, which is probably contemporary with the reign of King Ptolemy Soter.

3. *The Vintage*

Every garden contained at least a few vines set against a wall or bordering the central path. Their shoots were trained up stakes and poles and arched overhead, carrying in high summer a crop of luscious black grapes which were regarded as a great delicacy by the townsfolk. Viticulture was considerably more highly developed in the Delta than elsewhere, though less for dessert purposes than for wine-making. The traditional vintages were those of the Marshes (*meh*), of Imit, north of Faqous, of the Fishery (*ham*), of Sin in the Pelusium district, and of Abesh. This last was stored in special jars protected by a pad of basketwork, which are mentioned in the list of delicacies. Even before the compilation of this list, wine from the vineyard of Sebahorkhentipet was being transported in sealed jars to the residence of the Thinite* Pharaohs. The Ramesside dynasty, coming, as they did, from Avaris, between Imit and Sin, were keen connoisseurs of wine and did much to encourage both viticulture and the wine trade. Most of the dockets from wine jars discovered in the Ramesseum, at Qantir and in the Theban tombs date from the reign of Ramesses II, and we could even draw a tentative map of the Egyptian vineyards if our knowledge of the geography of the Pharaonic kingdom were less rudimentary.[5] Ramesses III indeed actually says: 'I created for thee vineyards in the oases of the south and the north, and many others besides in the southern districts. In the Delta their numbers increased by hundreds of thousands. I appointed gardeners from among the foreign captives to tend them and I dug pools of water for them filled with water lilies: wine and liquor from them flow

*Of the first dynasty, *c.* 3000 B.C.

like water, to be offered in thy presence in Thebes, the city of victories.'[6]

The only aspect of viticulture or the life of the wine growers of which we know is the actual vintage.[7] We can see the pickers scattered beneath the vines, using their hands (not knives) to pluck the fat black grapes. They put them in their baskets, taking care not to squash them, since the baskets are not watertight, and sing as they carry them on their heads to throw the bunches into the vat, before returning once more to the vines. I know of no instance of the use of an animal to carry the grapes. In countries where viticulture was practised on a really large scale it was found useful to transport the grapes from vineyard to stillroom in boats in order to lessen the risk of crushing the fruit and losing the precious juice.

We do not know the material of which the vats, which were round and deep, were made, but it cannot have been wood, since the Egyptians, who did not know how to make wooden barrels, could never have built wooden vats: though admittedly they were no more difficult to build than boats. I think that they must have been of stone. Plaster, pottery or faience would all have imparted some aftertaste, but some hard stone like granite or schist, capable of taking a high polish, could have been used to make vats which were both watertight and easy to clean. These vats occasionally stood on raised bases about three feet high and were sometimes decorated with bas-reliefs. On either side stood two small pillars, or, if the owner had no pretensions to grandeur, two forked sticks supporting a crossbar with five or six ropes hanging from it. When the vat was full enough of grapes the pickers would climb up and, probably because the bottom of the vat was not flat, would hold on to the ropes and vigorously tread out the grapes. At the home of Mera, the vizier of King Pepy I, we can see two musicians seated on a mat singing and clicking their wooden crotals to encourage the pressers to work harder and to tread rhythmically.[8] So useful a practice might well have survived, but by the New Kingdom the musicians have vanished; indeed the pressers could have sung to themselves at their task. The juice ran out of the vats through one, two or three holes into a large container.

When no more juice could be trodden out, the grape skins were put into a strong sack, attached to a bar at either end.

This was held over a trough by four men and the bag twisted in opposite directions, so as to squeeze the contents. This was rather an awkward method, as the four men had not only to support the weight of the sack but simultaneously to twist the bars, and if the sack got at all out of position the wine was spilt on the ground. Consequently a fifth man was required to stand in the middle and keep the sack steady or move the trough so as to catch the juice. Under the New Kingdom the pressers used an apparatus consisting of two uprights firmly embedded in the ground pierced at the same height by two similar holes into which the ends of the sack of grape skins were inserted. A bar was passed through a loop attached for this purpose to one end of the sack, and then had merely to be twisted. The whole strength of the pressers could be usefully applied and not a drop of wine was wasted.[9]

The wine was collected in wide-mouthed containers and then poured off into flat-bottomed vessels in which it fermented. When this process was complete it was drawn off into vessels designed for its transport, i.e. long and pointed, with two lugs and a narrow neck sealed with plaster. These jars were normally carried on the shoulder, but if they were very large and heavy they were slung on a pole and carried by two men. As ever, the scribe was on the job. He had counted the baskets of grapes as they were brought by the pickers, and now he recorded on the jar the particulars of the year, the growth and the grower, and duplicated these details in his own files. Sometimes the owner insisted on personally supervising the vintage and the pressing. He would immediately be observed and the workers would extemporize songs in his honour. On Petosiris' estate for example: 'Come, master, see thy vines which gladden thy heart, while thy vine dressers are busy pressing the grapes. The vines are heavy with fruit and never have they been so full of juice in any year before. Drink and heed not and take thy pleasure therein. All things will come to pass as thou desirest. The lady of Imit has caused thy vines to grow strong because she wishes thee well.'

'The vine dressers cut down the grapes and their children help to carry them. It is the eighth hour of the day, the "hour that folds its arms". Night falls, and the dew of heaven falls thick on the grapes. Make haste to tread them and bring them to our master's house.' 'All things are sent of God. Our master will drink sweetly, thanking God for thy *ka*.' 'Make a libation to Sha [the divinity of the vine], that he may grant thee plentiful grapes for another year.'[10]

The Egyptians did not lack a sense of gratitude, but they were shrewd folk, ready to take advantage of the divine good humour engendered by their piety, to ask for fresh favours. Beside the vat we often find a snake with distended neck poised ready to strike. Sometimes between its horns it wears a disk like Hathor or Isis: it may be enthroned in an elegant shrine or alternatively it may lie near a clump of papyrus. Its worshippers have placed beside it a low table standing between two cups, on which lie some loaves of bread, a bundle of lettuces and a bunch of lotus. This was in fact a snake-deity, the goddess Renoutet, lady of the harvest, on whose goodwill granaries, clothes, grapes and wine cellars all depended. Her main festival was celebrated at the beginning of *shemou*, which coincided with the opening of the harvest, and the vine dressers held their own celebrations in her honour when the last grape had been pressed.[10a]

4. *Ploughing and Sowing*

Under the Ramessids the staple agricultural operation was growing cereals.[11] The fields of wheat and barley stretched unbroken from the marshes of the Delta to the cataract. The peasants of Egypt were first and foremost ploughmen. They had comparatively little to do during the four months of *akhit* while the countryside was flooded, but as soon as the river had returned to its channel, while the ground was still soft from the flooding and could be easily worked, every hour was precious. In a number of pictures of ploughing pools of water in the background show that work was actually begun even before the Nile had entirely subsided. It was only these conditions that enabled the preliminary work on the soil, so vital in Europe, to be dispensed with. This was the moment when the author of the story of the Two Brothers elected to begin his tale. The older brother says to the younger, 'Let us prepare our team of oxen for ploughing, for the waters have uncovered the earth, and the ground is ready for the plough. Then thou shalt go into the fields with thy seed that we may begin to plough tomorrow morning.' The younger brother set to work at all the preparations which his older brother had ordered. Next morning at daylight they walked out into their fields with their seed and began to plough.[12] Pictures tell us that sowers and ploughmen worked together, or rather—in contrast to the normal European practice by which furrows are drilled first—that the seed was first sown and the ground then ploughed up to cover it over with soil.[13] The sower filled with grain a two-handled basket about eighteen inches long and the same in height. He carried it from the village hoisted on his shoulder: on reaching his destination he slung it round his neck on a cord long enough to enable him comfortably to take out the grain and scatter it on the ground.

In the Ramesside period the plough still remained the crude implement it had been in the most primitive phase of agriculture and even in the late period there was no apparent urge for improvement. It was in point of fact quite serviceable for scratching the surface of a light soil which contained neither stones nor weeds, consisting as it did of two upright handles joined by cross-pieces and ending in a curved sharebeam to which the ploughshare of metal or of wood was fitted. The shaft or beam ran between the handles, ending at the sharebeam, to which it was attached with a rope. A wooden cross-bar or yoke fixed to the other end of the long beam rested upon the necks of the pair of draught animals and was tied to their horns.

The small size of the cows—never oxen—which were used to draw the plough, suggests that the work can never have been very heavy. It is a well-known fact that cows which are working yield little milk, and this shows that there must have been enough cows both to supply as much milk as was required and to plough. Oxen were kept for pulling sarcophagi at funerals, and for hauling heavy blocks of stone. The use of cows for ploughing proves that the work was not too heavy for them, while the resulting loss of milk was only temporary and not a decisive argument against their employment.

There were usually two ploughmen. The man at the handles had the tougher job. When the plough moved off he stood upright and cracked his whip, with only one hand on the handles. As soon as the animals were on the move he gripped the handles with both hands, bending double and leaning forward on the plough with all his weight. His mate's job was only to guide the team, but instead of walking backwards in front of them he walked beside them facing forwards. Sometimes this job was done by a naked child, with a single lock of hair falling over his right cheek, who carried

a little basket. Both whip and stick were evidently thought beyond his power to manage and he had to rely on shouting to make
the animals obey him. Sometimes the actual sowing was done by
the ploughman's wife.

These long days of toil were not always uneventful. The two
brothers in the story used up all their seed and Bata had to hurry
back to the house as fast as he could. Elsewhere one of the annoy-
ing accidents foreseen by the scribe, who disliked agricultural
work, had just occurred. A cow had stumbled over some obstacle
and in her fall had almost broken the beam of the plough and
brought down her yokemate. The ploughman ran to the poor
beast's aid, disentangled her and helped her up. The team was
very soon ready to move off again quite undamaged.[14]

Although the Egyptian countryside does not wholly escape
monotony, there were as many trees then as there are today. The
green of the spreading sycamores, perseas, tamarisks, sidders and
balanites contrasted vividly with the blackness of the upturned
soil. Not only did they supply the wood which was required for
the tools of agriculture, but they afforded welcome shade to the
ploughman who, directly he arrived, had hung upon the branches
of a sycamore the water-skin to which he gratefully turned from
time to time, and had laid his basket of food and a big jar of cool
water in the shadow of its trunk. While the team have a much-
needed rest the ploughmen chat together. 'Lovely cool day. The
beasts are pulling well. Heaven is helping us. Let us work hard for
the prince.' At that very moment the prince, Paheri, comes to see
how the work is getting on. He climbs down from his chariot
while his groom holds the reins and steadies the horses. One of
the ploughmen sees him coming and warns his mate, 'Quick,
number one, get the animals moving, and the prince will stop and
watch.' Paheri had not got in his byres enough cows to pull all
his ploughs, and everyone was afraid that if they had to wait an
extra day the soil might become too dry. Four men take the place
of the animals and seize hold of the beam, consoling themselves
for their hard work by singing: 'Look at us working! Fear nothing
on earth: it is so lovely!' The driver, an obvious Semite who
might well, like his mates, originally have been a prisoner of war,
is content with his lot and cracks a joke in reply. 'Very neat, my
lad! It's a good year when nothing goes wrong. The grass grows
thick beneath the calves. (It's) better than anything!'[15]

At night all the beasts are unyoked and fed and spoken to kindly. '*Hou* (eloquence) is in the oxen, *sia* (wisdom) in the cows. Give them some food quickly.'[16] The herd gathers and moves towards the village, the ploughmen carrying the ploughs. If they left them in the fields they could not be certain of finding them again. To quote the cynical scribe: 'He will not find his team where he left it and will spend three days looking for it. He will find it lying in the dust, but he will not find the skin that was there for the wolves have torn it in pieces.'[17]

Other implements besides the plough, such as hoes or mallets, according to the condition of the soil, were sometimes used to cover over the seed after sowing. The former was as crude an implement as the plough, being merely a handle, a flat piece of wood and a cross-bar, the whole forming a capital A with one leg longer than the other. It wore out even faster than the plough and took a whole night to mend, a prospect which was accepted philosophically. 'I am going to do more than my master's work,' says one labourer to his mate, 'so keep quiet.' 'My friend,' replies the other, 'hurry up at your work. You will have us free in good time.'[18]

On ground which had long been under water, the whole of this laborious process could be shortcircuited by simply scattering the seed and then turning a herd of animals loose over it. Oxen and donkeys were too heavy for this purpose, and in the early period a flock of sheep was generally used. The shepherd would take a handful of fodder and feed the bell wether, which would obediently follow him and bring all the other animals along behind. For some unknown reason under the New Kingdom pigs were preferred for this work and it was a herd of these animals that Herodotus saw at work.[19]

The burial of the grain in the earth turned the Egyptian mind to thoughts of higher things—or, more accurately, to thoughts of death. The Greeks had not failed to observe that during this period they performed various ceremonies clearly related to funerary ritual and the observance of days of mourning. Opinion was divided about their propriety.[20] The Pharaonic documents on which we can draw, and which I have followed in my description of the operations undertaken during the season of *perit*, contain but few traces of these practices. When the shepherds arrived with their flocks at the chosen area they chanted a lament which they would repeat while the sheep were treading out the heaps of grain on the threshing floor.

'The shepherd is in the water, the fish are all around.
He has speech with the sheat-fish*
And greets the mormyr.§
O West! Where is the shepherd, the shepherd of the West?'[21]

Alexandre Moret was the first to suspect that this verse held a deeper significance than the crude jesting of peasants sorry for the shepherd floundering in the mud, for mud is not the habitat of fish, far less the comparatively dry threshing floor strewn with grain. The 'shepherd of the West' should be identified with Osiris, the victim of drowning in the first line, who had been cut in pieces by Seth and thrown into the Nile, where the tigerfish,† the lepidotus‡ and the oxyrhynchus had swallowed his genital organs. The time of sowing and of treading out the corn was the occasion for calling to mind the god who had procured useful plants for mankind and was so closely identified with plant life that he was sometimes symbolized by shoots of corn or trees sprouting from a mould shaped like his dead body. ‖ (p. 323).

Herodotus in his innocence believed that when ploughing and sowing were done, the peasant could sit back and wait with folded hands for the harvest. Had he done any such thing he would have risked his crops, for even in the Delta the rainfall is too light to make irrigation unnecessary. Particularly in Upper Egypt the soil would soon have dried right up and the crops have withered, like the barley in the 'gardens of Osiris' when they were left untended. Irrigation was therefore an absolute necessity, as Moses reminded the Israelites when holding before them the dazzling advantages which awaited them in the land of Canaan. 'For the land whither thou goest in to possess it is not as the land of Egypt from whence ye came out, where thou sowedst thy seed and wateredst it with thy foot like a garden of herbs. But the land whither ye go to possess it is a land of hills and valleys, and drinketh water of the rain of heaven.'[22] This passage has been taken to mean that the water was

*Silurus or *Schilbe mystus.*
§*Mormyrus oxyrhynchus* or *M. kannume.*
†*Hydrocyon,* or possibly *Alestes dentex.*
‡A river fish with brilliant scales, *Barbus bynni.*
‖A reference to the sprouting Osiris images or 'gardens of Osiris' set in tombs. See Budge, E. A. T. Wallis: *The Mummy.*

raised to the level of the fields by some mechanism worked by foot, but neither known texts nor illustrated documents give any warrant for inferring the existence of such a device. The probable explanation is that the engineers who controlled the sluices of Lake Moeris opened them when the farmer needed water, so that the canals filled up. By means of the *shadūf* or, more laboriously, by filling jars, the water was channeled into the irrigation trenches. These were opened and closed and new ones were constructed and dams built all 'with the feet', for, as we can see in a painting from Thebes, the mud which was used to make pottery was kneaded by trampling.

5. *Harvest*

When the corn began to turn yellow the peasant apprehensively watched the invasion of his fields by his natural enemies—his masters or their agents—accompanied by a swarm of scribes, surveyors, servants and representatives of civil authority. Their first task was to measure the fields;[23] their second to reckon the number of grains to the bushel. These two operations enabled them to calculate very accurately the taxes the peasant would have to pay either to the agents acting for the Treasury or to the administrators of gods like Amūn, who owned the richest land in the whole of Egypt.

The owner of the land or his agent has left home early in the day. He drives his own chariot with a firm grasp of the reins while his servants follow on foot, carrying seats, mats, sacks and boxes —everything, in fact, (and a good deal more) that will be required for the inspection and survey. The chariots draw up by a clump of trees and some men, appearing from out of the blue, take charge of them and unharness the horses, which they tether to the foot of a tree and then feed and water. They also erect a stand for three water jars. From boxes they take loaves and other kinds of food which they serve out on plates and in baskets, and they even bring out a toilet set. The groom, in the comfortable certainty of having the next few hours to himself, lies down and goes to sleep in the shade. Meanwhile his master is surrounded by his surveyors. He is dressed in his best clothes—wig, short-sleeved shirt gathered at the waist over a loincloth, necklace, stick and sceptre. He is wearing sandals on his feet, and laced-up

E.L.E.–I

leggings protect his calves from being pricked by the grass. His underlings wear nothing except a loincloth: a few have sandals but the rest are barefoot. On Menna's estate the surveyors, like their master, wear a short-sleeved tunic over their loincloth and a pleated skirt.[23a] Between them they carry all the implements of their profession—rolls of papyrus, writing palettes and briefcases containing inkpots and pen-cases, as well as balls of string and stakes four or five feet in length. If these operations are taking place on estates belonging to Amūn, who was both the wealthiest and the most acquisitive member of the Egyptian pantheon, the string is wound round a piece of wood terminating in the head of a ram—the god's sacred animal.

The chief surveyor ascertains one edge of the field and, authenticating its precise position by invoking the 'great god who is in heaven', he then sets up his staff (which resembles the sceptre symbolizing the nome of Thebes), and the string is unrolled and stretched taut. The children shout and wave their arms to scare away the quails flying over the corn stalks which are already heavy with grain. The scene is a source of interest to others beyond those directly concerned, for a crowd of inquisitive onlookers, ready to offer unsolicited advice, has gathered beside them. The actual workers would soon have been exhausted if an attentive servant girl had not brought them refreshments, and a large meal is being prepared beneath the sycamore tree.

Workers on the land would have to spend several weeks over the harvest and treading out the grain, and there were not always enough local inhabitants for the job. On large estates that belonged to the State or to the great gods, gangs of mobile labour were engaged. These began work in the southern districts and when they had finished there they only had to move gradually northwards to find fresh fields always just ready for harvesting. By the time that all the cereal crops in Upper and Middle Egypt had been gathered in, the harvest was only beginning in the Delta. Evidence for the existence of such gangs moving from one district to another to gather the harvest is to be found in a decree of King Sety I declaring the staff of his 'House of a Million Years' at Abydos to be exempt from conscription.[24]

Corn was cut with a short-handled sickle which fitted comfortably in the hand.[24a] Its blade was fairly wide near the handle and tapered to a point. No attempt was made to cut the corn stalks near ground level: the reaper stood almost upright, grasped a good bunch of corn in his left hand, cut it just below the heads and laid it on the ground, leaving the headless stubble still standing. The reapers were followed by women with baskets who picked the bunches up off the ground and carried them to one end of the field, while some also collected in bowls the grains that had fallen on to the ground. The straw is not likely to have been left to rot, but we do not know what became of it. Pictures sometimes show the owners of the land themselves harvesting and gathering the corn, without having even bothered to remove their smart white pleated robes. It might be tempting to suggest that they are formally inaugurating the work before promptly handing it over to the paid harvesters. The truth is, however, that we are looking at a scene of the future life in the 'fields of Yalou'—a place of plenty, but one where everyone had to cultivate his own land[25] (p. 311). Generally speaking the owners of property were content merely to be present at the harvest. We see Menna, for example, sitting on a cross-legged stool in the shade of a sycamore tree, with some food within easy reach.[25a]

Work began at daybreak and continued uninterrupted until nightfall. When the sun was at its height the harvesters would sometimes break off and take a long drink from a jug of water, tucking their sickle under their arm. 'Give the peasant plenty and give me some water to quench my thirst.'[26] In an earlier period, men had demanded more. 'Beer,' said one of them, 'for the man who cuts barley' (*besha*, from which, of course, beer was made).[27] The foreman was quick to jump on anyone who paused too frequently. 'We all know the sun is shining. You haven't handed in anything yet. Have you finished a sheaf? Don't stop for a drink today before you have done something worth doing.'

While the harvesters are toiling away a number of men are sitting in the shade with their heads on their knees. We do not know what they are doing; perhaps they are labourers who have managed to keep out of sight, or merely curious onlookers or personal servants waiting until their master has finished his inspection. There is also a musician sitting on a sack and playing his double flute. He is an old acquaintance: on the tomb of Ti, dating from the Old Kingdom, we find a musician with a flute some three feet long following behind the line of reapers. Before him stands a labourer, still holding his sickle and clapping his hands and singing

first the 'song of the oxen' and then a song of which the opening words were 'I'm on my way!' Perhaps his overseer's bark was
worse than his bite. On Paheri's estate the flute player is missing,
but the reapers chant an improvised song: 'It is a lovely day. Come
forth from the earth. The north wind is rising. Heaven works for
our pleasure. We love our work.'[27a]

Even before the whole of the field is reaped, the gleaners,
women and children, have set to work picking up the fallen heads
and begging for a little extra. We see a woman stretching out her
hand and reinforcing her gesture with the words: 'Give me just
one handful. I came last evening. Don't make my luck as bad today as it was yesterday.' In reply to similar entreaties, a harvester
roughly answers: 'Off with you and what you are carrying. People
have been turned off for that before now.' In very early times it
had been customary at the end of the harvest season to let the
workers have as much barley or spelt as they could reap in a day,
and the custom had persisted through the Pharaonic period. On
the estate of Petosiris, while the harvesters were working for their
master's benefit, they used to say: 'I am the good worker who
carry the grain and even in the bad years fill my master's two
barns, by the work of my arms, with all that grows in the fields
when the season of *akhit* comes.' But now it is their own turn and
they say: 'Twice happy are those who make good use of this day
in the field! The peasants leave their task.' Another group declares
that the wages are small, but that their share is worth collecting.
'A little sheaf a day is what I work for. If you take the trouble
to harvest for a sheaf, the rays of the sun will fall upon us to over-
whelm our work.'[28]

As a precaution against losing too much either to thieves or to
marauding birds, the crop was removed as quickly as the harvesters advanced. In the district round Memphis it was carried on
the backs of donkeys. Led by their drivers, the herd of donkeys
would come trotting up, kicking up clouds of dust. The sheaves
would be packed into a rope pannier, and when both sides were
full, still more sheaves would be tied on with cord. The foals
would gallop freely in every direction in front of the donkeys,
while their drivers plodded behind, joking or wrangling as they
plied their sticks. 'I've brought four pots of beer.' 'That's nothing: I loaded my donkeys with two hundred and two sacks while
you were sitting on your backside.'[29]

In Upper Egypt donkeys were occasionally employed[30] but most of the carrying was done by men. It may have been in order to set some limit to the resulting labour that the practice had grown up of cutting the corn high up the stem and of leaving the straw standing. The carrier used a network bag stretched on a wooden framework and fitted with a pair of suspension rings.

When the bag was packed absolutely tight with corn, a pole about six or seven feet long was inserted through the rings and tied firmly into place. Two men will shoulder this load and carry it to the threshing-floor, singing as they go as if to prove to the scribe that their lot is as good as his. 'The sun is shining on our backs! At Shou we shall be paid for our barley in fish.' A wag affects to think that if the porters don't go a bit faster they will be caught by the floods. 'Hurry up. Stir your stumps. The water is rising: it is nearly up to the sheaves!'—a considerable hyperbole, for the first sign of the flooding is still some two months ahead.[31]

As soon as the first pair has gone, another pair takes its place. One of the men has picked up the sack: his mate, who has got hold of the pole, seems anxious to slow the proceedings down, for he says, 'The pole will hardly stay on my shoulder. Oh dear, how hard it is.'

The floor of the threshing-floor is of beaten earth. When a sufficiently thick layer of grain has been spread, oxen are turned loose on it, accompanied by a number of men carrying whips and forks. While the oxen tread out the grain the men continually fork it over. The heat and the dust make this work very trying, but the ox-drover encourages his animals: 'Tread it for your own good, go on, tread for your own good. Your masters get the grain and you can eat the straw. Keep at it! It's quite cool.' Every now and again an ox lowers his massive head and takes a mouthful of mixed grain and straw, but no one seems to mind.[32]

Forking

As soon as the oxen had been led away, grain and straw could by roughly separated by forking. Next, a light broom was used: since the chaff was lighter than the grain, it tended to rise to the top, so that a large proportion of it could be removed. When it came to winnowing, the workmen would take in each hand an

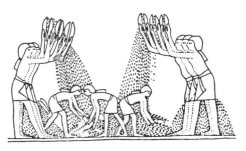

Winnowing

implement rather like a flat scoop and ladle up some grain; then, standing on tiptoe, they would lift it as high as they could and let it fall. The grain fell to the ground, while the chaff was carried away by the wind.[33]

Once the grain was clean, the scribes got busy with all the tools of their trade, accompanied by the measurers with their bushels.

There was no mercy for the peasant who held back part of his crop with intent to deceive, or who, even if he were perfectly honest, could not pay over to the authorized collectors every ounce which the survey had proved they could legally demand; he was stretched out on the ground and methodically beaten —if indeed he did not suffer worse. The corvée-labourers carried their bushel measures full of grain off the threshing-floor past the scribes and into a high walled courtyard containing the towering silos. The interior walls of these sugar-loaf buildings were carefully plastered, the outer walls whitewashed. A ladder led up to the opening through which the bushel measures were successively emptied. The grain could afterwards be drawn as required through a small door at ground level.

Generally speaking, this work, though hard, was cheerfully done, and the occasional clout with a stick was soon forgotten. The fellah was used to it and he could comfort himself with the reflection that nearly everyone got beaten sooner or later and that not all the victims had skins as thick as his. The words of the Psalmist were no less apposite in Egypt: 'Those who sow in tears shall reap in joy. He who weeps when he bears the seed shall come again in joy and bring his sheaves with him.'[34]

There had been lamentation over the divine shepherd when the seed was buried in the earth; now man might rejoice, but the gods must have their due share. The grain was winnowed under the protection of a curious image in the shape of a crescent swollen at the centre.[35] Even today at threshing time the peasants in the Fayyum fix on their roof-tops, or hang on their doors, a kind of doll decorated with ears of corn which they call the *arouseh* or 'bride', to which they offer a cup, eggs and bread. It has been plausibly suggested that the misshapen crescent was also an *arouseh*. Besides this, however, the owner of an estate had to make the snake goddess Renoutet (for her worship by vine-growers, see p. 108), a more elaborate offering of sheaves of corn, birds, cucumbers, water melons, bread and fruit of various sorts. At Siout every tenant farmer had to offer his first fruits to Wepwawit, the god of the district, and no doubt every local deity received a similar offering. The king in person, in the presence of a great concourse of people, offered Min, the god of fertility, a sheaf of corn during a festival held during the first month of *shemou*.[36] Everyone of high or low degree gave thanks to the gods, the lords of all, and awaited with confidence the new floods which would usher in a fresh cycle of work on the land.

6. *Flax*

Flax grew thick and tall, and was usually picked while still in flower. Agricultural scenes in colour in the tombs of Apouy and of Petosiris show the stalks growing among the cornflowers and terminating in a little patch of blue.[37]

The method of pulling flax was to grasp a handful in both hands fairly high on the stalks, taking care not to break the fibres. The handful was then turned upside down to shake off the loose earth and the stalks were levelled at the lower end. The handfuls of flax, with stalks pointing in both directions, were then laid on the ground, so that the finished bundles, when tied in the middle with improvised string made from some of the flax stems, had flower heads at each end. It was well known that the quality and toughness of flax was improved if it were picked before it was fully ripe, and this is confirmed by a definite statement to this effect in a text; but part of each crop had naturally to be kept for seed, which was needed partly for sowing next season and partly for pharmaceutical purposes.

Men carried the bundles of flax on their shoulders while children balanced them on their heads. The fortunate owners of donkeys packed their load into the panniers and warned the drivers sharply not to drop their freight. The porters carried it to a point in the shade where a man was hatchelling a handful of flax on a sloping board. To the porters' shouts of 'Hurry up, old man, don't talk so much: the men are coming quickly from the field', he would answer 'Bring me one thousand one hundred and nine bundles if you like, and I will comb them all!'[37a] Roudidit's serving-girl (p. 52) must have been urged on by some imp of mischief, for she chose the moment when her brother was busy at this work to confide her mistress's secrets to him. The young man made her pay for her choice, for he had in his hand a most effective instrument for inducing people to keep their mouths shut.[38]

7. *Harvest Pests*

As we have already seen, the crops were at the mercy of a host of potential enemies. When the barley was nearly ripe and the flax in flower, thunderstorms and hail might 'smite throughout all the land of Egypt all that was in the field, both man and beast'.* This was the seventh of the plagues and as Pharaoh's heart remained unmoved, since corn and spelt were late-ripening crops and had therefore escaped damage, the east wind brought a cloud of locusts which devoured everything that the hail had left undamaged, so that 'there remained not any green thing in the trees, or in the herbs of the field, throughout all the land of Egypt'.

In the face of enemies like these all the peasant could do was call upon the gods, and in particular the locust god. But among the marauders that assailed the gardens there were two—the golden oriole (*genou*) in spring and the roller† (*sourout*) in the autumn—against which he could take effective counter-measures.[39] Both these birds were useful because they destroyed a large number of insects, but being fruit eaters they also did much damage, and the tomb artists often show them fluttering round the fruit-trees. They could be snared by spreading a very large net, supported by poles at each corner, over the tree in such a way that the Birds still had room to perch. When a flock had settled, children crept up and knocked the poles away so that the net collapsed over tree and birds alike, whereupon the trappers ducked under the net, gathered the birds like ripe fruit and caged them. This method did not supplant spring traps, which had been invented at a very early date and always remained in common use.[40]

During their migration season dense clouds of quails arrived in Egypt in such a state of exhaustion that they would fall to the ground. It was naturally preferable, however, if possible, to capture birds in full vigour. A painting in the Berlin museum shows six trappers with a fine-meshed net stretched over a rectangular

*Exodus. ix. 25.
†A bird of brilliant plumage allied to the crow.

framework. Their clothes deserve some study, for they are shod with sandals as a protection against the stubble and a white scarf is wound round their bodies. When vast flocks of quails were flying over the harvested field the trappers would suddenly show themselves and flap their scarves, thus causing such panic among the birds that they would stop flying and alight on the net. Here many of them would find their feet caught in the mesh and they were too crowded to be able to flutter free in time. The final stage was for four of the trappers to lift the net and for the remaining pair to catch as many quails as they wanted.[41] These birds were very popular among the peasants and their families and even the gods found them acceptable. During the reign of King Ramesses III, for example. Amūn was the recipient of no fewer than 21,700[42] —almost one-sixth of the total number of birds of all kinds offered to the god over the same period.

8. *Cattle Breeding*

The primitive Egyptians had made a long series of unsuccessful experiments before discovering which animals would best repay domestication. Man and dog were natural allies in hunting, and ox and donkey were recognized to be valuable beasts of burden. The Bedouin prized sheep's wool highly, but the Egyptians disliked using it for dead or living and in general preferred goats to sheep. Besides these animals which, like the pig, had been quickly domesticated, the Egyptians hunted and caught, and then bred in captivity, gazelles, stags, oryx, antelope, addax,* ibex and even the later much hated hyena.[43] As late as the Middle Kingdom the governor of the Oryx nome was breeding in his stud some of the graceful creatures from which the district took its name. By the period of the New Kingdom however such experiments were a thing of the past. We find a schoolboy saying, 'You are worse than the antelope that lives in the desert and is never still. It never learns to plough, nor treads out grain steadily on the threshing-floor. It lives on the labour of the oxen, but it cannot be counted among them.'[44] The breeding fraternity now confined its activities to the real 'friends of man'—horse, ox and donkey, goat, sheep, pig, goose and duck.[45] The camel was scarcely known except among the population of the eastern Delta, and domestic fowls

*A species of antelope, resembling the oryx.

were not introduced until a later date.[45a] We should remember that if other animals were tended with care or even devotion, this only happened in the temples and from religious motives. We are here concerned solely with breeding for agricultural purposes.[46]

The horse had not been introduced into Egypt long before our period, and was still a comparative rarity, despite the tribute exacted from defeated Asiatic people. Houy had a stable as distinct from his ox byres and his donkeys' stalls, but then, as the Royal Son and Viceroy of Kush, he was a person of great importance[47] and a member of the privileged group who rode in a chariot when summoned to the palace or when they went out or visited their estates. The owners of horses hardly ever ventured to ride them and we only know of two or three representations by an Egyptian artist of a man on horseback.[48] The Bedouin were of sterner stuff, and when in war one of their chariots was brought to a standstill they would unharness the horse, jump on its back and gallop off. When horses were put out to grass they were kept separate from the other animals.

The ox byres were situated in the same enclosure as, and quite near to, the main dwelling-house and granaries.[48a] Oxherds lived in the byres with the double object of guarding them from theft and of being ready for work more quickly in the morning. In these squalid mud hovels, black outside and in, they kept a corner in which to prepare their evening meal and store their food. We can see them, heavily laden, walking at the head of the herd of oxen or bringing up the rear. For the sake of comfort they would have divided their load into two equal parts which they slung from a yoke in jars, boxes or hampers; if they had only a single bundle they carried it slung from the end of a stick over their shoulder. This was the kind of life that Bata led, but then he was a tough and cheerful character and popular with women. Most stockmen were poor enough specimens, worn out by a life of toil, bald-headed, likely enough, with matted beard, some paunchy, some thin as rakes, but all of them weaklings. There is a tomb at Meir in which the artist has depicted them with brutal frankness,[49] (p. 124).

A herdsman's life was never dull. He grew to love his beasts and would talk to them all day long. He knew where their favourite grass grew and led them to it, and his grateful beasts repaid his care by growing big and fat and producing many young, while sometimes they could even do him a good turn. Crossing the marshes was always rather a tricky business, for a calf might drown where a man and a full-grown beast could walk firm-footed. Here then the herdsman would hoist the calf on his back, grasp its legs firmly and step out boldly into the water, followed by the lowing mother, her eyes dilated with fear, and by

the other cows. The wise old oxen would move in an orderly group, marshalled by other herdsmen. In the deep water near the clumps of rushes and papyrus the dangerous crocodile lurked. In olden days cowherds knew the proper spells for turning it into a harmless plant or for blinding it,[50] but though I should not imagine that this knowledge was lost, later documents do not mention it. The song of a herdsman who had travelled over much of Egypt is preserved in a tomb at El Bersheh, 'You have driven oxen along every road. You have trodden the sands, and now your feet tread grass. You are eating tufted plants, and now you are well satisfied, and here is goodness to nourish you.'[51] The cowherd on the estate of Petosiris gave his cows fanciful names—'Golden', 'Brilliant' and 'Beautiful'—as if they were the living incarnation of the goddess Hathor, to whom all these epithets belonged.[52]

Mating time, the birth of the calf, the battles between the bulls and moving from one place to another were the main occasions which called for proof of the stockman's skill and devotion, and if he failed in his job he received short shrift. He would be given no chance of explaining away the seizure of a calf by a crocodile, the theft of an ox or the losses of a herd by disease. If things went wrong it was his fault and he was stretched on the ground and beaten.[53]

Branding, which was one of the most effective precautions against theft, was practised mainly on the estates of Amūn and the great gods and on the royal domains. The cows and calves were herded into one corner of the field and then lassoed in turn. Each animal was turned on its back with feet tied as though it was going to be slaughtered. The brand was heated over a stove and applied to the right shoulder. It goes without saying that the scribes were in attendance with their writing materials, and the herdsmen would kiss the ground to signify their respect for these symbols of authority.[54]

In another scene we see goats forcing their way into a clump of trees destined for felling. In an instant they have stripped them bare.[55] They are wise to eat greedily while they may, for the wood-cutter is already on the scene and has struck the first blows with his axe on a tree: even then the goats will not leave it. The kids are skipping about, but the he-goats are eating against time. But here comes the goatherd, proudly carrying a stick shaped like the sceptre of Thebes, to collect his herd again. He has slung a large bag on one side of his yoke with a kid on the other as a counter-weight. He carries a flute as well: but alas there was no Theocritus, no Virgil on the banks of Nile to sing of the loves of shepherds and goatherds.

Birds were bred in aviaries whose plans, consisting of a court-yard embellished with a stele and some statues of Renoutet, had hardly changed between the Old and the New Kingdoms. On one side we see a storehouse, full of jars and bales, and scales for weighing the grain: on the other, a piece of ground, surrounded by a railing, with a pond in the centre. A poultryman is bringing grain to feed the geese and ducks that are swimming or walking round its edge.[56]

9. *The Marsh Dwellers*

A large part of the Nile valley was covered by marshes. When the river subsided into its bed each year it left behind big stagnant pools on the edge of the cultivated areas, which did not dry up until the end of *shemiou*, the summer season. The marshes were carpeted with water-lilies and fringed with reeds, papyrus and other water plants. The thickets of papyrus were sometimes too dense to admit the least glimmer of light and tall enough to induce a sense of security among the birds that nested amid their spreading umbels.

The creatures of the marsh world are a favourite subject for the artist. Some, like winged acrobats, perform wonderful feats of daring in the sky above. A hen-bird is hatching out her eggs. A screech owl sits motionless, waiting for nightfall. Yet the birds' natural enemies, the genet, the mongoose and the wild cat can climb high enough up the stems to reach the nests. The parent birds defy their assailants with the courage of despair while the nestlings utter agonized cries and flap their featherless wings. Fish glide swiftly between the stems—grey mullet, sheat fish, mormyr, the fat Nile perch and the scarcely smaller *chromis*, and the fahaka,* which, in Maspero's phrase, nature must have created for a joke. The batensoda is swimming upside down: it has done this for so long that its back has become pale while its belly has darkened. Here a female hippopotamus has found a quiet corner to give birth to her young, while close by a crocodile watches her with a wary eye, waiting for his chance to gobble up the new-born calf—unless the male hippopotamus comes back first, in which case there will be a battle royal, with the crocodile the eventual loser, for the hippopotamus will seize him in his terrible jaws. Then the crocodile will vainly attempt to bite his enemy in the foot, but loses his balance and is crushed to death.[57]

The farther north one went the wider stretched the marshes and the thicker grew the clumps of papyrus. The word for Delta —*mehit*—also means a papyrus-fringed marsh. The Egyptian language was rich in synonyms for natural phenomena, and there were other words which signified respectively a marsh covered with water-lilies (*sha*), marshes where the reeds grew (*sekhet*), marshes haunted by birds (*ioun*) and the pools left behind when the floods receded (*pehou*). The marshes were the hunter's and fisherman's paradise. At various times virtually the entire population of Egypt, even boys destined for the sedentary life of the scribe, enthusiastically went fishing and hunting in the marshes, while the women and girls cheered their skill, happy if they could bring a plump bird home alive. Quite young boys became expert at throwing the boomerang and harpoon. This was all sport for the

Tetraodon fahaka, more correctly *Tetraodon lineatus.*

amateur: but in Lower Egypt the marshes afforded the population their livelihood.

First and foremost they supplied the materials for building and industry. When the men had gathered large bundles of papyrus they tied them in trusses and, bent double beneath their heavy load, slowly, sometimes stumbling, made their way back to the village.[57a] There the trusses were untied and spread out and those stems picked out which could be used for building huts. In this part of Egypt papyrus replaced brick for house building, the interstices being filled up with mud. The walls were thin and the plaster often fell down, but it was a simple matter to make good the cracks.

Gathering and stripping papyrus

Papyrus fibre was used to make ropes of different gauge, mats, seats and the bird cages which were bought by landowners. Papyrus stems and ropes also supplied the material for the graceful and well-designed skiffs which were indispensable in both hunting and fishing. But before it was safe to go out after game, the new equipment had to be tested. Each man, wearing a garland of wild flowers and a wreath of lotus round his neck, climbed into his boat, which was steered with a long forked pole. The contest—that is really what it was—began with an exchange of fairly uninhibited insults, and threats and blows were soon flying. It might look as though the occasion was going to degenerate into a brawl but in fact each participant was merely trying to upset his adversary into the water and overturn his boat. When at last only a single contestant was still upright the game was over, and winners and losers, the best of friends again, returned to the village to resume what the Egyptian satirist calls the hardest occupation of all.[58]

If a fisherman wanted to go for a long expedition, he would use a boat with a mast, and with ropes stretched between the stays

where split fish could be hung to dry. A bird of prey would sometimes perch on the mast.[59]

There were many different methods of fishing.[59a] The fisherman
who went out on his own would settle down in a small boat with
his provisions and, when he had found a quiet spot. drop his line
into the water. When he got a bite from a good-sized cat-fish he
hauled in carefully and killed it with a blow from a club. Where
the marshes were shallower, bottle-shaped traps, or sometimes
more complicated double traps with two pockets, were employed.
The mullet would push through the narrow reed neck of the trap
in search of the bait—they could get in easily enough, but not out
again, and the trap would soon be alive with fish. Sure as he might
be of success, the fisherman's only anxiety was lest some unsport-
ing rival might have spied upon him and forestalled him by
emptying his traps. The use of the landing-net demanded both
patience and a steady hand. A spot with plenty of fish had first to
be chosen; then the net was lowered into the water and a period
of waiting ensued. When the unsuspecting fish were well and
truly in the net, it had to be lifted quickly but at the same time
smoothly, for otherwise it would be found to be empty. For seine-
netting a dozen men or so were needed, as well as a couple of boats
and a huge net fitted with floats along one edge and stone weights
along the other. The net was lowered into the water, the fish were
driven towards it, and then net, fish and all were hauled slowly to
the bank. The moment of landing the catch was rather tricky, for
the synodont* was a very lively fish which would jump out of the
net back into the water, and the fisherman had to grab it in mid-
air.[60]

Harpoons were the best equipment[61] for catching the enormous
Nile perch, which were so large that when they were carried slung
on a stick between two men their tail brushed the ground. Harpoons were also used in hippopotamus hunting—though not of
course the ordinary fishing harpoon, which would have been
snapped like a matchstick on the beasts' hide. The weapon in
question was a solid object consisting of an iron gaff set on a
wooden shaft with a string of floats tied to it. When the harpoon
struck home, the wooden shaft might break, but the iron head
remained embedded in the great beast, which at once made off.
The hunters recovered the floats and hauled on the ropes to get

Synodontis schall, which, unlike the batensoda, swam right way up.

close to their quarry. The hippopotamus would turn its huge head towards the hunters, baring its jaws that were powerful enough to crush a boat; but it would be dispatched with further harpoon thrusts.[62]

Hunting with the boomerang was more a rich man's sport than a regular job for boatmen. We see Apouy comfortably ensconced in a boat shaped like an enormous duck,[62a] but most people who went in for this kind of hunting simply used the normal papyrus skiff. It was advisable, if possible, to have on board a Nile goose as a decoy. The huntsman takes his boomerang tipped with a snake's head, hurls it, and weapon and quarry fall to the ground at his feet. The hunter's companions, his wife and children, quickly grasp them both. A little boy in an ecstasy of excitement shouts to his father: 'Prince, I have caught an oriole!' True enough; but a single wild cat has caught no fewer than three (p. 66).[63]

By using nets a hunter could catch alive a large number of birds simultaneously. Several helpers were required and even princes and noblemen were ready to participate, either as leader or as look-out. A fair-sized rectangular or oval pond on level ground was selected. On either side of this pond rectangular nets were spread out, big enough, if joined, to cover the whole surface of the pool. The problem was to bring the two sides of the net together quickly enough to trap the birds that had settled on the water. Four posts—two on each side of the pool—were stuck in the ground. The two halves of the net were attached to them at the corners nearest the pond. The outer corners were tied at one end to a heavy post set in the ground some distance beyond the pond and in a line with its centre, and at the other to running ropes which might be up to twenty-five or thirty yards in length. Now the trap was set, and the look-out would hide in a thicket a little way off with his legs in the water or sit behind a screen with holes cut in it. Some decoy birds that had been trained to work with the hunters then walked by the edge of the water, which was soon covered with duck. Three or four of the hunters already held the end of the running ropes. They were far enough away from the pond not to scare the birds, which would have taken flight at the slightest sound. The look-out raised his arm or waved a scarf, and at the signal the hunters pulled sharply together, leaning their weight on the rope and so shutting the trap. The two

E.L.E.–K

halves of the net rose into the air, met and then closed over the whole swarm of birds, trapping the lot. Even the liveliest birds could not flutter free. The hunters jumped up quickly and rushed forward with their cages before they could escape. When the cages were full the wings of any birds still left in the net were broken and their wing feathers plucked, which would ensure that none would be lost on the way back to the village.[64]

These various operations demanded skill, patience and, on occasion, courage: but these qualities would have been of no avail if the hunters had not been regarded with favour by a goddess called Sekhet or 'Meadow', represented as a peasant woman in a close-fitting robe, with long hair falling over her shoulders. The net itself also belonged to a god, 'Net', the son of 'Meadow', but the latter was responsible for the operations just described. The fish and the birds were hers, but she was generous and ready to share the bag with her allies and friends, the hunters and fishermen.[65]

10. *Hunting in the Desert*

Hunting in the desert was a sport for princes and nobles as well as being a professional occupation. On the one hand there is hardly a decorated tomb without its scene of the owner launching showers of arrows with unfailing accuracy at gazelles and antelopes in a fenced-in park rather like a zoo. On the other, when the archers who patrolled and policed the deserts, or the guards who were responsible for the mountain of the gold of Coptos, went to make their report to Menkheperrê-senb, the high priest of Amūn, they were accompanied by the officer in charge of hunting, who would present a magnificent series of trophies—ostrich eggs and feathers, live ostriches and gazelles, as well as dead game.[66] King Ramesses III organized teams of archers and professional hunters with instructions both to act as escorts to those who gathered honey and resin and also to catch and bring back oryx for presentation to the *ka* of the god Rê on every feast day: for animals from the desert continued throughout the historical period to be as much the most acceptable of offerings to the gods as they had been at a date when hunting was man's principal source of food.[67]

All hunters, amateurs and professionals alike, were constantly looking for ways of saving themselves the labour involved in the indefinite pursuit of game which nature had endowed with good legs, without risking their own exhaustion and the consequent possibility of becoming victims of hyenas and carrion birds. Thanks to their knowledge of animals' habits and their favourite water holes they schemed to lure as many as possible on to ground of their own choice, where they could capture or kill them as they preferred. A favourite place for such an ambush was the bed of a valley or wadi, where perhaps a trace of moisture encouraged the growth of some sparse vegetation, and whose steep sides precluded flight to right or left. Two barriers of netting were hung on posts at what experience had proved to be the right interval, but which we cannot properly judge from the paintings. There were no gaps in the farther net, which effectively barred any flight, but the nearer one contained an opening through which animals and men could pass. Inside the enclosure between the nets food and water were placed,[68] and it would soon be full of animals feeding with a pleasure unshadowed by any suspicion of imminent death. We can see wild oxen trotting hither and thither, ostriches dancing to greet the rising sun and a gazelle suckling her calf. A wild donkey lies relaxed in sleep and on a tiny hillock a hare scents the wind.[69]

On other occasions the hunting expedition might set out afoot. The nobleman carried nothing, but his escort divided between them the load of provisions, bows and arrows, cages, nets and game baskets, and a kennelman held on a leash the harriers and hyenas, specially trained for hunting, which had already had a big feed. After chariots had come into general use, a nobleman would ride to the hunt as though he were setting off to war, fully equipped with bow and arrows. The personal servant (*shemsou*) followed on foot, carrying the jugs, full water bottles, boxes, bags and ropes slung from a yoke. When the little cavalcade had arrived at its destination the leader would step down from his chariot with his weapons. The pack of harriers were held on a leash,[70] but the use of hyenas, which the Egyptians of the Old Kingdom had succeeded in training, had long been abandoned.

The game are rudely awakened by a hail of arrows and the attacks of the savage harriers. The luckless beasts vainly seek a way of escape, but the steep sides of the valley and the nets hem them in and they must die where they stand. Deer and wild oxen are soon struck by arrows. An ostrich attacked by a dog strikes back vigorously with its beak. A terrified doe gives birth to her young in her attempts to escape, but a harrier immediately seizes the newborn calf by the throat. An oryx makes a desperate leap in its efforts to escape, but falls straight into its enemy's jaws. A greyhound has pulled down a gazelle and is killing it instantaneously. If we can believe the evidence of the paintings in the tomb of one Ousir, it looks as if traps were set inside the enclosure, but the painting is not well enough preserved to make out how they worked. Nevertheless these snares must have existed, for if the

Returning from the chase

hunters had had nothing beyond dogs and arrows it is not easy to see how they could have taken as many animals alive as Ousir and a certain Amenemhat.[71] These last return from the chase with an ibex, a gazelle, an oryx and an ostrich, all tied by the leg, but all able to walk. A servant carries an antelope fawn slung across his shoulders, while others are carrying by the ears what look like dead hares. A hyena with dangling head, slung by its four feet from a pole, is certainly dead. These hunters have much to show for their efforts, but others, like the tireless Prince Amenophis, whether because they scorned easy gain or were deliberately making it harder for themselves, were bold enough to chase the swift antelope in their chariots, which could fly like the wind. A man named Ousirhat also hunted with the bow alone in his chariot in the vast expanses of the desert. Before him he drives a flying herd of antelopes which have been joined by hares, a hyena and a wolf, and he will return laden with trophies of the chase.[72]

CHAPTER VI

THE ARTS AND THE PROFESSIONS

EGYPT was something more than a nation of farmers, scribes and priests. If this had represented the whole truth, there could have been no pyramids, temples or sculptured tombs, no diadem of almost magical delicacy to grace the raven hair of Princess Khnoumit. To hew a needle of granite nearly a hundred feet long from the living rock: to convey it from Aswan to Thebes: to dress it to the tapering shape of an obelisk: to carve it with hieroglyphs of faultless accuracy and finally to set it upright on its base—the whole astonishing achievement took a mere seven months and was repeated several times during each reign throughout the New Kingdom. Yet the scribes looked down on the craftsmen who performed these feats as a race of inferior beings. It is time for us to survey briefly their life and work.

1. *Quarrymen*

In the two deserts which lay on either side of the Nile Valley the Egyptians possessed supplies of stone equally well suited to the most grandiose conceptions of the architect or sculptor and to the most delicate work of the jeweller.[1] A continuous belt of limestone ran between Memphis and Iounyt,* south of Thebes. The finest and whitest limestone came from the quarries of Roiaou,† not far from the thermal springs of Helouan, and limestone of good quality was also quarried from the 'Mountain of Thebes'. Red quartzite (*mery*), almost the colour of cedar wood, came from the Red Mountain, the goddess Hathor's especial domain, to the north-east of On. This quarry was in full production under the twelfth dynasty, and it was by merging with the crowd of workmen who went to it from their village that the

*Hermonthis, the modern Armant.
†Modern Tura and Ma'sara.

fugitive Sinuhe succeeded in escaping from Egypt. Operations here reached their peak during the reign of Ramesses II, and one day a single block longer than a granite obelisk—unparalleled since the dawn of history—was actually brought to light in the presence of the monarch in person, who was travelling in the desert near On in the outlying purlieus of the estate of Rê. Everybody believed that His Majesty had created it himself with the rays of his presence. The king set picked craftsmen to work on it

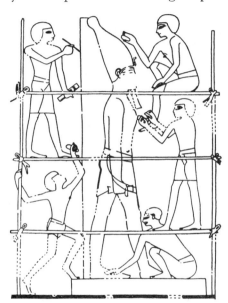

and in just a year it had assumed the form of a colossal statue which was named Ramesses-the-God. The superintendent in charge of the work was rewarded with gold and silver, and all the workmen who had been engaged on it shared in the royal favour. The king encouraged them to redouble their efforts by watching them at work every day. A second quarry, which was discovered beside the first, yielded stone for colossal figures for the temple of Ptah of Memphis and the temples of Ptah and Amūn of Ramesses.[1a]

Large quantities of fine quality sandstone, though it lacked the beauty of Red Mountain stone, were to be found in the three southern nomes. Aswan was the centre of the granite country and the red, grey and black varieties were all obtained in the vicinity of the town as well as from the islands of Abou (Elephantine), Satit and Senmout. An obelisk, a sarcophagus or a colossal figure of Osiris still testifies to the activities of the quarrymen of antiquity and signs of their preliminary workings can be seen on every side. The granite area extends a good way south. Three days' journey west of a place called Idahet lay the diorite quarries, in an area of such desolation and requiring such prodigious efforts and hardships to work that they had been abandoned since the Middle Kingdom. The Ramesside monarchs, who had hardly any prisoners-of-war at their disposal, never attempted to resume operations there.[2] Middle Egypt yielded a cheap supply of excellent stone: there was alabaster at Hatnoub, a few hours' journey from Akhnaton's abandoned capital, while farther south in the valley of Rohanou,* three days' journey from Coptos, there were deposits of a black gritty schist (*bekhen*) which took a beautiful polish, as well as of green breccia and of ordinary breccia or 'pudding stone'. Practically every ancient quarry contains groups of inscriptions, but those carved in the valley of Rohanou are the only ones which go beyond lists of names and titles and contain a mass of entertaining detail.[3]

The quarries were not worked intensively all the time. When a Pharaoh required *bekhen* stone the expedition which he dispatched would rank as one of the outstanding achievements of his reign, since it involved the assembling of many thousands of men. Such operations reached their climax when Ramesses IV mobilized no less than 9,368 men for one such huge-scale enterprise.[3a] The monarch had made elaborate preparations, both by consulting the books of the House of Life and by sending an advance party to undertake a reconnaissance. What might be called the headquarters staff of the expeditionary force comprised thirteen exalted personages, including the high priest of Amūn, together with his cupbearers, as well as some twenty army scribes. These highly skilled experts were expected to be equally capable of solving such technical engineering problems as the erection of an obelisk, the setting up of a figure fifty feet high or the construction of a ramp of unbaked brick, and the administrative questions arising, for example, from the organization of an expedition to Syria. There were ninety-one masters of the horse, equerries in ordinary and equerries in charge of baggage trains, fifty police officers of various ranks and a further fifty miscellaneous officials. It is surprising to observe the presence of 200 foremen of fisher-gangs: they can no doubt be accounted for by the fact that *shemou*, during which the expedition took place, was a bad season for fishing. The main body of the expedition consisted of 5,000 soldiers, 2,000 members of temple staffs, and 800 foreign auxiliaries

* The modern Wadi Hammamât.

(*Aperou*). Nine hundred officials of central government were included in the total strength, though they remained well to the rear. This army—for such in effect it was—was equipped with a number of ox-carts. The real experts—one chief artist, three master quarrymen, 130 quarrymen and stone dressers, two draughtsmen and four sculptors—represented only a minute fraction of the total force. The great majority were required either to haul the stone on sledges or to carry the necessary provisions. One of the main problems facing the commander of such an expedition was the commissariat—how to feed so many thousands of men in mid-desert and to ensure that each man got his ration of water, beer and bread, while at the same time supplying the experts and the leaders with a slightly more substantial diet and not forgetting to give thanks in a suitably dignified fashion to the gods of the mountain of *bekhen*, principally Min, Horus, and Isis, without whose goodwill the expedition was doomed to failure.[3b] The Egyptians picturesquely called this process 'making the desert blossom' or 'changing a road into a canal'. But it was a source of profound satisfaction to be able to record on a stele that not a single donkey had fallen by the wayside, not one man had suffered from thirst or even momentarily lost heart.[3c] Indeed the men who were conscripted for this job, with beer to drink and bread to eat as on a feast day in Egypt, had little enough to grumble about.[4]

Quarrying methods were primitive in the extreme.[4a] No attempt was made to attack a vein of rock and extract from it blocks of stone of uniform size. Instead the choice fell on any boulders which happened to be lying about and were large enough to yield a sarcophagus or its lid, a statue or a group. The first comers removed the blocks which lay closest to the side of the road, while the later arrivals had to scramble up the slopes and roll the great lumps of stone to the bottom. Not infrequently they got shattered in the process. Then an overseer named Mery had the brilliant idea of building a sloping road beside the hill and letting the blocks slide down it. The device worked perfectly and the ingenious engineer brought back on his own account ten statues of some seven feet in length—a quite unprecedented achievement. It had taken a mere thousand years to discover.[5]

The Egyptians were quick to see signs of divine intervention in everything, and those of them who had ventured out into the desert would seize on any unusual incident, however trivial, and magnify it so that it rapidly assumed the proportions of a miracle. While the quarrymen were wandering round the mountain of *bekhen* looking for a ready-made sarcophagus lid for King Nebtawi-Rê Mentuhotep, a she-gazelle—guided no doubt by the god—put them on the right road, for a 'gazelle great with young' appeared in their path and confronted the men. She stared at her would-be captors, but 'she did not turn back until she had reached the place on the august mountain where a sarcophagus lid lay and on it she gave birth. The king's soldiers, who had seen this, cut her throat and then they took up their place and made a solemn burnt offering and came down from the mountain in peace. Now surely it was the majesty of this august god, the lord of deserts, who had granted this gift to his son Nebtawi-Rê—may he live for ever—in order that his heart might rejoice, that he may dwell in life upon his throne for ever and ever and may celebrate jubilees without end.'[6]

When a block of stone had been found, got down to the road intact and loaded on a sledge in readiness for departure, the leaders of the expedition could not give the signal to move off until a fitting monument had been erected to the gods of the mountain of *bekhen*, the most august of whom was Min, the lord of Coptos and Ipou. This was all the more essential because the miracle of the gazelle had been quickly followed by a second. A cistern some ten cubits square had been discovered in the middle of the valley, full to the brim with water. Precautions were taken to prevent the antelopes from fouling it and to conceal it from the desert nomads. 'Yea, in earlier reigns soldiers had come and gone past where it lay, but no eye had ever seen it, no man's gaze had lighted upon it . . . it revealed itself only to His Majesty . . . when those who dwell in Tomery, the *Rekhyt**-people that are in Egypt, in the north and in the south, shall learn of this they shall bow down to the ground and shall acclaim the perfection of His Majesty for ever and ever.'[7]

By His Majesty's command 'This stele was erected in honour of Min his father, lord of the deserts, on this holy primeval mountain, placed first in the land of the rising sun, the divine palace endowed with the life of Horus, the divine nest in which this god delights, his pure abode of joy upon the deserts of the divine land, that his

---

*A generic name for the inhabitants of Egypt. Its precise significance is uncertain (p. 219).

ka may be satisfied and that the god's heart may be uplifted at wielding the royal might on the great throne which is above all thrones, that the monuments of the perfect god may be established, the lord of joy, greatly to be feared and greatly to be loved, the heir of Horus in his Two Lands, whom Isis, the divine mother of Min, the mighty Enchantress, reared for the dominion of Horus of the two banks, king of the South and the North, Nebtawi-Rê —may he live like Rê for ever.'

'He says, "My Majesty sent forth Amenemhat, the hereditary prince and vizier, chief of the works, who fills the king's heart,* with an army of 10,000 men from the nomes of the south as far as Wabout,† in order to bring him back a block of precious stone worthy of reverence, the finest that is in this mountain which Min hath set firm, to make therefrom a sarcophagus, an emblem of eternity fitter than all the monuments in the temples of Upper Egypt, on a royal expedition of the king, lord of the Two Lands, to bring from the deserts of Min his father what his heart desires".'[8]

Eventually, after duly sacrificing antelopes and oxen and burning turpentine resin in honour of the god's benevolence, the expedition set out again for Egypt twenty-two days after its arrival in the valley, bringing with it this wonderful stone, some twelve feet long, six feet wide and three feet deep.

The Egyptians did not like unnecessary hard work and whenever possible they got their stone by this simple method. They had some excuse for thinking that the block of sandstone taller than an obelisk found in the quarries of the Red Mountain was likewise a gift of Hathor. But when they had to dig and hew out galleries in the living rock, they were quite prepared to do so.[9] The labour involved in hewing rock tombs in the mountain of Thebes yielded a double dividend in the shape of 'houses of eternity' for the dead and blocks of stone of every shape and size for the living. A large number of quarrymen and stonedressers were either prisoners-of-war or convicted criminals, but we know that many free Egyptians also followed this occupation. Nevertheless when they learned, under the last of the Ramessids, that the country was torn in two by civil war, all broke their chains, joined the enemies of Amūn and scattered throughout the

*i.e. his favourite.
†The Oxyrhynchus nome.

country, committing countless deeds of sacrilege and brutality, which hardly suggests that they had previously been content with their lot.

2. *Miners*

There were a number of rich deposits of gold in the desert between the Nile and the Red Sea. Three points should be noted. There are numerous references in texts as well as in the Harris papyrus to gold of Coptos,[10] and we must realize that this gold was found in the mountain of *bekhen*. It was a fortunate combination of natural conditions that gold-mines and quarries yielding a stone so highly prized by sculptors—besides being capable of use as a touchstone—were both to be found near a source of water, at the junction of several tracks across the desert and equidistant from the Nile and the sea. The area was regularly visited by the overseers of the gold lands of the Coptos mountains, by the chief huntsmen in pursuit of ostrich, hares and gazelles, and by the police authorities of Coptos, who were responsible for the safety of those who travelled through the desert with their load of precious metals.

There were other gold-bearing areas, but they were less richly endowed by nature than the mountain of *bekhen*. One day King Sety I, who was engaged on a study of the problems connected with the high desert, expressed the desire to see the mines from which his gold was conveyed.[11] After starting from Edfou and exploring the canals which intersected the region, the monarch halted to reflect upon the matter in the following words, 'How wearisome is the waterless road! How can man walk when his throat is parched? Who will quench the traveller's thirst? The lowland is far away, the high desert is vast. The man that is thirsty on the hills laments. How can I order matters for them aright? I will find out the way to make them live and they will thank God in my name throughout the years to come. Future generations will glorify my energy because my foresight makes me consider the needs of the traveller.'

After uttering these reflections the monarch travelled through the desert in search of a place to dig a well. God guided his footsteps aright and the stone cutters were commanded to dig a well in the mountain for the comfort of the exhausted and the refreshment of travellers parched by the summer's heat. So successful was the venture that the king could write: 'Lo, God hath answered my prayer, and hath brought forth water from the mountain for me. In my reign the road that had been perilous since the beginning of time has been made kindly.'

But this was only a beginning. The king planned to found a proper town with the impressive name of 'Menmaatrê who pours forth abundance of water like the twin abysses of Elephantine.'* Since a town without a temple was unthinkable, the superintendent of the royal building work was ordered to build one. The quarrymen of the necropolis set to work and soon at the mountain's foot there rose a temple which, though small in scale, rivals any building of the period in the quality of its statuary and its inscriptions. Many divinities—Amūn, Rê, Osiris, Horus and 'the Nine Gods who are in this temple'—these included the king himself—were all worshipped there together. King Sety came to its opening and addressed the following prayer to his ancestors the gods. 'Homage to you, mighty gods, who have founded heaven and earth after your design, who look upon me with favour throughout all eternity and cause my name to endure for ever. For I am well disposed towards you, I do good on your behalf, I am watchful for those things that you delight in. Happy is he that follows the gods' words, for his purposes never fail. Let man observe your commandments, for you are all-powerful. My life and my strength have I spent on your behalf and in you I have sought my good. Grant that my monuments may endure for me and that my name may abide upon them.' Meantime for their part the grateful miners ceaselessly offered prayers to the gods on behalf of the king for his unparalleled achievement in digging a cistern and in building a temple in which the gods delighted. To each other they said: 'Amūn grant him eternal life, may he long endure. Ye gods that dwell in the spring, you shall grant him to endure as you, for he had opened for us a way to travel which before was impassable. Now we can fare on it in good health, and when we reach it, there we find life. The road which was inaccessible to us is become a good road. Thanks to our king the passage of the gold is become like the sight of the falcon.'†

The mines were put under the ownership of the temple, to

---

*The caves which Herodotus calls Krophi and Mophi, the fabled sources of the Nile. (Hdt. II. 28.)
†i.e. 'as the crow flies'.

which all the gold that was mined from the mountain had first to be conveyed before going to swell the royal treasury. An officer and a body of archers were detailed to protect the temple and those who worked there. None of the other seekers for gold who travelled through the desert, nor the archers, nor the guards must make any change in the arrangements which the king had ordained. No one was empowered to requisition for any purpose any of the workers engaged on washing the gold on behalf of the temple nor to touch the gold 'which is the flesh of the gods'. Succeeding kings who should have due regard to the wishes of Sety would be strengthened by Amūn, Harakhté and Ptah Tatenen. 'They rule the earth with mildness. They shall have dominion over the desert and the Land of the Bow. Their *kas* shall endure. They will sate those that are on earth. . . . But woe to all them, kings or commoners, who are deaf to my words! Osiris will pursue them. Isis will harry their wives and Horus their children, with the help of all the princes of Todjeser* that will execute judgement.'

The plight of the miners whom the king dispatched to Nubia was even worse.[12] To quote: 'There were large amounts of gold in the land of Ikaita [which lay to the east of the second cataract] but the lack of water made the journey there excessively arduous and not more than half the foremen who went there to wash the gold succeeded in reaching their destination, the others dying of thirst on the way, together with the donkeys they drove before them. They could not find enough liquid to drink, either to go or to return, from the water in their leather bottles. Therefore, for lack of water, no more gold can be brought from that land.' According to a report of the Prince Viceroy of Kush, kings in bygone times had tried to dig wells to a depth of some 200 feet, but the attempt had been abandoned before any water had been struck. However, the engineers at the beginning of the reign of Ramesses II, relying confidently on the support which they were sure that Hâpi, the father of the gods, would lend to his beloved son, were undaunted by this setback. They resumed operations and this time met with success. The water in the *Douat*† did the king's bidding and rose in the well. The miners no longer died by the roadside, although the working conditions in the mines remained terribly

*The necropolis.
†The underworld.

hard. We possess no source earlier than Diodorus,[13] according to whom the rock was made friable by heating and then attacked with metal wedges along the line of the gold-bearing vein. Lumps of ore were then carried to the entrance of the shaft and there crushed and washed until the gold dust was clean and bright. Chemical treatment of this dust resulted, he says, in gold of a very high degree of purity. In actual fact, however, the gold used in Egyptian jewellery is generally alloyed with silver, copper and other impurities.[14]

The precious turquoise (*mafaket*)[15] used by jewellers was found at Sinai together with such other compounds of copper as malachite (*seshmet*).[16] The mines had begun to be worked as early as the reign of King Sanekht* and operations were intensified in the Ramesside age. There was no lack of water here, and the Bedouin, who in the past had more than once attacked the miners and their escorts, had either mended their ways or had been subdued. In the nature of things there were always liable to be the kind of difficulties we hear of from an engineer in the twelfth dynasty called Horourrê. This man, who was in charge of exploration in the mine, had arrived on the scene in the third month of *perit*, when the best of the season was already over. The day after his arrival he had held a conference with the most experienced of the technical experts, who had unanimously advised him: 'There is unlimited turquoise inside the mountain, but the colour is what is important in this season. We have always heard the same thing said: the stones in the mine look splendid in this season, but their colour goes [fades] in the bad season of *shemou*.' Horourrê adds: 'During *shemou* the desert heat is scorching. The mountains are like red-hot metal and the stones become discoloured.' Horourrê was in fact at the end of the winter season: the worst of the heat had not yet begun, but it could not have been far ahead, and it would have struck when the work was in full swing. But keenness to serve the king and confidence in Hathor, the Lady of Heaven (who was also the Lady of the turquoise and the protectress of miners) kept his spirits up.

All Horourrê's workmen arrived without casualties. After the first yield there was no further hesitation. The work proceeded steadily and he completed his work in the first month of *shemou* without having experienced the heat which discoloured

*c. 2750 B.C.

the turquoise. In high glee he ends his story: 'I had gathered these precious stones. I had succeeded better than any man before me and I had done even more than I had been ordered. Assuredly I would wish for nothing more. The colour [of the turquoises] was flawless and my eyes rejoiced [to see them]. The gems were even more beautiful than at the usual season. Put then your trust in Hathor. If you do so, it will be the better for you. You will have even more success than I have had. I wish you good luck.'[17]

Thus it was that, thanks to the energy of her engineers, to the toughness of well-tried labour and to the enterprise of her traders (of which we shall speak in a later chapter) the warehouses of Egypt were full of materials that could be used in manufacture— stone, metals and wood. Let us now turn to watch the craftsmen busy in their workshops.

3. *In the Workshops*

An examination of the many paintings in tombs of the New Kingdom showing work being carried on in workshops, together with the descriptive texts, might suggest that the whole range of craftsmen—carvers in stone or wood, drillers of stone vases, goldsmiths, jewellers and lapidaries, makers of metal vessels, armourers, joiners and chariot builders—all plied their trades in a single workshop. But this impression may well derive from a pictorial convention. The whole range of diverse activities is supervised by an overseer represented as a colossus, and the workmen toiling under his vigilant eye are midgets by comparison. His figure is framed in an hieroglyphic text which defines his duties: a certain Douaouneheh, for instance, the overseer of the estate of Amūn, is described as 'coming to carry out an inspection of the workshop, to open the two houses of gold and silver, to organize all tasks, to put in hand all the work for which the overseer is responsible . . .'[18] It is possible that all the workshops specializing in a particular craft were grouped along one street, as they are in modern Cairo or Damascus, and that the director inspected each in turn: on the other hand, it is noticeable that wooden, and perhaps even stone, statues were decorated with inlay, that some parts of chariots, furniture and weapons were carved and set with gold and precious stones, and that a stone vase might be mounted with gold and inlaid with turquoise and lapis lazuli. Either one craftsman must have been master of several crafts or else a number of experts must have worked side by side, passing the object in question from hand to hand until it was finished.

4. *Sculptors*

We know, however, that the stone carvers liked to work on their own. In the scene in which Douaouneheh appears, we can see them at work simultaneously on a monolithic doorway comprising two uprights, a lintel and a cornice, on the façade of a building with a pierced front, and on a pillar, hewn from a single block of stone, with a palmiform capital similar to those at Tanis or Ahnas. Some of the workmen are using adzes, others chisels, and others again polishers; some are standing, while others are sitting on stools or on the block of granite itself. Although they have not finished their work, draughtsmen, reed pen in one hand and palette in the other, are already tracing in the outline of the hieroglyphs which will later be incised in the stone and painted blue or green. In the workshop of Rekhmarê, which also belonged to the domain of Amūn,[19] we can see the colossal seated statue of a king on a square low-backed seat, a colossal upright figure standing against a pillar, a sphinx and an offering table, all in the process of manufacture. The sculptors are standing equally comfortably on the paws or the back of the sphinx, the top of the offering table, and on a movable wooden scaffold from which they can work on the faces or hair of the colossal figures. Some are busy with mallet and chisel, while others are polishing the surface of the granite. The draughtsman is outlining with his pen the hieroglyphs on the pillar behind the figure, while the painter is dipping his brush in a bowl before colouring them. One cannot help wondering whether so wide a range of activities could have taken place simultaneously. In actual fact the sculptor chiselling certain details of the face and the engraver at work on the hieroglyphs on pillar and base need not have been in each other's way, but the polishing must have been left until after the sculptor and the engravers had finished, and the painting must have come last of all. This all suggests that the artist responsible for the scene may have shown in a single studio a number of craftsmen whose operations were in fact performed successively.

We shall find the same convention applied to other objects. The Egyptians no doubt liked to tackle several different processes simultaneously. Sooner or later the polisher would knock against the chisel or the burin, there would be a shout, and the aggrieved party would curse the interferer, who would reply with a joke. The statue would be finished in record time and was then ready for dispatch to temple or palace, there to bear witness before an admiring crowd to the favour with which the king regarded his servant or the love which the god bore to the Pharaoh.

The actual removal of the statue to the temple provided an excuse for a festal celebration: it was also, particularly when the statue was of colossal dimensions and the road was rough, a major technical and administrative achievement. For instance, an alabaster statue some twenty feet high had to be transported from a suburban workshop, on the road to the alabaster quarries, to a building known by the name of its founder, 'the love of Thoutyhotep is enduring in the Hare nome.'[20] It was an act of almost unprecedented royal graciousness which had permitted both this building to be given the name of a private individual and a statue of this size to be carved and conveyed to its destination with such ceremony. It was first place on a stout sledge, consisting of two massive baulks of timber curving upwards at one end and joined by strong cross-pieces, firmly braced with ropes. Since alabaster was a brittle stone, all the points where the friction of the ropes might have caused damage had been carefully padded. To this sledge, with its five- or six-ton load, four very long ropes were attached. These were to be hauled by porters divided into four groups, comprising respectively men from the east and from the west of the province, soldiers of the line and temple servants.

Two men did not hesitate to add their weight to that of the statue. One of them sat on its knees and directed his censer so as to wreathe the alabaster face in terebinth smoke, while the other sprinkled water from his ewer drop by drop, just as was done in the temple before the gods' statues. Water carriers stood close at hand, pouring water on the ground to make it slippery, while yet more men carried a huge baulk of timber: this seems to have been used to help in pulling the statue, but we do not know exactly how it was employed.

The order was given to move off. The superintendent of the

manufacture of the statue and his associates were responsible for the operation. They transmitted their orders to a number of men who had the knack of addressing, or perhaps it would be truer to say, of catching the interest of, the army of men on the ropes, and of rousing them with a harangue which concluded in a stirring shout of *haya*! The statue got under way and began to move along the road, from which the quarrymen had removed the worst of the stones. The road was lined with soldiers holding back an immense concourse of eager sightseers, while boats on the canal which ran parallel to it kept pace with its progress, crews and passengers alike adding their voices to those of the crowd. Some street altars had been set up on the quays, and there was plenty of food to keep up the strength, both of the workers and of the spectators who merely shouted. The central figure in the whole scene, Thoutyhotep himself, had come in a litter carried by porters, with an escort of his sons, soldiers and servants bearing feather fans and mats, to be present at this, his crowning hour. He believed that no comparable spectacle had ever been presented in his province: 'The princes who had laboured of old, the administrators who had worked for eternity within this town wherein I have set up altars on the river bank, had never dreamed of what I have done, had never thought of what I would do for myself. Behold, I have completed my work for eternity after this my tomb was completed in its works of eternity, yea, for ever.'

The foregoing scene, which took place under the Middle Kingdom, was a good deal less unusual than the governor of the Hare nome supposed. Comparable festivities took place every time a king permitted a private individual to have his statue transported to a temple, as well as when royal statues were conveyed there. The Egyptians enjoyed these opportunities for doing things in a big way, with their excuses for shouting loudly and drinking heavily, which sent everyone home happy at the end of the day. An individual named Qenamūn received an even more signal mark of royal favour in as much as he was given permission to bear no fewer than three statues in procession.[21] They were accompanied by a multitude of people, shouting and gesticulating among clouds of terebinth smoke. The men carried fronds of papyrus, priestesses of Hathor, the Lady of Thebes, shook their sistra and crotals, and dancing girls and acrobats whirled through the crowd.

5. *Goldsmiths, Jewellers and Lapidaries*

The manufacture of stone vases, which had already reached a high degree of perfection as early as the first dynasty, was still flourishing in the Ramesside age. Alabaster, schist and breccia were cut into jars and jugs, amphorae, bowls, cups and basins, sometimes ornamented with human or animal figures. The tools employed were extremely simple, the most characteristic being a drill hafted on a wooden shaft which was tipped with leather at the upper end. The craftsman gripped the block of stone between his knees and rotated the drill in his hands. Sometimes there were

Making metal vases

failures: the wall of the vessel might for instance be pierced by over-vigorous drilling, but this damage was reparable by neatly cutting out the affected area and inserting a patch. The tomb of Tutankhamūn has yielded a number of alabaster pieces which are more remarkable for virtuosity than for taste, and many people will find more pleasure in the beautiful amphora depicted in the tomb of Pouyemrê,[22] whose sole ornament is a short hieroglyphic inscription.

Large numbers of craftsmen were engaged in metal working. Admittedly the treasure of Bubastis, with its gold and silver vases, dishes, earrings and bracelets, or the jewellery from the tomb of Siptah or the Serapeum (now in the Louvre) which date from our period, are less magnificent and less varied than the staggering collections of Tutankhamūn and Psousennes. Yet for a truer picture we should examine the Harris papyrus, which lists the offerings which Ramesses III made to the gods, in a monotonous recital of gold and silver, copper, lapis lazuli and fine turquoise. The doors of the sanctuaries of Thebes were either of gold or of burnished copper which shone like gold. Some of the statues wore garments of gold; many offering tables and libation vessels were of silver. Royal decrees issued in favour of Amūn were engraved on great tablets of gold, silver or copper. The Great House* itself and the sacred barque of Amūn were of an opulence which beggars all description. The temple of Atum at On owned a pair

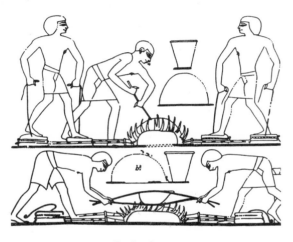

Casting bronze

of golden scales, said to be absolutely unique, on which a solemn cynocephalus ape cast in gold presided over the weighing. There were statues of the Nile god in no less than twenty-one different materials: 13,568 were of pure lapis lazuli and turquoise, and half as many of gold and other materials—a staggering figure. Every temple had its own treasury, while in order to get an idea of the scale on which metal workers practised their craft we must keep in mind all the royal and private collections of regalia and *objets d'art* as well.

The first step in the workshops was the weighing out of the gold and silver before it was handed on to the craftsmen who worked it.[23] This is what the scale balance was used for on earth; in the underworld a similar balance was employed by the god

*The temple sanctuary.

Thoth at the judgement, to weigh the soul in the presence of Osiris and the gods of *Amentit.** Cereals were measured by the bushel. Ingots of Asiatic copper were counted though it was not considered necessary to weigh them. The balance took the form of an upright column ending in the head of Maât the goddess of truth, who carried a metal fulcrum and a flail with a point at its centre, from either end of which two identical pans were suspended by triple cords. When anything had to be weighed the flail and its appendages were balanced across the fulcrum to see whether the pans were in equilibrium. The weights were shaped like kneeling oxen, while the metal to be weighed was in the form of rings. The operator checked any movement of the pans with his hand and bent over the scales to verify that the upright was vertical. Meanwhile the scribe had taken his reed pen and palette from their case and recorded the results in the presence of the foreman of the temple workmen, who took the gold after it had been weighed and distributed it to the craftsmen.[23a] They would need wire for making chains, flat plates and narrow strips for cloisonné work jewellery, large sheets of metal for vases and cups, tubular sections for bracelets, and solid bars as bullion,[24] and so the metal had first to be melted down for fabrication into these various shapes. For this purpose it was poured into a crucible, which was placed on the hearth.

The Egyptians melted gold and silver over an open flame, half a dozen men standing in a circle round the hearth and making the fire glow brightly by blowing down long blowpipes ending in a pottery nozzle with a very small aperture. It is to their credit that they could joke about it, for it was exhausting work. This method had been traditional from very early times, but an improvement was introduced at the beginning of the New Kingdom, whereby the flues were attached to skins fastened to the ground and each fitted with a string which opened or closed, as required, an aperture at the top. Each blower stood on a pair of these skin bellows, holding a string in either hand, and put his weight on them alternately. At the same time he pulled on the string of the skin which was not in use, while slackening the string of the skin on which he was treading, thus forcing the air down the flue. Two men using this device could quite easily do the work of six.[25] When the metal was molten, two men, undeterred by the heat and

*The underworld.

smoke, seized hold of the crucible with metal tongs, broke off a corner and poured off the metal into a line of moulds on a table. It was removed from them in the form of smallish lumps, which were then handed to craftsmen whose tools consisted of a large stone which formed an anvil and a smaller one which made a handy hammer. With this simple equipment they beat the metal into lengths of wire, bars or strips, or flat plates. The hammering process would eventually harden even an unalloyed metal, which was then made malleable again by reheating: the craftsman grasped the sheet in a pair of tongs and brought it over to a char-

Jeweller stringing a necklace

coal fire, which he fanned into flame with a blowpipe. Wire was rendered progressively finer by being drawn through a draw-plate. Simple though these processes were, they yielded metal in practically every shape which the goldsmith required, and it only remained to cut and assemble it. A craftsman engaged on making a gold or silver cup would sit on a stool in front of a support firmly embedded in the ground and shape the metal sheet by judicious hammering. Once the body of the object had been made,

it had to be decorated, and the Egyptian repertoire of decorative forms was unlimited. They were equally fluent in covering a cup or a jug with floral or geometric patterns enclosing a religious or a secular scene and in engraving, with the utmost restraint, a short hieroglyphic inscription on an exquisitely simple vase. After the finishing touches had been applied and the final polish given, the completed object would be exposed to view on a shelf which by the end of the day would be laden with a wide variety of products.

6. *Wood Work*

The varieties of wood employed by the joiner included acacia, carob, juniper and other native types not so far identified, together with ebony, which came from the lands to the south, and

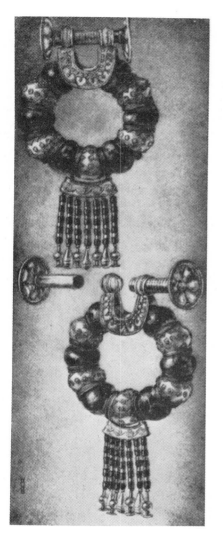
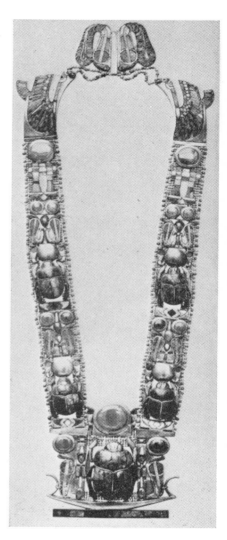

Plate VI   Ear-rings and pectoral of Tutankhamūn

the woods from Syria—pine (*āsh*) and the fir (*mer*) which resembled in colour the quartzite from the Red Mountain. The trunks were sawn into planks and sections with handsaws, but beams were hewn by carpenters with long-handled axes. The adze, a metal cutting blade shafted at right angles to the end of a

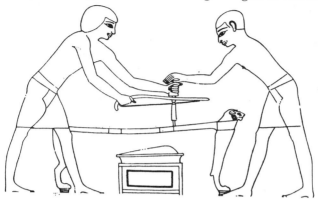

Using a bow-drill

wooden handle varying in length from a palm's breadth to a cubit,* was used for the same purpose as the modern plane or scraper. Round holes were made with a bow-drill, and mortises were cut out with a hammer and chisel, which were also employed for joinery work.

Carpenter's benches had not been invented, and a piece of wood which was to be cut lengthwise had to be lashed to a post firmly embedded in the ground. The motion of the saw was nevertheless liable to cause the wood to slip and 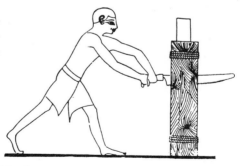 eventually to split, and this difficulty was got over by tying the post and the plank together at the top and fixing a heavily weighted stick between them. If the piece of wood was not too large, however, the craftsman held it firmly against the ground

*i.e. about 6 to 18 inches.

with one hand and sawed with the other. He did the same when working with an adze, using his feet as well as his hands to steady the wood. For joining pieces of wood, pegs, tenon joints and glue were preferred to metal nails, which were more commonly employed for fixing sheets of metal on wood. The adze was also used for planing down minor blemishes after the parts had been assembled. The final process was polishing. The complete chest or piece of furniture would often be handed over to a painter responsible for its decoration.[26]

Two great wooden shrines made by order of Apouy for the temple of the deified King Amenophis I show us both how rich the ornamentation could be and how the craftsmen set about their job.[27] These pieces stand about twelve feet high, one of them being raised still farther by a dais reached by a flight of five steps. Papyriform columns support a cornice decorated with uraeus heads,* and the roof is of the usual convex form. On the front panel Horus and Seth are twining around the deified king the symbolic plants of north and south. The other shrine is composed of three tiers, each supported on a row of miniature columns. The lowest stage or floor is left empty to receive a bed and its head, stool, table and mirror. At the other levels the front is pierced and carved. Among the decorations can be observed the emblem of Hathor, several royal cartouches, the symbols of Isis and Osiris, crowned falcons, Bes playing on his tambourine and Toueris holding her amulet. The craftsmen engaged on making these two shrines are obviously talented acrobats. The engravers of the hieroglyphs on the two great pillars need not leave ground level: but two others working on the cornice have climbed right to the top of the column, carrying their tools. One rests his foot on the streamers wreathed below the capital, the other perches on the capital itself, and both are holding on to a uraeus on the cornice and wielding a mallet with their one free hand. On the second shrine the unexpected arrival of a foreman has taken the workmen by surprise. At the bottom a man sitting on the top step seems in no hurry to pick up his tool. Another is climbing rapidly away, using the small columns in order to remove himself as far as possible from the representative of authority. On the other side the painter is amusing himself by daubing his neighbour's face, greatly to the latter's delight. The foreman has passed close by

*The sacred royal cobra, emblem of the goddess Būto.

them without noticing them, his whole attention fixed upon a workman who has stretched out at full length and gone to sleep in front of his unfinished work. The foreman shouts at him; whereupon one of the men clinging to the next stage up gets so excited that he loses his balance. On the roof two men have

A carpenter's shop

already made a dash for their tools, the first boring a hole, the second polishing the wood, while a third man is shaking the sleeper. In ancient Egypt, no less than nowadays, men preferred working in a gang to working by themselves. To get results called for a large number of sharp-eyed foremen, with rich vocabularies and no fear of using the stick—and more foremen to keep these last up to the mark.

From the beginning of the New Kingdom onwards a new trade —that of chariot builder—was very popular. It was essentially no more than a specialized branch of joinery.[28] Chariots were basically of wood, and the wheels were never shod with metal tyres, though sometimes sheets of metal were applied to the body. They contained a large number of component parts and we possess a poem which enumerates a good fifty of them without being exhaustive. The circle of the wheel was made by joining several segments sawn from a plant of the proper thickness, and the trickiest problem was to get the wheels, which had either four or six spokes, perfectly round.

Other specialized aspects of the joiner's craft were the manufacture of bows, arrows and javelins, sticks and sceptres of all kinds for the use of Pharaoh and high religious, military and civil dignitaries, and musical instruments.[29] Sometimes the aim was to get staves that were perfectly straight, sometimes to give them a graceful and permanent curve. In the workshop of Menkheper-rê-senb we can see a man testing a bow, while his mate tries the weight of an arrow and checks it for perfect straightness. Branches of trees were curved by heating before being stripped of their bark, and were then fixed in a kind of primitive carpenter's bench consisting of a forked post stuck in the ground, with two arms very firmly bound together. Once the heated branch had been fixed in this vice, it could be bent as necessary with the help of a lever.[30] Staves, sceptres and musical instruments were often decorated, like pieces of furniture, with inlay or veneer, or by the addition of a carved head. A female head, in wood, now in the Louvre, once graced the top of a harp.[31] Tutankhamūn's walking-sticks are fitted with ivory or ebony crooks ending in the head of a negro or an Asiatic.

7. *Leather Work*

The leather industry was flourishing as early as the Old Kingdom. Outa, who lived during that period, manufactured sandals,

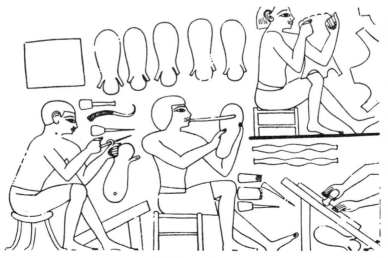

Leather workers

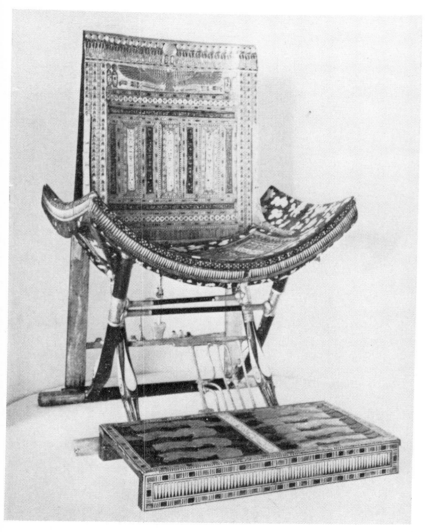

Plate VII   Tutankhamūn's throne and footstool

sheets of parchment for the use of the official who, programme in hand, directed religious or secular ceremonies, and satchels.[31a] These objects continued to be made, along with an increasing quantity of helmets, accoutrements, quivers, and leather bucklers reinforced with studs and metal borders or plates.[31b] The art of embossing leather had been discovered, and quivers and bucklers were decorated with ornamental themes partly borrowed from Syrian motifs but executed with a delicacy and grace unknown in their native land.[32] Yet the Egyptians never used any tanning process save oiling—now known as chamoising—in which the skins were first stretched taut on a board, and thereafter left to soak in a pot of oil. They were then taken out and when they had begun to dry were hammered to ensure that the oil was completely absorbed by the leather. This process gave the skins the qualities of leather—suppleness, impermeability and durability.

8. *Artists and Craftsmen*

In any kind of workshop completed objects were spread out on tables, or stacked on shelves, for inspection by the head of the establishment and, if he approved, pronounced worthy to find a place in the repositories of god or king. In addition there were also what might be described as general exhibitions of arts and crafts which displayed all the products of Egyptian industry. The tomb of Qenamūn contains a kind of illustrated catalogue of all the New Year gifts offered to the king (p. 28),[33] and the temple of Karnak displays another excellently carved pictorial handbook of all the objects dedicated by the king to Amūn.[34] There are lavish examples of statuary: lines of royal statues in shrines, each standing on a boat of archaic design: statues of men and women standing, sitting and kneeling: sphinxes with human or falcon heads, both crowned and uncrowned, and animal figures in the shape of gazelle, oryx and ibex. There are stone vases reminiscent of the early period as well as round-bellied amphorae on tiny feet, besides some charming mixing bowls and stemmed cups with fluted bodies, containing miniature artificial gardens where lotus, papyrus, marguerite and pomegranate surround a frog squatting on a pedestal. Some of the sauce boats are in the shape of birds, the handle occasionally being in the form of a duck's head turned towards the interior, either because the contents were so appetizing or because a duckling swam within the bowl. Even more remarkable are the great goblets crowned with a Syrian fortress complete with its garrison, or a house with a beautiful bird perched on the roof being stalked by panthers. The main articles of furniture were chests, arm-chairs and stools. The goldsmiths displayed necklaces with several tiers of ornament and a clasp with a spray of flowering plants. Armourers and chariot

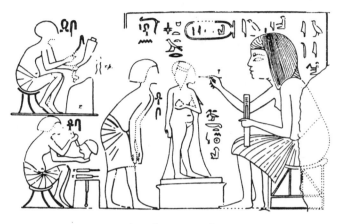

A sculptor at work

builders had sent chariots complete with full equipment, harness, horse rugs, bows, knives, whips, swords, bucklers, coats of mail, bow-cases, quivers, axes, daggers and helmets. Household objects included mirrors, ostrich feather parasols with gold-mounted ebony handles and curious objects like birds' heads with long beaks and immensely long necks, the function of which is impossible to imagine, doubtless because they were of no practical use whatever. Moreover there was a continually growing fashion for elaborate pieces of furniture and objects designed for no purpose beyond display, their surface sprouting palm-trees laden with fruit and with colonies of monkeys gambolling in their branches. It was indeed a magnificent show, and the craftsmen in the workshops of the king and of Amūn truly deserved well of their master, human or divine.

But were these splendid craftsmen, many of them true artists in their own right, paid as they deserved? When Pouyemrê, the second prophet of Amūn and director-general of the works of the temple of the god, calls for the work which had been executed in the workshops and receives the head artist and the head craftsman, they greet him with 'All hearts rejoice at your fortune', but Pouyemrê utters not a word of gratitude. To him these miracles of invention and skill were of no greater interest than the baskets of offerings, the miscellaneous goods, ores or foodstuffs gathered in by the tax collectors.[35] There is no evidence that he ever spoke kindly, or offered a word of congratulation, to even the most skilful of his craftsmen. Rekhmarê makes it clear to us that when he visited the workshops of the temple of Amūn, his responsibility as director was to assign each man his task: but, though he remembers to tell us all his own titles and dignities, we are not told which of the craftsmen had done the best work. The overseer addresses the artists like common labourers: 'Come on, men, get busy. Let us do what this magistrate praises in completing monuments for his master in the domain of his father Amūn whose name shall endure over them, established for all the years to come.'[36] The assembled craftsmen had worked for the glory of Amūn or the king, the vizier or the high priest, but their achievement was anonymous, and history was never to know the names of those supremely accomplished masters of their craft. Everyone seems to have accepted a great sculptor as a gift of the gods.

However, in the eighth year of his reign, on the occasion of the discovery of a colossal block of stone during his visit to the Red Mountain quarries (p. 134), King Ramesses II had a stele erected in the temple of On, on which he made a special declaration of his interest in all those who had shared in the execution of the sphinxes and the statues of standing, seated or kneeling figures with which he had filled all the sanctuaries of Egypt. 'Hear my words. Here are the riches you possess. What I commanded has come to pass. It is I, Ramesses, that create and give life to the generations. Food and drink, all that your hearts could desire, are before you. I improve your lot that I may say that you work for love of me, who am strengthened by your greetings. I have caused plentiful supplies of food to be dispatched to you for your labours, in hopes that you will live to bring them to completion. . . . There are barns full of corn so that none of you may go hungry for even one day. Each man of you has been paid for a month.

'For your benefit I have filled warehouses with stores of every kind, pastries, meat and cakes for you to eat, divers perfumes for you to anoint your heads every tenth day, sandals that you may be well shod each day and garments that you may be clad all the year round: all these things that none among you may pass the night in fear of want. I have appointed many men of divers rank to feed you even in years of famine: men from the marshes to bring you game and fish, and other men as gardeners to reckon up [what is due to you]. I have built a workshop where pottery vessels can be shaped to keep your water cool in the season of *shemou*. For your benefit boats sail ceaselessly from the south to the north, from the north to the south with barley, starch grain, corn, salt and bread. All this have I done saying "As long as you live you are of one mind to work for me".[37]

This is all highly commendable. The king may be anxious that his name should endure on monuments which will outlast eternity, but he is no less concerned that his workmen should be well fed and clothed and happy to work for a generous monarch. Louis XIV granted positions and pensions. Ramesses in effect did what it lay in an Egyptian king's power to do, namely to establish a huge estate, developed by vast human resources, the income from which was used to support the artists in a workshop like that of On. All the same we should be even more grateful to the greatest of the Pharaohs if he had singled out one outstanding artist from among the mass of competent craftsmen and had shown him receiving his due reward along with those inevitable recipients of the royal favours, the senior official, the courtier and the high priest. The scribe may well have been right when he said: 'I have never seen a sculptor sent on an embassy, nor a bronze founder leading a mission: but I have seen the smith working in the furnace's mouth. His fingers are like a crocodile's claws; he stinks worse than fish roe.'[38]

There are nevertheless scraps of evidence to show the esteem in which artists of the highest creative talent were held. The inscription which such a one had engraved on his stele under the Middle Kingdom tells us first of all how he appeared in his own eyes.

'I know the secret of the divine words, and the conduct of festivals. I have practised all magic and left none undone, and no secret that touches on these things is hidden from me. I am the master of secrets. I see Rê in his epiphanies.'[39]

The artist had to be familiar with liturgy and mythology, as well as all the attributes of kings and gods—no small achievement. The Phoenicians, who were eager to copy Egyptian models, made a number of mistakes in this field which would certainly have upset the Egyptian public. Our artist next praises his own skill:

'Moreover I am an artist that excels in my art, a man above the common herd in knowledge. I know the proper attitude for a statue [of a man], I know how a woman holds herself, the stature of the   . . ., the way a man poises himself to strike with the harpoon, the look in an eye at its moment,* the bewildered stare of a man roused from sleep, the way a spearman lifts his arm, the tilt of a runner's body. I know the secret of making inlays that fire cannot melt or water dissolve.

'There is no man famous for this knowledge other than I myself and my own eldest son. When god has given his order, he sets to work and achieves it. I have seen his handiwork in the employment of the director of the works, in every kind of precious stone, from gold and silver to ivory and ebony. . . .'

We can only hope that such transcendent merit was recognized by others than its possessor. The tomb of one of the innumerable Amenemhets of Thebes contains an unusual—indeed perhaps within our present knowledge unique—picture.[40] Amenemhet by word and gesture is inviting four men, seated on mats before him, to share in the rich offerings exposed before them—loaves and meat, birds, vegetables and fruits, drink and perfumes. One of these four men is Ahmosé, the artist of the scene, and one of the others a sculptor of statues, whose name is lost. This representation of a banquet was offered as the highest reward that could be given to the artists responsible for the decoration of the tomb, and they must have derived from it the same advantages as those gained by Amenemhet from the spectacle of the riches depicted therein. Earlier than this when the pyramids were being built, a chief steward called Menna prided himself on having rewarded generously those who had helped to build and decorate his tomb. 'No man who took part in it shall ever regret it. Be he artist or stone cutter, I have given him his reward.'[41] In the reign of Ramesses IX, Setaou, the First Prophet of the goddess Nekhabit, entrusted the decoration of his tomb to a famous artist called Mery-Rê, whose originality and merit he proclaimed: 'With

*i.e. how to catch the expression of a fleeting glance.

his own hands did he make the inscriptions when he came to decorate the tomb of Setaou . . . as for the scribe of the divine books, Mery-Rê, he is no [mere] copyist. His inspiration comes from his heart. No master gives him a model to copy, for he is a scribe of dexterous fingers and of good understanding in all things.'[42]

Houy the painter

We can in short safely assert that kings, princes, priests and public alike were duly grateful to those who had worked so well to ensure their glory, and paid and thanked them according to the practice and resources of the day. An artist who lived under Ramesses III and Ramesses IV and who had had to decorate a great tomb in Deir el Medineh,* depicted himself busily painting the statues of King Amenophis I and his mother.[43] He has abandoned the conventional restraint which he had largely observed when executing his commission, and has drawn himself in an entirely natural pose, squatting on a plinth, his bare feet crossed, the left, which is seen sole uppermost, over the right, his long hair falling over his shoulders, brush in one hand and palette in the other. This picture attracted some attention, and we possess a copy drawn by a schoolboy on a chip of limestone.[44] It is in-

*In western Thebes.

ferior to the original, but extremely valuable since it gives us not only the artist's name, but also his titles 'prince' and 'scribe'. Artists of the period of Akhnaton, such as Thutmosé and Houy, seem to have been men of wealth and position: while here at the end of our period we find a painter who was of such high standing that he was regarded as the equal of a provincial governor.

9. *Masons and Minor Craftsmen*

It is now time to turn to more arduous or menial occupations, which never earned their practitioners the title of 'prince' and were generally performed by foreigners, whether prisoners-of-war or free men.

The main job of an Egyptian builder's labourer was to mould and stack unbaked bricks. Every Egyptian town was surrounded by an encircling brick wall about fifty feet wide and sixty high, the gates alone being made of stone. Administrative buildings and private houses, and their enclosure walls, also contained far more

brick than stone. When King Ramesses II began to build his favourite town of Ramesses (generally called Pi-Ramessu by the Egyptians) and the warehouses of Pithom, he gathered the Israelites, set gangmasters over them and forced them 'with hard bondage' to mould bricks.[45] As work it was tedious, but not at all difficult. Nile mud was mixed with sand and chopped straw, and

E.L.E.—M

to obtain the right consistency the substance had to be moistened, trodden out for a long time and stirred at intervals with a mattock. The workman exactly filled his mould, which stood close beside him, with the damp compound, removing any surplus with a wooden scraper, and then quickly lifted it off, thus leaving the brick intact. After being left to dry for eight days it was ready for use. For choice, brickmakers settled to work near a pool and water-carriers kept them supplied with water. Other workers would go and collect the stubble from the harvested fields, in order to prepare the chopped straw. Pharaoh's order to the children of Israel to go and fetch their own straw, without reducing their daily quota of manufactured bricks, was a very real additional hardship, but grumbling would only have meant a beating from the gangmasters. The bricks were carried on a pair of flat trays slung on a yoke.[45a]

One word—*iqdou*—was used to describe two occupations which seem at first sight widely different—those of the bricklayer and the potter. The former was known as *iqdou inebou* or 'builder of walls' and the latter was *iqdou nedjesit* or 'small-scale builder'.[46] Both in fact used Nile mud, but the real reason for their common name derives from the Egyptian language, in which the root *qed* means 'round'. The primitive form of house was round like a pot—which in essence it was. The potter kneaded his material into a paste with his feet, and then put a lump of it on his wheel, which was merely a flat circle of wood revolving freely on an [upright] pivot. Beneath the craftsman's supple fingers the lump would take the form of a round-bellied pot, a bowl or pitcher, a goblet or a basin, a big jar with a pointed bottom used for keeping wine or beer, or one with a rounded bottom like a bag.[47] When the wheel could no longer be usefully employed, the potter gave the object its final shape with his fingers. The finished pots were then taken to the kiln, which was a kind of round chimney about twice the height of a man and, if the pictures of them are reliable, about two or three feet in diameter: but we must remember that Egyptian draughtsmen were not very particular about the relative magnitudes of persons and objects. By the time of the New Kingdom the potter had grown more ambitious. No longer content to manufacture monochrome pottery whose elegance was derived from shape alone, he was now technically competent to paint his products with patterns borrowed from the engravers or inspired by their decorative repertoire, adding borders of geometric or floral patterns, vine branches, plant motifs, a wading bird eating a fish, or a charging bull.[48] Even the poor who could not afford metal dishes could own pottery vessels which possessed a certain intrinsic beauty.

The barber was an itinerant craftsman, who would settle down at a cross-roads in a shady spot where he could be sure that his patrons would gather quickly.[49] Sometimes there looked like being a long wait, in which case a song or a storyteller might help to pass the time quickly. Argument was one way of killing time and this is presumably what two men sitting back to back on the same stool but not equally comfortably—are doing, for while one of the barber's clients is sitting in comparative ease, the other is most precariously perched on the extreme edge. Another customer, indifferent to their bickering, prefers to sleep with his chin on his knees and his head buried in his folded arms.

The customers would follow one another on the barber's three-legged stool, where they sat quietly with their hands soberly on their knees and surrendered their heads to his ministrations, which would relieve them of hair and beard. A stemmed bowl held the soapy water. The razor was a blade about eight inches long with a curved edge and fitted with a guard.[49a] The barbers who attended wealthy families, some of whom were also doctors, owned a variety of bodkins, tweezers, scissors and razors carried in leather bags and kept in elegant ebony boxes. They worked at their patrons' houses, and enjoyed a certain standing. The court of the gods possessed a barber god. But the barber who shaved the common people was an object of pity rather than envy.[50]

10. *Patrons and Workers*

As a pattern of enlightened patronage in Egypt we may take Romeroy, the high priest of Amūn. 'Oh priests, scribes of the house of Amūn, excellent servers of offerings to the gods, bakers, brewers, makers of sweetmeats, all who shall come into this workshop which is in the house of Amūn, utter my name each day and remember me with kindness, glorify me for my good deeds, for I was a man of virtue.

'I found this building an utter ruin, with crumbling walls and rotting woodwork, its wooden door frames decaying like the paintings on its bas-reliefs. I restored it all, yea, greater than it had been before, both higher and broader. I made its door frames in sandstone and I fitted it with doors of fine fir wod. I made a workshop where the bakers and the brewers could work in comfort. I laboured at these improvements for the protection of the servants of my god Amonrâsonter.'[51]

Bakenkhonsou, another of the high priests of Amūn, seems to have been equally admirable. 'I was as a good father to those underme, teaching those that were young, giving a helping hand to those in trouble, keeping alive those that were in need, and making useful objects in his temple in my capacity as the chief director of works in Thebes on behalf of Ramesses II.'[52] We can only hope that if his subordinates had been questioned they would have confirmed this testimonial. The ethics of the time forbade workmen or servants from being compelled to work unreasonably hard;[53] nevertheless the ordinary workers had occasion to complain more than once, while sometimes their protests looked not unlike revolt. Workers might receive their allowance of food and clothing anything from one to four times a month. The less thrifty—and they were not necessarily extravagant—always managed to exhaust their supplies before the next distribution. 'We are aching with hunger, and there are still eighteen days before next month.'[54] The workmen assembled near a monument. 'Tell your masters that are gathered over there that we will not return.' An employee sums the matter up: 'We went to hear them, and they told us true words.' A hungry mob made for the warehouses, though without attempting to break open the doors, and one of them made the following speech. 'We have come because we are desperate with hunger and thirst. We have no cloth, no oil, no fish, no vegetables. Send to our lord Pharaoh, send to our lord the king that he may give us the necessities of life.' This complaint was repeated before a magistrate, but already the spokesman's friends had begun to lose their nerve and were ready to say that things were not so bad after all. Others, however, refused to disband unless there was an immediate distribution. Confronted by this situation, the magistrates called a bookkeeping scribe and said to him 'See what grain thou hast received and give some to the workers in the necropolis.' 'So Pémontounebiat was sent for and we were given rations of corn each day.'

By this means the threatened strike was averted. The lot of the workmen was tolerable when their masters, like Romeroy and Bakenkhonsou, took the trouble to provide them with accommodation which was clean, decently ventilated and comfortable, to distribute food and clothing at regular intervals and to allay the anxiety of the feckless by an occasional extra distribution. There were frequent holidays and feast days, and the more highly skilled and responsible workers might very likely become foremen or overseers, put by some money and end their days as small proprietors or even as patrons themselves. When troubled times came—for example during the conflict between the followers of Amūn and Seth—the workers felt the pinch sooner and more acutely than other elements in the population, and powerfully swelled the forces of disorder.

11. *Business and Finance*

On the estates which belonged to the State or to the great gods very strict accounts were kept of the daily intake of provisions and produce and of the quantities consumed by the staff employed. They were what might be called closed corporations. Although stores and warehouses were full to bursting with goods, they were destined to reach only a small fraction of the population. When all the needs of this community had been satisfied, then and only then might the surplus be released on the market. Alternatively two large estates might exchange their products direct, or else the produce from an estate might be sold to business men who were ready to take the risks involved in reselling it. Along with the great corporately owned estates very many private owners operated on widely varying scales, breeding cattle or growing grain, fruit or vegetables. They needed clothes, furniture or articles of ornament or luxury and their only means of getting them was by selling the surplus of the stock they bred or the crops they grew. Equally there were independent craftsmen, making what they could from some workshop they owned, and getting their living from their products. Finally there were merchants, who produced nothing, but bought and sold everything in common use all over the country. The market was where all these characters—buyers, sellers and middlemen—met. The peasant in the story loaded his donkeys with all the good produce of the salt oasis.[54a] But for his being robbed on the way he would have reached the good town of

Nen-Nisou with his wares, and offered his soda, water birds and
dried fish for sale in the market place, bartering them for cakes,
linen and clothes. He was quite unusually unlucky, for in normal
times, when the police were vigilant, travellers arrived safely at
their destinations. The tomb of Khâemhat[55] contains pictures of
merchants standing and sitting, who have spread out their bales

A market scene

and baskets and are gesticulating and shouting. They are men of
most unusual appearance, with very large heads and long untidy
hair. Those who have come to do business with them, their bags
slung over their shoulders, are full of gestures also, and we may
be sure that their vocabulary was no less rich or picturesque. The
arrival of a foreign ship, perhaps from the Upper Nile or Syria,
would attract not merely the inquisitive who never ceased to
delight in the spectacle of the tawdry wares of the strangers in
their motley clothes, but merchants as well, quick to set up stalls
and sell provisions to the Phoenicians, who would offer in payment a decorated horn or a head mounted on an elephant's tusk.[56]†

Commerce had been simplified by the adoption at an early stage
of a system of valuing provisions and manufactured articles in
terms of a unit called *shat*.* A document as early as the fourth
dynasty expresses the value of a house as so many *shat*,[57] while a
papyrus of the eighteenth dynasty uses the same terms to value a
female slave, that is, her services over a given period.[58] It was,
however, a purely imaginary unit. It never occurred to anyone
in an official position to cut and stamp round pieces of metal of
an exactly controlled and uniform weight; yet business men and
the public generally knew the weight of gold, silver or copper

†See Plate VIII.   *Literally 'seal' or 'signet-ring', $\frac{1}{12}$ of a *deben*.

which was equal to a *shat*. Goods could not therefore be exchanged for money: but an intending seller of a house who had succeeded in reaching agreement with his purchaser on its value in *shat* would accept in payment corn or cattle to an equal value. This was fairly simple, but if the objects or animals exchanged were not of equal value, the difference had to be calculated in so many *shat* and some commodity discovered which the one party could supply and the other was willing to accept. This led to a good deal of argument. The *shat* seems to have fallen out of use in the later New Kingdom, because it was not found to facilitate the conduct of business. It is never referred to in the great Harris papyrus, in which precise quantities are recorded by weight in terms of the *deben* (about 2½ oz.) and the *qite* (¼ oz.) of gold, silver, copper and precious stones, without any reference to their value. In this document, as elsewhere in the calendar of Medinet Habu, cereals are reckoned by the bushel, fruit by the basket, and other types of produce by bags or baskets of varying capacity. Animals and trees are enumerated by species. When we are told the number of oxen or wild oxen, oryx, antelope and gazelle, their numbers are all totalled to give the full number of livestock: and the same is true of birds, without any apparent attempt to fix their value. Anyone who wanted to do so would have done it in terms of a weight of gold, silver or copper of equivalent value. The price of an ox ranged between 30 and 130 *deben* of copper: a sack of emmer wheat (*bôti*) was worth one *deben* of copper.[59] Usually, however, the buyer was not in a position to offer payment in copper and still less in silver or gold. This method of settling accounts in precious metals only developed under the later Ramessids, when the looting of temples and tombs had brought back into circulation large quantities of these three metals which had for centuries lain hidden in vaults or had been kept locked up in temples. One robber spent one *deben* of silver and five *qite* of gold on a purchase of land: another paid two *deben* of silver for a pair of oxen. The slave Dega was paid two *deben* of silver and 60 of copper. Five pots of honey were bought for five *qite* of silver and an ox for five *qite* of gold.[60]

Before this period of anarchy set in, buyers who did not own the requisite quantities of metal, paid for what they bought in commodities which the seller was ready to accept, their value being expressed in terms of given weights of gold, silver or copper.

The scribe Penanouqit sold an ox valued at 130 *deben* of copper and received in payment a linen tunic worth 60 *deben*, ten sacks and 3½ bushels worth 20 *deben*, some beads for a necklace worth 30, and two more tunics worth ten *deben* apiece.[61] A woman of Thebes, who had bought a female slave from a merchant at a price of 41 *deben* of silver, recited before the magistrates a list of different articles, offered in exchange: some were pieces of material which she was providing, others were objects of bronze and copper, to be contributed by a number of different people.[62]

The State itself had perforce to employ this method of settling accounts. Wenamūn, who had gone to negotiate the purchase of some wood at the court of King Zekerbaal of Byblos (p. 180 ff) immediately obtained seven baulks of timber, leaving his boat as security. He hurriedly obtained from Tanis some gold jugs and basins, five silver jugs, ten pieces of royal linen, 500 rolls of papyrus, 500 ox hides, 520 bags of lentils and 30 baskets of dried fish, while a second consignment consisted of five lengths of royal linen, a sack of lentils and five baskets of dried fish.[63] History unfortunately does not relate how much this omnium gatherum was worth in terms of gold and silver. The king of Byblos does not seem to have cared. He sent an order for the trees to be cut down, hauled down the river on to the beach, and finally handed over to the envoy of Amūn, but not before the latter had made a tremendous fuss. It seems highly probable that the Syrian and the Egyptian had each converted these items of merchandise into their corresponding weight of gold and silver and that the two parts were equal in value. Be that as it may, the lack of any true money made the conduct of business a very laborious affair. This explains the expressive gestures of the sellers in the tomb of Khâemhat and the endless arguments which took place before the bargain between the king of Byblos and his Egyptian buyer was finally concluded.[63a]

CHAPTER VII

TRAVEL

1. *Travelling Inside Egypt*

CONTRARY to popular belief, the ancient Egyptians were great travellers. There was a ceaseless coming and going between village and district capital and between the latter and the Residence city. For the great festivals pilgrims would gather from all over Egypt. Certain towns—Coptos, Silé, Sounou,* Pi-Ramessu, Memphis— were thronged all the year round by travellers on their way to the mines, the quarries and the' oases, or bound for Asia or Nubia, and by those returning with their loads of foreign goods.

The poor had only one means of transport the means which Jean-Jacques Rousseau regarded as the most delightful of all— namely, walking. It required no equipment beyond stick, loin-cloth and sandals.[1] This was all that Sinuhe carried when, in fear of his life, he made his devious way from west to east across the Delta and reached the Bitter Lakes. Anpou, in answer to his brother's appeal, left his village with sandals, stick, one garment and his weapons, and arrived at the valley of the *ash*-tree, near Byblos.[2] The peasant from the salt oasis bound for Nen-Nisou walked behind his donkeys, which were laden with every kind of produce, though, had he liked, he could have mounted one and risked, like Aesop's miller, the gibes of the passers-by. In fact he met with a more unpleasant adventure: a man who lived in an isolated spot, and was evidently no novice at the job, robbed him of everything he had. Soldiers were a perpetual menace to tra-vellers. When they met an unarmed man carrying a sack of flour and a fine pair of sandals, they were as likely as not to strip him and leave him naked on the road. Ouni took steps to remedy this state of affairs,[3] and a district governor of Siout records that in his day a traveller overtaken by night could sleep without anxiety,

*Greek Syene, modern Aswan.

leaving his goods and his goats safe beside him on the road, protected by the fear which the local police inspired.[4] It is a pleasant thought; but the precautions taken by various administrators are clear proof of the existence of brigandage and the hazards that attended travel.

There were as many roads as there were canals, for wherever one of the latter was dug, the excavated earth was used to build a dyke above flood level. Moreover roads and canals were kept in repair by a single process, since dredging the latter provided the earth needed to repair gaps in the former. These dykes served as roads for pedestrians and livestock and as towpaths for boats. No word for 'bridge' is known in Egyptian, but it features in at least one picture, a bas-relief depicting the triumphant return of King Sety I from his campaign in Palestine. This bridge, spanning a sheet of reed-fringed water thickly infested with crocodiles, unites two military buildings, on the 'Asiatic' and the 'African' banks respectively,[5] and must have comprised piers, architraves and traverses. There can clearly never have been any bridges over the main stream of the Nile or even over its smaller branches in the Delta, and even stone or wooden bridges spanning canals must always have been rarities. Faced with the necessity of crossing a canal or a shallow marsh, man and beast alike would unhesitatingly plunge in. Many Egyptians could swim. The inhabitants of Tentyris (Denderah) were ready to dive into the Nile and cross it without any apparent fear of the crocodiles, but not everyone could display comparable *sang froid*[6] and, if the satyrical papyrus deriding their occupations is any guide, fishermen and fowlers after water birds went in terror of the brutes. People of rank acknowledged as an obligation, as pressing as that of giving bread to the hungry or clothing the naked, the duty to provide a passage over the water for the boatless traveller, and in Thebes and the large towns ferrying was a recognized occupation. We find a reference to a ferryman accused of being concerned in tomb robberies (p. 263),[7] while after the gods had withdrawn to their island in mid-stream they instructed the god Anti, the divine ferryman, to refuse to let Isis across.[8] The fugitive Sinuhe found a rudderless boat on the bank and took it to cross the river.

For going short distances the rich for a long time used a kind of carrying-chair or litter. This looked imposing but had the disadvantages of being slow, expensive and uncomfortable. The carriers would walk in time to a chant of 'We would rather [carry it] full than empty', but they had to be paid, or at least fed. [9] By the period of the New Kingdom, the king only took his seat in his chair on certain ceremonial occasions, such as Horonemheb's celebration of his triumph. For everyday purposes the monarch, like his subjects, preferred to use a chariot which, with its team of horses, was by this time reasonably common, being indeed what

Nobleman on donkey litter

everyone wished for his friends and hoped to own himself. 'Thou enterest thy chariot, thy golden whip in thy hand. Thou carryest new reins; colts of Syria are harnessed to the chariot, and negroes run before thee to do thy bidding.' [10] We have a picture of Amenhotepsisé, the Second Prophet of Amūn, setting out for a drive [11] in his elegant and well-built chariot, decorated with figures in high and low relief and drawn by a pair of horses wearing neither bit nor blinkers. The main feature of the harness was a pair of great leather straps, one fastened round the horse's neck, which must have been very uncomfortable, the other round its body, while the reins were attached to a headstall. Amenhotepsisé, who has no coachman, holds the reins himself and drives standing; several grooms run in front, while a posse of *shemsou* (servants) are strung out behind him, carrying everything that their master would need when he wanted to rest or refresh himself.

A chariot came in handy for paying a visit to the royal palace or the vizier, for going on a tour of inspection in the country or for hunting, but even in the most favourable conditions it could not be used for a long journey. The staple form of transport in ancient Egypt was the boat. It was by boat that Prince Dedefhor left Memphis and went past Khentkhetyt on his way north in search of the magician who dwelt in Dedi Snefrou, and by boat that he brought him back to the court. When Sinuhe, after his pardon by the king, received his safe conduct at the frontier posts of the Roads of Horus, it was by boat that he travelled all the way from the isthmus of Suez to the royal residence at Ithy-Tawi,

Ladies driving in chariots

south of Memphis, and he whiled away the voyage by watching good meals being prepared and eating them. An Egyptian making the pilgrimage to Abydos would often mobilize a regular con-voy.[12] On these occasions travellers would embark on a vessel of archaic design, built up very high at bow and stern—a sign that the voyage was strictly religious in character. Once on board they would take their seats in a cabin shaped like a shrine, as if they were in a summer-house in their own gardens, with food laid out on a tray in front of it. The forepart of the boat served as both slaughter-house and kitchen, and here an ox would be cut up and beer prepared so that the travellers could enjoy it fresh. The pilgrims' boat had neither oars nor sails and carried a crew of only two, one at the bows to watch the tow-rope and keep it taut, while the other manned the twin rudders at the stern, which were of painted wood and terminated in a head of Hathor, the patron goddess of distant countries and protectress of travellers. It was towed by a vessel fitted with a mast braced by two cables attached to bow and stern respectively The centre of this second boat was taken up by a large cabin decorated with a cornice and with walls covered with paintings. The rudder was attached to a small mast and passed through a narrow slot cut in the stern, and the steersman moved it by means of a handle. Sometimes two eyes were painted on the rudder blade—a very useful precaution, since its function was to keep the boat away from trouble. When travelling downstream or crossing large expanses of water without a helping wind, there was no escape from the necessity for rowing. The rowers might number anything from ten or a dozen upwards. The captain stood in the bows with a long pole to take soundings, while another officer was posted on the roof of the cabin carrying a whip to lay across the shoulders of any idle oarsman. The third and only other officer was the steersman. When going upstream sail was hoisted.* This consisted of a single large rectangular piece of fabric, quite frequently greater in width than in height, stretched between two yards and raised and lowered by a number of ropes. Meanwhile the rowers stayed sitting on their benches. The officers would climb the rigging to get a better look out. When sailing on the Nile it was reasonable to hope for a comparatively quick and uneventful voyage, but anyone who planned to use the canals, which were not always navigable all the year round, had to make some preliminary investigations. When King Khoufou wanted to go to the temple of Rê, the lord of Sakhebou, somewhere in the second nome of the Delta, there was no water in the Canal of the Two Fishes. His friend the magician told him not to worry. 'I will cause there to be six feet of water in the Canal of the Two Fishes.'[12a] Ouni had no magician at his beck and call, but he was none the less able to travel by boat during the season when the waters were low. Work had been undertaken at Lake Moeris to supply water for both navigation and agriculture, though we do not know precisely what feats of engineering this involved.

The boats which were designed to make the long voyage up the Nile as far as Nubia were regular floating houses. The *dahabieh* of the Viceroy of Kush was a long crescent-shaped vessel rising clear out of the water at both bow and stern,[13] and with an enormous sail attached by numerous ropes to a single mast. Instead of a central rudder, a pair of rudders were set against the hull

---

*The prevailing wind is northerly, so that 'to sail' meant also 'to sail southwards, go upstream'.

slightly forward of the stern, and fastened to great posts to port and starboard respectively. The passengers' quarters were in a big cabin amidships, with an extension in the form of a shelter for the horses, and two smaller cabins were placed at bow and stern respectively.

Landed estates seem to have been very widely dispersed. Rich citizens of Thebes owned property in the Delta, while the god Amūn owned farms and even towns not only all over Egypt but in Nubia and Syria as well. The temple of Abydos, a foundation of Sety I, also owned estates in Nubia. In order to be able to collect their produce at a central point and to facilitate the import and export of goods, these large corporations and rich individuals owned regular fleets of crescent-shaped flat-bottomed cargo boats,

A cargo boat

with one or two cabins placed amidships.[14] The illustrated documents at our disposal cannot convey an adequate idea of the number and variety of the vessels which plied on the Nile, for the Egyptian language contains a large number of words for 'boat'. Barges were used for the transport of great blocks of stone hewn from the quarries, obelisks and colossal statues. A tomb painting in Thebes shows a statue of Tuthmosis III, during its voyage, being treated with scarcely less consideration than the monarch himself, for it is housed in a shrine, incense is being burned before it, and the boat in which it is being transported is towed by another vessel.[15] Cattle were generally carried in cabinless barges: cereals in barges with a central cabin. The boats were brought alongside the quay, and a sloping gangplank, braced with cross-bars at regular intervals, was lowered. The porters formed up in single file to unload their bales one by one, singing to keep in step and pass the time: 'Are we going to spend the whole day carrying barley and wheat? The weather is fine, the barns are full to bursting, there are piles [of grain] to fill them. The boats are full and brimming over with barley. We are being told to walk quicker. Do they think our hearts are of metal?'[16] When the convoy reached its destination, the gangplank would be lowered to the quay and cattle and goods disembarked. Merchants would arrive, set up a table or some shelves and light a fire, and the sailors would soon be celebrating the end of their voyage with food and drink.

2. *Travelling in the Desert*

The Egyptians regarded the desert with a mixture of awe and fear. Even quite late in their history they never forgot that their prehistoric ancestors had wandered through its length and breadth, before finally settling in the Nile valley. Min, who was one of the great gods of Egypt, and whose principal cult centres were Ipou and Coptos, was the ruler of the entire region between the latter place and the Red Sea. His favourite residence was 'a mountain venerable and primordial, occupying the first place in the land of the *Akhetiou* (the *Akhit* was the country beyond the known limits of the world), the divine palace endowed with Horus' life, the divine retreat where this god prospers, his holy place where he takes his pleasure, which is the queen of the mountains of the divine land.'[17] Perils of every kind—hunger, thirst and enemies—awaited the traveller bold enough to penetrate unprepared into this sacred region. The lion no longer, as formerly, ventured up to the Nile valley to attack cattle, but wolf, panther and leopard were still lively dangers. One day the warrior Horemheb found himself face to face with a huge hyena. Fortunately he both knew its ways and was well armed. Stretching forth his left arm towards the beast and holding his spear in his right hand, he stared it in the eye and was able to force it to turn tail.[18] East of On the country was infested with snakes which hid in the sand. Travellers claimed to have seen strange creatures in the desert— griffins with human heads on their backs, winged panthers, cheetahs with necks longer than a giraffe's, and greyhounds with square ears and tails as stiff as arrows.[19] There was always the chance of meeting some of the Bedouin tribes, like that which one day appeared in the presence of the prince of Menat Khoufou, and included fighting men armed with wooden throwing spears, bows and javelins, women and children led by a sheikh and a priest who played on a zither.[20] This tribe was peaceable and only asked to be allowed to exchange for corn the green and black powder used for making cosmetics and eye paint (p. 70). But there were other Bedouin who had no thoughts for anything but pillage. Various shrines had been set up for the protection of those who travelled over the desert, and in one of them, on the edge of the tracks which run between On and the Red Sea, there has recently been discovered a sculptured group representing Ramesses III and a goddess, entirely covered with inscriptions for the most part derived from an early compilation in which the wives of Horus play a leading part.[21] No doubt passers-by read these inscriptions if they knew how to, or perhaps it was enough if they looked at them or touched them. At any rate they would go on their way in confidence of benefiting from the favour in which the king himself was held by the gods.

Some travellers, whether from ignorance of how to assure themselves of the immediate protection of the gods or from an inability to pick good guides, got lost in the desert. In the words of a certain Antef, who had been sent in the reign of Amenemmes I on an expedition to the *bekhen* quarries (p. 135): 'My master had sent me to Rohanou to bring back this marvellous stone, the like of which had never been brought back since the days of the god. There was no hunter who knew where it lay nor how to reach it: and so it was that I spent eight days in journeying through the desert, not knowing where I should find it. So I cast myself down prostrate before Min, before Mout the great enchantress and all the gods of the desert. In their honour I burned terebinth resin. Dawn broke and a second day came and we appeared on this mountain of Upper Rohanou.'[22] He adds that despite their wanderings his party had kept together and there were no casualties. But it had been a near thing.

This worthy expert had paid a high price for his apprenticeship in the life of the desert. There were some Egyptians who spent their whole life there investigating its natural resources and their exploitation and also, no doubt, because they enjoyed the nomadic

life. A certain Sankh, who was commandant of troops for the
desert region, the overseer for Egypt and chief of the river har-
pooners, led a number of expeditions which were so lavishly
equipped with water bottles, clothes, bread, beer and fresh
vegetables that he seemed to have changed the valley of Rohanou
into a fertile meadow and the mountain of *bekhen* into a lake.
Sixty years of age and, like Jacob, the patriarch of a family of
seventy children, he ranged ceaselessly over the desert from
Taaou to Menat Khoufou, as far as the 'Great Green',* hunting
birds and animals.[23] It is to these tireless explorers that we owe
maps like those now in the Turin Museum, which have been truly
called the oldest maps in the world. They were designed to cover

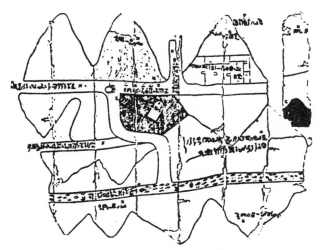

Map of a gold mining region

the region of the quarries and gold mines lying near Coptos.
The flat areas are painted brilliant red, the mountains dark ochre.
Footsteps dotted along the roads mark their direction. A castle
was drawn to mark the site of the ruins where King Sety I had
erected a stele.[24]

We have already mentioned the efforts of this monarch and his
son to discover water in this thirsty land (p. 139). Ramesses III
recalls with pride how he built a great cistern in the desert of

*The ocean—here the Red Sea, elsewhere the Mediterranean.

E.L.E.—N

Ayan, which he surrounded with a wall 'as solid as a mountain
of bronze . . . its doors were of pinewood, its bolts and locks
of bronze'.[25]

An extremely valuable tree grew in some of the wadis of the
eastern desert. This was the turpentine or terebinth, whose resin,
known as *sonté*, was burnt in temples, palaces and private houses.[25a]
No doubt frankincense from the land of Punt was even more
acceptable to the gods. When the shipwrecked sailor was finally
persuaded that the serpent which ruled over the island where he
had been cast away was less alarming than it looked, he promised
it terebinth resin; but the serpent, amused by his *naïveté*, replied:
'Though you may possess terebinth, you have little enough
frankincense. But as for me, I am the lord of Punt!'[26] Frankincense
was indeed not always to be had: but in its place terebinth gum,
when thrown on glowing coals in incense burners, produced a
scent which pleased both human and divine nostrils. It was a useful
thing to burn when animals were being slaughtered in temple
courtyards, and even private individuals used it to fumigate
their houses, as an antidote to vermin and insects, and for their
toilet. Bees frequented clumps of terebinth, and so two sets of
hunters would meet there, the one intent on gathering the gum
and taking cuttings which could be planted out in the temple
gardens, the other collecting the wild honey which was consumed in large quantities. Ramesses III had commissioned a corps
of police and archers to protect his caravans, and thanks to him
the traveller felt as safe in the inhospitable desert as in Tomery,
the Beloved Land itself.[27]

3.   *Travelling to Byblos*

In Egyptian eyes the sea, *iôm*, was a jealous god who, when he
saw the beautiful creature that the gods had given Bata as his
companion, invaded the earth to make her his own. But they
were as ready to brave this terrible deity as they were the perils
of the desert. Egyptian sailors had had long experience of the
Syrian seaboard. While the gods still dwelt upon earth the coffin
of Osiris, which had been cast into the Nile by Seth, had floated
through the Delta down the Tanitic mouth of the river, and had
been carried by the sea to Byblos, where a tree had miraculously
enclosed it. In due course Isis repaired there and, taking up her

position beside a fountain at the hour when the queen's servants used to come to fill their jars, she dressed their hair for them, allowing them the while to perceive the exquisite perfume emanating from her body. The queen of Byblos, captivated by such kindness, granted the goddess the sacred tree enclosing her husband's body. The relations thus established on so friendly a footing were destined never to be disrupted. The Egyptians would disembark at the little port of Keben with their offerings for the lady of Byblos. With the consent of the inhabitants they built her a temple. They would present the king with gifts of welcome—alabaster vases, jewels and amulets—and would set off home again laden with resin, baulks and planks of timber and even boats completely fitted out—so much so, indeed, that the word *kebenit*, derived from *Keben* the Egyptian name for Byblos, signified exclusively sea-going vessels. Generally speaking Egypt and Asia fought wherever they met—Sinai, Palestine, Carmel, or Upper Retenou;* but in Byblos, and only in Byblos, the Egyptian was made welcome. Even so, one day some Egyptians were massacred there; but their assailants were neither local traders nor Byblite sailors, but Arabs, 'sand rovers', the eternal and treacherous foes of Egypt.[28]

Gradually the Egyptian zone of influence spread, and by the Middle Kingdom their emissaries were travelling as far as Beirut, Qatna† and Ugarit‡ leaving a trail of statues and sphinxes to mark their passage. But Byblos still kept its special position: its king was proud of his title of Prince of Egypt, and boasted of his Egyptian culture. He had a tomb built in the Pharaonic style and furnished it after the Egyptian fashion, even to the extent of partially filling it with precious objects sent directly from the Residence city Ithy-Tawi. We have nothing to tell us whether, during the Hyksos invasions, the inhabitants of Byblos stood by their friends in the hour of trial: but, for whatever reason, the sea voyages lapsed and the pious were at their wits' end to acquire the fir trees (*āsh*) which provided timber for the priests' coffins and the resin to embalm them. The interruption of this traffic had other serious consequences: for the sacred boats and the flagpoles with their streamers which stood before the temples, overtopping the

*Syria.
†Probably the modern Mishrifé, near Homs.
‡The modern Ras Shamra, north of Latakia, the most northerly city of Phoenicia in the 2nd millennium B.C.

cornice of the pylons by several feet, as well as various articles of furniture, were all made of deal. But the bad times passed, and as soon as Egypt was once again mistress of her own soil she returned to Byblos. Tuthmosis III made a point of halting there during his triumphant campaigns and got from his allies more wood and more boats than the Pharaohs of old times had ever asked for. Later still, when Syria was intriguing with the enemies of Egypt, Ribaddi remained faithful to Amenophis III and his successors. Ramesses II engraved steles on the banks of the Dog River between Byblos and Beirut, and he actually founded a town bearing his own name in the valley of the *āsh*-tree, where a contemporary story-teller had set the adventures of Bata, and even erected stelae in the temple of Byblos itself. His contemporary as king of Byblos was called Ahiram. Like all his subjects Ahiram both spoke and wrote Egyptian, and for writing his native language he used an alphabetic script which may actually have been invented at Byblos by a simplication of the hieratic script.[29]

The warlike Pharaohs of the eighteenth dynasty laid great stress on the fact that their messengers could travel the length and breadth of Syria without let or hindrance, and doubtless they were made welcome at Byblos; but a little later, under the last of the Ramessids and at the beginning of the twenty-first dynasty, matters stood very differently. King Zekerbaal, the distant descendant of that Melkander who had treated Isis so kindly, was insolent enough to offer to show the Egyptian envoy the tombs of several messengers of Khâemhat, tenth in the line of the Ramesside kings, who had died at Byblos after long captivity.[30] Wenamūn himself was luckier, since by the exercise of patience he succeeded in leaving the port with his cargo of wood, but he ascribed his success to the protection of his god Amūn of the Way, whom he had had the happy idea of carrying with him in his baggage.

Moreover it must be admitted that Wenamūn was in a rather special position. He was under instructions from the high priest of Amūn to bring back a load of wood for the god's sacred barque, *Amonousirhat*, which during the season of floods plied on the Nile between Karnak and Luxor to the plaudits of an immense crowd (p. 290 ff). He had gone first of all to Tanis, to the court of Smendes and his wife Tentamon, who were already the effective rulers of the land though not yet recognized as its king and queen.

Here he was fitted out with a boat commanded by a certain
Mengabouti and within a fortnight he was navigating the 'great
Syrian Sea'. He put in at Dor, a town of the Sakkal people, but
while he was getting some provisions on board—ten baskets of
bread, a jar of wine and a shoulder of beef—one of his crew deserted with the treasure, consisting of five *deben* of gold and 31
deben of silver. Greatly upset, Wenamūn went ashore to call on the
king of the country, Badil, and told him what had happened.
'Whether you like it or not,' replied the Sakkal monarch, 'I know
nothing of what you are talking about. If the thief from your ship
who has stolen your silver belongs to my country, I will make
good your loss from my own treasury until he can be arrested. But
if he is one of your people and is a member of your crew, stay
here a few days so that I can look for him.' The reply was well
meant; but after nine days there was no trace of either the thief
or the money. Wenamūn managed to borrow 30 *deben* of silver and
landed at Byblos from a ship which he had picked up at Tyre.

For twenty-nine days King Zekerbaal refused to receive him
and only made up his mind to do so when Amūn, the god of
Thebes, took possession of a young man in his entourage and,
speaking through his mouth, gave him the following orders:
'Bring the god up here! Bring the messenger of Amūn that ac-
companies him. Send him on his way and let him go.' On the
following day Wenamūn made his way to the palace, where he
found the king seated on his throne, with his back to the balcony
beyond which the waves of the 'great Syrian Sea' were breaking.
The interview was strained: the facts were all against Wenamūn.
Instead of arriving in the manner befitting an official emissary in
a ship chartered by Smendes, and duly presenting his letters of
credence, he had disembarked without any papers from a boat he
had picked up by chance. Wenamūn managed to explain that he
had come in search of wood for the sacred boat of Amonrâsonter.
The king replied: 'Once upon a time my servants discharged this
mission because Pharaoh (Life, Health, Strength!) sent hither a
convoy of six boats loaded with the produce of Egypt, which were
sold in my warehouses. Are you he that shall bring me what I am
owed?' The discussion went on: 'He caused the account book of
his fathers to be brought. He caused it to be read in my presence.
Altogether in his book 1,000 *debens* of silver were found. He said
to me "If the king of Egypt was my master, if I were his servant,

he would not have sent gold and silver saying 'Do the bidding of Amūn' without bringing him gifts (*barakat*,) for that is what he did to my father. But as for me, I am not your servant, and most assuredly I am not the servant of him that sent you. . . ." Wenamūn replied by emphasizing the power of Amonrâsonter, the lord of life and health—'and he is the lord of thy fathers,' added he to the king, 'who passed their lives in the service of Amūn. And you too,' he continued, 'are the servant of Amūn. If you say, "I will do it, I will do it for Amūn," if you busy yourself on his behalf, you will live in strength and good health. You will be the benefactor of all your country, and your men will wish you the things of Amonrâsonter.'

After this exchange of views Zekerbaal loaded a ship with timbers for stem and stern, one other piece and four beams, which he dispatched to Egypt with a letter from Wenamūn. Smendes and Tentamon then sent various goods together with some gold and silver, and food and clothing for Wenamūn's own personal use. The king was satisfied. Dispensing with the blessings of Amūn, with which the envoy had wished him to be content, and without paying overmuch attention to his threats, he took the Egyptian goods into store, raised a body of 300 men, and the same number of oxen, and appointed leaders to command them. The trees were felled and after the winter was over they were dragged down to the water's edge. Wenamūn might now seem free to go off with his wood, but there were still further complications. Zekerbaal considered himself underpaid. Wenamūn, very seriously, induced him to have engraved on a stele the words: 'Amonrâsonter has sent to me his messenger, "Amūn, of the Way" (Life, Health, Strength!) together with his human messenger Wenamūn, for the timber for his sacred vessel of Amonrâsonter. I have cut the wood and put it on board ship. Thanks to my ships and my crew I have removed it. I have caused them to journey to Egypt that Amūn may grant me fifty years of life beyond my allotted span. So be it.' 'In time to come,' adds the jocular Wenamūn, 'when another Egyptian shall read your name on this stele, you shall receive the water of *Amentit* and of all the gods that are here.' The outmanoeuvred king of Byblos admitted that this was fair, and Wenamūn promised that the high priest of Amūn, on receiving his detailed report, would send him some presents.

Modern commentators have generally taken this story as evidence of the impotence of Egypt and the contempt in which she was held at the time of Smendes. But in fact, even when she was at the height of her power, Pharaoh never regarded the king of Byblos as a subject or vassal under an obligation to hand over his timber without payment. The Egyptian envoy would present himself armed with official letters and with gold, silver and merchandise, and the king of Byblos would pocket these gifts and hand over the timber. The business completed, thanks and good wishes would be exchanged. Pharaoh would send in addition a few trifling personal presents such as amulets and a statue of himself. The king of Byblos would accept them with gratitude and would have engraved upon the statue, in Phoenician, a prayer that the goddess of Byblos might lengthen the years of his reign. This had been the traditional procedure from time immemorial.

On leaving the port of Byblos, Wenamūn had a very narrow escape from the Sakkals who were lying in wait for him, only to fall into the hands of Cypriots who wished to kill him. The end of the papyrus is torn, so we do not know precisely how he managed to escape from this new danger, as there is every reason to think that he did. We first hear of the Peoples of the Sea in the reign of Ramesses II, and from then onwards their presence represented an additional menace to Egyptian navigation, though sea traffic was never brought to a complete standstill. On this subject we have the formal testimony of Ramesses III. 'I have made for thee (Amūn) vessels, transports, sea-going boats with hogging ropes (p. 185) equipped with their tackle on the Great Green. I have appointed archers and their commanders and captains together with many crews, yea beyond number, to carry goods from the land of Phoenicia and foreign countries of the ends of the earth to thy great storehouses in Thebes the Victorious.'[31] It is noticeable that Pharaoh did not rely simply and solely upon Amūn. A few companies of well-armed and well-led archers were detailed to protect the ships from attack from any quarter and to ensure respect for his envoys ashore.

4. *Voyages in the Red Sea*

The destination of voyages in the Red Sea was the land of Punt —the land of incense—which lay beyond the straits of Bab el Mandeb on both the Somali and the Arabian coasts. The Good

Serpent, whom we have already met in the story of the shipwrecked sailor (p. 178), declared himself both ruler of Punt and
lord of incense (*ânti*). The Egyptians had been visiting the
country from time immemorial. As early as the Old Kingdom
they had succeeded in organizing a service of boats connecting
Byblos on the Syrian coast with the coast of Punt, the Terraces of
Fir with the Terraces of Incense.[32] From Byblos the vessels
would sail to the Egyptian Delta, go up the Tanitic arm of the
Nile to Bubastis and proceed thence by canal to the Wadi Toumilat, which can be regarded as the most easterly arm of the Nile.
This was not navigable all the year round, but when the river was
in flood it was deep enough to give passage to the shallow-draught
Egyptian vessels, which, after crossing the Bitter Lakes, reached
the end of the Gulf of Suez and sailed slowly on to their destination in Punt. The Bedouin, known to the Egyptians as 'those who
dwell upon the sand', who, for all their barbarity, used to convey
passengers and goods overland from Syria to Arabia, would try
to interrupt this service of boats. King Pepy I sent several expeditions against them, but the attacks always broke out again. It
appears that after the reign of King Pepy II these voyages were
temporarily abandoned, and that after being restarted in the
Middle Kingdom and suspended for a second time during the
Hyksos occupation, they were undertaken once again by Queen
Hatshepsut and continued by Tuthmosis III, Amenophis II,
Horonemheb and Ramesses II and III.[33] It was with the object
of opening direct communications between his residence in the
Delta and the Red Sea that Ramesses II spent much money in
restoring the 'canal of the two seas', traces of which were discovered during the digging of the modern Sweet Water Canal. Its
course was marked by the towns of Pi-Ramessu, Bubastis and
Pithom and by the erection of granite stelae on lofty bases, which
declared to the awe-struck navigators the glory of the king and
the boldness of his conceptions.[34]

Let us imagine the scene: the boats newly come from Syria
have disembarked their passengers and cargoes on the quay of
Pi-Ramessu and are about to take on board others bound for the
land of Punt. These boats are *kebenit*—i.e. typical Byblos craft,
either built in that city and sold to the Egyptians by the Lebanese
or constructed in the Egyptian shipyards 'Byblos fashion' of
timber imported from Syria. We have two pictures of them, the

earlier dating from Sahurē's time, and the other, and later, from the reign of Queen Hatshepsut.*[35] Though they are separated by nearly a thousand years there is very little difference between them. Both have a long hull with a ram projecting from the bow and a raised stern curving inwards and ending in a huge papyrus head, with two look-out posts at bow and stern. There are twin rudders on either side of the ship near the stern. A huge hogging cable supported on four forked uprights spans the length of the hull. Nearly amidships a single mast, stayed by four ropes, supports a single sail greater in width than in height.[35a] The crew was large

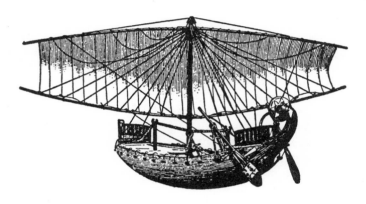

Model of sailing ship

since, unless there was a wind, the sailors had to take to the oars. They were experienced sailors—'men who had seen the sky, who had seen the earth, who were more prudent than wild animals, who could foretell the coming of the storm before it broke'. Representatives of the king, as well as scribes and soldiers, would be on board, and the cargo would include some of the fine wares of Egypt most highly appreciated by the inhabitants of Punt—articles of clothing, mirrors and weapons. After the king had greeted the convoy it would enter the canal system, pass by Pithom where the Hebrews were toiling at their brickmaking, and reach the Great Green.

A look-out, posted on one or other shore of the 'God's Land', would observe and report the arrival of the Egyptian ships,

*i.e. about 2500 B.C. and 1500 B.C. respectively.

whereupon king, queen and chieftains would emerge from their huts which stood on piles in a lagoon and mount their donkeys to ride to meet the Egyptians. They were as tall as their visitors and broad-shouldered, with round heads and beards dressed like those of gods and Pharaoh in the Nile valley, the only difference being that, whereas the Egyptian beard was a creation of the wig-maker, theirs was natural. About their necks they wore a round medallion after the Syrian fashion. The queen is an extraordinary figure—a mountain of quivering flesh, apparently almost incapable of walking, while her daughter, though young, displays a strong family resemblance. The Egyptian artists who recorded it all must have stared wide-eyed at so novel a scene. One wonders whether they made a surreptitious sketch of their hosts on the edge of a sheet of papyrus or whether they waited to fix the scene in their memory until they were safely back on board. In any event they certainly depicted it all most vividly, and have shown us faithfully everything worth observing—the king and the queen, the village and its inhabitants, even the cattle and the crabs.[35b]

A tent was soon pitched and greetings exchanged. With the deepest reverence the natives did humble obeisance to Amon-Rê, 'the primordial god who is throughout all foreign lands'. They were without exception delighted to see the Egyptians and perfectly well aware of what they wanted, but they would affect astonishment and ask: 'Why have you come here to this land that few men know? Are you come down from heaven? Have you travelled over water or land? The divine earth is fertile where your feet tread. Rê, he is the king of Tomery. His Majesty sits on no distant throne. We live by the breath that he gives us.' In obedience to the orders of the Palace (Life, Health, Strength!) their majesties would be offered bread and beer, wine, meat and fruit and all the produce of Tomery, the Beloved Land.

The list of cargo to be loaded on to the Egyptian boats shows that they would not have been the losers by the exchange; for it included all the best tree trunks of God's Land, heaps of dried incense, trees of fresh incense, ebony and ivory, gold fresh from Amou, three types of perfume (*tishepses, khasyt* and *ihmet*), terebinth, black eye-salve, two breeds of monkey, greyhounds, panther hides from the south and slaves with their children. The whole cargo was valuable, but while the caravans from the Upper Nile also brought ebony and ivory, panther skins and other pro-

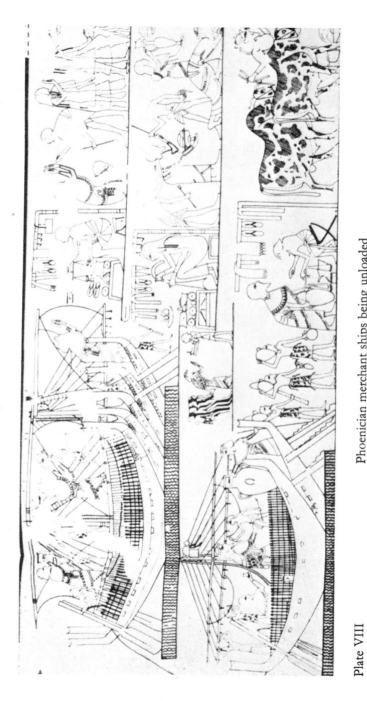

Plate VIII   Phoenician merchant ships being unloaded

duce, what they did not bring, and what made the laborious and dangerous voyage worth while, were the trees of God's Land, the frankincense and, above all, the thirty-one incense trees complete with their roots and the soil in which they grew, as if they had been packed up by the most skilful of nurserymen. No wonder that the successful navigators were cheered when they tied up to the quay of Apit Esout (Karnak). The porters, happy to work hard in the king's service, address the green trees as though they were sacred beings: 'We bid you welcome, you incense trees who have left your home in God's Land to come and dwell in this realm of Amūn. Makarê (the queen) will set you to grow in her garden on either side of her temple, as her father has commanded.'[35c]

One of the questions which the people of Punt had asked their visitors was whether they had come by land or by sea. There were for practical purposes two alternative routes from Egypt to Punt. Before Ramesside times—long indeed before the time of Queen Hatshepsut, in the eleventh dynasty—an explorer by the name of Henou had travelled from Egypt to Punt and back partly by land and partly by water. He had been instructed to buy fresh incense from the desert sheikhs and also to inspire fear of the Pharaoh in the inhabitants. His journey was therefore undertaken with both political and commercial objects: in his own words: 'I left Coptos by the road which His Majesty had commanded me to take. The soldiers that accompanied me came from the south, from the realm of Wabout, between Gebelein and Shabit. Every royal official, the men of the town and the country, followed me in a single band. Scouts cleared the way before me to overthrow the king's enemies. The children of the desert formed my bodyguard. All the staff of His Majesty were put under my command. They corresponded with the messengers. By giving a single order His Majesty could hear millions.'

'I set out with an army of three thousand men. I changed the road to a river, the red land* into a corner of meadow land. To each man each day I gave a waterskin, a stick, two jars of water and twenty loaves of bread. Donkeys carried the jars, and when one was tired another took its place. In the wadi I made twelve cisterns and at Idahet two, each measuring twenty cubits by thirty. At Iaheteb, where the waters meet, I made another cistern ten cubits square.

*i.e. the desert.

'Lo, I reached the Great Green. I made this boat and fitted it out thoroughly and on its behalf I made a great oblation of wild oxen, of African oxen and of small animals. After I had gone down into the Great Green I did His Majesty's bidding and brought him all the products which I found on the shores of God's Land (To noutir). I returned by Wag and Rohanou. I brought back for him [i.e. the king] splendid stones for statues in the sanctuaries, such as had never before been seen in the king's house. Never had any comparable achievement been accomplished by any Royal Friend since time began.'*[36]

The expedition had evidently been on the grand scale. Henou had crossed the desert with no fewer than 3,000 men. Guided by the children of the desert and keeping in touch with the palace, he moved south-east instead of taking the normal easterly route. Digging water cisterns as he went, he reached the coast at the point which was later to become the small port of Berenice. There, according to his own account, he built a vessel, no doubt with material brought by sea from the Lebanon. He then reached Punt, visited both coasts of God's Land and bought incense and all their produce. On his way back he left his ship at Qosseir, and made his way to the valley of Rohanou. His halt there was not for the purpose of resting, but in order to prepare a consignment of stone bound for the sculptors' studios. Henou certainly made the most of his time and fully deserved to be numbered among the explorers of antiquity, for when the Roman Aelius Gallus came to repeat his exploit in the reign of Augustus, he met with the utmost difficulties.[37]

Expeditions to Punt under Ramesses III profited by the experience thus acquired, and made use of both the land and the sea routes. This monarch organized expeditions on a considerable scale. The fleet consisted of several large ships and escort vessels, while the crews included not only sailors but also archers under their officers, together with supply troops. Huge quantities of foodstuffs and merchandise had been simultaneously embarked, both to feed the expedition and to encourage trade. According to the Egyptian chronicler this fleet did not sail from the Red Sea but from 'the sea of Mou Qedi', which must have been the Persian Gulf, for Mou Qedi, 'the water of the country of Qede' in Naharina, was the Egyptian name for the Euphrates.[38] It is possible

*Literally 'since the time of the God'.

that Ramesses III had managed to haul fir trees from the Lebanon to the Euphrates, as Tuthmosis III had once done,[39] and had built a fleet on the banks of the river. Alternatively he may have concluded a treaty with the king of Babylon which gave his troops and officials, after reaching the Euphrates, the right to embark and continue their voyage in Babylonian bottoms. Whatever the truth, the fleet which bore the expedition which Ramesses III dispatched must have sailed down the Euphrates and doubled the enormous Arabian peninsula, so as to reach, without mishap—thanks to the fear which the name of Pharaoh inspired—the land of Punt.

On that occasion matters turned out as they had in the reign of Queen Hatshepsut. The Egyptians established contact with the natives and handed over Pharaoh's presents; in return the ships and their escort vessels were loaded with the produce of Punt and all the mysterious wonders of that mountainous land, especially dried incense. Then they sailed northwards through the Red Sea to the Gulf of Suez and reached Egypt again by the Pithom canal. But during the voyage the children of the chieftains of God's Land had left the ships with their produce, in the neighbourhood of either Berenice or Qosseir. They formed themselves into a caravan and loaded their wares on donkeys and on porters. They arrived in excellent shape at the Mountain of Coptos, transferred to water at Coptos itself and eventually arrived at Thebes in high fettle. 'The produce and marvels were paraded before me,' ended the king. 'The children of their chieftains hailed my presence, kissed the earth and fell flat on their bellies before me. I gave them to the Ennead of all the gods of Egypt to satisfy their princes in the morning.'[39a]

It is quite possible, though it is not explicitly stated, that the caravan arrived at Coptos or at Thebes at least as soon as those who had made the whole journey by boat. The decision to use two different methods of transport was evidently intended to improve the chances of the safe arrival of the produce of Punt, for the risks of the journey by sea were great. The shipwrecked poet may tell how many ships went down with their crews and cargoes. 'The storm struck us while we were still in the open sea, before we had reached land. The wind rose with redoubled force, driving before it a wave twelve feet high. I saw a plank and seized hold of it. Thus the ship sank and of all who were in her not a soul survives.'[39b]

This itself was a notable journey, but in the reign of Ramesses II the Egyptians had travelled even farther and more adventurously. Stories of their odysseys were still current in the time of the classical authors. Since virtually the beginning of their history the Egyptians had worked the blue lapis lazuli, a stone which is not found in the deserts of Africa.[40] The sole source known to antiquity was Bactria, whence the precious material could have been brought overland through Syria to Egypt, or, perhaps rather more easily, by a route which ran down the Indus and so along the Makran coast to the mouth of the Euphrates. This was the route that Nearchus must have followed. The Egyptians did not go all the way to Bactria to get their lapis lazuli; it suited them to buy it at a town known to them as Tefrer,[41] which I identify with some confidence as Sippar, lying in a strategic position on a canal which linked the Tigris and the Euphrates at a point where the two rivers run very close to each other. It was common knowledge in Egypt that lapis lazuli came from Tefrer, and the name of this city was given to another unidentified stone from the same district.

It so happened that one year while Pharaoh was in Naharina receiving homage from some foreign princes, he was apprised of a personal visit from the king of Bakhtan (Bactria), during which the latter sought an alliance, offering in return magnificent gifts and the hand of his own daughter. Pharaoh accepted his offer and returned with the princess to Thebes. Some time later an envoy arrived from the king of Bakhtan and sought an audience, at which he told Pharaoh that the princess's sister was ill. Pharaoh dispatched one of his most skilful doctors, nominated by the House of Life, to Bakhtan, but the princess got no better and a second envoy made the long journey from Bakhtan to Egypt. After the failure of the doctor there was nothing for it but to send a god to Bactria and the choice fell on Khonsou, the ruler of destinies. He left Egypt in a great ship with an escort of five small vessels and arrived in Bakhtan one year and five months later—a not incredible length of time, remembering that the convoy had to traverse the whole length of the Red Sea, round the Arabian peninsula, follow the coast of the Ichthyophagi* and sail up the Indus to the point where the emissaries disembarked to reach the

*'Fish eaters', a name given by the Greeks to the inhabitants of the coast of Baluchistan.

capital of the king of Bakhtan. Here the god remained for three years and nine months, at the end of which time the king rather reluctantly allowed him to return to Egypt with many presents and a powerful escort of soldiers and horses. The first messenger from Bakhtan had arrived in Thebes in the fifteenth year of the Pharaoh's reign: Khonsou finally returned to Egypt in the thirty-third year, the intervening eighteen years being taken up by the first envoy's journey and his return with the Egyptian doctor, the second envoy's journey and his return with the god and finally, after an interval of three years and nine months, the god's return to Egypt. In all, there had been five journeys between Thebes and Bakhtan.

The stele in the Louvre on which these events are recorded reads in every particular like an official document.[42] In its opening passage the three first names are part of the royal protocol of King Tuthmosis IV, the first New Kingdom Pharaoh to marry a foreign princess, while the two names in cartouches are identical with those of King Ramesses II. In my opinion this gives no grounds for regarding the document as late or for considering the whole story a fabrication. In the ancient world kings often corresponded and the services of Egyptian doctors were often sought outside Egypt.[43] Memories of the expeditions of Sesostris in the Erythraean Sea* were still vivid in the time of Alexander.[44] There is nothing intrinsically improbable in Ramesses having been anxious to establish direct contact with a country which had for centuries been the source of a precious stone which was highly valued by both sculptors and popular taste.

*The 'Red Sea', the Greek name for the Indian Ocean.

CHAPTER VIII

THE PHARAOH

1. *The Monarch's Essential Duties*

THE art of government—of ordering human life in society—was conducted in Egypt on somewhat unusual principles. Provided that the gods appointed as sovereign (Life, Health, Strength!) the issue of their divine flesh, then the land would enjoy peace and prosperity. A swelling Nile would cover the earth with wheat and barley, flocks would multiply, and from every quarter gold, silver and copper, rare woods, ivory, incense, perfumes and precious stones would flow into the country. But all depended on the fulfilment of this basic condition. If that were not satisfied, the land of Egypt would drift aimlessly; none would wield authority, for all would be striving to command. Brother would slay brother until—final and utter degradation—a foreigner occupied the throne. Then no longer would the Nile flood the land. Starvation would stalk the earth. No imports would enter from Syria or Kush, no offerings be presented in the temples to the gods, who would in consequence avert their eyes from those who had deserted their faith.

Thus the Pharaoh's prime duty was to demonstrate his gratitude to the divine rulers of the universe. Many texts on official monuments open with the statement that His Majesty was at Memphis or On, at Pi-Ramessu or Thebes, engaged on tasks that rejoiced the gods, restoring what had fallen into decay, building new shrines, reconstructing and strengthening the walls surrounding them, filling them with statues, renewing their furnishings and sacred boats, erecting obelisks, heaping the altars and offering-tables with flowers and generally outrivalling all his royal predecessors. To quote the prayer and confession of Ramesses III: 'I offer you homage, ye gods and goddesses, masters of heaven and earth and ocean, great of step in the boat of millions

Plate IX   Pharaoh Sety I offers incense to Sokaris

[*sc.* of years], beside their father Rê, whose heart rejoices when he sees their beauties, so that the Beloved Land, Tomery, is made glad . . . he is joyful, his youth returns to see them great in heaven, waxing strong on earth, filling with air the nostrils that could not breathe.

'I am your son, whom your two arms have brought forth. You have set me up as sovereign (Life, Health, Strength!) over every land. For me you have made perfection on earth. I perform my duty in peace. My heart never rests from searching for what will serve our sanctuaries to good purpose. By great decrees laid up in every hall of writing I endow them with men and land, with cattle and with boats. Their barges sail on the Nile. I have restored prosperity to your sanctuaries that had fallen into decay. I have instituted for you divine offerings beyond those which were previously displayed before you. For your honour in your Houses of Gold I have wrought with gold, silver, lapis lazuli and turquoise. I have counted your treasures and I have completed them with many things. I have filled your granaries with barley and wheat piled high. I have built you castles, sanctuaries, towns, whereon your names are graven for all time. I have furnished you with companies of men and have added many to their numbers. I have not removed men or captains of ten from the shrines of the god, since there were kings to do so, in order to enrol them in the infantry and chariotry.* I have made decrees to establish them on earth, for the use of the kings who shall come after me. I have consecrated to you offerings of all choice things. For you have I laid up stores for your feasts, full of food. For you have I made vases inlaid with gold and silver and copper by the hundred thousand. I have built your barques which are upon the river together with their great Dwelling† overlaid with gold.'[1]

This introduction was followed by a recital of what the king had done in the principal temples of Egypt. He had already expatiated at length on the gifts which he had made in favour of 'Amūn, lord of the Thrones of the Two Worlds', of 'Atum, lord of the Two Lands of On', and of 'Ptah the mighty, who is to the south of his wall', and their consorts. In his voluntary surrender of his own and his country's wealth to the gods, Ramesses III was not breaking new ground. Since the first Pharaoh had sat on the

---

*i.e. I have exempted the priests from military service.
†The shrine in which the divine barque was kept (p. 291).

E.L.E.—O

throne of Egypt, the words on the stele of Amada* could have been applied, practically without exception, to all Egyptian monarchs, 'He is a king bountiful by virtue of the works which he undertakes for the gods, in building them temples and in making images of them.'² Ramesses II had scarcely been crowned before he conceived the ambition to display no less filial piety towards both his spiritual fathers, the gods, and his earthly father Menmaatrê Sety-Merenptah, the suspension of whose immense building operations in the city of Anhour and Ounnefer† had caused some parts of it to resemble a builder's yard and others a ruin. The precise boundaries of the royal domain, which had never been firmly delimited, were constantly being torn up. The king accordingly commanded his royal chancellor to summon the courtiers, the princes of the blood royal, the leaders of the army, the overseers of building work and the keepers of the house of books and addressed them in the following terms: 'See, I have called you together because of an idea that I have conceived. I have seen the buildings of the necropolis and the tombs in Abydos, which have been left unfinished from the days of their master until now. For hitherto, when a son succeeded his father he has allowed the monument which his sire had built to fall into decay. So I have said to myself "It brings good fortune to raise up again that which has fallen, and it is rewarding to do good. Therefore my heart bids me to do what is profitable in honour of Merenptah." Throughout all time to come men shall say of me "It was his son who caused his name to live".' The king continued for some time in this strain, ending with the words: 'It is a fine thing to raise one monument on another, to do two good things at one stroke. Such is his son, and such was he who begat him.' The monarch's scheme aroused the enthusiastic support of his audience, and after hearing what they had to say, he ordered the work to be entrusted to the architects. He chose soldiers, masons, engravers, sculptors, draughtsmen and skilled workmen of every guild to build the Holy of Holies for his father and to restore every ruined building in the necropolis. He had a complete and definitive inventory compiled of all the lands, serfs and herds. He appointed priests, and assigned them their exact tasks, besides a chief priest. Ramesses then addressed the king his father directly, rehearsing what

---

*Erected by Amenophis II (*c.* 1447 B.C.) in the temple of Amada in Nubia.
†Abydos.

he had done for him and for his temple. 'All will go well for thee while I am alive, as long as the son of Rê, Ramesses Miamūn—may he be granted life like Rê—shall live.' And King Sety Menmaatrê, addressing him as a father speaking to his son, assures him that he has pleaded his cause in the presence of Rê and that all the gods—Rê, Atum, Thoth and Ounnefer and the Divine Ennead—are rejoicing at what the king has done.[3]

The king made only one mistake: he should not have charged all his predecessors with negligence. A century and a half earlier Tuthmosis III Menkheperrê had found the temple of Ptah of Thebes in a condition unworthy of so great a god, its brick walls and wooden doors and pillars fallen into decay, and had commanded its complete reconstruction in fine white sandstone. The surrounding wall was built to stand for ever. New gates were made of pinewood, with hinges of Asiatic copper. In his own words, which echo the illusion so dear to all Egyptian hearts, 'The like had never been seen before my time. I made it greater than it had been before. I purified his great abode with gold from the mountain country, all its vases of gold and silver and precious stones, the cloths of white linen, the fragrant unguents of divinity to give him pleasure in the feasts to mark the beginning of the seasons that are held in this sanctuary . . . when My Majesty returned from the Mountains of Retenou[4] I filled his temple with all manner of good things, oxen, birds, incense and wines, presents and vegetables.'

But even after the king had showered gifts upon the gods, even after he had restored the ancient sanctuaries and built new from the rarest materials and had endowed them, his work was still incomplete. He must take the personal trouble to supervise the execution of his orders and, when the work was completed, ceremonially consecrate the temple and dedicate it to the gods.[5] He must scatter grains of *besin* round it, knock twelve times on its door with his mace, consecrate the shrine with fire and run round the walls bearing in either hand a vase or possibly an oar and an architect's square rule. Sometimes Apis, the sacred bull, ran at his side. The king had also to participate in several of the great religious feasts. At the time of the great festival of Opet, for instance, it was incumbent on him to show himself on the sacred vessel, more than 100 cubits in length, which was towed upstream from Karnak to Luxor. No less popular was the festival of Min at the beginning of the season of *shemou*, when the monarch had to reap a handful of *bôti*-wheat. It was out of the question for King Ramesses III of all monarchs to depute anyone else to perform this task, since it coincided with the anniversary of his coronation. When the Ethiopian Piankhi embarked upon the conquest of Egypt, he began by celebrating the New Year at Napata in his own country, and on his arrival at Thebes, which coincided with Amūn's great river procession, he acted as escort to the god.[6] Thenceforward battles and ceremonies alternated until the final victory was won. He proclaimed to the inhabitants of Memphis: 'Do not shut yourselves up and do not fight against the residence of Shou in the first time. When I enter, he enters, and when I go out, he does the same. No one can halt my progress. I will make offerings to Ptah and the gods of the White Wall.* I will honour Sokari in his mysterious shrine. I will contemplate him who is to the south of his wall. And I will return thence in peace, leaving the region of the White Wall unscathed so that even the children shall not weep. Behold the southern nomes: none has there been slain save the impious who had blasphemed against God.'[7] After the capture of the city he purified it with salt and perfumes and then repaired to the temple of Ptah, where he cleansed himself in the chamber of purification and performed all the ceremonies which Pharaoh alone might celebrate; then entering into the temple, he offered a great oblation to his father, Ptah South of His Wall.

Soon afterwards the ceremonies recommenced at On. After a number of preliminaries designed to enable him to make a fitting appearance in the Holy of Holies, and after receiving homage from the high priest and listening to the prayer which kept the king's enemies at bay, Piankhi ascended the staircase of the great terrace to see Rê in the Castle of the Pyramidion.† Alone he drew back the bolts, opened the leaves of the door and gazed upon his divine father and upon the sacred boats of Rê and Atum. Then he closed the doors again, sealed them with clay and stamped them with the royal seal, whereupon the priests fell down before the king and wished him long life and prosperity.[8]

Piankhi wanted to show the Egyptians that he was no whit less pious than they and even more punctilious in his respect for

---

*i.e. Memphis.
†i.e. the temple of the sun-god Rê at On. (See Glossary.)

ancient tradition. But the Ramessids had anticipated him at every point. When they passed through a town, they never failed to visit the temple and worship its gods. Wherever he went Pharaoh was at home, for on the walls of any temple he would see the image of a Pharaoh offering the gods water, wine and milk, proffering the symbol of truth and burning grains of terebinth resin in the censer. Moreover, before coming to the throne Ramesses I and his son Sety I had been the high priests of Seth and had been connected with various aspects of the cult of the ram of Mendes and Wadjit, the serpent goddess who was worshipped in their native city and in the surrounding countryside (p. 277).[9] At the outset of his reign Ramesses II assumed the title of high priest of Amūn, though this was no impediment to his nominating a titular high priest, to whom indeed a young king so obviously destined for pleasure, hunting and war would doubtless be happy to leave the more meticulous observances of his office.[10] But even so he was as scrupulous as his predecessors and his successors in discharging the obligations towards the gods which every Pharaoh must acknowledge. By these means he could buy—high though the price no doubt was—the peace of the country at a time when the mass of the workers was, generally speaking, content with its lot and incapable of raising a serious revolt, while those who might have caused trouble had everything to gain from preserving order.

2. The King's Toilet

The king's rising must have been an occasion of considerable ceremony. We know from a high official named Ptahmosé that he got up early every day in order to be the first person to greet his master.[11] I do not know of any picture of the royal levée, but the tomb of Ptahhotep shows a man of high rank undergoing the attentions of his barber, manicurist and chiropodist, surrounded by his family and his servants, and the king's toilet must have been at least as elaborate.

Not only was the monarch's attire more sumptuous than that worn by princes and civil and military leaders, but it was designed to emphasize the unique status of its wearer. The king never appeared in public bareheaded: even in private he almost always wore some kind of head-dress, his hair having been cut short to enable him to change it easily. The simplest form was a round wig decorated with a diadem knotted at the back and loose ends hanging down the back of the neck. Round the diadem was twined a golden uraeus with its swollen throat rising at the centre of the front. The northern or southern crowns, or the double crown, were worn only on ceremonial occasions. The northern crown was a tall tapering cap swelling outwards at the top; the southern was a flat-topped mortar cap with a tall stiff projection at the back, from the base of which a spiral of metal ribbon projected forward: the double crown was a combination of both. The king always liked, especially for military parades or for war, to wear his blue helmet with its clean curving lines. This too was decorated with a uraeus and had two streamers hanging down at the back of the neck (Plate I).

Both crowns and helmet were worn directly on the head. The *nems*, which was sufficiently large to go over the round wig, was a white headcloth with red stripes, passing over the forehead and behind the ears, and tied at the back; the cloth hung down over the wearer's shoulders to his chest, on either side of his face, falling behind in a point to the middle of his back. Sometimes the king wore a made-up *nems*, anchored with a circlet of gold, which was particularly necessary when it served as the foundation for the northern or southern, or for the double, crown. In another varia-

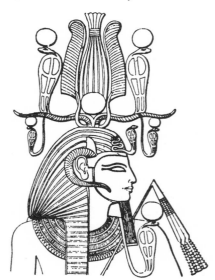

tion the *nems* might be surmounted by a pair of tall stiff feathers, or by an *atef*, which consisted of the crown of Upper Egypt flanked by two swaying feathers and resting on two ram's horns enclosing a glittering golden disk and supporting a pair of uraei, each in turn crowned with a disk. The use of these more elaborate head ornaments must clearly have been confined to ceremonies in which the king remained virtually motionless.

The Pharaoh's ceremonial costume included an artificial

beard, plaited in imitation of that favoured by the inhabitants of Punt—the 'Divine Land', so called since so many of the gods of Egypt had sprung from its soil—and joined by a chin strap to whatever head-dress he was wearing. Kings were usually clean-shaven, but occasionally grew a short beard, trimmed square.

The basic garment, for Pharaoh and commoner alike, was the loincloth, but that worn by the king was pleated and was kept up by a broad belt with a central metal buckle adorned with his personal cartouche beautifully engraved in hieroglyphs. A bull's tail hung down behind. Occasionally a sort of apron in the shape of an elongated trapezoid was hung on the belt, sometimes made entirely of metal and sometimes of rows of beads in a metal frame-work, with uraei crowned with disks along the bottom or flanking either side of the apron. The king sometimes walked barefoot, though he owned a rich assortment of sandals of metal, leather and basketwork.[12]

This brief sketch of the monarch's wardrobe must be com-pleted by a reference to his jewellery and ornaments (Plate VI). He had a vast selection of necklaces, often consisting of strings of tiny pendants of gold, or beads, or large balls, ending in a flat clasp which lay on the wearer's neck, from which was suspended a very striking kind of decoration formed of chains and tiny flowers. These necklaces were a comparatively late innovation. The classic form of necklace in Egypt consisted of several rows of beads strung between two falcons' head terminals, fastened at the back of the wearer's neck by cords tied in a knot. The lowest rows of beads were tear-shaped pendants; the others were cylindrical or olive-shaped. Such necklaces might weigh several pounds. As if that were not enough, the king might also suspend from his neck by a double chain a pectoral in the shape of a temple façade, and would wear at least three pairs of bracelets: on the upper arms, at the wrists, and at the ankles.[13] Sometimes on top of everything else he would wear a long light robe, trans-parent and short-sleeved, with a girdle of the same material tied in front.

3. *The King at Work*

Diodorus, who claims to have made a careful study of the events recorded in the annals kept by the Egyptian priests, asserts that every aspect of the king's life, both public and private, was governed by strict rules. On waking in the morning, he would first read his correspondence and then, after bathing and donning the insignia of royalty, he would offer a sacrifice and listen to the prayers and exhortations of the high priest and to improving literature. The remainder of his time was divided between holding audiences, delivering judgements, walking abroad and relaxation. He had to practise strict moderation and to observe the laws scrupulously. Since in this he was following established tradition, he did not find it irksome and was quite content with his lot.[14] Although not all Pharaohs can have maintained a standard of conduct quite as high as Diodorus liked to think, none the less his account of the way in which the king spent his time is no doubt substantially accurate, and the facts that we know fit easily enough into the picture.

There is no doubt that many kings performed their duties conscientiously, listening to dispatches, keeping abreast of current affairs, dictating replies and, on occasion, summoning their council. We find a large number of official inscriptions on stelae beginning with the phrase 'It was brought to His Majesty's notice. . . .' This more often than not referred to the activities of his enemies. For example King Psammetichus II was at Tanis, occupying himself with activities of which the gods of the country approved, when the news reached him that the negro Kouar had taken up arms against Egypt.[15] The king was the arbiter of peace and war; but he was also interested in strictly practical questions. We have already (p. 139) seen King Sety's interest in ensuring a supply of water for the gold prospectors in the area east of Edfou, and so keen was his concern that he went there in person to gain first-hand experience of the sufferings of those who had to labour, without water, beneath a pitiless sun.[16] When King Ramesses IV wanted to erect monuments to his ancestors the gods and goddesses of Egypt, he began by studying the books in the House of Life to discover the routes which led to the mountain of *bekhen*-stone; and he himself travelled across the holy mountain (p. 135).[17]

Although Ramesses II was too obsessed with his own grandeur to leave the banks of the Nile, he went to much trouble in his palace of Hatkaptah in studying ways and means of finding water in the terrible desert of Ikaïta. Seated on his golden throne and wearing on his head the diadem and plumes, he said to the keeper of the royal seal at his side: 'Call the lords who are outside [my audience chamber, that] my Majesty may take their advice about this land. I will lay the problem before them.' They were immediately haled like criminals into the presence of the good god, for no one, not even a member of his council, could possibly behold the august countenance of the Pharaoh without terror. They kissed the earth and the problem was explained to them. The most elementary tact required them to avoid giving a straight answer or attempting to display their wisdom. The whole of the glory of the project must belong to the king. They accordingly followed the example of the courtiers assembled by Ramesses a few months earlier to listen to the announcement of his intention of completing the temple of Abydos: they uttered an extravagant eulogy of this unrivalled monarch, who had but to conceive a scheme during the night for it to come to fruition at daybreak and after recalling the failure of previous attempts in both the recent and the distant past, ṭhey ended, 'If then thou thyself sayest to Hâpi thy father, father of the gods, that thou wouldst that the water should flow high on the mountain, he will do all that thou dost wish, in accord with the plans which thou hast explained to us, for all thy fathers the gods love thee more than any king that hath reigned since Rê.' On this note the audience ended, anḍ it only remained for the experts to get to work. They would keep the king informed of progress and a granite stele would eventually commemorate the success of the undertaking.[18]

The appointment of high officials and great dignitaries was evidently within the royal prerogative. The choice of the high priest of Amūn was a matter of the utmost importance. No Ramesses had forgotten the dispute which had led to open strife between the monarchy and the priesthood attached to the richest and the most ambitious member of the pantheon. At the outset of his reign Ramesses II had personally assumed the title of high priest. Very soon he resolved to nominate someone else to this office, and his choice not only went outside the priesthood of Amūn, but fell, moreover, on one who was not particularly distinguished—the high priest of Anhour in the Thinite nome, whom the king must have noticed when visiting the buildings put in hand by his father in this region of particular sanctity. Before making his final choice he had engaged in some kind of consultation, the details of which we cannot quite follow, in the presence of the god himself, to whom before them all he had recited the names of all the members of the court, the leaders of the army, the prophets of the gods and his household officers. Amūn was not satisfied with any of them and only signified his pleasure when the name of Nebounnef was uttered. 'Be gracious to him,' said the king in conclusion, 'for he entreats thee.' On hearing these words the courtiers and the thirty counsellors united to praise the goodness of His Majesty, bowing repeatedly before this good god and exalting his 'souls' to the vault of heaven. When the chorus of praise had died away, the king handed to the new high priest his two gold rings and his staff of electrum, thus signifying to all Egypt that the whole domain of Amūn had been delivered to him, lock, stock and barrel.[19]

4. *The Royal Pardon*

The Memoirs of Sinuhe contain the only instance known to us of a criminal's being pardoned by a Pharaoh. But the narrator has explained to us at length how this came about. The king, not content with merely remitting Sinuhe's punishment and allowing him to return, was anxious to see him. The adventurer arrived at the frontier post of the Roads of Horus, where he parted from his Bedouin friends, after distributing among them the presents which he had been sent by the court, and surrendered to the soldiers who had orders to bring him by boat to the Residence of Ithy-Tawi. He was duly awaited in the palace, where the royal children stood in a group among the bodyguard, while the courtiers responsible for ushering newcomers into the pillared audience chamber directed him until he found himself in the presence of the sovereign seated on his great throne in the hall of electrum. Overcome by the magnitude of his crimes, Sinuhe fell prostrate. 'I was like a man caught in the shadows. My spirit failed, my limbs quaked. My heart was no longer in my breast. I knew [not] life from death.'[19a]

Sinuhe was raised from the ground and the king, who had interrupted him sharply, calmed down and urged him to speak. He did not presume on this permission and closed his brief remarks with the words: 'Here I stand before thee. Thou art life: let Thy Majesty do as he will.'

The monarch commanded the royal children to come in. While

they were getting ready he could not help observing to the queen how much Sinuhe had changed; indeed, from living among Asiatics, he had come to resemble them. The queen uttered a cry of astonishment and the royal children all applauded the king's remark. 'In very truth, your Majesty, my lord, it is not he!' Thereupon they brought out crotals and both kinds of sistrum (p. 95) and presented them to the king. 'Hold in thy two hands these beautiful things, take the ornaments of Hathor! May the Golden Lady grant life to thy nostrils, may the Lady of Stars be made one with thee.' After reciting a fairly extensive string of compliments they ask for pardon for Sinuhe, whose misdeeds had been due to lack of judgement. The goddess of the sistrum and the crotal, the Golden Lady of the Stars, was in fact a goddess of joy, dancing and feasting, and her role in this scene is to prepare for the act of clemency which the king is to perform towards the wanderer. Intervention of this nature was no doubt generally expected in similar circumstances. In the upshot Sinuhe eventually left the palace not merely pardoned but a man of wealth, and the owner of a house, destined henceforward to live on choice viands from the royal table.[20]

5. Royal Rewards

A courtier once defined Pharaoh as 'he who causes good things to multiply, who knows how to give. He is god, yea, the king of gods. He knoweth all that know him. He rewards him that does him service. He protects those that support him. He is Rê whose visible presence is the disk and who lives for ever.'[21] During the wars of liberation and the conquest of Syria Pharaoh was moved to award the Gold of Valour to more than one war hero. The practice caught on and soon it was the turn of the civilian population.

Occasionally a single individual was rewarded, but it was more usual to wait and then to summon a number of recipients to the palace simultaneously. They would be wearing their best clothes and, when they left their houses to mount their chariots, their servants and neighbours would form a cheering crowd round their doors. The chariots would gather in a park in front of the palace and the grooms would gossip or chat with the guards, each boasting of his own master and the favours to be showered on him.

'Well, my lad, who is all this celebration in honour of?' 'It is in honour of Aÿ, the divine father, and of his wife Taia. See, they have become people of gold.' A bystander, who has not heard, asks in his turn: 'Who is this rejoicing for?' and the answer comes: 'Listen to him! Pharaoh (Life, Health, Strength!) is holding it for Aÿ, the divine father, and Taia. Is Pharaoh (Life, Health, Strength!) giving them millions of gifts to take away? Look over at the window. We shall see what is being done for Aÿ, the divine father.'[22]

When everyone is present, the king takes up his position on the state balcony leading off one end of a pillared hall. From outside the building the range of royal apartments, furnished with arm-chairs and rich chests, is visible. The gifts to be presented are spread out on tables which will be placed at the king's side, and replenished as often as necessary, while in the remainder of the palace the servants continue to go about their usual tasks. Some people are talking quietly, and a number of women are singing and dancing and playing the harp. In the courtyard sunshade bearers, fan bearers and officers of the household are marshalling the prospective recipients and leading them one by one to the foot of the balcony. Each in turn salutes the king with his arms but without prostrating himself, and delivers a laudatory address, to which the king replies in kind, enlarging upon the faithfulness, skill and devotion of his servant. Sometimes he advances him in rank with such words as: 'Thou art my great servant, who hast faithfully carried out thine orders in all the tasks that thou hast performed, and I am well satisfied with thee. I therefore give thee this office with the words "Thou shalt eat the bread of Pharaoh (Life, Health, Strength!) thy lord, in the temple of Aton",' simul-taneously tossing down to him valuable golden cups and neck-laces, which the waiting officials catch in mid-air. The necklaces, sometimes three or four in number, are forthwith clasped round the neck of the recipient who, bowed beneath their weight and overcome with joy and gratitude, makes his way out, followed by the officials carrying everything that he cannot wear, and by subordinates bearing gifts of food, while scribes record the whole proceedings. Once outside the palace the recipient rejoins his friends, servants and attendants, all of whom clearly demonstrate their joy. He gets into his chariot again and returns home, escorted by a noisy throng which increases in size at each step. On

his arrival his wife welcomes him, throwing up her arms in astonishment at such wealth, while other women play the tambourine
and sing and dance. His parents and friends come to join the celebrations and the festivities are evidently destined to continue long.[23]
  These investitures were not confined to men. We have already
met Aÿ, the divine father, receiving honours from Akhnaton. He
in turn has become Pharaoh and now he is distributing the rewards. He has just decorated Neferhotep, the scribe and master
of the flocks of Amūn, and has decided also to confer an honour
on his wife Meryt-Rê. The setting is one of the king's country
residences, a square stone building with a row of little oblong
windows on each side, and in front a large window with a projecting balcony supported on pillars. The garden round this unpretentious house is planted with rows of vines running parallel
with the pathway, their branches twined round low columns
similar to those of the house. At the foot of the wall we can see a
pile of vases, baskets and plates. Meryt-Rê, looking very attractive
in her transparent dress, and wearing a scented cone on her head
(p. 94), comes to stand in front of the house and catches in both
hands the necklace which the king tosses down to her from the
window. There are only a few witnesses of this intimate scene.
One woman is applauding, another is kissing the ground. Bunches
of flowers are brought, while a female musician engaged for the
occasion manages to drink without interrupting her sistrum-
shaking. Two children who have managed to creep into the garden
and are staring at the scene in fascination, have been noticed by a
gatekeeper, who is shaking his stick at them. After leaving the
king's presence Meryt-Rê makes her way home on foot, leaning
on the arm of a man whom we cannot recognize: possibly her
husband, possibly some official assigned by the king to see her
home. She walks with a proud gait, wearing all the king's necklaces round her neck. A procession has formed behind her, and in
it we can recognize the sistrum player, who has been joined by two
little naked girls. Servants have shared out the jars, bundles and
baskets which will ensure that a memorable day is duly celebrated
with an equally memorable feast. The most valuable gifts have
been stowed in a chest.[24]
  Investitures were sometimes held in the open air, either because
the recipient was too important a person merely to have a few necklaces tossed down to him by the king from a balcony, or because

the crowd of spectators was too great for it to take place indoors. On these occasions a light canopy—a miracle of richness and taste —would be erected in a large open courtyard by the master cabinet-makers. On a low platform decorated with bas-reliefs of Syrians, Libyans or Negroes kneeling and lifting their hands in supplication or trampled underfoot by the king in the guise of a griffin, four papyriform pillars would be erected, carved and inlaid from top to bottom, supporting a many-tiered cornice and surmounted by a convex roof. Pharaoh would climb the steps, which were guarded by sphinxes with falcons' heads, and take his seat upon a chair of unexampled magnificence. In the scene now to be described the recipient of honour is Horonemheb, himself destined to

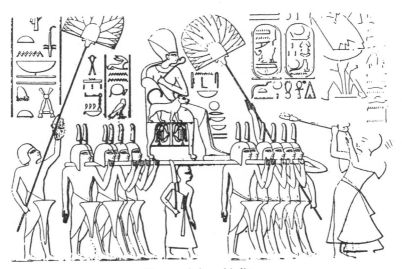

Horonemheb on his litter

sit upon the throne and already the occupant of an important military command. He had come to the assistance of the Bedouin when they were hard pressed by other nomads, captured the whole tribe of their assailants and brought to the king's residence both his prisoners and those whom he had rescued, the latter of whom had come to beg the favour of being permitted to cross the frontier into Egypt with their herds, in accordance with age-long tradition. Prisoners and rescued alike were destined to witness

Horonemheb's hour of triumph. The general, wearing full dress, raises his arms in acknowledgement of his honour, while officers clasp necklace after necklace round his neck and others, stooping as they walk, bring more necklaces on dishes. Horonemheb's subordinates point to the long lines of prisoners, with well-marked features, and wearing long hair and beards. Their hands are tightly bound and their faces distorted with pain. The women, who are unbound, are walking with dignity. A soldier has seized the hand of one mother of a family, who is wearing a flounced dress and carrying one child on her shoulder and another small child in a sling, while another woman seems to be trying to get into conversation with the soldier walking in front of her. These captives are destined for brickmaking or stone-quarrying and perhaps the horses, held on leading reins by an Egyptian officer, are of even greater interest.

After receiving his own reward Horonemheb in person pleads the cause of the nomads, who, without his advocacy, were in danger of forfeiting their flocks and all their possessions. Still wearing his necklaces and holding his long-handled fan upright, he addresses Pharaoh directly, first extolling his might and next explaining the situation. Then he turns to the interpreter and bids him tell the nomads that Pharaoh is graciously pleased to permit them to remain in Egypt. They are recognizable as Libyans by the feather set on the top of their heads and the hair cropped short over their foreheads, a large lock covering the whole of one side of their face. There is also a sprinkling of Syrians wearing long-sleeved garments and wide sashes. They demonstrate their gratitude with eloquent gestures, lifting their arms to the sky, or stretching them out towards Pharaoh or throwing themselves prostrate. Some, in their transports of delight, are rolling in the dust.[25]

Though Horonemheb had earned his reward, the same could hardly be said of Amenhotep, the high priest of Amūn, whom Ramesses IX received as an equal, only to end by losing his all to him. The ceremony was held in a state pavilion. The king and the high priest stood facing each other on either side of tables piled high with gifts. Although the king is shown in the temple of Karnak wearing the blue helmet and standing on matting, while the high priest is bareheaded, the sculptor of this relief represents them as of equal size. The presents were enormously valuable—10 *deben* of gold, 20 *deben* of silver, enough food for a banquet and 20 *arouras* of cultivated land: but the concessions which had been extracted from the king were worth far more, for Amenhotep had secured for himself unprecedented powers which removed the immensely wealthy realm of Amūn from all external control, so that it became a State within the State. Thus long years of patient effort had at last resulted in the priests of Amūn—slighted by Akhnaton, and objects of suspicion to Ramesses II—regaining all the influence which they had succeeded in winning in the time of Queen Hatshepsut and her successors, Tuthmosis III and IV.[26]

6. *Reception of Foreign Ambassadors*

The reception of foreign ambassadors, in an even higher degree than investiture ceremonies, provided an excuse for the utmost pomp and for flattering Pharaoh's pride, more especially when envoys from all the corners of the world attended a single audience. There was a constant stream of Nubians, Negroes, missions from the land of Punt, Syrians, Libyans and envoys from Naharina. In the Ramesside age, Cretans with long curly hair and wearing particoloured loincloths no longer made their appearance bearing

Tribute from the Cretans

their rhytons, tapering vases, handled cups and flowered bowls, and begging the favour of being 'on the king's water'. But though no more embassies came from Crete, the fame of the king of Egypt had spread eastwards to countries whose very names would have been strange to the Tuthmosis and Amenophis dynasty—Media, Persia, Bactria, and the banks of the Indus. These ceremonies were held in a pavilion specially constructed for the king in the middle of an open space and surrounded by his bodyguard, the bearers of his sunshade and his scribes. The envoys would form a hollow square, with the precious gifts which they had brought piled before them. After the scribes had listed the treasure, it would be carried off to the storerooms of the neighbouring temple.[27] In return the king would grant them the breath of life—and sometimes substantial gifts worth even more than those which he had himself received. It was the Pharaoh's pleasure as it were to regard himself as an inexhaustible source of gold for the whole world. He was bound to go on subsidizing the impoverished princes who wished to conclude alliances with him—by marriage or any other means—but who were, if times were propitious, never above flirting with his rivals.

7. *Royal Pleasures: Sport*

A king's time was largely taken up with war, and princes were trained for this pursuit from their childhood. The young Ramesses II, like his companions, had been accustomed by his father to continual exercise and physical endurance. None of these boys, says Diodorus, was allowed to eat until they had run 180 stades,* with the result that by the time they grew up they were all accomplished athletes.[28] The poem of Qadesh and many other texts expatiate on the king's physical strength, endurance, skill and courage. We can ascertain the details of the sporting education of the young princes from a stele of that valiant warrior Tuthmosis III,[29] and in even greater detail from a stele of his son and successor Amenophis II,[30] who, in the opinion of the doctors who have studied his mummy, must have been a man of unusual strength. His contemporaries used to say of him: 'So mighty of arm is he that none can bend his bow, no, none among the soldiers nor the chieftains of foreign countries nor the great men of Retenou.'[31]

*About two miles.

E.L.E.—P

Let us see then how a prince of the blood, heir to the throne of Horus, spent his time. 'At the age of eighteen he was full grown in strength. He had learned to know all the works of Mōnth. There was none to equal him on the field of battle. He had learned horsemanship. He had no rival in the whole of this great army. Not one man could draw his bow, nor could any man run as swiftly.' It is the epitome of the all-round athlete, equally proficient as oarsman, archer and horseman.

'He was strong of arm and tireless for as long as he manned his oar and took the helm at the stern of his royal boat, as captain of a crew of two hundred men. When they rested after half an *atour** of sailing, they were exhausted and their limbs were slack and feeble, but His Majesty, unlike them, kept up his stroke with his oar of twenty cubits. When they halted and when His Majesty made fast his royal boat, he had performed three *atours* at the helm without taking rest from start to finish. Everyone rejoiced to see His Majesty doing this.'[31a]

We should not, however, forget that the steersman's job was easier than formerly, since the rudder was kept upright by a pole near the end and a mortice cut in the stern, in the axis of the ship or, when there were two rudders, at either side of the stern. In the Old Kingdom the steersmen unaided had to use both hands to hold the oars which formed the rudder, and it required an immense effort to go athwart the current or to alter course. There is nothing to suggest that the prince had reverted to the former system, but even so, and despite the improvements just described, the feat undoubtedly demanded great strength and endurance.

A good archer was expected to be a connoisseur of bows. 'He drew three hundred powerful bows in order to compare the craftsmanship of their makers and to tell the incompetent maker from the skilled.' Then, having selected a bow that was beyond criticism, and one, moreover, which no man but he could draw . . . 'he entered his northern butt and found that four targets of Asiatic copper had been set up for him, each a hand's-breadth in thickness. Each post was twenty cubits from its neighbour.

'When His Majesty appeared on his chariot, like Mōnth in his might, he seized his bow, grasped four arrows together and

*A measure of distance, the Greek σχοῖνος, rather more than 5 miles.

advanced with his accoutrements, shooting like Mōnth
at the targets. Each shaft
passed clean through the target. He then aimed at the
next. This was a feat which
no one had ever performed
before and had never been
heard of, to shoot an arrow at
a copper target so that it went
right through and fell to the

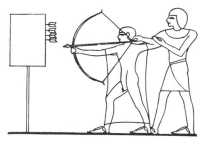

Prince Amenophis is taught to shoot

ground: none had done such a thing save this strong and mighty
king to whom Amūn had granted victory.'[31b]

In actual fact Prince Amenophis was merely repeating an exploit of his father Tuthmosis III, who could also pierce a copper
plate with his arrows, though it was still a remarkable achievement. If Amenophis, like Ulysses, had had to return home in the
guise of a beggar, his irresistible arm and his matchless bow would
have enabled him to wreak vengeance on those who were looting
his palace and lusting after his women.

A true warrior loved his horses—and indeed, horses in general
—better than life. Although Prince Nemarot's kingdom comprised only part of Middle Egypt he had a stable in his capital of
Shmoun. Men and horses alike had suffered during the siege of
this town. When Piankhi made his victorious entry (p. 196) he
visited the stables and saw the fodderless barns and the famished
horses. He was seized by pity and anger to think that his enemy's
folly had brought these beautiful animals to so sorry a state. 'By
my life, by my love of Rê and as my nostrils are rejuvenated with
life! To see horses so hungry grieves my heart more than all the
evil that thou hast done in thy wickedness. Knowest thou not
that the shadow of god is over me and that I am guiltless in his
eyes? I was born of the divine womb, divinely conceived, and the
seed of the gods is in me. I call his *ka* to witness that I do nothing
without his knowledge. It is he that bids me do as I do.'[32]
Ramesses III would never rely on his officers' assurance that his
horses were in good condition and fit for operations. Wearing
full uniform, carrying his shield in one hand and his riding-whip
in the other, escorted by retainers bearing his fan and his parasol
and followed by his orderly officers, he would make his way to

the royal stables. The royal trumpets would ring out and the grooms would leap to their posts, each grasping the reins of a pair of horses, while the king inspected them in turn.[33]

From his earliest childhood and long before he was fit to undertake the works of Mōnth, Prince Amenophis trained himself assiduously. He loved horses and was proud of his love, which made him expert at horse-breaking. His father, the terrible Tuthmosis III, came to hear of his successes and was happy and proud at the reports of his eldest son. He said to his courtiers: 'Give him the finest team from my royal stable in the nome of the Wall (Memphis) and say to him "Make it your business to break them and train them and make them strong. This is your father's wish".' With this encouragement and with the help of Reshef and Astarte, deities of Syria, the horses' homeland, the young prince did as he was bidden. Drive them as he might, they had no equals for endurance, and even in a long gallop they never lathered with sweat.[33a]

Most of these long rides took place in the district west of Memphis, near the great pyramids. When the uraeus had shone forth on his forehead* Amenophis ordered the construction of a shrine to form the base of the great stele of white stone on which we can still read of his exploits. Tuthmosis IV, his son, was ambitious to emulate them. He loved shooting at a target near the great Sphinx, and going out into the desert to hunt game. One day while he was asleep between the Sphinx's paws, it appeared to him in a dream and bade him clear away the sand which was choking it, and so earn the right to sit upon the throne of Geb. The prince had to obey and was naturally bound to record so marvellous a dream for posterity.[34] It is to the piety of these young men that we owe our knowledge of how they prepared themselves for the responsibilities of kingship.

8. *Royal Hunts*

A prince might amuse himself by shooting at a copper target or hunting antelope in the desert near the pyramids under the protection of Harakhté, but beyond the Euphrates, or south of the cataract, sterner sports awaited the king who chose to pit

---

*i.e. when he became king.

Plate X

Rameses III hunting wild bull

himself against wild beasts which he could never hope to meet in the two deserts flanking the Egyptian Nile.

This was how King Tuthmosis III and his escort came to make their bold attack on a herd of 120 elephants at a placed called Niy in the Euphrates valley, at a point where the river runs between two rocks. The fighting began in the water. 'No king had ever done such a thing since the world began.' It was no doubt providence which placed the very largest of the elephants directly opposite the king, who found himself in great danger. Luckily his old comrade-in-arms Amonemheb was at hand and cut off the elephant's trunk. Although the king rewarded him with a gift of gold, he made no mention of Amonemheb's devotion in the official account of the episode which was carved by his command on the stele of Napata, despite his assertion 'I have told everything frankly, and I have uttered no lie'; and the truth would have remained unknown to us had not Amonemheb in his turn composed a short—too short—account of this remarkable hunt.[35] Had it been not Amonemheb but a soldier of less exalted rank, we should have known nothing about it.

The texts we have do not tell us whether Sety I and Ramesses II hunted elephant on the Euphrates and rhinoceros between the third and fourth cataracts, but on the bas-reliefs of Medinet Habu we can see Ramesses III in full fighting equipment, hunting lions, wild bulls and antelopes.[36] The king is riding in a chariot, while beneath the horse's belly a wounded lion lies on its back, trying to claw out the arrow sunk in its breast. A second lion, struck with two arrows and a javelin, is roaring as it seeks a hiding-place in the reeds, while a third springs from a thicket behind the chariot. But the king, spear in hand, has turned to face it and his would-be assailant cannot escape the death blow.

Another relief shows the royal party hunting a herd of wild bulls near a reed-fringed marsh amid tall vegetation. A line of soldiers are equipped as though for battle with bows, pikes, swords and shields. The frenzied animals, forced to fly headlong, are overtaken by the chariot containing the king, who is armed as for war with a triangular bow and pike. One bull, riddled with arrows, has fallen on its back in a thicket and paws the air: a second has rolled beneath the horses' feet, while a third, with tail outstretched and tongue protruding in its desperate leap, has failed in its attempt to reach the water and sinks in exhaustion to its knees.

By comparison with the drama of this kind of hunting, ante-lope hunting in the desert seems a mild form of amusement, pur-sued by the king alone in his chariot and unescorted. Unlike the citizenry of Thebes or professional hunters, he makes no attempt to corral the gazelles, but if he sees a herd of wild asses or ante-lope in the distance he drives at top speed until he can overtake them.

9. *The King's Private Life*

On returning from a long journey or an expedition across the desert, the king would find much enjoyment in his palaces of Pi-Ramessu,[37] Memphis or Thebes. Akhnaton was so delighted with his brand-new palace of Akhetaton that he hardly ever left

it. The sole pleasure of this devoted father, loving hus-band and affectionate son was found in the company of the queen and princesses, who were his inseparable companions—on his walks, in the temple, at investitures, at the reception of foreign missions—and who prepared his drinks and sweetmeats. The queen herself would take the pot and strainer to serve him his warm drink with her own hands. His happiness was complete when the queen mother came to visit his child-ren. Both lunch and dinner

Akhnaton and his family

were taken *en famille*.[38] But we do not know whether all the Pharaohs followed these habits, for Akhnaton had reacted against many ideas and customs of the period preceding his reign, and they were resumed after his death. At the beginning of the eighteenth dynasty the king's private life with his family was much more restricted. King Ahmosé, on going to rest on his private couch, found there the most excellent, most gracious royal daughter, royal sister, divine consort, the Great Royal Spouse Ahmosé

Nefertari. And what, we may wonder, did they talk about? Why, how they might minister to the inhabitants of the underworld, the dead who demand water and tables covered with offerings at the feasts of heaven and earth. In some astonishment, the queen, who may well have expected something a little more romantic, cries: 'Why do you have such thoughts? What is the object of such talk? What has come into your heart?' The king replies: 'I have called to mind Tetisheri, my mother's mother, my father's mother, the Great Royal Spouse, the royal mother, her of the true voice, whose tomb and monument are even now in the dust of Thebes and Tini. This I have said in your presence since I, the king, wished to build for her a pyramid and a castle in the necropolis Todjeser, near to My Majesty's own royal monument, that its pool should be dug, its trees planted, its food offering assured, that they may be for ever staffed with men, endowed with land, and with herds, with *ka* priests (p. 331ff), with men appointed to perform the ceremonies in their own charge, every man knowing what he must do.'[39]

We can admire the king's piety, the dignity of his language and the respect he displays towards his wife, but we cannot help thinking that the queen might perhaps have preferred a conversation on some other topic. Ramesses II was less austere. The constant theme of the numerous texts which refer to Pi-Ramessu, the palace which he founded on the ruins of Avaris in the eastern delta, is its charm and gaiety. Food and drink alike were good. The wine was sweet as honey. Those who dwelt there garlanded with flowers acclaimed the king each day. It was a veritable earthly paradise.[40] At Akhetaton, too, life was a long series of feasts, but with a perceptible difference. The heretic king practised what we regard as the domestic virtues. The Ramessids, generally speaking, liked variety: and in the reign of Ramesses II, to our certain knowledge, five separate women bore the title of Great Royal Spouse. This in itself is not necessarily surprising in the case of a king who reigned for sixty-seven years, but his 162 children are clear evidence that he did not confine his attentions to his official wives. Our documentary evidence is too scanty to tell us how the members of this large establishment got on with each other: but we know of one instance of the great king's chivalry. Although he had made peace with his enemy Khattousil, the Hittite king, fighting was still going on, and wherever Egyptian

and Hittite troops ran into each other, an engagement took place.
Khattousil took a big decision. He divested himself, we are told,
of all his possessions and, putting his well-beloved daughter at
their head, he sent them to Ramesses. The journey took place in
the season of bad weather, but at Ramesses' request the god
Sutekh, who was always well disposed towards his distant descendant, performed a miracle. There was a succession of summer
days, and the princess's long journey from the Hittite capital in the
middle of Asia Minor to Egypt took place in brilliant sunshine.
This was not all. Ramesses decided to build a strong fortress
between Egypt and Phoenicia which he named Ramesses-Great-
of-Victories (p. 18f), and placed it under the protection of four
gods, two Asiatic (Sutekh and Astarte) and two Egyptian (Amūn
and Wadjit). He stocked it with food, sent four statues and went
there himself to wait for the princess and her escort, in order to
conduct her thence to his great palace of Pi-Ramessu, whereupon
the populace loudly expressed their joy at the sight of so lovely a
princess, and for the first time Hittite and Egyptian soldiers
fraternized.[41]

Ramesses II's successors made no effort to outdo him in this
respect. Ramesses III, though eager to rival him in everything,
and fond of female society, contented himself with a mere three
wives and ten children. He liked playing draughts with pretty,
lightly dressed women, who brought him flowers, drink and
sweetmeats (fig. p. 13).

Egyptian kings also enjoyed the society of their companions
in war and in hunting, as well as of men distinguished for their
learning. Cheops summoned his sons and made each in turn tell
him a story, and it was the same monarch who, on learning that
there was living a wise man who could also work miracles, sent
one of his sons to look for him. Snefrou summoned to his court
a wise man who both knew the past and could foretell the future,
while at a much later date Amenophis III confided to a sage of the
same name as himself his anxieties and his desire to see the gods.

10. *Intrigues in the Harem*

For all Pharaoh's assumption of divinity as the legitimate son
of Amūn, there were plenty of godless people to plot his destruc-

tion and seek ways and means of cutting short his reign and interrupting the natural line of succession. Towards the end of the reign of Ramesses III one of his wives, Taïa, was scheming to secure the throne for her own son, known in the Turin judicial papyrus as Pentaour (though this is an alias),[42] by means of an intrigue with one of the palace officials, Pabakikamūn, whose name means 'the blind servant'. The latter was the intermediary between the women of the harem, who were devoted to Taïa's interests, and their mothers and sisters, who had undertaken to recruit adherents and to raise them in revolt against the king.[43] He believed he could secure a valuable ally in the person of one of the herd overseers named Penhouibin and in response to his request procured for him a book belonging to the king Ousirmarê Miamūn, the great god, his master (Life, Health, Strength!).[44] Once possessed of this book Penhouibin set to work to compose written spells and to construct wax figures designed to exercise a magical influence upon Pharaoh and his supporters, either by debilitating their limbs or by undermining their sense of duty. The plot was in fact a joint conspiracy on the part of women and officials. One of the conspirators, the commander of the archers of Kush, the brother of a woman of the harem whose addiction to letter-writing outran the bounds of discretion, is referred to in the report of the proceedings as Binemyat ('wickedness is in Thebes'), while another officer is called Mesedsou-Rê ('Rê abominates him').[45] Before the conspiracy they must have been called 'good is in Thebes' and 'Rê protects him' respectively, but they had forfeited the right to bear such propitious names. Many people—too many and too talkative—were privy to the plot, which Rê was concerned to thwart. By some means we do not understand, we learn that the principal conspirators and their accomplices, together with those who had been in the secret but had kept their mouths shut, were arrested. A court of inquiry was appointed consisting of two treasurers, a fanbearer, four cupbearers and a herald, for Pharaoh preferred to the regular magistrates men closely attached to his person. In his preliminary instructions, the beginning of which is mutilated, he directed them to show no mercy: 'Let all their deeds recoil upon their heads. As for me who escaped and was saved for eternity, I am of the company of the true kings who are in the presence of Amonrâsonter and Osiris, lord of eternity.'[46]

In nominating the members of his tribunal the king's choice had not been altogether happy, since two of them, together with an officer of the bodyguard, discarded their mask of loyalty when they learned that some of the women had fled, and went off to join them 'in a bad place'. Not for long, however: for they in turn were recaptured, this time by men who meant business, and as the first instalment of their punishment their noses and ears were cut off.[47] This was how King Horonemheb had dealt with magistrates and officers guilty of dereliction of duty.[47a]

The writer of the account uses a curious phrase to describe the final punishment of the ringleaders. 'They have put them in their place. They died themselves.' This may mean that the victims were left alone with their remorse in the room where the trial had ended, with a sharp knife lying nearby, knowing what was expected of them. But the examination of a mummy dug up at Deir el Bahari, and known as the mummy of the Unknown Prince, suggested to Gaston Maspero a more dramatic explanation. The mummy is that of a man between twenty-five and thirty years old, in good health and with no sign of injury, who had been interred without having undergone the processes normally associated with embalming. The brain had not been removed and the internal organs were complete. In Maspero's words: 'No face can ever have displayed more vividly the evidence of intolerable agony. The terrible distortion of the features makes it virtually certain that the unhappy victim must have been deliberately suffocated by being buried alive.'[48] This explanation may seem far-fetched: but against the alternative it can legitimately be argued that there is no evidence that in Egypt the guilty were ever given the opportunity of suicide; moreover no mercy could have been shown towards those who had lifted their hand against Pharaoh.

11. *Meditations of a King*

A long reign and a number of episodes like the preceding could on occasion combine to fire a Pharaoh with the ambition to bequeath to posterity his experience of human behaviour. Several monarchs, including Amenemmes I, the father of Sesostris I, have left instructions to their successors,[49] though we possess no intimate memoirs of Sety I, who 'entered *Amentit*' in the prime of

life, nor of Ramesses II, who never wearied of the role of god that
he played for so many years. But we do possess virtually the whole
of the long document which Ramesses III dictated at the end of
his life.[50] It breathes a consciousness of work well done, of the
devotion of the best of Egypt's resources to the enlargement and
embellishment of the temples of the gods—particularly those of
Amūn at Opet, of Atum at On, of Ptah at Memphis and of their
consorts—without having neglected to pay due honour to lesser
divinities. The king has supplied them with a numerous and well-
trained staff; at each of their feasts he has appointed for their
shrines what they should eat and drink: and with all this he has
not neglected the welfare of his human subjects. He has established order and peace throughout his kingdom. He has slain and
thrown into prison the Libyans who had settled all along the strip
of the Delta which lay between the western Nile and the Sahara,
for all the world as though they owned it. The Peoples of the Sea,
who had attempted to make a frontal assault on the Egyptian
coastline, had been taught a lesson they would not soon forget. He
had built and fitted out fleets and sent expeditions to every point
of the compass in quest of incense, turquoise, gold, copper, ebony,
ivory and the conifers of the Lebanon. Egypt had become a
garden and peace reigned in the land.

'I gave life to the whole earth with its inhabitants, *Rekhyt, Payt*
and *Henmyt*,* both men and women. I raised mankind from his
wretchedness. I gave him breath and protected him from the
oppression of the strong. . . . Since my reign began the earth
hath been full of good things and joyful. To gods and men alike
I have done good. I have never seized for myself what was the
common property. I have ended my earthly reign as Ruler of the
Two Lands. You were my servants, beneath my two feet. You and
your excellent deeds were precious to my heart. May you be able
to read my command and my words. Here now I lie in the city of
the dead, like my father Rê. I have mingled with the Great Ennead
of the Gods, in heaven, on earth and in the *Douat*.'[51]

But despite his implicit trust in his gods, the king was uneasy
about his son, 'whom Rê himself had begotten, the son of Amūn
and issue of his loins, crowned Lord of the Two Lands like
Tatenen.' There was no doubt that the world lay at his feet and
that men kissed the ground before him; but who could say if the

*Words of uncertain meaning, denoting the various inhabitants of Egypt.

Egyptians would follow the advice of one who was now one with the gods from whom he sprung, for all his demands that mankind should at all times follow his son, should adore him, exalt him and magnify his beauty as is done each morning for Rê? Almost as if he knew by instinct that the great days of Pharaonic Egypt were gone, never to return, the king piles request upon request to the gods to be gracious to his son.

To Amūn he cries: 'Hear my prayers, my father, my lord. I am alone among the Nine Great Gods that are beside thee. Make my son the acknowledged king in the dwelling of Atum . . . it was thou that didst proclaim him king when he was young, who hast set him up as sovereign (Life, Health, Strength!) of all the world, to rule over mankind. . . . Grant him to be king for millions of years. . . . Grant youthfulness to his limbs, grant him children each day. Thou art the shield that dost protect him each day. Make the peoples of Asia cower in fear beneath his sword and his club as if he were Baal. May he extend the frontiers of Egypt at his pleasure. May the lands and the deserts stand in fear of him. Grant him Tomery, the Beloved Land, and let men sing his praises. Keep far from him all evil, all catastrophes and disasters. Grant that his heart may be joyful, and that men may shout and dance and sing before his beauteous face. Plant love of him in the heart of the gods and the goddesses, fill the heart of the *Payt* with love and honour towards him.'

'What thou foretellest cometh to pass and none can gainsay it. That which thou sayest is marvellously fixed. Mayst thou be able to grant me the kingship for two hundred years, making it secure for my son that is on earth. Forget not the good things that I have done towards thee and make him endure longer than all other kings. He will act as king upon thy command, for it is thou that dost crown him. He will obey thee in all things, O master of the gods. Grant that in thy good time the Nile may flow great and strong to feed his kingship with abundance of food. Make those kings that know not Egypt to come his sacred palace, heavy laden. . . .'[52]

No less fervent are the prayers that the king addresses to Atum, Ptah and the gods and goddesses of the Great Ennead. The concluding lines of the document must have been a supreme appeal to men and gods alike for this well-beloved son. Had some wise man—so common in Egypt—warned Ramesses III that the disasters kept at bay by his skill, courage and good fortune, were going to burst upon the Beloved Land? In times long past Cheops had received from such a source the warning that his dynasty would fail after three generations. The Ramesside dynasty had but seventy more years to run, and the last of them were to be sheer disaster; but under other rulers Egypt was destined to rise again.

CHAPTER IX

THE ARMY AND WARFARE

1. *Pros and Cons of the Military Career*

THE scribes regarded the profession of arms as far inferior to their own, but their pupils, dazzled by the mirage of glory, not infrequently came to prefer the sword and the bow, and, even more, the chariot with its pair of fiery steeds, to the reed and the writing-board. It was accordingly necessary to demonstrate to these young hotheads the miseries of the soldier's life, and the surviving stylistic exercises of the period largely consist of variations on this theme. To judge from them, a prospective infantry officer was dedicated to his career almost from birth. As soon as he was three feet tall he was immured in a barracks, where he was put through so severe a course of training that soon his head and body were scarred with wounds that never had a chance to heal. If he dared to rest he was beaten like a carpet,* and when at long last he was considered ready to go to the wars his life became a nightmare. 'Come, listen to my stories of his campaigns in Syria, and his marches over the mountains. He carries his bread and his water on his shoulders like an ass's burden; his spine is dislocated. He drinks brackish water and sleeps with one eye open. When he encounters the enemy he is like a bird caught in a snare and there is no strength left in his limbs. When the time comes for him to return to Egypt he is like a worm-eaten piece of wood. He is ill, paralysis seizes him and he has to be led on a donkey. His clothes have been filched by robbers and his orderly takes to his heels.'¹ The chariot-borne officer is spared these labours. In his early days, when he has been issued with two magnificent horses from the royal stables and five orderlies, he is cock-a-hoop and hurries

*Literally 'like a parchment'.

off to his own town to show himself off, issuing challenges to anyone bold enough to withhold their admiration. But he has had to supply two of his five orderlies, and now he has got to buy a chariot. The pole costs three *deben* of silver and the body five more, which accounts for the whole of the little fortune he has inherited from his parents. He gets involved in fresh quarrels, he falls and is injured, and his vehicle is abandoned in a ditch at the very moment when his superior officers are on their rounds of inspection. He is arrested and sentenced to be beaten. He is laid out on the ground and given a hundred blows.[2]

All this is an obvious caricature which proves, if it proves anything at all, that men of learning disliked the soldiers, who may well have reciprocated their sentiments. Veterans of many a campaign in Syria, Nubia or Libya who could return to Egypt and end their days in comfortable retirement like Ahmosé, the son of Abana, or could secure a sinecure about the court like Ahmosé of Nekhabit, did not in retrospect think their active service career ill spent. 'The name of a man of brave deeds,' says the son of Abana, 'shall never perish from the earth.' Besides, it was a profitable profession, with a distribution of booty after each victory. Anyone whose courage had been reported to the royal herald received not only a grant of land in his own town but, as a result of confiscations from the king's enemies, slaves of either sex as well.[3] Ahmosé, for example, was granted nineteen slaves and on several occasions, in recognition of his courage, was given gold in the form of necklaces and cups. They must have resembled the cup of Thouty which bears the following hieroglyphic inscription: 'Presented by favour of King Menkheperrê to the noble prince, divine father, the beloved of God, who rejoices the king's heart throughout all foreign lands and the islands of the Great Green, who fills the warehouses with lapis lazuli, with silver and with gold, overseer of foreign lands, commandant of soldiers, the man praised by the good god, whose future the lord of the two lands assures, the royal scribe, Thouty.'[3a]

Another regular soldier called Didou, who successively held the posts of commandant of the deserts west of Thebes, king's messenger to all foreign countries, standard-bearer to the king's personal bodyguard, captain of the vessel *Mery Amūn* and finally chief of police, also on a number of occasions received 'Gold of Praise'. He used to wear a number of gold bees and a lion passant on a ribbon round his neck above his necklace;[4] while another standard-bearer, a contemporary of his who rejoiced in the high sounding name of Nebkêmi (Lord of Egypt) had been given an electrum bracelet.[5]

More fortunate still was the standard-bearer Nebamūn, who had grown old in the service of the king; a man of courage and loyalty, who had never been punished or reprimanded in the whole of his long career. The king, in recognition of his services, took steps to ensure that he should enjoy an honoured old age in an elegant two-storied house with an inner courtyard shaded by a palm tree. It was to be furnished with servants, herds, land and serfs, while the whole estate was to be given special immunity from requisition by officials acting on the king's behalf, and the dignity of *amakhou** was conferred on Nebamūn himself. Pharaoh, who did not want to see him retire altogether from public service, appointed him chief of police on the western side of the town. These dignities and properties were bestowed upon him at a full ceremonial parade. When Nebamūn had been a standard-bearer he had served, like Didou, on the warship *Mery Amûn*, and his standard accordingly bore the device of a ship with central cabin, rudder and rigging. The whole of the crew had come by water to see their former commander honoured, the officers sitting on cross-legged stools and the men standing shoulder to shoulder in four ranks. Nebamūn handed over the standard which he had carried when he accompanied the lord of the two lands in the foreign countries of the south and the north, and did obeisance to it. An officer, one of the king's fan-bearers, then handed him a new standard with the device of a gazelle bearing an ostrich feather on its back, which was the insignia of the police force operating to the west of Thebes, together with a small palmiform column slightly longer than his hand, which may have contained a copy of the royal decree confirming Nebamūn's appointment. After this presentation the *Medjaiou*† moved off to march past their new commander, while two of their officers, Captain Teri and Lieutenant Mana, touched the ground before him with their knees and elbows. Nebamūn was then presented with a number of small flags, some square and some semi-circular, which no doubt bore

---

*An honour which entitled the holder to burial at the king's expense (see footnote, p. 260).
†The Nubian desert patrol.

the names, numbers or badges of the units comprising the *Medj-aiou* corps. Finally the bugle called the parade together and the march past began. At the head marched the standard-bearer followed by the archers, behind whom came the heavy infantry armed with spears and shields. As the archers passed in front of Nebamūn they 'presented arms' by holding out their bows in their right hands. Then they hung them round their necks so as to leave their arms free, and marched with clenched fists.[6]

Although we can be sure that men like this had no complaints about their treatment by their sovereign, we know far less about the junior officers and other ranks who could not afford to build themselves great tombs painted with scenes from their military careers. However, these very pictures give us some information about the life of the ordinary soldier. It is clear that the senior officers, the royal scribes and the recording scribes, men like Tjanouni, Horonemheb and Amenemheb, took a great deal of trouble over feeding their men. The general issue of rations usually consisted of bread, beef, wine, cakes, vegetables and a wide range of nourishing food. We can see the troops parading in good order, under the command of their non-commissioned officers, each man carrying his haversack. They open a door leading into a courtyard where they find jugs, baskets full of flat cakes, small rolls and pieces of meat. Some elderly men wearing white cloaks—clearly cooks and bakers—are seated on the ground behind the baskets. Scribes are recording the issue of the rations to the men.[7]

One of Nebamūn's responsibilities, on promotion to the command of the *Medjaiou*, was to supervise the training and welfare of recruits. He was fortunate in being able to perform this duty while sitting comfortably on a stool, assisted by two orderlies who are standing by with a second stool, a bag, sandals and walking-sticks. Under his supervision scribes are bringing and recording provisions, sealing wine jars and branding oxen.[8] This food was presumably not intended for Nebamūn's personal consumption, but for the troops under his command, since he was responsible for the welfare of the recruits.

Like earlier monarchs the Ramessids were anxious that their soldiers should be well fed and equipped and they did everything in their power to make them contented. This was the reason why Ramesses II reproached his army so bitterly for having abandoned him in the midst of his enemies with nothing save Amūn's help to rely on (p. 243).

'What cowards you, my charioteers, have shown yourselves! Truly I can feel no pride in you at all. Yet I have treated every one of you well in my own country. Did I not rise up like a lord? Were ye not poor? Each day, by my *ka*, I made you great. I set the son over the possessions of his father. I averted all evil from this land. I relieved you of your taxes and I gave you other things which had hitherto been taken from you. If any man uttered a wish, I saw that it was fulfilled. . . . No ruler has ever done more for his soldiers than I, your king, did for you. I allowed you to live in your towns without performing service as officers, and I did the same for my charioteers. I allowed them to go to their towns, saying, "Yet I will always find them ready in the time of battle and when the hour for marching strikes".'[9]

The king might well have asked himself whether he had not allowed the army to live too softly; but King Ramesses III held the same ideas. For several years after he came to the throne the defeated enemy did not venture into the open, and the soldiers had long lived with their families on what might be called unearned income, in the towns of their choice, and with plenty of spare time on their hands. 'In my reign I have allowed the soldiers and the charioteers to settle down. The Shardana (p. 234) and the Qahaq* slept at full length in their towns. No more need they fear the Nubian fighting men nor the enemy from Syria. The weapons and bows hung unused in the armouries. They were sated with food and drink and they never ceased to rejoice. Their wives and children lived beside them, and they looked not behind them, for their hearts were at ease. I was with them as the safeguard and shield for their bodies.'[10] In short, Herodotus's comments on the Egyptian army in the time of Psammetichus would have applied equally to the same army under the Ramessids. There were, he says, two kinds of soldiers, known as *calasiries* and *hermotybies*, a distinction corresponding to that drawn by Ramesses between infantry (*meshâou*) and charioteers (*tentheteri*). Soldiering had become a hereditary profession, son succeeding father in families who learned no other trade. They all owned property, while members of the royal bodyguard were entitled to extra rations of corn, wine and beef.[11]

*Mercenaries who originally came from Lybia.

2. *Service Inside Egypt*

Although when the kings of Thebes began the war of liberation against the Hyksos their army was composed solely of Egyptians, the practice of conscripting prisoners soon developed. The regiment commanded by Tjanouni, a royal scribe in the reign of Tuthmosis IV, contained a squadron of tough characters not in the least like Egyptian recruits.[12] The Egyptians are tall and

Egyptian infantry

slim, with broad shoulders and flat stomachs. These others are sturdy of limb and their hair grows down over their necks. Their belts emphasize the size of their stomachs—by any reckoning their most distinctive feature. They wear panthers' tails hanging down behind their backs to the calves of their legs. Although they clearly come from the south, they are not negroes. They march in perfect step, with long strides, each holding a staff in his right hand. Akhnaton actually preferred foreigners, and in his personal bodyguard in attendance on his way from the palace to the temple, Syrians, Libyans and Nubians visibly outnumber Egyptians.[13]

The first recorded appearance of Hittites serving in the Egyptian army occurs in the reign of Horonemheb, and that of the Peoples of the Sea in the reign of Sety I. The bodyguard of Ramesses II consisted entirely of Shardana,[13a] tall, slim, well-built men. Egyptian artists were very accurate observers and managed to catch the characteristics which distinguished the

Egyptians with their regular features and clean-cut profiles from the prognathous Negroes, the bony Libyans and the hook-nosed Semites. When one sees a band of mercenaries on a wall of the temple of Abydos, one is tempted to think that they are Europeans whom Pharaoh had enlisted in his army against the coalition of his enemies.[14] The successful campaigns of Ramesses III against the Libyans and the Peoples of the Sea enabled him to take a large number of prisoners who immediately on capture were branded like cattle, stamped with the king's name, sorted into squads and subjected to discipline on the Egyptian model.[15]

Training took the form of route marches and single combat. The king liked watching the fights and competitions organized among the best trained of the soldiers and would invite the Court to enjoy the spectacle.[16] At Medinet Habu a military tournament, organized for Ramesses III, is well depicted. The princes walk fan in hand, a pendant in their hair hanging across their cheek. They are accompanied by a few foreign princes, like, at a later date, the refugee Hadad, David's enemy. The Syrians are identifiable by the long scarves knotted round their body, their long hair held in place by a ribbon, and their beards. The Negro wears massive earrings and has an ostrich feather stuck in his hair. The Hittite and the Libyan have put on their finest clothes. All address Pharaoh in unison. 'Thou art like Mōnth, O Pharaoh (Life, Health, Strength!), our gracious lord. Amūn hath cast down those evildoers, the strangers that came against you.'

Now the contestants are in the arena. The first two antagonists are armed with sticks and wear the military loincloth, its ends forming a huge triangular apron, pointing downwards. Their left forearms are strapped up, and their right hands padded by a leather gauntlet, while their chins and both cheeks are protected by a thick bandage attached to a band round their foreheads. One of the contestants bows towards the royal prince, the commander-in-chief of the army, who encourages him by calling: 'To your heart, to your heart, O fighter!' The other of the pair lifts both his arms to heaven. Then they fall to, belabouring each other with their sticks, guarding their faces with their left hands the while and hurling insults at each other: 'Take care! I will show you the hand of a fighting man!'

The single-stick fighters are followed by wrestlers. An Egyptian lifts his Libyan opponent off the ground, while the latter retaliates by biting his hand. The Egyptian cries: 'Take care what you are doing, you biting Syrian! [*sic*] My master Pharaoh (Life, Health, Strength!) is on my side and is against you!' This may mean either that Pharaoh was going to intervene to stop the fight and punish the man who committed the foul, or merely that this unsportsmanlike behaviour was not going to prevent the Egyptian champion, backed by Pharaoh, from winning. In another scene two Egyptians are wrestling: the man on the left has lifted his opponent's leg off the ground and is announcing in barrack-room terms that he is going to throw him on the ground in front of Pharaoh.

In the last scene an Egyptian, possibly the winner of the last bout, is matched against a Negro. In defiance of normal convention the Egyptian referee is encouraging his compatriot: 'Remember that our good lord Pharaoh (Life, Health, Strength!) is watching you!' The Egyptian lifts up the Negro by the waist and is on the point of hurling him flat on the ground, saying as he does so: 'That's thrown you, you filthy nigger! I'll smash you to smithereens in front of Pharaoh!' It is the final throw: the Negro, who is on the ground on his knees and shoulders, must have thrown up the sponge, for his conqueror is standing upright and with arms uplifted is claiming victory. 'Amūn, the verdant god, the conqueror of strangers. The great regiment "Ousirmarê is the guide" has vanquished every land.'

On this occasion Egyptian pride was gratified, but we may perhaps speculate on what the Court would have thought if the foreigners had happened to win; we may guess they would not have been best pleased. But the author of the bas-relief of these scenes from the soldiers' life does not tell us explicitly either how the public reacted or what the winners received by way of prizes. On the other hand he has made a careful study of the foreign princes watching the spectacle from the second row of the spectators, and the impassivity of their countenances does not suggest that they found it particularly enjoyable.

3. *The Army in Wartime*

During the nineteenth and twentieth dynasties the Egyptian army had plenty of opportunities to display its prowess. To judge from official accounts and bas-reliefs, notably those recording the achievements of Sety I in Palestine and of Ramesses III against the Libyans and the Peoples of the Sea, military expeditions are presented like dramas in four acts; the first covering the issue of weapons and departure of the army; the second, a great battle in open country; the third, the siege and capture of a town; and the fourth, the triumphal return. Under the Ramessids, this sequence of events was common: nevertheless victory was as chancy a business as it is today. Although the Egyptians were reluctant to mention their defeats, we know that in fact they met with several severe reverses. For example, in the closing years of the eighteenth dynasty the troops of the Hittite King Subbiluliumma not only defeated the Egyptians but pursued them right across Syria in revenge for the murder of the prince who had gone to Egypt in response to the appeal of Pharaoh's widow.[17] But the period was, generally speaking, one of success for Egyptian arms. Let us follow them on their victorious way.

4. *The Collection and Distribution of Weapons*

Before beginning operations Pharaoh would usually consult his advisers, even if he had already decided on his line of action. This was the course followed by Kamosé, one of the liberators of Egypt, when, under the inspiration of Amūn, he decided to attack the Hyksos who had been in occupation of the whole of the Delta and Upper Egypt as far as the fourteenth nome, and whose ultimate aim was to extend their domination and forcibly impose the worship of their god Sutekh over those parts of Egypt which still remained independent. The counsellors, who were nervous, would have preferred to wait, for they were frightened of making even worse a situation which, though pretty bad, was at least familiar. But the king had his way and war was decided upon.[18] We do not know whether a messenger told the Hyksos of Pharaoh's designs or whether the invaders were only apprised of the Theban intentions when they saw them advancing northwards in battle order. The kings of the ancient Near East were indefatigable correspondents, for ever sending each other riddles, threats, claims or complaints, or informing each other of births, bereavements, or intrigues on someone's part. The end of hostilities between the Egyptians and the Hittites was finally marked by the conclusion of a treaty, duly signed, sealed and delivered, and containing a preamble, numerous articles and a conclusion, in the twenty-first year of the reign of Ramesses II.* For a long time this was regarded as the most ancient surviving treaty. We now possess several of greater antiquity, but not, as yet, any document constituting a formal declaration of war on another power. I think, however, that such documents must have existed, since, as we shall see, we know that the two sides were in communication during the progress of hostilities.

When war appeared imminent Pharaoh began to prepare his infantry and his personal bodyguard, the Shardana whom he had captured and brought back to Egypt in earlier campaigns, and armed and drilled them in fighting tactics. They formed a special unit under the king's personal command. The bulk of the army, comprising Egyptians, Syrians, Libyans and men from the southern regions, was divided into a number of regiments. Texts dating from the reign of Sety I refer to the regiments of Amūn (also known as Valiant Bows), of Rê (the Numerous Arms) and of Sutekh (the Powerful Bows).[19] A fourth regiment, that of Ptah, makes its first recorded appearance at the beginning of the reign of Ramesses II.

The issue of weapons and equipment was a solemn occasion, attended by the king in person.[20] Ramesses III, after taking up his position on a dais with a balustrade and resting his arms on a cushion, would take the salute and hear addresses from his officers. He would then speak himself: 'Bring forth the weapons, bring them out into the open so that the courage of my father Amūn may humble the rebellious lands that know not Egypt!' On these occasions he would stand wearing full dress costume including an elaborate loincloth and sandals on his feet, in the midst of a group consisting of the heir to the throne, the royal scribe and a number of senior officers. The different weapons would be stacked in piles. One would contain helmets of a design which completely covered both the head and the back of the neck of the wearer, with a visor and two strings falling from the crest and ending in tassels; a short distance away lay the javelins, triangular bows, quivers, short-sleeved coats of mail which protected the whole of the wearer's body, and swords with blades curved like sickles and long handles ending in a pommel, known in Egypt at *khopesh* (forearm). The soldiers would advance in single file, empty-handed

*c. 1280 B.C.

and wearing nothing but the loincloth with a triangular flap, receive their issue of arms and move off, while a large number of scribes made a note of their names and their weapons.

By the thirteenth century the Egyptians had come to adopt the weapons of their old adversaries the Syrians—indeed they had only been able to defeat them by doing so. The helmets which Ramesses III had issued to his troops (and of which, incidentally, we possess a picture in colour in one of the chambers of his tomb) are very like those worn by the Syrian soldiers and so are familiar to us not only from the battle scenes on the chariot of Tuthmosis IV, but also from pictures of foreigners bringing offerings and indeed from original Syrian works of art.[21] They are identical in shape, the only difference being that in the Egyptian version the horse's tail has been replaced by strings ending in tassels. The god Seth—commonly known in this period as Sutekh—the most Asiatic in character of the Egyptian deities, can be seen wearing a similar helmet with the additional frontal decoration of a solar disk, two sharply pointed horns and a long ribbon attached to the crest and falling almost to the ground, ending in a triangular flower. Since Sutekh was a warrior god, we might imagine that the military version of the helmet was simply that worn by the god with the necessary modifications to make it practical; but we must remember that Sutekh's equipment is oriental and that he has very close affinities with Baal (p. 277).

While the triangular bow had been in general use in Asia for a very long time, Egyptian practice had been far from consistent. Their original form of bow, with a double curve, had never been entirely abandoned but had been largely replaced, under the Old Kingdom, by a bow with a single curve. It was with this double-curved bow that Tuthmosis III and Amenophis II had pierced their copper targets (p. 210 f). By our period the entire Egyptian army had been issued with the triangular bow, possibly because it was easier to produce in quantity. It is well established that the curved-blade sword was a weapon whose origins lie far back in Asiatic history.[22] During the Middle Kingdom every king of Byblos had a ceremonial *khopesh*, of the finest workmanship, deposited in his tomb, while we possess a scene showing Syrian soldiers presenting an example to Menkheperrê-senb, the high priest of Amūn. Curved swords had been acquired in Syria by Tuthmosis III, and were recognized by the Egyptians as a formidable weapon. The king carried one for his personal use and his example was generally followed.

The coat of mail, in the form of a leather jerkin covered with small metal scales, was also a Syrian invention.[23] Most of the Syrians depicted on the chariot of Tuthmosis III are wearing this garment, though some instead have two wide straps crossing over the wearer's chest. Although the coat of mail could not preserve the 'vile soldiers of Retenou' from Pharaoh's arrows, the Egyptians had observed that it was not without its uses.

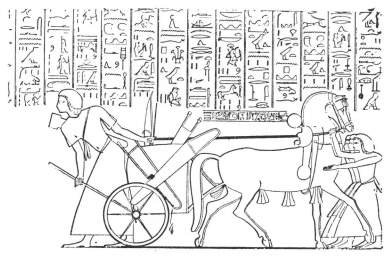

Pharaoh's chariot and groom

The chariot—a weapon of major tactical importance—had been borrowed by Egypt from Syria.[24] We do not know precisely when the horse became known in Syria, nor the exact date of the invention of the chariot: documents of Middle Kingdom date, from Syria as well as from Egypt, contain no reference to either.* They are not mentioned in the story of Kamosé, but we find both sides using horse and chariot from the beginning of the eighteenth dynasty onwards. The Syrians must have initiated the practice, since the Egyptian words both for the chariot itself and for its parts, as well as for horse and harness, are linguistically of Semitic

*But documents from Mari on the Euphrates now show that horses were known and prized by the rulers of states in Syria at least as early as the eighteenth century B.C.

origin, as are the decorations most commonly found on chariot bodies—palmettes, animals heraldically opposed and interlacing spirals. The chariots of Pharaoh and the Egyptian princes, however, with their gold overlay and embossing, represent a degree of luxury quite beyond the resources of the nobles of Retenou.[25] The harness too was decorated with gold plaques and reinforced with metal. Nevertheless we should not be so dazzled by their elegance and opulence as to forget that they were ill designed for their prime purpose—to make the fullest possible use of the horse's strength while still retaining full control over it. The head harness consisted of a noseband and two upright pieces which met at a cockade, together with a front, a headstrap and blinkers. The horse's head was surmounted by a flat covering containing a spray of artificial flowers or ostrich plumes. The reins and martingales were fastened to the bit and the place of the modern collar was taken by a harness consisting of three main pieces, namely a fairly wide rounded strap covering the withers, a thinner strap passing beneath the body, which was left fairly slack, and a tighter band round the horse's chest. The remainder of its body was left free. Streamers fluttering in the wind were attached to the harness and golden plaques glittered on the leather. The blinkers were engraved with figures of Sutekh, the lord of horses.[25a]

The crew of the chariot consisted of the driver and a fighting man. The former carried a whip which was often richly ornamented, while the latter was equipped with a bow and arrows and a dozen or so javelins, carried respectively in a quiver and in a container fixed to the body of the vehicle, the floor of which was about thirty inches above the ground, and rested directly upon the axle, unsupported by springs. Vehicles of this design were very liable to upset on the stony Syrian roads, though, provided they were not taken unawares, both the occupants would have time to jump out, since the chariot was open at the back. When a chariot came to grief, the best thing to do was to follow the Syrian practice of unharnessing the horses and jumping on their backs. The Egyptians did the same when circumstances demanded—or so at least I imagine; for in fact their artists, when depicting a battle scene, never envisaged the possibility of an Egyptian chariot being overturned.

When the Shardana were embodied in Pharaoh's army they used the same equipment as they had when they were fighting

Chariot of State of Tutankhamūn

Plate XI

against him. They still kept the loincloth, round shield, triangular-bladed sword and helmet, somewhat reminiscent of a round bowl worn upside down and surmounted by a disk and crescent crest. So did the Philistines, whose circlet of feathers made them easily recognizable in Pharaoh's armies. The Syrian panoply was sufficiently close to the Egyptian to cause no difficulties. A few Syrians continued to wear the pectoral and tasselled loincloth. The Negroes remained faithful to their immemorial double-curved bow, and many also carried throwing-sticks.

5. *The Order of March*

Let us imagine the Egyptian army marshalled on the plains of the Delta, and ready to move into action. Once again it is about to form column of route, starting with a brisk crossing of the bridge of Silé over the crocodile lake, a scene depicted in a relief of the time of Sety I on a temple wall at Karnak. At Medinet Habu we see the order of march of Ramesses III. At the head of the column an infantry regiment[26] is drawn up in ranks seven or eight deep. Next come the trumpets—though the straight instruments of copper or silver, a mere eighteen inches or so long, could only sound a few not very rousing notes. The drum had been invented, but I have never seen it depicted in scenes of active campaigning, although we can see it in use at such occasions as the enrolment of recruits or at festivities. This makes me think that it was only employed by the army at home.

Next comes a group of officers forming the king's personal staff, followed by a single chariot bearing the standard of the sacred ram crowned with the disk, thus ensuring that the entire army was under the protection of the great god of Thebes. Behind this chariot follows a second group of officers and finally, behind two parasol-bearers on foot, the royal chariot, driven by King Ramesses in person. Near the horses walks an unleashed lion. The entire army is on foot: first the various types of infantry, then the chariotry followed by the supply echelons marching behind their asses laden with bundles and jars or driving wagons drawn by six oxen. The Egyptians had had enough experience of the vastness of the desert and the poverty of Palestine to know that for a long time the army would have to live on what it had brought with it.

Eventually the long columns of fighting men and chariots, stretching endlessly along the road, reach the first watering point, known as Houpana, lying beside a *migdol* and a building called 'Lion fort'.[27] According to which route was followed, a series of watering points led either to Beersheba and Hebron or to Gaza on the coast. A succession of beaches, sand dunes and palm plantations stretched as far as Megiddo, from which point onwards the ground began to rise in a rocky outcrop. Beyond that, the gardens of Tyre and Sidon afforded a chance of welcome repose. There was plentiful refreshment to be enjoyed on the plain of Beirut, beyond which the snowy peaks of the high mountains began to come into view above the pine- and fir-clad hill slopes. Less than a day's march away the road ran beside a swift-flowing ice-cold torrent, past the stele engraved at the beginning of Ramesses' reign and already partly weathered away. Some distance farther on, beyond villages inhabited by fishermen, woodcutters and husbandmen, lay another river very much like the former, whose waters each year ran red with the blood of a god.* At this point the route turned up into the mountains, but a further short stage along the coast led to the holy city of Kapni (Byblos) whose shrewd and mercenary inhabitants were always on the lookout for a chance of selling their timber or hiring their boats to the Egyptians. It was worth halting at Kapni and invoking the protection of the goddess of the city, who bore a marked resemblance to Hathor of Memphis and Iounit. From here onwards the road led directly away from the sea, climbing steadily over the mountains towards the desert. The snow-clad ranges, so remote to a traveller on the coast, seemed scarcely higher than the pyramids seen from Memphis, while here at last there was a cool breeze to refresh the weary troops. The plateau ended in a steep drop down to a smiling plain, as richly cultivated as the valley of the Nile, dotted with many a town, and richly watered with fresh streams. Everyone knew that Qadesh was not far away.

6. *The Battle*

The enemy could, if he chose, conduct a purely defensive war from the shelter of his strongholds. If, however, he felt con-

---

*i.e. the Adonis river (Nahr Ibrahim) associated with the legend of Adonis and Astarte.

strained to meet the invader in the open field, convention required him to propose a fixed day and place for the battle and to have regard to his opponent's convenience. When Piankhi of Ethiopia dispatched his army northwards against Egypt, he recalled this convention—or rather this law—in a famous order of the day:

'Let neither side attack by night, but fight in full view, in obedience to the rules of the contest: give your adversary notice of the conflict from afar. If he says that his infantry or the cavalry from some other town are behind their time, then wait until the whole of his army has assembled and fight only when he gives the word. If his allies happen to be in some other town, wait for them. Let the Libyan princes, his faithful fighting men, whom he is summoning to his aid, be warned in advance of the struggle with the words "Do thou, whoever thou mayst be, who commandest the troops, harness the finest steeds from thy stable, and draw up thy line of battle. Thou shalt learn that Amūn is the god that hath sent us".'[28]

Piankhi's orders have sometimes been misunderstood.[29] In actual fact they represented strict compliance with the laws of warfare as the ancient world and the Middle Ages observed them—or at least subscribed to them. We are reminded by Montaigne of how, after the legate Lucius Marcius had practised a stratagem, 'the elders of the Senate, mindful of the ways of their fathers, condemned this ruse as hostile to their ancient practice, which, said they, relies on courage, not on subtlety: neither on surprises and encounters by night, nor on deliberate flights and unexpected counter attacks: not making war without having first proclaimed it and, often, having agreed upon the hour and the place of the battle.'[30] From the Egyptians to the ancient Romans, custom had not altered and, thanks to Montaigne, we can understand what the Ethiopian leader meant by his 'rules of the contest'. The two adversaries must take up positions openly facing each other without any attempt to conceal either their strength or their intentions and the struggle must be on purely equal terms, precisely as two chess players begin the game with an equal number of pieces. God would grant victory to the better side.

Proof that the Egyptians had adopted this sporting practice well before the time of Piankhi can be found in the epithet often applied to Seth, the warrior god, of 'announcer of battle',[31] and

even clearer evidence is afforded by the account of the battle of
Megiddo when the army of Tuthmosis III engaged a coalition of
Asiatic powers.[32]

The Egyptian army had arrived at the town of Yiehem on the
sixteenth day of the first month of *shemou*. The king summoned his
warriors to a council at which he told them that the 'vile Fallen
One' of Qadesh had set up his headquarters at Megiddo, where
he had gathered round him the leaders of those countries

The Egyptian camp near Qadesh

that were formerly vassals* of Egypt as far as Naharina and had
said to them: 'I shall wait here at Megiddo to engage the Egyptian
king in battle.' 'Give me your advice,' added the Egyptian monarch. His councillors suspected a trap. The direct road from
Yiehem to Megiddo narrowed sharply. Both men and horses
would have to move in single file, so that the advance guard
would be in action before the rear guard was clear of Alouna.
It would be much wiser to take a roundabout road which would
enable the army to reach Megiddo from the north in a compact
formation. This highly sensible advice was rejected by Pharaoh,
who cried: 'By my life and by Rê who loves me, by my father
Amūn's favour to me, by my nose that breathes life and duration,
My Majesty will march by the high road from Alouna. Let him
among you who wishes, take the road of which you speak, and
him who will, follow My Majesty. Our foes, whom Rê abhors,
would think "the king goes by another road afar for fear of us".'

*Literally 'on the water of . . . .'

This outburst disarmed all opposition. In the king's presence they declared: 'Lo, we will follow Thy Majesty whithersoever thou goest; where the master leads the servant will follow.'

In the light of the procedure defined by Piankhi, the situation confronting the council of war seems quite clear. The Fallen One of Qadesh had sent Pharaoh a message proposing a definite day and site for the battle. The councillors suspected a trap, but Tuthmosis considered that it would be unworthy of both himself and the divinities who loved and protected him to seek to evade a challenge couched in the due and traditional form. Events proved him right. Led by the king, the army entered the narrow valley, which it completely filled. The officers, who were still keenly suspicious, implored the monarch to heed them at least to the extent of not himself advancing until the rearguard had safely passed the danger point. This precaution, however, proved to be superfluous. From their positions between Taanach and Megiddo the enemy made no attempt to interfere with the manoeuvres of the Egyptian army, which was able to take up its battle positions south of Megiddo towards midday and there prepare at leisure for the battle which was scheduled for the following morning. The rules of warfare had been properly observed.

In urging Pharaoh to be cautious, however, his councillors were doing their duty. The army facing them, though commanded by the king of Mitanni, included a large number of *Aamou*,* the age-old and treacherous foes of Egypt, of whom an early king of the eleventh dynasty had said, in the instruction which he drew up for his son, Merikarê, 'The accursed *Aamou* . . . can never stay still, his feet are always on the move. Since the beginning of time he has fought, never victor, never vanquished; like a man of evil intent he never says when he will strike. . . .'[33] The *Aamou*, familiar as they were with the woods and mountains, always avoided fighting in open country, where they would be at a disadvantage, preferring to harass the Egyptian army and then vanish, and relying primarily on stealth and stratagem. None the less, even when the Egyptians engaged an enemy of their own size, the element of surprise was not wholly eliminated, and it was destined to play a decisive and, for the Egyptians, disastrous part before Qadesh when Ramesses II and his army met the Hittite army in battle.[34]

*A general name for Asiatics.

Let us now return to our army approaching Qadesh. The vile Fallen One of Hatti* had marshalled against Egypt all the northern countries as far as the farthest shores of the ocean. Besides the traditional enemies of Egypt, who occupied the whole of the area from the Syrian coast to the Euphrates, there were the people of Asia Minor, Dardanians, contingents from Ilion (Troy), Kashkash and Qarqesh, Lycians and European peoples like the Mysians. The Hittite king had spared no expense in his efforts to bring them over to his side. So great were their numbers, so thickly were they spread over mountain and valley, that they seemed like a swarm of locusts. All these troops lay in concealment north-east of Qadesh. The Egyptians, whose spies had entirely failed to discover them and who therefore thought that they were still delayed somewhere near Aleppo, advanced confidently along the Orontes valley. Ramesses himself, after fording the river, led the march with his bodyguard, followed by the regiment of Amūn. The regiment of Rê was only fording the Orontes at Shabtoun, while the regiment of Ptah was waiting in its quarters at Irnam until the ford was free. The regiment of Sutekh, a long way in the rear, was straining to make up lost ground, but was still several days' march away.

While the king was at Shabtoun two of the Bedouin *Shasou*, who were in the habit of attacking caravans passing between Syria and Egypt and farmers in the Delta near the isthmus of Suez, sought an audience to say, on behalf of their kinsmen, that they wanted to defect from the king of the Hittites and take service with Egypt. In reply to Pharaoh's question, 'Where are your kinsmen and what news have you to tell?' they replied that they were in the same place as the hated Hittite king; the Fallen One of Hatti was in the country of Aleppo, north of Tunip, too frightened to move southwards since he had heard that Pharaoh (Life, Health, Strength!) was making northwards. This was quite untrue. The Bedouin were actually spies sent by order of the Hittite king to discover the Egyptian whereabouts and to try, by giving misleading information, to lull them into a sense of false security.

The upshot was that the king decided to encamp north of Qadesh on the west bank of the Orontes.† A huge rectangle was

---

*The name given by the Egyptians to the Hittite king Mutallu.

†The description which follows is of the relief in Luxor depicting the army encamped.

marked out on the plain, and round it a stockade of shields, or of objects resembling shields, was erected. In the centre we can see that one large tent has been put up for the king's use besides three smaller ones, while still smaller tents are dotted about all over the enclosure. The king's lion lies dozing on the ground, tethered by the foot, while the horses have been unharnessed to feed. The donkeys have been unloaded and are rolling in the dust, kicking up their heels or galloping about. Weapons and bundles are being piled up, and fresh carts, drawn by oxen, are entering the camp. Senior officers for their part are making themselves comfortable in wooden huts with roofs resting on a single upright post, each fitted with a door, like a house, containing water jars and basins on stands. Stoves and tables, stools and mats have all been unpacked. Men on fatigue duty under the command of a N.C.O. are sprinkling water and sweeping up dust, while others are busy on a variety of errands, driving donkeys or carrying bundles slung on yokes. Beside the huts a horse has plunged its head in its manger. A groom is quieting down another pair of restless chargers, while the charioteer is comfortably ensconced in the body of his chariot and is sound asleep. One of the soldiers is drinking: no one has the slightest inkling of danger.[35] But an Egyptian patrol has captured two scouts sent out by the Hittite king, and they are led before Pharaoh on his golden throne mounted on a dais. The stick is an unrivalled method of loosening a man's tongue and the prisoners are ready to answer every question. 'We are in the service of the Hittite king who sent us to see where Your Majesty was.' 'But where is the Fallen One of Hatti? I was told that he is in the land of Aleppo, north of Tunip!' 'See,

E. L. E.—R

the accursed king of Hatti is coming hither with the many nations who are his allies . . . they outnumber the sands of the sea. Even now they are in position and ready to fight around Old Qadesh.' The king bursts out in fury: 'So! the enemy are in hiding round Old Qadesh and neither my foreign chieftains nor my Egyptian officers with them knew anything about it, and now we are told that they are upon us.' The councillors admit that shocking mistakes have been made. 'It is bad, it is a serious mistake on the part of the foreign commanders and the officers of Pharaoh (Life, Health, Strength!) to have failed to disclose the whereabouts of the accursed Fallen One of Hatti in their daily reports to Pharaoh (Life, Health, Strength!)' The vizier was ordered to bring up the laggard elements south of Shabtoun to the king's present position with all possible speed, but even while the king was discussing the situation the accursed Fallen One of Hatti was advancing with his troops and equipment and all his allies, and crossing an undefended ford south of Qadesh. The Egyptian troops and chariots were caught completely off their guard and fled in disorder and the enemy were actually able to capture some of the king's personal bodyguard.

In this crisis the king rose up like his father Mōnth, grasped his accoutrements, and donned his breastplate. 'He was like Baal in his hour.' When his squire Menna saw what a multitude of chariots were swarming round his master, he began to tremble, his heart failed him and he was sore afraid. He said to the king: 'My good lord, O my brave sovereign, great protector of Egypt in the day of battle, we are all alone in the midst of our enemies. Our soldiers with their weapons have deserted us. How will you save them? Make us pure. Save us, O Ousirmarê!'

The king, wholly unafraid, reassures him. Although his troops have deserted him, seeking for booty instead of standing their ground, and although neither prince nor squire, guide nor officer is at his side, not in vain has Ramesses built countless monuments, and erected obelisks without number in honour of his father, not in vain has he filled his 'Houses of a Million Years' with numberless captives and dispatched convoys laden with rare produce. The king's cry for help is heard even in Thebes; and it is answered by an ally worth more than any number of soldiers. Loosing a hail of arrows to his right, Ramesses parries the assault to his left. The twenty-five hundred enemy chariots are overthrown and their

horses laid low. No more will their hands avail them. Their hearts
are fallen into their stomachs; no more can they shoot nor grip
their swords. The king drives them into the water like crocodiles.
Those who are laid low do not rise again. The accursed Hittite
king who fought against the Egyptian monarch, surrounded by
his troops and his chariots each manned by three warriors, takes
to his heels in terror. His troops with their accoutrements, his
allies, the kings of Irtou, Mesa, Alouna, Lycia, Dardania, Carche-
mish, Qarqesh and Aleppo and his own brothers all flee headlong
in amazement at Pharaoh's courage, crying out 'Each man for
himself'. The king pursues them like a griffin, and charges against
them five times, like Baal in the moment of his might. He sets fire
to the countryside of Qadesh that the place which had been
trampled by the enemy host may be obliterated.

Now that the battle had been won by Pharaoh's strength and
courage—and by some other agency which the author of the poem
judges it inexpedient to disclose—the Egyptian troops make their
belated appearance. The king pours sarcasm on them. 'Not one of
you was there . . . not one man to lift his hand to help me in my
fight . . . I call the *ka* of Amūn my father to witness . . . no
man among you came that he may tell of his exploits hereafter in
the land of Egypt . . . the strangers who have seen me will tell
of my valour, yea, to the very unknown ends of the earth.'

Humbly the troops give thanks for their lord's bravery, and his
nobles and attendants praise the strength of his arm. 'Glorious
lionhearted warrior, thou hast saved thy army and thy chariots.
Thou art the son of Amūn, who dost great deeds with thy arms.
With thy strong arm thou hast bound the land of Hatti. Thou hast
broken the back of Hatti for ever.'

The king merely answers with fresh reproaches: '. . . fair is
the name of him who has fought bravely. Since the beginning of
time men have earned respect for deeds of their arms, but I will
not reward any man among you, for you deserted me when I was
alone in the midst of my enemies.'

These reprimands were not very alarming: they merely meant
that the army had forfeited its chance of reward. It was left to
another king, Piankhi, completely to lose his temper with his army
—despite the fact that it had fought well. Although it had forced
Tef-nakht to fly northwards with the enfeebled remnants of his
forces, the king had set his heart on the capture or annihilation of

all his enemies at one stroke. When the troops realized their king's disappointment, they took three strongholds in the teeth of a desperate defence. But even this news did not mollify Piankhi. One day the king made an appearance in his two-horsed chariot on the deck of his river-boat, whence, raging like a panther, he lashed the soldiers with his tongue. 'Are you waiting for a messenger from me to fight these men? Must I wait till the year's end before my fear is felt throughout the Delta?' All his soldiers smote themselves in an extremity of distress.[36]

Now after the victory at Qadesh the accursed Hittite king, the Fallen One, sent a messenger to praise the name of Pharaoh as highly as that of Rê, saying: 'Thou art Sutekh, yea, Baal himself, the fear thou inspirest runs like a fire through the land of Hatti.' The messenger was the bearer of a letter which was nothing more nor less than a request for an armistice. 'This thy servant speaks and acknowledges thee as the very son of Rê. He hath granted thee all the lands together. The land of Kêmi (Egypt) and the land of the Hittites stand ready to do thy pleasure; they lie at your feet. Prâ, thy honourable father, hath granted them to thee to exercise dominion over us . . . is it good to slay thy servants? . . . see what thou hast done yesterday, when thou didst slay millions . . . thou shalt leave no inheritance. . . . Despoil not thy possessions, O mighty king, glorious in battle. Grant us the breath of life.'[37]

The king immediately summoned the leaders of the army and his staff and the nobles and informed them of the message he had received from the accursed Hittite king. Without a moment's hesitation they unanimously exclaimed, 'Yea, peace is good, yea, exceedingly good, our sovereign lord.' This was their heartfelt conviction; but they immediately corrected themselves. 'There is no harm in peace if thou dost make it. Who shall greet thee in the day of thy wrath?'[38]

This was the advice the king wanted to hear, and the Egyptian army peacefully retired southwards without having captured Qadesh, whose crenellated battlements were plainly visible beyond a branch of the Orontes.

The truth was that Pharaoh had narrowly escaped complete disaster. Badly briefed on the Hittite dispositions, without sending forward scouts or covering his flanks he had thrust his army forward into hostile territory. He owed his escape to the fighting qualities of the royal bodyguard, mainly consisting of Shardana, for it is noteworthy that his criticisms are solely directed at the Egyptians. Perhaps when the Hittites had forced their way into the Egyptian camp they had been distracted by plunder so that their greed had changed their initial success into defeat. Their king was well satisfied to get this great army to depart so cheaply.

Other military ventures—for example the great battle won by Ramesses III against the Libyans—led to more clear cut results.[39] Like his forebear and namesake the king was in the thick of the fight. He drove his chariot at full gallop, tying the reins to his belt to leave his arms free to draw his bow. He wore a military helmet on his head, bracelets on both arms and circlets on his wrists. Two broad straps crossed on his chest and an open quiver was slung over his shoulder, while the sheath fixed to the side of the chariot was full of javelins. The officer who rode in the chariot behind the king did not take part in the fighting but carried the golden jug and cup which we noticed when the expedition left Egypt (p. 28). The royal chariot was followed by others, each manned by two fighting men. The Philistines who had enlisted in the Egyptian army performed prodigies of valour in this engagement. The Libyan chieftain Meshesher, son of Kapouro, whose horses had been slain and whose companion had been transfixed by a spear and had fallen from his chariot, realized that all was lost. He turned to Pharaoh and, raising his arms with his little finger upright, admitted defeat. Whole detachments of his troops surrendered together, holding their long swords upright like candles and stretching out their left arms with hands turned palm downwards.[40]

Again, in the reign of Ramesses III, countless hordes of the Peoples of the Sea had made their appearance on every sea and overland route that led to Egypt.[41] The women and children travelled in buffalo-drawn carts with solid wheels secured by linch-pins. Their long ships, high pooped and with lion's or bird's head prows, were packed to the gunwale with warriors. There was bitter fighting both by sea and land. The king jumped down from his chariot the better to wield his bow, accompanied by the whole of his personal staff—the officers who carried his bow, quiver, and javelin, the servants who between them bore all his toilet articles, his ostrich feather sunshade, and the bags containing changes of clothing: everything, in fact, that he might need to repair the ravages of battle.

After victory had been won the king mounted a dais to survey the battlefield. The bearers held sunshades at arm's length to give him shade, and the standards were ranked near by. Even while the princes and the military leaders were offering the king their congratulations a prolonged census, to estimate the magnitude of the victory, had begun. As in the time of Ahmosé, every warrior who killed an enemy cut off his hand and, if the victim were a Libyan, his male organ. All these trophies were presented to the royal heralds and then thrown with the weapons into a heap on the battlefield near the dais, where they were patiently sorted and counted by an army of scribes. The prisoners were bound or pinioned and paraded before the king. The most important were kept back to play their part in other ceremonies, while the uninjured were made to wait in little groups and thrust forward in turn to be branded. Soldiers armed to the teeth stood by ready to quell any flicker of revolt, but the defeated troops were resigned to their fate.[42] Once branded, the Danaoi and the Philistines were destined for embodiment in the Egyptian army, in which the proportion of native Egyptians was steadily diminishing. For the time being it paid to employ foreign troops.

7. *Siege Warfare*

Quite frequently war meant siege warfare, either because the enemy dared not meet the Egyptian army in open battle or because open fighting had still left him with enough troops for the defence of his fortresses, which were generally built on high ground, sometimes on precipitous mountains. The main defensive features were a moat filled with water and a stockade. The surrounding forest afforded shelter for fugitives and for those who had not had time to gain the walls before the gates were shut, and into it they would drive their herds of oxen, preferring the risk of being eaten by bears to facing the Egyptian arrows. The area immediately surrounding a fortress was generally cultivated, the slopes being covered with vines and fig trees, and the roads lined with flowering shrubs. Before finally retreating, the Egyptians would be sure to follow the normal practice of cutting down any valuable trees.[43]

In Syria the usual fortress plan consisted of high crenellated towers with projecting platforms and long walls following the

Plate XII   The Siege of Dapur

contours of the ground, pierced at intervals by windows and gates. Towns were quite often defended by two or three concentric series of defences, and examples are known of two or even three towers of diminishing size on top of each other, with a flag waving from the summit.[44] In temple reliefs depicting siege scenes, we can see the Egyptians raining a hail of arrows into the embrasures and driving the fugitives before them. Those who have already gained the safety of the walls are leaning forward and stretching out their hands to haul up a few laggards, while some of the defenders are hurling arrows, javelins and stones, and others, sword in hand, await the attackers. The priest is burning some resin in a portable censer, resembling the incense burner known in Egyptian as *akh*, to summon the gods of the city to its aid, his hands upraised like Moses during the battle against the Amalekites; from time to time he leans over the parapet to encourage the men fighting below him. But all the defensive measures are of no avail. The approaches to the fortress are strewn with corpses and the defenders die where they stand. It is not long before the Egyptians are at the foot of the walls, breaking down the gates with axe blows and setting up great scaling ladders, and soon the outer defences are in their hands.

When things had reached this point the only course open to the besieged, if they valued their lives, was to capitulate and to try to temper the ferocity of the victors by gifts. The ruler of Amor turns his censer towards Ramesses III, making a gesture of adoration with his left arm as he does so. 'Grant us the breath of life that we may breathe by thy might from one generation to another.'[45] One by one the chieftains emerge, some of them grovelling on knees and elbows, others bearing great bowls filled with artificial flowers, amphorae decorated with animal figures in high relief, or jewels. Objects of this character were greatly valued by the king and the chief priests, by whom they would ultimately be consigned to the temple treasuries. Other types of spoil—grain, wine, livestock and weapons—were matters of interest to the entire army, for they enabled the troops to eat and drink uninterruptedly on a scale equalled in Egypt only by the rich during festivals. The towns of Syria were rich in horses and the pick of the fighting men were mounted in chariots. In Megiddo alone Tuthmosis III captured the gold-plated chariots of the 'vile Fallen Ones' of that city and of Qadesh as well as 892 chariots of his accursed troops. True, these princes had assembled a considerable coalition against Egypt and allies had come to join them from as far as the Euphrates. But victory had put the king in a good humour and he sent these princes back to their distant lands riding backwards on donkeys.

Forests covered the hills of the Lebanon, and from time immemorial the Egyptians had made their way to Byblos in search of wood for their sacred ships, for the flag poles erected in front of the temple pylons, and for a multitude of other purposes, both religious and secular. The fir-tree (*āsh*) yielded the most highly valued timber, capable of taking a finer point than the beard of an ear of barley and straight as a lance: while other highly regarded species included the red wood of the cedar (*mer*), the carob (*sesnedjem*) and an unidentified species known as *wān*, which may have been juniper.[45a] Once they were masters of Syria, the Egyptians set methodically to work to exploit its forests. By Tuthmosis III's orders, his troops scattered over the mountains and felled the trees, whereupon the Syrian chieftains hauled them with oxen to the water's edge. A fleet of ships specially built for the purpose was used to transport the princes of Lebanon with the rich produce of the Divine Land.[46] By the nineteenth dynasty of Egypt, Lebanon was no longer a colony to be exploited, for the Hittites were trying to gain a foothold there, while the inhabitants themselves were better able to protect themselves. Nevertheless vast quantities of raw materials and goods found their way annually to Egypt, and Sety I was still in a position to force the rulers of the country to fell their fir-trees at his command.[47]

8. *Warfare in Nubia*

War against the peoples south of Egypt seems to have presented no military problems whatever, since the Egyptians had only to surround the dowars.* The Nubian men wore panther skins and were equipped with a shield and a large slashing sword; the women, who carried their babies in slings on their backs, would collect their children and run to try and hide in the palm groves. The one-sided struggle was bound to end in victory for the Egyptians and in a rich haul of loot, for the local population was extremely industrious and manufactured a considerable quan-

*Native encampments.

tity of furniture, at once luxurious and barbaric, of gold, ebony and ivory. Their huts were filled with masses of ostrich feathers, elephant tusks, panther skins, horns and perfumes.[48]

9. *The Triumphal Return*

Pharaoh has displayed his might in every part of the world, and every place where the sun shines has witnessed his success. He has fixed his frontiers where he pleased, as his father Amon-Rê and all the gods his fathers had decreed. Nothing now remains to do save to return to his Beloved Land Tomery and there receive the acclamations of his people and the adoration of the priests who are even now preparing to cover the pages of their ledgers with names and figures, to devote the pick of the booty to the gods, to reward the brave and to punish the rebellious as an example to the whole world.

On the homeward journey the army keeps more or less the same order as when it had first set out. The prisoners of high rank march in front of the royal chariot, their hands held fast in a pillory which was sometimes shaped like a panther, and with ropes round their necks. Most of them have their arms bound behind their backs or tied above their heads.[49] As soon as the Egyptian frontier is crossed the celebrations begin. Priests, gathered in front of the bridge of Silé, offer bunches of flowers.[50] It was necessary for some of the most important prisoners to be ceremonially killed. Amenophis II indeed, after the manner of Hercules, slew eight at the bow of his ship, six being hung in front of the temple wall at Thebes and the remaining two at Napata 'to bear witness to the victories of the king for ever and for aye, in all the lands and all mountains of the land of the Negro'.[51] At the last moment the vanquished once again make their gesture of submission, the Libyans by raising their first finger, the others by turning the palm of their hands towards their executioner. After the victory of Ramesses III, Kapouro, the aged Libyan king, had written to Pharaoh begging him to spare his son, who had been captured alive, and offering himself to be punished in his stead.[52] His request was not granted. The Libyan menace to Egypt had become so grave that Pharaoh was not prepared to show clemency. In the words of Pharaoh's political testament: 'They had established themselves firmly in Egypt, for they had captured towns in the west of the country from Hatkaptah as far as Qarban. They had penetrated as far as the whole bank of the great stream,* in many years plundering the towns of the district and seizing the oxen. But though they were in Egypt, I destroyed them, slaying them all at one time. . . . I drove them back over the frontiers of Egypt. The rest in their multitudes I gathered as my spoil, with blows of my sword, driving them like birds before my horses, yea, their women and their children by tens of thousands and their cattle by millions. Their princes I drafted into my army. I gave them commanders of the archers and leaders of their tribes. I branded them as slaves sealed with my name.'[53]

After the execution of those of the prisoners destined for punishment, another ceremony took place in the temple, at which not only was the fate of the remainder of the prisoners decided, but the booty was also consecrated to the gods.

A Shardana and a Philistine led prisoner

The treasures brought back from the cursed land of the Hittites were spread out in front of the images of the gods—cups and amphorae, rhytons and goblets of gold and silver, set with precious stones, like those offered by the Syrians when yielding their

*The Nile.

besieged city, or those brought in time of peace by emissaries from Retenou, Amor or Naharina as their military contribution or in token of vassalage 'upon the king's water'. In due course the king arrives, followed by the prisoners—Negroes, Libyans, Syrians, *Aamou*, Amorites, or Hittites—with hands bound and ropes round their necks.

The prisoners acknowledge defeat. Pharaoh is like a fire sweeping through waterless places. He suppresses every rebellion and every impious word. He can remove man's breath from his nostrils. Pharaoh for his part acknowledges that victory over his foes is a gift from his father Amūn, and in presenting part of the prisoners and treasure to the temples of the gods, he is but returning what they have given to him.[54]

CHAPTER X

SCRIBES AND JUDGES

1. *Administration*

FROM the dawn of her history Egypt had enjoyed sound administrative machinery. As early as the first dynasty officials of the royal household were using a cylinder seal to stamp their names and titles on the stoppers of jars. Every individual known to us, from statue, stele or tomb, possessed at least one title, while some ran to several dozen. During the Old Kingdom, indeed, there were enough names and official titles to fill a book. From our chosen period we possess a handbook or catalogue of the Egyptian hierarchy.[1] The list is headed by the gods and goddesses. Next come the spirits, the reigning king, the royal spouse, the divine mother of the king and the royal children, followed by the magistrates, with the vizier at their head, and all those who enjoyed the good fortune to live near the Sun,* namely the royal sons, the military commanders, scribes attached to the royal library, chamberlains, heralds, sunshade- and fan-bearers, royal scribes, officials of the White House,† the scribe in charge of the rolls of the supreme court, and the scribes concerned with taxation. Another list enumerates the king's representatives in foreign countries and in the provinces and towns of Egypt, the royal messengers in every land, the keeper of the seal for the House of the Sea, and the superintendent of the mouths of the canals. There was almost no limit to the number of specialized jobs. Each high official had a large personal staff. The governors of the various nomes lived, as far as they could, in their own residences like Pharaoh in his capital and maintained a household modelled on that of the king. The immense wealth of a god like Amūn had resulted in the creation of a highly specialized and minutely graded body of temple

*The king.
†The Treasury.

officials.[2] The entourage of the First Prophet included a major-domo, a head steward, a chamberlain, a guard of the chamber, a staff of scribes, a commander of sailors, and numerous servants. His deputy also had a personal staff, and even the Fourth Prophet would think himself gravely slighted if he did not have his own little retinue to accompany him on all his occasions. Nor must we forget the army of officials, foremen and scribes who shared responsibility for each of the operations and improvements which the leading priests decided to undertake. The most important of them were the directors and scribes of the Treasury, the chief officer of the Treasury seal, and the scribe of the divine seal of the house of Amūn. A deity such as Min, lord of Coptos and Ipou, less universally worshipped than Amūn, but still of considerable importance, possessed not merely a large staff of priests but a considerable administrative cadre of scribes, foremen of works, head herdsmen, linen-masters, superintendents of transport, store-keepers and accountants.[3] The Egyptian administrative machine shared the universal tendency to expand rather than to contract. Throughout the thirty-one years of his reign Ramesses III had consistently enriched the gods; and every extension of their pos-sessions meant the creation of more jobs. There was a constant demand for more scribes to raise and collect taxes, to muster slaves, or to see that canals, roads, quays and warehouses were kept in proper repair.

2. *Recruitment and Training of Officials*

The nineteenth dynasty was founded by a certain Paramses,* who, in the course of a long career, had held a number of im-portant civilian posts, religious offices and military commands in the eastern district of the Delta. When he was summoned by king Horonemheb to Thebes to supervise building in the temple of Opet, he devised most of his titles and positions to his son Sety, already a man in the prime of life.[4] The conduct of high officials was imitated by lesser ones. A certain Neferperit, who was a member of Pharaoh's personal staff on the expedition to the mountains of Retenou, had dispatched to Egypt four Phoenician cows, two Egyptian cows and one bull, all consigned to the House of a Million Years. He managed to get his brother put in

*Later Ramesses I.

charge of this little convoy and his son appointed as carrier of the milk jars. Jobs of this kind were not merely guaranteed during the holder's lifetime, but they generally became hereditary in the family and passed from father to son, and from heir to heir.[5] This practice aroused no criticism: indeed all fathers of families were anxious to do the same. A formula designed to be read by visitors to tombs runs: 'If you wish to bequeath your offices to your children, then say . . .' Anyone who misbehaved in a tomb was faced with a serious threat. 'He will not be. His son will not be in his place.' The law prescribed that a disobedient official should not merely himself lose his post and be severely punished but that in addition he should be punished through his children, who should be degraded to the status of labourers or serfs.[6] It would nevertheless be a mistake to conclude from these texts that as soon as their holder died jobs which involved heavy responsibility, and required considerable ability for their satisfactory performance, were immediately given to his son. In practice the children of officials started their career in the administration immediately on leaving school and were promoted according to their keenness and ability and in proportion to the influence of their patron.

Schools generally formed part of a temple. Bakenkhonsou, who afterwards became high priest of Amūn, studied for twelve years in the 'writing school' in the temple of the Lady of Heaven.[7] School exercises written on papyri have been found in the precinct of the Ramesseum, at Tanis, at Deir el Medineh and elsewhere. Education began early. Bakenkhonsou was sent to school when he was only five: but then his father, who was himself a distinguished priest and cherished ambitions for his son, may have forced him rather more than a normal child. However it is generally true that the day when little boys stopped going about naked and tied the knot of their first girdle more or less coincided with their first experience of school.

Although, as we know, the prospective official was taken from his parents at an early age, schools were usually day schools. The small pupil carried a little basket containing a crust of bread and a jug of beer prepared for him each morning by his mother.[8] The daily journey to school and home again gave him plenty of time to squabble and exchange blows with his small schoolfellows. In a recently published Egyptian story we read of a boy so clever that he got ahead of his older companions. They knew how to find his weak spot and asked him one day: 'Whose son are you? Haven't you got a father?' When he remained silent they went on laughing at him and hitting him, saying: 'Whose son are you? You haven't got a father at home!'[9]

The first lessons consisted of reading and writing. Papyrus was as a rule far too valuable to be given to schoolboys and they were issued instead for their exercises with highly polished limestone slabs ruled with lines or squares. At Thebes rough flakes of limestone were generally used. These served both as exercise books, in which the pupils were set to trace single hieroglyphic or cursive signs and make little drawings or copy out passages of gradually increasing length, and as text-books. Some surviving examples actually bear dates. If we had enough of these school books sufficiently well preserved we could work out how many days a pupil needed to study or learn by heart one of the Egyptian classics —a text such as the Hymn to the Nile or the Instructions of Amenemhat.[10] When he had spoiled enough of this cheap material the schoolboy—promoted thereby to the status of student—was allowed to use a whole lovely new papyrus to copy, no mere extract, but a complete work. He would kneel down and unroll an area of the virgin papyrus equal to a page of the model. He had already prepared his red and black inks and selected the appropriate size of reed pen from his pen-case: and now he began to

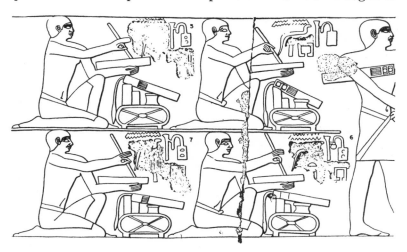

copy a story or a moral or poetical work or some model letters. Titles and chapter headings were written in red ink and the ordinary text in black. Every scribe, however, was also both draughtsman and painter and used green, blue, yellow or white inks for illuminating his text.[10a]

Education meant more than the study of grammar and writing, familiarity with classical texts and stories of the gods, and a little drawing. Egyptian officials might find themselves confronted by an immense range of jobs and were capable of switching from one to the other with remarkable ease. Ouni, for example, began his career as a police officer and judge, then made long journeys of exploration in search of stone, built boats and cleaned out the canals, and finally, when war broke out, served as chief of staff. Accordingly students had to familiarize themselves with the laws and regulations, with history and geography and with the principal technical processes. A study of the questions put by the scribe Hori to one of his colleagues whose incompetence he wanted to expose, strongly suggests that there may have been a system of examinations and diplomas. What are the rations for soldiers on campaign? How many bricks are required to build a ramp of given dimensions? How many men are needed to transport an obelisk? How is a colossal figure erected? How would you organize a military expedition? Finally, a variety of geographical questions about Syria. Such a range of topics must have involved extensive studies.[11]

Naturally enough, the keenness of these would-be scribes varied a great deal. We have frequent complaints from their masters about their idleness. 'Write with your hand,' says the scribe Amenmosé, over and over again, 'discuss things with those wiser than yourself . . . the way to get strong is by practising every day . . . if you slack for a single day you will be beaten. A youngster's ear is on his back; he only listens to the man who beats him. Listen carefully to what I say, since you will find it valuable. Monkeys have to be taught to dance, horses are trained. The young kite is taken on the nest, the falcon is made to fly. Always remember that discussion is the way to make progress, don't neglect your writing, and set your heart to listen to what I say, for you will find it valuable.'[12] The speaker, a schoolmaster, at least affects to think that the only obstacles to work in a boy's heart are laziness and obstinacy. But since animals can be broken and trained he is confident that a wayward pupil can be brought back to the royal road that leads to the highest distinctions by appeals to his ambition and good sense. But unfortunately young Egyptians were not so high-minded. 'I hear,' says another master, no less critical than Amenmosé, but rather better informed, 'that you are neglecting your writing and spending all your time dancing, going from tavern to tavern, always reeking of beer . . . you are like a shrine without its god or a house empty of bread. You are seen hammering on walls, and men fly from your path. If only you realized that wine is a thing of the devil and could forget your wine jars! But you neglect your own dignity.'[13] But this was not the worst. The ease with which concubines could be introduced into all Egyptian households, or slaves could be bought or hired, acted as a check on the development of bawdy houses. There were none the less establishments where the patrons were not only encouraged to drink too much but where they found dancing girls, singers and professional female musicians; and these, even if they were singers attached to the cult of Amūn, were generally of easy virtue. Here one could sample the pleasures of foreign music, singing and reciting to the accompaniment of tambourine or harp. And there were other pleasures as well to pass the time till one found oneself once more grovelling in the street and, after fruitless attempts to guide one's wavering footsteps straight, rolling in the dirt or involved in a brawl.[14]

3. *Magistrates—Good and Bad*

The arm of the law, even in the persons of its humblest representatives, was an object of awe to the section of the population represented by the workers and the *fellahin*. All too often their arrival foreshadowed a regular thrashing or the confiscation of their meagre possessions. No doubt the moralists advised the authorities and their agents to practise moderation and to show mercy. 'Do not cheat over the collection of taxes, but equally do not be too severe. If the list shows very large arrears standing against the name of the poor man, divide it in three, and remit two-thirds so that only one-third is left.'[15] Some officials have used stelae in their tombs or statues erected in the temples in the sight of their gods to record the fact that they were inspired by similar motives. In the words of the vizier Ptahmosé: 'I have done the

things that men praise and the gods approve. To the hungry I
have given bread and I have succoured the destitute.'[16] Another
vizier called Rekhmarê tells us of the care with which he has
administered the royal estates. He has filled the temples with
statues and has built himself a magnificent tomb; yes, but he has
also protected the weak against the strong, defended the widow
without kin and given children their father's inheritance.[17] If we
can believe Bakenkhonsou, the high priest of Amūn, his subordinates had little cause for complaint. 'To those under me I was a
father, teaching their young men, giving a helping hand to those
in trouble, providing for those who were in want. I never
frightened my servants, nay, I was a father to them. . . . I assured a funeral for those who had none to succeed them and a
coffin for him who was destitute. I gave protection to the orphan
that sought my help and I championed the cause of the widow. I
never deprived a son of his father's office. I never snatched a baby
from its mother. I always hearkened to those that spoke the truth,
but evildoers I would not let near me.'[18] Similarly Khâemhat, a
former royal scribe and superintendent of the granaries, took an
untarnished reputation to his grave. Never had any accusation
been levelled against him . . . when he came to the great judgement hall all his actions had been weighed in the balance and
found true by the gods that dwelt there. Thoth had found him
guiltless at judgement before all the gods and goddesses.[19]

Reassuring though this might seem, an elderly monarch, wise
in the ways of the world, warned his son against judges. 'You
know that they never show mercy when they judge the unfortunate.' The retired soldier Horonemheb, who occupied the
throne between the last of the followers of Akhnaton and the
first of the Ramessids, was under no illusions on the subject. He
knew well enough that during the years of unrest after the
religious revolution the scribes, the tax collectors and the minor
bureaucracy had hideously oppressed the poor and had robbed
the people and the king alike. When anyone appealed to justice,
those whose business it was to protect the taxpayer took bribes
to acquit the guilty and to condemn the innocent victim who
could not afford to purchase their favour. Horonemheb, always
seeking an opportunity to stamp out injustice and punish falsehood, issued an edict against those that betrayed their office. Any
magistrate convicted of having abused his position was sentenced

to having his nose cut off and was deported to a kind of concentration camp at Silé on the Suez Isthmus.[20]

In a decree we find Sety I speaking his mind in his address to the viziers, nobles, judges, viceroys of Kush, chief archers, keepers of the gold, princes, chieftains of the tribes of the north and the south, equerries, masters of the stables, sunshade-bearers, all the keepers of the king's house and all envoys sent on missions abroad. The object of this decree was to protect the House of a Million Years, which the monarch had just consecrated at Abydos and endowed with magnificent possessions, staff and herds, against this army of officials. He had good reason to fear that shepherds, fishermen, land workers and workmen might be forcibly requisitioned, that the staff might devote their time to hunting and fishing in its marshes and coverts, or that its boats, especially those returning from Nubia laden with the produce of the south, might be seized. Accordingly he announced that every official who appropriated any temple property would receive not less than a hundred blows from a cudgel, would have to restore what he had stolen and would have to pay a hundred times its value by way of penalty and interest. In certain circumstances the penalty would be 200 blows and five wounds. In extreme cases the penalties might involve the cropping of nose and ears and the seizure of the offender, who would thereupon be assigned to the temple as a labourer.[21] Although it is extraordinary to find the king acting with such severity against his own administrative officers in the interests of the privileged priestly class that formed a State within the State, there is no doubt that officials did not always pay unlimited respect to the privileges enjoyed by the clergy.[22] We may nevertheless question whether equally severe penalties were exacted for injustice to a free labourer or workman. Despite the gaps in the tale the story of the eloquent peasant of the Salt Oasis at any rate proves that the king was sincerely anxious to govern justly.[22a]

4. *The Maintenance of Public Order*

Under the last of the Ramesside monarchs conditions in Thebes, and no doubt throughout Egypt, were past belief. Theft, the abuse of power, crime—all these had been experienced in every period and even under the best kings; but never before had there been the spectacle of organized gangs looting temples and tombs, those repositories of vast wealth whose main protection in the last analysis was the simple faith of the common people. Ever since the Old Kingdom it had been customary to engrave, in large letters and in a conspicuous position, a warning to any who misconducted themselves in a tomb, or who damaged or stole statues, paintings, inscriptions or any of the articles of funerary furnishings, that their misdeeds would not go for ever unpunished. 'Whoever contravenes this in any way, may the crocodile attack him in the water, and the serpent on land. None shall ever perform his rites for him. God himself will judge him.'[23] At a much later period a governor of the Siout nome who had good reason to fear that his tomb might be violated, since he himself had taken possession of an earlier one, had an even more elaborate warning engraved on it. 'All men, all scribes, all learned men, all the middle and lower orders who raise their voices in this tomb, or who damage its inscriptions or break its statues, will be exposed to the wrath of Thoth, the most swift to anger of all the gods, they will be the victims of the knives of the king's executioners that sit in the Great Houses. Their gods shall reject their offerings of bread.' By way of contrast, rewards are promised to the respectful visitor: he shall grow old in his city and shall be an *amakhou** of his nome.[24]

During the New Kingdom the Egyptians still retained confidence in the efficacy of these minatory inscriptions. When Sety I found a spring of water in the desert in the vicinity of the gold mines, he built a shrine which he dedicated to Amon-Rê and a number of other deities, not merely in gratitude but also to ensure their protection for those who went there to wash the gold and were responsible for dispatching it to the royal treasury. As for kings in after times who would respect his decisions: 'Amūn, Harakhté and Tatenen will grant them to rule the earth mercifully and to overhrtow foreign lands and the Land of the Bow', but any monarch who thwarted these designs would have to answer for it at On before some nameless tribunal; while any prince who advised his master to remove the miners and put them to other work, 'the flame shall burn his flesh. The Clear One shall devour

---

*i.e. "privileged". In the New Kingdom, since the privileges were largely confined to the hereafter, this word came to mean little more than "deceased"

his limbs. If any man hearken not to his bidding, may Osiris stand behind him, may Isis stand at his wife's shoulder and Horus behind his children, together with the princes of Tod-jeser who fulfil their tasks.'[25] Herihor, a high priest of Amūn, had his statue erected in the temple that it might dwell near the presence of the god and greet him when he went forth in procession. He laid a curse on any man who should move it even after the lapse of many centuries. 'He shall be delivered to the wrath of Amūn, Mout and Khonsou. His name shall perish from the land of Egypt. He shall die of hunger and thirst.'[26] Amenophis III promulgated a decree relating to the foundation of a *ka*-mansion (mortuary temple) of his favourite Amenhotep, the son of Hapou. The foundation was placed under the protection of Amon-Rê, King of the Gods, for as long as it should endure upon earth, and anyone who did any damage to it would have to face the wrath of Amūn. 'He will give them over to the king's fire in the day of his wrath. His uraeus will shoot out flames at their face and will destroy their flesh and consume their body. They will become like Apophis* on the morning of New Year's Day. . . . No longer will they be able to consume the offerings of the dead. None will pour out river water for them. Their sons will not succeed to their inheritance. Their wives will be violated before their very eyes. . . . . In the day of the slaughter they will be put to the sword. Their bodies will shrivel and waste, for they shall be hungry and shall have no bread.'[27]

But all aspects of a country's government are interdependent. Fear of the gods or terror at the thought of punishment after death sufficed to protect temples and tombs just so long as an honest and vigilant police force kept guard in Western Thebes. But the day would dawn when the police would forget their duty and on that day the inscriptions, be they never so frightening, would lose all their efficacy.

The first lootings of which we know took place in the fourteenth year of the reign of Ramesses IX,† though others had doubtless occurred earlier. For many years the tombs were robbed without a finger being raised to stop it by the prince of the *kher* (mayor of the necropolis), who was responsible for the police, the *Medjaiou* corps, and a considerable body of guards. It was actually

*The serpent of the underworld slain by the god Rê.
†*c*. 1100 B.C.

Paser, the prince (mayor) of the town, who had no direct responsibility in the matter, who reported this shocking state of affairs to the vizier and to a great commission of high officials. The report caused considerable alarm and Paour-Rê, the prince of the *kher*, who was directly involved, was forced to instigate inquiries by his colleagues in the police. A group of tombs in the northern quarter of the necropolis was selected for checking, and a start was made with the tomb of Amenophis I, an extremely popular figure among the inhabitants of western Thebes. The report of Prince Paser alleged that it had been violated, but this was a mistake, for, in fact, the tomb of the royal saint was intact, as was another tomb close to the temple of this same Amenophis—a tomb very famous for its statue of King Antef with his dog Bahika between his legs (p. 65). The robbers had also made fairly determined attempts on two other tombs without reaching the funerary chamber. On the other hand they had had complete success in their operations against the tomb of King Sekhem-Rê Shedtawi, son of the Sun-god, Sobekemsaf, and the chamber in which the monarch lay with his spouse Queen Noubkhas was found to be entirely empty. Five other royal tombs were found intact, but two out of four tombs belonging to the singers of the 'House of Adoration' of Amonrâsonter had been robbed, while the neighbouring cemetery where other singers were interred, as well as various noblemen of much later periods, and 'people of the land', presented a deplorable spectacle, for every tomb had been violated. The robbers had torn the mummies from their coffins of wood or stone and had thrown them aside on the ground, after first stripping all the gold and silver and stealing all the tomb furnishings. Some of the robbers were arrested and questioned, and the transcript of their interrogation was also forwarded to the committee of inquiry by Prince Paour-Rê.

None of these high officials had any real justification for complacency. They ought to have devoted themselves single-mindedly to apprehending the robbers, and to dismissing and punishing everyone whose negligence or complicity had contributed towards these shocking events. In fact, however, their annoyance was principally directed at Paser, who had not only stirred them from their lethargy but was now threatening to send a report to Pharaoh and have them all arrested. To get rid of this awkward customer he was sent a false witness—a metal worker called

Pakharou—who told him that he and his gang had gone to rob the Great Dwellings (tombs). The prince of the *kher*, who clearly knew how unreliable this evidence was, held an inquiry, which proved it to be an utter fabrication. The committee of inquiry then met, with the vizier in the chair, and summoned before it both Pakharou and his alleged accomplices, together with his accuser and those witnesses whom it wished to cross-examine. The vizier summed the case up and announced the results of the inquiry. 'We have made a check of the places which the prince of this town claimed had been broken into by the workmen of the castle of Ousirmarê Miamūn, and we have found them intact. This proves that all his allegations are false.' The workmen were cross-examined and confronted with Paser. It became clear that in fact they did not know any of the Great Dwellings in the place of Pharaoh which had been referred to in the statement of the prince of the town. Paser was accordingly convicted of lying. The workmen, who belonged to the chief prophet of Amonrâsonter—among the most suspect of those concerned—were released and given back their jobs.[28]

Despite their strong inclination to turn a blind eye to the activities of the robbers, the police were obliged to arrest a number of those who had robbed the tomb of King Sobekemsaf. Thanks to the fragments of the inquiry which have come down to us, we can reconstruct their operations. A mason called Amenpanofer, an employee of Amenhotep the high priest of Amonrâsonter, joined forces with seven other men, either fellow masons or carpenters, together with a farm labourer and a boatman. The latter was an indispensable member of the gang, since the scheme involved crossing and recrossing the Nile with the loot without arousing the suspicions of the curious. The gang had already been at work for four years when they decided to make their attempt on the tomb of Sobekemsaf . . . 'which was quite different from the pyramids and tombs of the nobles which we had been accustomed to robbing'. With their copper tools they hacked out a passage in the thickness of the pyramid. It was a slow business, but eventually they reached the underground chambers. Here they lit their torches, and after succeeding in clearing away the final obstructions, found themselves confronted by the two royal sarcophagi belonging to the king and his queen. Their interest was not, however, archaeological, and they immediately lifted up the lids of the sarcophagi, inside which they found coffins of gilded wood, which they ripped open as well. The king's imposing mummy, lying in its coffin, was girt with a sword, decorated, likely enough, with palmettes and hunting scenes, like that of Queen Aahhotep. His face was covered with a golden mask and strings of amulets and necklaces encircled his neck. The whole of the mummy was covered with gold. The bandits made a pile of all the gold, silver, bronze and jewellery, and burned the coffins. They divided the gold, which weighed 160 *deben* (about 30 lb.), into eight equal parts and crossed the Nile with it. Perhaps they may have boasted, or perhaps their activities were observed—whatever the truth, Amenpanofer was arrested by the town guard and locked up in the office of Prince Paser. The thief thereupon collected his twenty *deben* of gold and sent them to the scribe of the quay, who released him without any further formalities. He then re-established contact with his accomplices, who, with exemplary honesty, made a fresh share-out of the loot, now regrettably reduced to seventeen and a half *deben* each. It was necessary to make up lost ground, so the gang restarted its operations and continued them until the decision to arrest them was taken. 'But,' added the thief, 'lots of other people robbed tombs like us and are just as guilty.' For some time they were kept in custody. The magistrates extracted a confession and brought them to the very pyramid they had robbed for a reconstruction of the crime. They decided to hand over the eight robbers to their superior, the high priest of Amūn, but when the actual moment of handing them over came, the eight had dwindled to three, plus one member of another gang of seventeen. The others had made themselves scarce. The magistrates made the high priest responsible for finding the missing culprits.

Three months later the mason Amenpanofer, whose mother had already been banished to Nubia, was re-arrested and brought to trial. The beating he duly received resulted in fresh confessions. With five companions he had robbed the tomb of a Third Prophet of Amūn, removing the sarcophagus of gilded wood and leaving the mummy in a corner. They had then foregathered on the island of Amonemopet where they stripped and divided up the gold and burned the coffin. Amenpanofer continued his career of crime until he was captured and then released: thereupon he began again until the fresh arrest which resulted in his being brought to trial.

The thieves who robbed the tombs of kings and commoners were originally recruited from the quarrymen, stonemasons and labourers who worked in the necropolis, but they were soon joined both by minor officials employed in the temples on the west bank and by members of the priesthood. It was a gang consisting of a priest, Penounheb, and four Divine Fathers (p. 278)—Mery the old, his son Paisem, Semdy and Pakharou—which succeeded in removing the necklace from the statue of Nefertoum, the great god, which when melted down produced four *deben* and six *qite* of gold. The distribution was done by Mery the old, no doubt because he was the eldest. Another gang, which included priests, scribes and oxherds, broke into the golden house of King Ousirmarê Sotenperê—the precise significance and exact site of which are unknown to us. The outer door, which was made of granite of Abou, had bronze bolts, and the inner doors were covered with gold. It must have been extremely inefficiently guarded. The priest Kaoukaroï, together with four accomplices, visited it on several occasions, on each of which they brought back a quantity of gold which they exchanged in the town for grain. One day a shepherd, trying to pick a quarrel with them, asked, 'Why do you give me no more?' They repaired to their inexhaustible gold reserves and returned with five *qite* ($1\frac{3}{4}$ oz.) of gold, with which they bought an ox and gave it to the shepherd. As it happened, however, Setouimosé, the scribe of the royal books, had overheard the quarrel between the priests and the shepherd, and seizing his opportunity, declared: 'I shall report this at once to the chief priest of Amūn.' The priests took immediate steps to ensure that this went no further and in two further visits they acquired four and a half *qite* of gold with which they bought Setouimosé's silence. The priest Toutouy, who was a trusted servant of the golden house, wanted to extend his operations. He ran to the gates of the sky with the priest Nesiamūn and after stripping all the gold off them he set them on fire. The same agency was responsible for the disappearance of a considerable quantity of valuable furniture. On one occasion robbers stole the portable shrine of Ramsesnekht, the First Prophet of Amūn who had died shortly before; on another, a second gang stole the portable shrine of the great god Ousirmarê Sotepenrê, together with the forty 'houses' of King Menmaatrê (Sety I), which formed part of the treasures of the Mansion of Ousirmarê.

Although the reports and cross-examinations relating to these robberies would fill a thickish file, they are nevertheless comparatively unimportant, since they refer to the violation of only a single royal tomb. We should remember however that practically every tomb in the Valleys of the Kings and the Queens had been broken into and robbed before the beginning of the twenty-first dynasty, that is to say, within thirty years. To protect the actual mummies of the Pharaohs the viziers and the high priests of Amūn were obliged to remove them from their coffins and to lay them, wrapped in bandages and devoid of jewels and golden masks, in plain wooden coffins, which were then hidden. Practically the sole survivor was the tomb of King Tutankhamūn, together with that of Queen Aahhotep, which lay in the area in which the first robbers had commenced their operations. I think it unlikely that the tombs of the kings named Amenophis, Tuthmosis, Sety and Ramesses should all have been robbed by labourers, even working in gangs—with whom in normal conditions the police could easily have dealt. During the reigns of the last Ramesside monarchs, Egypt was rent by the horrors of a hideous civil war, in which the priests and adherents of Amūn fought those of Seth, who were scattered throughout the whole of Egypt, but were particularly numerous and active near Coptos, Oxyrhynchus, Tell Modam and Pi-Ramessu. I think that it must have been during this war that these great tombs were robbed by one side or the other, or indeed by both successively, each on the pretext that it could not leave such huge quantities of precious metal to the mercy of its opponents. In the face of this example on the part of their leaders, the impoverished populace continued to take what they could when they could find it, more especially since the anarchic conditions had resulted in severe inflation, in which goods were scarce and could only be obtained for fine silver or gold. An ox, for example, cost nearly $1\frac{3}{4}$ oz. of gold (p. 167). The accomplices of a certain Boukhâf asserted that with their share some of them had bought land and others grain, cloth or slaves. The purchase of a slave was bound to attract attention, since it had to be officially registered, and a member of the working classes who was observed to have done so would be questioned by a judge about his means. We find the scribe of the court asking a Theban woman called Arynofer, 'What have you to say about this money brought by Panehsy your husband?' 'I never saw it!' The vizier pressed his questions. 'How did you get the servants he had with him?' 'I never saw the money he paid for them with. He was travelling when he acquired them.' One last question from the bench. 'What was the source of the money on which Panehsy got interest with Sobekemsaf?' 'I got it by selling barley in the year of the hyenas, when everyone was short of food.'

The bench regarded it as quite unnecessary to ask the defendant what she meant by 'the year of the hyenas'. But although the phrase was in common use it is a source of some difficulty. Some scholars think that it refers to a year during which hyenas had actually been seen at Thebes, much as wolves are occasionally seen at the present day roaming the streets of large towns. Others have been inclined to think that the phrase is metaphorical, and that it may have signified the year in which the enemies of Amūn captured Thebes and sacked its temples and cemeteries. Law and order had completely collapsed. We hear of a thief shouting to the father of a woman who was a member of Boukhâf's gang: 'You good for nothing old idot, if you were killed and thrown into the Nile, who do you suppose would look for you?' Well might Ramesses III, with pathetic insistence, implore the gods to grant his son a prosperous reign. He could see the coming storm. It broke some seventy-five years after his death, and after a quarter of a century or more of events unprecedented since the time of the Hyksos—the gods and the dead being robbed by labourers, scribes and priests—Egypt emerged from it but a shadow of her former greatness.

5. *The Law Courts*

The re-establishment of order was followed by severe measures. It is certain that as early as the reign of Ramesses IX a committee of inquiry was appointed under the chairmanship of the vizier, the most important man in the country after the king, to ascertain the extent of the damage. It gives the impression of being less anxious to discover the truth than to hush it up. Various robbers were arrested, but they purchased their freedom with a little gold and resumed their operations, having taken advantage of their removal from the prison of the mayors of the town to that of the high priest to make their escape. However, after the recrudescence of robberies which broke out during the last years of Ramesses

IX, a second committee of inquiry, which included not only the vizier but also some of the royal cupbearers, a lord of the treasury, two fan-bearers, scribes and heralds, set to work. This time it meant business. It was quite normal for plaintiffs to consult the statue of some sainted monarch in order to secure the restitution of an object that had been stolen or to get a rent paid in full. But this was no time for such measures, and the sainted Pharaoh was left in his corner. The judges preferred to rely on well-proven methods of eliciting the truth.

At one session, devoted to the examination of the leaders of the gangs of robbers who had broken into the great tombs, the vizier opened the proceedings by addressing the shepherd Boukhâf in the following terms. 'You and your gang were on this job. The god caught you and has brought you here and delivered you into Pharaoh's power. Tell me the names of all your companions in the Great Dwellings.' Boukhâf needed little persuasion to name six of his accomplices. The court, however, was not satisfied and he was beaten, as a result of which he swore he would speak. He was accordingly interrogated afresh. 'Tell us exactly how you entered the revered Great Dwellings.' Boukhâf's assertion that the tomb he had entered had already been open earned him a fresh beating, which he ended by swearing to speak. Thirteen names were dragged out of him after which he declared: 'I swear by Amūn and the king that if I am found to have concealed the name of any of my companions, I will be punished in his stead.' This was followed by a monotonous parade of his accomplices together with some other individuals whose names had been mentioned during the proceedings. The defendants all swear to tell the truth on pain of banishment to Nubia, or mutilation or 'being placed on the wood'. We meet this phrase in other contexts. Several of the conspirators against Ramesses III were condemned to suffer this punishment. Some scholars think that it refers to impalement, but this is doubtful, for although scenes of impalement are found on Assyrian bas-reliefs they are unknown in Egypt, though occasionally a man is shown tied to a stake to be beaten.[29] I think that condemnation to be 'placed on the wood' meant to be tied to a stake and perhaps to be left there to die.

Sometimes in reply to the judge the defendant answered: 'Woe to me! Woe to my flesh!' The judge, quite unmoved, would put another question and if, as generally happened, the answer was unsatisfactory, a beating ensued. There must have been different types or degrees of beatings, for we find three different terms—*badjana, nadjana, manini*—all in use. Some victims actually suffered all three successively, but we do not know exactly how they differed. Prisoners were generally beaten across the back, but sometimes on the hands and the feet. These measures were generally drastic enough to loosen the victims' tongues—generally, but not always: for the record often shows that a defendant had not confessed even after being beaten two or three times, in which case he was probably kept in custody at the court's pleasure. Sometimes a judge, after failing to extract a confession or any information, and uncertain where the truth lay, might invite the unfortunate prisoner to name a witness who could confirm his story. Only rarely was a prisoner released. A trumpet player called Amonkhâou was brought into court and asked by the vizier, 'How did you, in company with Shedsoukhonsou the resin burner, manage to get into the Great Dwelling from which you removed the silver after the expedition of the robbers?' Amonkhâou replied, 'Woe is me! Woe to my flesh! I said to my companion, Perpajaou the trumpet player, with whom I was arguing, "They will kill you for the thefts you have perpetrated in the *kher*." ' He was beaten on the hands and feet, but said, 'I haven't seen anyone except the person I told you of.' He suffered *nadjana* twice and *manini* once, but continued to repeat, 'I have told you all that I saw.' He was re-examined on the tenth day of the fourth month of summer, and was acquitted of the thefts and set at liberty. The poor man had certainly earned it.[30]

The mass of documentary evidence which we possess enables us to eavesdrop at a number of such interrogations, but we have no record of the court's decisions, nor do we know what sentences were passed, nor whether the wretched victims died under torture or dragged out a miserable existence in the mines and quarries.

6. *The Reception of Foreign Tributaries*

As we have just seen, public officials' time was mainly spent in maintaining the value of the royal estates, suppressing banditry, dispensing justice and collecting taxes. When food was scarce they fed the population. All this was routine, but every now and again a few were fortunate enough to share in tasks that flattered their self-esteem, and none seems to have been more agreeable than to welcome envoys from foreign countries on their arrival in Egypt and to introduce them into the Pharaoh's presence, whether they came to deliver their quota of tribute as a war indemnity, to express their desire to be 'on the king's water', or to make known in exalted quarters that in some distant land a princess lay incurably ill and that only an Egyptian doctor, or the presence of a compassionate god, could restore her to health (p. 190).

From Retenou or Naharina or the farthest confines of Asia envoys had the choice of travelling either overland, in which case they would be met by the frontier guards at the Roads of Horus, or by sea. Their boats were very like the Egyptian in design, which is natural enough when we remember that in shipbuilding Egypt was the pupil of Byblos.

Once safely in harbour, the Syrian chieftains would burn incense and gesticulate vividly in token of their joy at the successful conclusion of their long voyage. While they would make haste to unload their cargoes, the Egyptians for their part would have opened eating and drinking stalls on the quays; and soon the newcomers would make contact with an Egyptian official responsible for bringing them before the vizier. They formed a most attractive procession and in all likelihood a crowd gathered to watch them pass. They were keenly observed by the artists who would one day be called upon to depict them on the walls of the vizier's tomb. The men wore either loincloths embroidered with multicoloured wool and fringed with tassels or long gowns with sleeves, laced up on hooks down the front, or they might be swathed in long woollen scarves. A few of them wore a medallion round their necks. The women were dressed in flounced gowns. Servants led horses, bears, and pygmy elephants scarcely larger than calves and shouldered jars of turpentine oil, pitch, honey and oil, or baskets laden with gold or lapis lazuli. The Egyptians valued even more highly articles such as chariots and weapons, ornamental objects and metal vases, in the manufacture of which the Syrians had attained an astonishing degree of skill. They were no longer content, as they had been at the beginning of the eighteenth dynasty, to make amphorae with floral handles, gadrooned cups and bowls containing sprays of artificial flowers. By now they were producing huge standing vases, their entire surface engraved or embossed and further ornamented with plants or human or animal heads clustered round belly or lid. We possess amphorae with three separate bellies and three necks. The lids might be modelled in the shape of a mask of Bes or a griffin's head. Sometimes a multi-storied construction, or a female-headed sphinx, would spring from a cup-shaped base; sometimes the bowl of the goblet itself would be supported by two male figures back to back. Human heads, sometimes of Bes, sometimes of a woman, with an ivory handle in the shape of a natural or artificial elephant tusk richly ornamented, are particularly striking. Objects of this kind were purely ornamental and of no practical use whatsoever, and this seems to have enhanced their attractiveness in the eyes of the Egyptians, who had the less elaborate of them copied in their own workshops. The popularity of these foreign products is clear from the care with which they are reproduced, notably, for example, in the tomb of Amiseba[31] (p. 28).

For sheer picturesqueness, processions of men from the south rivalled, if they did not surpass, those from Asia. The negroes would dance forward to the sound of tambourines, wearing necklaces and with panthers' tails tied to their arms, their heads shaven except for three tufts of hair. Their women wore skirts or flounced dresses and carried anything up to four children in baskets slung on their backs. The men would carry leather shields, ivory, ostrich feathers, eggs, panther skins and jars and bundles, or would lead monkeys, cheetahs and long-necked giraffes on cords. By far the most magnificent of all these processions was that presented to King Tutankhamūn by Prince Houy.[32] We can see the viceroy of Kush, still wearing the gold necklaces presented to him by his sovereign, receiving his Egyptian colleagues who kneel to greet him, and touch his garment or his feet. Most Nubians adopted Egyptian dress, while still retaining some of their traditional ornaments. They wore their hair in a long bob like a kind of skull cap kept in place by a diadem crowned by an ostrich feather. Heavy rings hung from their ears, and their necks were encircled by a bead collar and their wrists by massive bracelets. A few of them wore a panther skin on their backs beneath an outfit comprising a belt, baldric and apron ornamented with a pattern of suns with rays. The princes moved at ease in their transparent pleated gowns, Egyptian-type head collars and sandals, while their children, like those of Egypt, wore a thick plait of hair hanging down by their right cheek. They had panthers' tails tied to their arms. Plain rings dangled from the ears of the men who carried the offerings, but princes wore earrings in the shape of golden disks with pendants.

The company included soldiers who knelt on the ground and besought the breath of life, and porters to carry the offerings and present bags of gold-dust and gold rings on dishes, panther hides, live giraffes and oxen with huge ivory-tipped horns. A group of princes walked before the king of the country, who rode in a chariot like those used in Asia or Egypt, except that it was fitted with a magnificent sunshade of ostrich plumes and was drawn by two hornless oxen instead of horses. Behind it walked prisoners with manacles on their hands and halters round their necks. The rear of the procession was brought up by negresses bare to the waist, carrying their babies slung on their backs and leading their older children, whose heads were shaved according to the custom of the country. The women wore earrings like their menfolk, panthers' tails and heavy bracelets.

Although the people of the south were less industrious than the Phoenicians there were some extremely skilled craftsmen among them. There is evidence to suggest that Egyptian governors of Nubia, who were known by the title of 'King's Son' or 'Viceroy of Kush',[33] took some trouble to encourage native arts—witness the satisfaction with which Houy regards the articles spread before him before personally presenting them to the king. Nubia made not merely articles copied from Egyptian originals, such as chairs, beds and bedheads, and chariots, but also weapons of quite individual design. Their leather shields rimmed with metal and studded with nails sometimes displayed such conventional patterns as a ram-headed sphinx trampling its enemies or Pharaoh impaling a Nubian on his lance. More popular with the Egyptians, however, were models of negro villages in gold, on trays or stands. In one of these models a hut in the shape of a very tall pyramid is overshadowed by date palms and *dōm* palms. Children and monkeys climb the branches to pick the clusters of fruit, while giraffes and their attendants are moving about the village and negroes are doing obeisance at the edge. The foot of the stand is decorated with a motif of negroes tied to a post and with royal cartouches. Panther skins and golden chains hang from the table top. This was the showpiece of the whole exhibition, and represented the high-water mark of Nubian gold work under the inspiration of Egyptian originals.

Indeed, the governor who brought back such rareties from the south, not to mention ingots of gold and ebony and ivory, and who could also claim that peace reigned there, had fully deserved his reward.

CHAPTER XI

IN THE TEMPLES

1. *Piety*

In the opinion of Herodotus the Egyptians were the most scrupulously religious of mankind.[1] They regarded the gods as the owners of the entire universe and the fount of all prosperity, aware of all human desires and capable at any moment of taking a hand in mortal affairs. Ramesses II's escape before Qadesh when abandoned by his troops and surrounded by his enemies was attributable to the fact that his voice reached Thebes and was heard by Amūn. A spell of fine weather during the bad season for the journey of the Hittite princess who was to be his bride must be ascribed to the fact that Sutekh could deny him nothing. Did his well-diggers find water in the desert of Ikaïta? His father Hâpi loved him more than any of his predecessors on the throne.

This conception of divine favour bestowed on particular individuals sometimes inspired quite immoderate ambitions. King Amenophis is said to have wished to see the gods during his lifetime.[2] Prince Hornekht, son of King Osorkon II and Queen Karōm, wished the divine vulture to help him when he consorted with the antelopes in the desert and the birds in the sky,[3] no doubt so that he might be able to understand their private language—a secret confined to a few initiates—and to comprehend the important messages which the gods chose to entrust to them. There were many who came near to believing that specially favoured mortals could issue their commands to nature and earth, to sky and night, to mountains, rivers and seas, and could transcend the bounds of time and space.[4] But these were but passing follies. When Ramesses III dictated the Harris papyrus he asked for nothing from the gods, greatest and least alike, but what was simple and reasonable; for himself happiness after death, for his son a long reign full of power and honour and abundant Nile floods: favours of which he believed himself worthy, for the gods had set him firmly in his father's place, just as they had established Horus in the place of Osiris, and he had neither robbed nor oppressed any man nor disobeyed the gods' commandments.[4a]

The wishes of private persons, of high or low degree, were modest enough. Parents who had no son prayed to Imhotep to grant them one. When Bata was fleeing from his brother's violent rage he reminded himself that Harakhté knew truth from falsehood. Everyone knew that god had pity on the poor and that though every man's hand might be against them, god, the judge who took no bribes and did not seek to suborn witnesses, would sustain them. In the law courts the poor man who had no gold or silver with which to cross the scribes' palms, nor clothes to give their servants, might find Amūn transformed into a vizier so that the truth might blaze forth and the weak triumph against the strong.[5] We find a scribe appealing to Thoth for help in reaching the top of his profession. 'Come to my aid, O Thoth, sacred ibis, O god beloved of Shmoun, secretary of the nine gods . . . come to me, guide my counsels, give me skill in thy craft which excels all other crafts, for men have found that he that excels therein becomes a prince.'[6]

We are often disconcerted by this blend of pious ardour and self-interest. The desire to provide the rich and rare in honour of the gods is universal, but in the New Kingdom the wealth of the temples beggars all description. Since Ahmosé's accession they had been the repositories of every manifestation of extravagance and opulence. As we have already seen, the main preoccupation of every king was the creation of new shrines, and the enlargement and embellishment of those that already existed by restoring the outer walls and doors, the construction of sacred boats, the erection of statues and the replacement of brick with stone and of native wood with timber from foreign lands; by covering the pyramidal tops of obelisks and the walls of the Great Dwelling with gold leaf, and filling each room with furniture inlaid with gold and semi-precious stones. We cannot doubt that in Akhnaton's reign and perhaps in the obscure years before the accession of Set-nakht there was some damage and what might be called a preview of what was to happen on a large scale under the last monarchs of the Ramesside dynasty, but the kings whose reigns were successful and prosperous energetically and lavishly made good previous losses.

We cannot but share the astonishment felt by the Greeks and the Romans at the number and the curious diversity of Egyptian divinities. The vignette of a papyrus in the Cairo museum portrays a priestess, Isitemheb, a daughter of the king, prostrating herself with a charming gesture on the bank of a pool before a crocodile who basks on the farther side at the foot of a willow tree.[7] The priestess drinks, with every appearance of enjoyment, from the pond where the animal wallows, while it watches her unmoved. The crocodile is in fact the widely worshipped god Sobek, who had two principal cult centres, one in the Fayyum (the Greek Crocodilopolis) and one at Soumenou* south of Thebes, as well as scattered shrines throughout the country.

The inhabitants of Memphis and On, on the other hand, gave the place of honour to the bull, worshipped as Hâpi (Apis) in the former city and Merwer (Mnevis) in the latter. We know the distinctive characteristics of Hâpi from Greek authors.[8] When he had been identified his birth was carefully recorded and he was ceremoniously conducted into the temple of Ptah. For the rest of his life he was overfed with delicacies and loaded with honours, and when he died the entire populace went into mourning. His mummified body was interred in princely fashion in a special tomb. At Shmoun the ibis was a sacred bird,[9] and one especially privileged specimen receive divine honours. Mummified corpses of ibis were brought from every part of Egypt and laid in a huge underground cavern. Falcons were regarded as sacred all over Egypt and not merely in the town of Nekhen (later known to the Greeks as Hierakonpolis†) but also at Nekheb opposite Nekhen and in all the modern Egyptian Damanhours (town of Horus) or Sanhours (protection of Horus), besides other centres like Hathirib (Athribis) where their necropolis was entirely restored by the saviour Djedher, or Tanis where our expedition recently found the skeletons of falcons in little jars. Bubastis was the centre of a cat worship, Amit that of the cult of the formidable serpent Wadjit (Būto). The peasants of the Thebaid offered the first fruits of their harvest to this same serpent, which they called Renoutet.

*Near Hermonthis, the modern Rizzeigat.
†Greek ἱέραξ—a falcon.

Not only animals but some plants enjoyed this veneration of the pious. We see men and women, singly or in pairs, approaching the sycamore with hands reverently outstretched to receive the holy water sprinkled by a goddess concealed in the tree. Every town had its sacred tree, just as it had its local deity, but the worship of the latter did not afford sufficient outlet for religious enthusiasm. In every city, small or great, the local god was associated with companion divinities who had been imported at some date from other localities near or far. On establishing his residence in the eastern delta, Ramesses II assembled a whole pantheon there. Amūn and Seth—age-old foes whose enmity was later to be renewed—found themselves side by side with Toum of Heliopolis and Ptah of Memphis, with the gods of the Delta and those of Syria and Phoenicia, for, as though their own pantheon was too small, the Egyptians set about adopting the gods of neighbouring countries. Seth the Slayer of Osiris changed the greyhound's for a human head and assumed the dress and the attributes of Baal, namely a pointed headdress resplendent with the solar disk, from which projected two sharp horns, with a long ribbon hanging from its tip to the ground, and an embroidered loincloth fringed with tassels. His consort was no longer the sister of Isis but Anta (Anath), a goddess of Canaan.[10] When

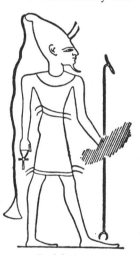

Baal-Seth

Astarte first arrived in Egypt she was honoured as a queen by all the gods.[11] Ramesses was bound to place the castle he built to await his bride between Egypt and Syria under divine protection, and for the purpose he chose two Egyptian deities, Amūn and Būto, and two Asiatic, Sutekh and Astarte.[12] From the reign of Tutankhamūn onwards Houroun, a falcon-headed Canaanite deity, seemed anxious to supplant Horus, the ancient supporter of the monarchy.[13] Memphis, in which an entire quarter was inhabited solely by Tyrians, was a microcosm of all Egyptian and foreign cults,[14] while 'Thebes of a hundred gates' might well have been called 'Thebes of a hundred gods'.

2. The Priesthood

As we have already seen, every temple was a miniature town, within whose walls officials, police, craftsmen and land workers lived as though in an ordinary community. Although their livelihood depended on the temple, they were laymen. The only people who could claim the title of religious were the *wâbou* (pure ones) the *it neter* (divine fathers), the *hemneter* (divine servant) the *kheryhebet* (the man with the scroll, who held in his hand a parchment scroll showing the order of ceremony), and the members of the *ounuît*, which must have been a group of at least twelve persons since the word *ounut* means 'hour'. These priests worked on a kind of shift system so as to ensure a sort of perpetual adoration by day and by night.[14a] Many temples contained a superintendent of the mysteries, who was responsible for the sacred dramas of which we shall have more to say later (pp. 294ff). A priest known as *sem*, though unknown in the cult of Amūn, was an important figure at On and Memphis. The Theban priesthood was headed by four *hemneter* priests. The first 'divine servant', despite the apparent humility of his title, was in fact one of the leading figures in Egypt. In On the head of the priesthood of Atum was known as the 'great seer', *our ma*; the comparable official of Ptah at Memphis as the 'chief artist'; at Shmoun the head of the temple at Thoth was known as the Great One of Five. In many other temples, as in that of Amūn, the leading figure was a 'divine servant'. Modern usage has followed Greek practice in calling these *hemou neterou* προφῆται, 'prophets', inasmuch as their duties sometimes included the interpretation of the divine will; but this was not their sole function and we cannot be sure that only they were allowed to perform it. Whatever their religious titles, in the New Kingdom the priesthood were coming to be distinguished from the majority of the citizens: they had discarded the long pleated gown with sleeves and had taken to wearing instead a long loincloth which left the upper part of their bodies naked, and, to shaving closely their hair, beard and moustache.

Just as a temple might extend its hospitality to several deities, so the priesthood were not bound by any oath to the lifelong worship of a single god. Sety, the high priest of Seth, was also responsible for the festivals of Banebded and was in charge of the ritual of Būto, judge of the Two Lands. Nebounef was nominated by Ramesses II to be high priest of Amūn although he had never belonged to the priesthood attached to that god: he was in fact high priest of Anhour at Tjiny and of Hathor at Denderah. A Second Prophet of Amūn by the name of Anen was consoled for his failure to reach the highest office by his appointment as head of the seers and *sem*-priest at On of Mentou (Hermonthis), a town in the nome of Thebes.

Many women participated in cult observance.[14b] Every temple had a corps of female singers whose job it was to sing and shake the sistra or crotals during services. These women lived at home with their families and did not reside in the temple, since they were only required to attend at certain times and on certain days. On the other hand the women comprising the *khenerit* must have lived in the temple, since '*khener*' means both 'prison' and the 'innermost sanctuaries of a temple or a palace'. Women of higher position still were known as 'divine wife of the god'. 'God's hand' or 'divine adorer'. It is sometimes suggested that the members of this divine harem formed a kind of corps of sacred prostitutes such as is known to have existed at Byblos, a town steeped in the traditions of Egyptian civilization, but there is no proof that this practice was ever followed in Egypt. In actual fact the behaviour of the singers of Amūn was sometimes distinctly forward and they were not always over-particular about where they went, but it would no doubt be quite unfair to assume that all the singers of Amūn behaved like this on the evidence of the only example preserved in a papyrus now in Turin.[15] It could not in any case prove that women attached to the temple were obliged to follow the example of the women of Byblos during the feast of Adonis, namely to give themselves to strangers and to hand over any resulting profits to the temple treasury.

Priesthood, like officialdom, was nearly always a matter of family tradition, and priests were nearly always the sons of priests.[16] Bakenkhonsou, the son of a Second Prophet of Amūn, was sent to school at the age of five with an eye to his one day entering the priesthood. Both the sons and grandsons of the high priest Romeroy followed his profession, the elder son acting beside his father as a Second Prophet and the younger officiating in a temple to the west of Thebes, while the grandson became a 'divine father'. Sometimes, however, a son wanted to follow a career in opposition to his family's wishes. From an official letter we learn that the vizier had presented three boys with the intention of their becoming priests in 'the Castle of Merenptah which is in the temple of Ptah', but that an official who had but scant respect for the privileges of religion (like those mentioned in the decree of Sety I, p. 259), got hold of the young men and sent them north to become officers. This was a flagrant abuse of authority and a scribe immediately wrote to draw attention to the fact and to demand their return.[17]

Schoolboys destined for the religious life learned grammar and writing like all their fellows, but they had to learn a lot of other things as well: they had to know not only the images of the gods but also their titles, epithets, attributes and legends, and to be thoroughly familiar with ritual. All this took a deal of learning.[18] At the end of their course they took an examination. A candidate adjudged successful, and so entitled to become a member of the priesthood, took off his clothes and was bathed, shaved and anointed with perfumes. Then he put on his full priestly regalia and was 'admitted to the horizon of heaven'. Awestruck at the thought of the divine majesty, he could at last approach the god in his sanctuary.[19]

3. *The Cult*

The daily rites performed in all Egyptian temples, in the king's name and at his expense, were conducted in the innermost shrine and in secret. The public were debarred from all participation. The proper priest first purified himself in the House of the Morning and then took and lit the censer and moved towards the sanctuary, purifying the area through which he passed with the scent of turpentine-resin. The naos, or shrine containing the gilt wood statue of the god or goddess, would be shut and the priest would break the seal of clay, draw back the bolt and open the two leaves of the door to reveal the divine image. He would prostrate himself before it, anoint it with unguents, cense it and chant hymns of adoration. Up to this point in the ceremony the statue was still inanimate: it was endowed with life when the priest offered it first a model of the eye torn from Horus by his enemy Seth and recovered by the gods, and then a statuette of Maât (Truth), the daughter of Rê. The statue of the god was then drawn forth from the naos and the officiating priest would proceed to perform its toilet as though he were doing the same service for the king—washing it, censing, dressing and perfuming it and finally replacing it in the naos and laying before it articles of food which were then completely burnt. A final purification with natron, water and terebinth-incense concluded the ceremony and it only remained to close the naos, draw the bolts and seal it up. Thereupon the priest withdrew backwards, removing with a broom all traces of his footprints.[20]

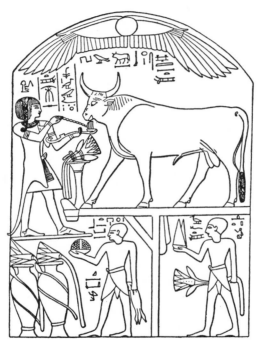

High priest offering incense to Mnevis

In return for these attentions and offerings the god granted the king not merely life on earth, but life in union with god, together with a future of ceaseless happy jubilees throughout all eternity. For the populace who played no part in this daily worship, it was enough to know that Pharaoh enjoyed the favour of his fathers the gods and that all manner of blessings would in consequence descend upon Egypt.[20a] They would make the most of the god's public appearances (p. 286) but in the intervals of waiting for those days of rejoicing, anyone who wanted was certainly free, perhaps in consideration of some small offering, to enter the god's domain and to cross the courtyard and the sacred grove to the park where the ram or the bull, the specially chosen representatives of the god incarnate, were free to play, or the pond where the crocodile of Sobek wallowed. There was nothing to stop an Egyptian of humble birth from laying at the foot of the statue of Amūn in Thebes, or of Ptah in Memphis, a little limestone stele engraved with a picture of the god himself, and with eyes and ears as well: perhaps a single ear, but more commonly three, nine or possibly forty-eight or even 378. This was a naïve way of ensuring that the god should hear and see the petitioner, who might then ask every kind of grace and favour. From death alone prayer could win no repieve.[21]

Every temple also contained statues or stelae with a reputation for healing.[22] The surface of stelae of this type was engraved with a figure of the naked child Horus standing on a crocodile and holding serpents in his hands, and with a grinning figure of Bes above. On the back or the base was engraved the legend of how, while his mother was away, the divine child was bitten by a snake in the swamps of Akhbit. On hearing the mother's cries, the lord of the gods had bidden Thoth to cure the injury. Alternatively the text might tell how the goddess Bastit was cured by Rê of a scorpion's sting: or how Osiris was cast into the Nile by his brothers and miraculously preserved from the jaws of the crocodiles. The statues, on the other hand, represented holy men who during their life had won renown as snake charmers. Each such statue and stele stood upon a pedestal in the middle of a basin full of water, connected by a channel to a second pool cut in the lower level of the pedestal. When anyone had been bitten, water was sprayed over the statue or the stele and thus became impregnated with the virtues of the magical texts and legends engraved thereon. It was then collected from the lower pool and given to the injured person to drink. 'The poison does not enter his heart, it does not burn in his breast, for Horus is his name and his father's name Osiris and his mother is called Neith who weeps.' As soon as the patient had recovered he had only to offer a prayer of gratitude to the saint who had been the instrument of his cure, although this naturally did not relieve him of

Plate XIII   Magical Stela: Horus on crocodiles

the obligation to give a small gratuity to the Pure One or the Divine Father who had sprinkled the water.

None the less, when these humble folk preferred their modest requests they felt somewhat ill at ease in the splendour of the Divine Houses in Thebes, Memphis or the great cities. They believed implicitly in Amūn or Ptah, but they preferred to commune with these great gods without the presence of officials and in shrines as humble as themselves. The workmen in the necropolis had adopted as their protectress a serpent-goddess whom they called Mertseger, the Friend of Silence. Her chosen habitation was the summit of the hill overhanging their village and a reference to the Peak was equally likely to signify the goddess herself or her dwelling place. One day a worker in the necropolis called Neferâbou called upon Ptah and the Peak goddess to witness his statement in a court of law. In fact he was lying and soon afterwards he was struck blind. He confessed his sin before Ptah, who had cast him into darkness in the full light of day, and testified aloud to the justice of this god whom nothing escaped. Yet in spite of all this he was not healed. Then he made his humble confession before the great and mighty Peak of the West. She came to him with a refreshing breeze and cured him of his affliction. 'For the Peak of the West is merciful to him that entreats her.'[23] The popularity of the little shrine of Mertseger can be judged from the large number of stelae and votive offerings found there. But the goddess did very well from being so near a neighbour of the other great gods whose shrines lay beside her own. When one of the workmen decorating a tomb fell ill, his father and brothers addressed their prayers to Amūn, who saves even him who is in the world beyond. The lord of the gods came like the north wind, 'yea like a cool breeze to save the sufferer, for he never lets the sun go down upon his wrath—his anger lasts but for the twinkling of an eye and leaves no trace behind'.[24]

Not content with having adopted a female patron in the person of the Friend of Silence, these workmen chose as their male protector Amenophis I, the first of the monarchs of the New Kingdom to have his tomb cut in the Valley of the Kings,[25] who had indeed been the first employer and benefactor of the population centred on Deir el Medineh. His cult soon became so widespread that he possessed many shrines in Western Thebes. Traces have been discovered of a temple of Amenophis (Life, Health,

Strength!) of the Garden, and we know of at least three others
—Amenophis of the Forecourt, Amenophis sailing upon the
Water and Amenophis the Favourite of Hathor. The festival in
their good patron's honour lasted for four days during which the
workmen and their families drank and sang incessantly. All the
priests in this cult—those who shaded the god, those who fanned
him and those who censed him—were workmen.

The workers trusted their god so implicitly that they used to
invoke him to settle their disputes. The justice he dispensed was
both swifter and more merciful than that of the vizier and his
scribes. In the word of a woman plaintiff, 'Come to my aid, my
lord! My mother and my brothers have started a quarrel with me.'
The father of the family had died, leaving the plaintiff two 'por-
tions' of copper and an allowance of seven measures of grain. The
mother had appropriated the copper for herself and was only letting her daughter have four measures of grain. In another case a
workman had made a coffin out of wood which he had himself
supplied. The value of the materials and labour was estimated at
31½ *deben*, but the client would not pay more than 24 *deben*. In a
third case an engraver's clothes had been stolen and he uttered
his complaint before the statue of the sanctified king. 'My lord,
come to my help today, for both my garments have been
stolen!' A scribe read out a list of houses: when he came to read
out 'the house of Amonnekht' the plaintiff asserted that his clothes
were in the house of Amonnekht's daughter. The god, on being
questioned, signified assent. Finally, a workman called Khâemwâs
was involved in a dispute over the ownership of a house. The
statue was appealed to and signified an affirmative answer by
nodding vigorously.

Perhaps in imitation of the kindly deeds of the sainted king,
even the greatest gods would sometimes deign to grant humble
mortals a piece of sensible advice or to settle a thorny dispute. A
chief of police was present one day at a procession in honour of
Isis when the image of the goddess, seated high in her boat, bowed
towards him. The recipient of this mark of favour was rapidly
promoted. In Thebes, the capital, it was the great god of the city
(Amūn) who was most frequently consulted. When a senior
official of his cult was accused of embezzlement the god was placed
in his boat and carried to the appropriate place in the temple.
Two mutually contradictory texts were written out: 'O Amonrâ-

sonter, this Thutmosé is said to have concealed the missing objects' and 'O Amonrâsonter, this Thutmosé is said not to have any of the missing objects in his possession.' In reply to a question the god signified his willingness to judge the case. When the two texts were laid before him the god twice indicated the one which pronounced the accused man innocent. Thutmosé was immediately restored to his former dignities and new honours were conferred upon him. On another occasion during a procession the high priest asked Amūn whether the sentence of guilt passed upon some condemned criminals deported to the great oasis could be remitted. The god replied 'yes' with his head.[26]

Although the king of the gods would condescend to reply to ordinary mortals, it was more consonant with his dignity to address himself to great matters of state. When at the outset of his reign Ramesses II had to appoint a high priest of Amūn, the god attended the Council at which the names of the candidates and of all those who were in the running for the job were read out. The only name to win his approval was that of Nebounnef (p. 201f). The high priest Herihor used to consult Khonsou on a variety of topics. When the throne of Nubia was vacant, the princes paraded in line before Amūn, who signified the candidate whom he wished to see enthroned.[27]

The surviving documents which describe exactly how the god made his choice known are not, unfortunately, as clear as we could wish. Some scholars, with an echo, perhaps, of Don Quixote in mind, think that the statues were mechanically jointed and that while they did not utter their reply, they could raise or lower their arms, move their heads and open and shut their mouths. The Louvre contains what is perhaps a unique example of a talking statue in the shape of a jackal's head with a movable lower jaw. The mouth of this Anubis figure was normally kept open, but it could be shut by pulling a string.[28] On other occasions the god whose opinion was sought would be carried in by the priests. A forward inclination signified approval: a backward movement, the reverse.[29] The implications of these consultations are occasionally somewhat obscure. When the god pointed to a particular candidate we may be sure that the matter had been arranged beforehand. When he asserted the innocence of a defendant the affair had no further consequences, and the victims simply had to continue to search for the criminals elsewhere. But what if the god named someone as guilty? He would be well advised to restore the stolen property or pay what he was asked for. If he still refused he ran a serious risk of being treated as a liar as well as a thief and of getting a double beating. When it was a matter of settling a dispute we may assume that both parties had agreed to accept the decision, whichever way it went. The temple of Amūn contained both policemen and a prison, while on the left bank of the Nile the *Medjaiou* police were no doubt ready to make arrests at the god's direction.

4. *The God's Public Appearances*

Believers could approach their god at any time by going to the temple and there confiding in him their difficulties, their anxieties or their gratitude. And at least once a year the Lord of the locality left his abode with full ceremony and made his progress through the town and the surrounding countryside. With breathless impatience the whole population awaited these excursions, some of which were recognized occasions for crowds to gather from far and wide. Herodotus had seen boats crowded with men and women travelling to Bubastis for feasts of the cat-goddess Bastit, the women tirelessly shaking their crotals and some of the men playing flutes, while the rest sang and clapped their hands. The excitement rose to fever pitch as the procession passed through a town and the pilgrims shouted coarse jokes at the expense of the local inhabitants, who replied in kind. Many folk, carried away by the spectacle, would leave their own towns and businesses to make their way to the festival, a rewarding journey since, when once the sacrifices were concluded, the 700,000 pilgrims abandoned themselves to enjoyment. They took their pleasures strong and perhaps a trifle intemperately, for, if we may believe Herodotus, who may have been exaggerating a little, more wine was drunk in one week of the festivities in Bubastis than during all the rest of the year.[30]

5. *The Public Appearance of Min*

In the capital the presence of the king and his court conferred upon some of these divine progresses the prestige of a national festival. The anniversary of the coronation of Ramesses III coincided with the festival of Min, lord of Coptos and the desert regions and god of fertility, which was celebrated in the first

month of *shemou* at the beginning of the harvest season.[31] Both
king and god were thus the central figures of the festival. Ramesses
III would emerge from his palace of Life, Health, Strength, shining in his splendour like the rising sun, and ride in a litter to the
dwelling of Min his father, there to contemplate his beauty. The
litter, which needed at least a dozen bearers, consisted of a large
arm-chair mounted upon a dais surmounted by a cornice and supported on four long poles. The sides of the chair were decorated
with heraldic figures of a lion passant and a sphinx, while the back
bore a protective symbol of two winged goddesses. A cushioned
footstool stood in front of the arm-chair. The honour of acting
as one of the bearers was a matter of eager rivalry among the
king's sons and the highest dignitaries, who shielded the monarch
from the sun with sunshades of ostrich plumes, holding their long-
handled fans level with his face. The procession was headed by an
impressive group, comprising the king's other sons and various
high officials, who between them carried the other items of the
royal insignia—sceptre, flail, staff and axe. Among the priests we
can see one with a roll in his hand who must have been responsible for the detailed organization of the proceedings.

Another priest extended an incense burner towards the Pharaoh
throughout the journey, for he was celebrating millions of
jubilees and hundreds of thousands of years of eternity on his
throne. The eldest son of the king, as heir apparent, walked
directly in front of the litter-bearers. The rear half of the procession comprised servants and troops equipped with club, shield
and spear. Among others we can recognize some whom we have
already encountered among the king's suite when he assumed
command of his army, when he sprang into battle or galloped off
in pursuit of the wild bulls. One of them carried a stool for the
king to use when alighting.

When the procession arrived at the dwelling of Min, the king
descended from his litter and stood facing the shrine containing
the statue of the god. Here he first performed the ceremonies of
incense and libation and then presented his father with offerings,
in return for which he received the gift of life. The doors were
then opened and everyone could gaze with wonder at the beauty
of the god standing before his shrine. His body and limbs, not yet
dismembered by Isis, were tightly held in a sheath; on his head he
wore a flat-topped cap from which two feathers stood stiffly

upright and a ribbon hung to the ground. A plaited beard was tied to his chin and he wore a pectoral around his neck. His shrine included features as diverse as a pointed hut shaped like a beehive, closely resembling the dwellings of the natives of Punt, attached to a slender column crowned by a pair of horns, a pole held upright by eight ropes with negroes climbing up them, and a square plot of lettuces. Min was a deity of extreme antiquity who had travelled far before arriving at Coptos with a somewhat miscellaneous assortment of attributes.

A hymn was then chanted while the statue was taken from its shrine and placed on a litter borne by twenty-two priests. Practically nothing can be seen of them beyond their heads and feet: their bodies are invisible behind hangings decorated with rosettes and fixed to the frame of the litter. On all sides more priests are waving bunches of flowers and long-handled fans and brandishing sunshades, while yet others are carrying chests containing the canonical attributes of the god. A little group of priests is carrying the box of lettuces on a kind of stretcher.

At this point the king assumed the leadership of the procession. He had exchanged the blue headdress which he was wearing when he left his palace for the crown of Lower Egypt and carried a long staff and a club. The queen had also made her appearance. The procession had been joined by a newcomer in the shape of a white bull, bearing between its horns the solar disk surmounted by two tall feathers. This animal was an incarnation of the god, who was frequently known as 'the Bull of his Mother.' A priest with shorn head, naked to the waist, sprinkled in one motion the king, the bull and the god's statue.

Immediately behind this group we can identify the bearers of offerings and of the emblems of the gods who had accompanied Min on his wanderings and were now associated with all his festivals: jackals, falcons, an ibis, a recumbent ox, several nome signs, including that of Khemmis, the second nome of Lower Egypt, which was Min's home, a whip and a club. Next, and as it were the counterpart to the ancient companions of Min, came the royal ancestors, each in the form of a gilded statue carried on the shoulders of a priest, the leading figure being that of the reigning monarch and the next that of Meni (Menes) the founder of the monarchy, followed by Nebkherourê who reunited the country, and by most of the kings of the eighteenth and nineteenth dynasties. Neither Queen Hatshepsut, for whom her nephew Tuthmosis III had had a deep and well-founded hatred, nor Akhnaton and his successors, who had brought little glory to Egypt, were included in this company.

The procession moved off, but it was destined to halt several times before reaching the temporary shrine which was its destination; during these halts the company would hear a second hymn danced. We know little of this save that at this comparatively late epoch even the most erudite priests found most of the text incomprehensible—a fact which merely enhanced its sanctity. We need remember only that the gods danced for Min and that they were followed by a negro—the negro of Punt. Indeed Min was sometimes known as the father of negroes and is represented with a black face, since his original subjects had a varying admixture of negroid blood.

At long last the statue and its accompanying procession would reach the temporary shrine, where Min was to be installed. Two priests bearing the insignia of the genii of the east would stand before him while Pharaoh proffered a fresh offering. Light is thrown on the significance of this culminating moment by a passage from a hymn which was recited later: 'Hail to thee, Min, that makes his mother to bear! Marvellous deeds hast thou done to her in the darkness': as well as by a passage in a second hymn to the effect that Min, the Bull of his Mother, caused her to bear and consecrated his heart to her while his thigh was for ever beside hers.[32] In fact it was not his own mother whom the god got with child, but Isis, who would in the fullness of time give birth to Horus, destined to wear the crowns of Upper and Lower Egypt.

To commemorate this great event the king had assumed his double crown, while for his protection the vulture of Nekhbet had replaced the uraeus of Wadjit. He must shoot arrows north and south, east and west to lay his enemies low: and then he must release four birds, named after the children of Horus, Amset, Hâpi, Duamutef and Qebehsenouf, to carry throughout the world the tidings that the king, in renewal of Horus's original deed, had placed on his head the white crown and the red. The birds were rollers, which came from the north each autumn and left again in the spring.

The accession of a king who was both pious and beloved of the gods secured all manner of blessings for the land of Egypt. Now it was time to glorify the fertility of the earth. The statues were placed on the ground, and the company formed a circle round the king and queen. An official handed the king a sickle of copper damascened with gold together with a clump of the cereal called *bôti*, still rooted in the soil in which it grew. This symbolized the fields which stretched endlessly from the sea coast to the Nile cataract. The king cut the stalks high up, just below the ears, like the reapers round Thebes, while one of the celebrants chanted a new hymn in honour of 'Min who is in the cultivated fields'. Before his conquest of Coptos, the former lord of the desert had established himself in the once fertile valley which ran from that town towards the valley of Rohanou. He had created the grass which gave life to the flocks. The sheaf of *bôti* was offered to the god and to the king, who would retain a single ear of it, and a last hymn was chanted, in which the mother of Min lauded the strength of her son and his conquest of his foes.

This twofold liturgy concluded the ceremony. The statue was replaced in its shrine and the king took his leave of the god by presenting him with the censer, pouring a libation and making fresh offerings, for which Min briefly returned thanks. The king resumed the blue headdress which he had worn when the ceremony opened, and returned to the palace.

As far as we know no one except the god and the king, members of the royal family, priests and high officials, is portrayed participating in the great progress of Min. The artists responsible for the pictures of the main features of the ceremony on the walls of Karnak and Medinet Habu completely ignore the common people. Admittedly it took place at a time of year when there was much agricultural work to be done in the fields. None the less, there were doubtless plenty of folk with time to spare to line the streets while Min and his white bull passed by.

6. *The 'Beautiful Festival of Opet'*

The magnificent festival of Amūn at Opet was much more of a genuinely popular occasion than that of Min.[32a] It was held during the second and third months of the season of inundation, when the floods were at their height. The farmers had nothing to do and boats could sail without difficulty not merely up and down the main stream of the Nile but also along the canals and even outside their channels, since the whole of the countryside was under water.[33] It was no longer possible to move from place to place on the dykes, which had been eroded by the rising waters; every boat and every raft was pressed into service.

The starting point for the festivities was the temple of Karnak.[34] Here itinerant merchants had taken up strategic positions against the huge temple pylon from which they offered the passers-by water melons, pomegranates, grapes, Barbary figs, trussed fowls ready for the oven or already cooked, and little loaves of bread. Within the temples every member of the religious staff was astir. The first task was to go and fetch the portable boats of the Theban divinities from the rooms where they were kept on their stands. The largest of these—that of Amūn—was recognizable by the ram's head ornaments at bow and stern. The boat of his consort, Mout, carried two women's heads, each wearing a vulture skin, for her name was written with the sign of a vulture. The third boat, distinguished by its two falcon heads, was that of their son, Khonsou. The boats were carried on the shoulders of bearers through the courtyards, past the pylons and along the processional way flanked by ram-headed sphinxes which led up to the huge building. The priestly bearers, who wore long skirts held up by belts, were clean-shaven and bareheaded; a man playing a tambourine went before them, while priests with panther skins draped over their shoulders burned turpentine-resin in the censers they carried in their hands, and scattered sand and waved sun-shades and fans as they went.

At the quayside a considerable flotilla was drawn up. The vessels of Amūn, Mout and Khonsou bore little resemblance to the portable boats so recently removed from their repositories, for they were virtually floating temples, anything up to sixty or seventy yards in length—longer, that is, than most of the boats that plied on the Nile—and were decorated with indescribable magnificence. They were built of deal—'the finest firs of the Terraces' (of the Lebanon)—and were designed to be capable of sailing in spite of the prodigious weight of gold, silver, copper, turquoise and lapis lazuli ($4\frac{1}{2}$ tons of gold alone) used in their construction. The decoration of the hull, on the model of bas-reliefs in temples, depicted the king performing familiar rituals in honour of Amūn. From the centre of the bridge there rose the Great House, while beneath the shade of its canopy stood the

portable boats, statues and other objects which had been ceremoniously fetched from the temple. In front of this lofty cabin,
as if before a real temple, stood a pair of obelisks and four poles
gay with pennants. Sphinxes and statues could be seen on every
side, while bow and stern were surmounted by two enormous
rams. The boats of Mout and Khonsou, together with the royal
vessel, while perhaps slightly smaller, were decorated in very
much the same fashion.

These vessels were too heavy to be capable of unaided motion,
and to get under way they had to be towed. This operation demanded the mobilization of a regular army of uniformed soldiers
wearing military loincloths and armed with clubs, short axes and
shields, under the command of their standard-bearers, as well as
sailors. The proceedings opened with a hymn to Amūn, after
which the men detailed for towing duty grasped the ropes, encouraged not merely by their foremen, but, even more effectively,
by the crowd which had gathered on the quayside. Women shook
sistra and crotals while the men clapped their hands and beat
tambourines in time with the songs of the Libyans and the
soldiers. Negroes danced and tumbled while other soldiers, some
carrying trumpets and others wearing feathers in their hair, moved
among the crowd.

Once the boats had been hauled to the main stream of the Nile
the worst was over, and to the crack of the overseer's whip they
were made fast to the sailing or rowing boats which were to tow
them. The whole fantastic armada was surrounded and escorted
by a swarm of boats of every shape and size, including an attractive little craft in the shape of a bird with a human-headed rudder,
loaded to the gunwale with food. We can see one member of her
crew rearranging his cargo, and another building a pyramid of
fruit and vegetables.

Both banks of the Nile were lined with spectators who had
come from far and wide to watch and take part in the festival as
best they might. Innumerable tents and drinking stalls had sprung
up and food was arriving in a steady stream in the shape of herds
of oxen and calves, gazelle, ibex, oryx and birds, besides baskets of
fruit and incense to sweeten the air. No sooner had the oxen been
slaughtered than they were cut up in the open-air slaughter-houses
which lay only a few steps from the little colonnaded and gaily
decorated building where the cooks were at work. The Libyan

troops incessantly thumped their drums and dancing girls, naked to the waist, spun to the all-pervading rhythm of sistra and crotals.

The goal of the voyage was Southern Opet—the modern Luxor—where Amūn of Karnak was going to stay for nearly a month as the guest of the city. We have no detailed knowledge of how this time was spent. Amūn was a comparative new-comer to the huge Egyptian pantheon, and it was not until well into the historic period that he settled in Thebes. Egyptian mythology assigned him Mout as a consort and Khonsou as a son, because the mightiest of the gods must have a family, but we know of no myths associated with him. He had inherited a number of epithets and attributes from Min, and he may equally have borrowed certain features of his legend. It is quite possible that the interminable festivities may have included representations of some more or less original episode in the legend of Amūn: perhaps some scene performed in Pharaoh's presence, recalling the miraculous aid with which he succoured Ramesses II when beset by the cursed soldiers of the Hittites.

Whatever took place, the festival closed with the return of the sacred fleet. The portable barques were unshipped and carried back to the shrines which they had left twenty-four days previously. Once more the homeward-bound procession formed up, the tambourine players at its head, and passed down the ram-lined way, this time, perhaps, more quietly. The king could rely with redoubled conviction on the enjoyment of every divine blessing that man could expect to receive. 'The time Rê endures, the functions Atum performs, all the years of eternity on the throne of Horus in joy and strength, victory over all countries, the might of his father Amūn each day, sovereignty over the Two Lands, bodily youth, monuments that abide like the sky for ever, the whole people of Egypt, the circle of the sun's disk are within the orb of his countenance.'*

Meanwhile the man in the street had had nearly a month of excitement—eating, drinking, gesticulating and shouting. He had enjoyed a splendid view of a magnificent spectacle and he felt convinced that not only his prosperity but his very life and liberty were inseparably bound up with the god-like mortal who had escorted his father Amūn on his journey between his two great shrines.

*lit. 'under the place of his face'.

7. The Festival of the Valley

There was still another occasion, namely the Festival of the Valley,[35] when the sacred boat of Amūn left its anchorage. This time it crossed the Nile 'towed by the gods'. A number of scholars have explained this phrase by suggesting that the figures that can be seen wearing grotesque masks and looking like the witch doctors of Equatorial Africa were impersonating the towing deities. But this is altogether too literal an interpretation, equivalent to supposing that the doctors, midwives, guards and nurses who looked after the queen and her new-born child assumed the aspect of the gods depicted on the walls of the temples of Luxor and Deir el Bahari. In fact the scenes in question are purely symbolical and show nothing beyond the depth of the care and interest of the gods in all Pharaoh's actions, and the warmth of their appreciation of the trouble he took to beautify the city of Amūn.

The Festival of the Valley was shorter than that of Opet and lasted only ten days. The king left his palace simply dressed and escorted by his fan-bearers and servants. Before entering the temple he changed into a richly ornamented loincloth and placed on his head the most elaborate of all his headdresses, in which the solar disk, feathers, uraeus and ox and rams' horns were conjoined. The purpose of his journey was to invite Amūn to pay a visit to the buildings on the west bank, during which the god's main resting place would be the hypostyle hall of the Ramesseum, where the king of the gods would receive visits from the deities who protected the dead. This was the occasion for a statue of the sainted King Amenophis I to leave his temple in a litter borne by a number of priests and surrounded by others carrying the royal flails and waving long-handled fans and sunshades. A sacred boat was waiting in a nearby canal to carry him to Amūn's great barque, the *Ousirhat*.[36] When the gods were all assembled, the ensuing ceremonies were performed on behalf of the countless dead who lay at rest in the rock-tombs of the 'mountain of the west'.

8. The Mysteries

The progresses of the gods would not have taken so many days or have attracted such enormous crowds if those responsible for the organization had not been ready to introduce an occasional note of variety. The spectacle of a golden boat, or even dancing to the tambourine, palls in the long run, and to quicken the interest of the spectators the idea had been conceived at an early date of enacting the most stirring episodes in the lives of the gods, or, better still, of having them performed by the pilgrims in person. Every Egyptian knew that Osiris had been a good king and knew also how Seth had murdered him and thrown him into the Nile, how his body had come to land at Byblos, how it had returned to Egypt, and the rest of the legend, and everyone was interested in seeing a performance of such an exciting drama. Besides, many could play minor parts in the story, leaving the leading roles to be taken by professional actors.

The most striking performances of the Osiris drama took place at Abydos and Busiris, where the producers had taken infinite care over every detail both of costumes and production.[37] The performances included a great procession under the leadership of the god Wepwawit, the 'Opener of Ways'. His enemies tried to bar his progress but the procession entered the shrine in triumph. During a second festival, or possibly a second act, the murder of the god was either acted or perhaps simply narrated. The audience displayed unrestrained grief and a great procession made its way to the tomb. Another play represented the slaughter of the enemies of Osiris, and there was general rejoicing at the sight of the god restored to life and returning in the boat called *neshmet* to re-enter his palace at Abydos. At Busiris the pillar of Osiris was erected with ropes and the crowd danced and jumped with joy. Two groups representing the inhabitants of the two adjacent towns of Pé and Dep boxed and kicked each other as a preliminary to the accession of Horus to the throne. At Saïs, when Herodotus saw performances given by night on the circular lake, the whole story of the god's passion was probably performed, including the miraculous voyage to Byblos and his transformation into a column.

Herodotus also took the opportunity of paying a visit to Papremis, a town in the north-east of Egypt sacred to Seth, the murderer of Osiris, where he saw a performance of the same character—naturally enough, for Seth was a god of battles. The god's statue, escorted by priests, was carried in its shrine outside the consecrated area. When the time came for its return it was placed in a four-wheeled chariot. More than a thousand men armed with cudgels made a rush at the small body of priests protecting the statue. The latter were joined by reinforcements and a tremendous rough house ensued. When it was all over there were innumerable black eyes and broken heads, though the inhabitants maintained that it was only a game. Its purpose was to recall that Seth had wanted to enter his mother's house in defiance of the servants who had failed to recognize him. He had accordingly sought outside help and had routed those who were trying to bar his way.[38]

Juvenal was an eyewitness of a comparable performance at Ombos in Upper Egypt, though since he was less perceptive than Herodotus and neither liked nor attempted to understand the Egyptians, he was under the impression that he was watching a real battle between two warring tribes. According to him the towns of Ombos and Denderah were divided by an ancient enmity, since each detested the gods of the other. One of them was *en fête*: tables and couches had been set up for a week and the population were dancing to the sound of flutes when the inhabitants of the other town suddenly burst in. A fight instantly began, first with fists, then with stones and finally with arrows. The inhabitants of Denderah eventually took to flight, leaving on the ground one of their number, who was seized by the men of Ombos, cut in pieces and eaten raw.[39] In point of fact Ombos (Noubit in Egyptian) belonged to Seth, while Denderah was the domain of Hathor, and several towns in the district had been the scene of the struggles between the mother of Horus and her adherents and the lecherous and pugnacious Seth.[40] What Juvenal saw was a late representation of one of those struggles, with more noise than real damage.

In every province and town religious observances and local legend provided plenty of material for drama. If one judged simply by the luxury of the temples and the number of priests and officials who took part in the ceremonies, one would hardly suspect that the Egyptian people possessed a wry and irreverent sense of humour. Even Pharaoh himself, the god who cannot be approached without trembling, appears in various stories as suffering five hundred blows from a stick,[41] cuckolded by his wives, incapable of taking personal responsibility, the slave of his counsellors and magicians and the dupe of his architects. Similarly the gods exhibit all the failings, vices and frailties of humanity and no more dignity. When they met in council to decide whether Horus or Seth should succeed to the tasks of Osiris, eighty years passed without a final answer being given. Seth's lechery was equalled only by his stupidity and credulity. When Horus was beaten he cried like a child. When Neith was summoned to the presence of the lord of the universe, she found no better way of showing what she thought of his decisions than to lift up her dress at him.[42] One day the god Shou got tired of ruling the world and took flight for heaven. His successor Geb conceived the notion of wearing on his head the uraeus which had enabled Shou to win all his victories. He paid the price of his vanity, for as he stretched out his hand to seize the box in which the uraeus lay, the serpent, child of earth, suddenly struck with its poisoned fangs at the god, who in agony ran wildly hither and thither in search of a remedy.[43]

We may be sure that the gods were treated with equal familiarity in the popular dramas which were performed in a variety of settings—in the temples or their precincts, before the temple pylons or on the sacred pools. These scenes from the legends of the gods were not confined to miming: the gods and heroes were made to speak. Not a single Egyptian drama has survived, and we have to be content with a number of texts such as the dramatic Ramesseum papyrus copied by King Shabaka from an ancient original, which gives only the title of several scenes and some of the cues, or a few snatches of conversation transcribed above scenes of private life in the tombs—especially those of the Old Kingdom. We need not doubt, however, the existence of the Egyptian theatre, the more especially since the French Institute has discovered at Edfou the stele of a professional comedian with an inscription reading: 'I accompanied my master on his travels, and never failed to recite. I gave my master his cues in all his speeches. If he was a god I was a king. If he slew, I raised to life again.'[44]

These theatrical performances were unquestionably one of the main attractions of festivals and accounted for their continuance for so many days without boring the populace.

9. *The House of Life*

Most temples contained schools somewhere within their precincts—not merely schools for teaching little boys reading and writing, but institutions where those who planned to spend their lives as draughtsmen, engineers and sculptors, devoting their talents to glorifying Pharaoh and the gods, passed their apprenticeship. They also housed libraries, containing not merely the temple archives and a mass of texts copied by an army of scribes, but also books on ethics and the literary works which the young scribes might well need, as well as technical literature. When King Neferhotep wanted to consult the books of Atum he was advised by his courtiers, 'Let your Majesty go to the libraries where he can see all the sacred utterances.' In point of fact the king found the book of the house of Osiris Khentiamentiou, the lord of Abydos.[45] Certain temples in addition owned more elaborate establishments known as the House of Life.[46]

We know from Ramesses IV himself that he was an assiduous frequenter of the House of Life of Abydos. By reading through the Annals of Thoth which were kept there he could learn that 'Osiris is the most mysterious of the gods. He is the moon; he is the Nile; it is he that reigns in the other world. Each evening the god of the sun sinks towards him and forms the united soul which governs the world and Thoth sets down his orders in writing.' As he read through these Annals, with which he was as familiar as if he had written them himself, he was struck by the range of their subject matter and of the information which they contained. When he wanted a sarcophagus of *bekhen* stone from the valley of Rohanou for himself, it was in them that he found accounts of previous expeditions which had returned with numerous sarcophagi and statues for the Place of Truth* and the temples. When he came to appoint the princes, soldiers and high officials who comprised the headquarters staff of his expedition, he was careful to attach to them a scribe from the House of Life. The king who received the ambassador from the prince of Bakhtan felt obliged to consult the priests of the House of Life before replying. When a new sacred ram was discovered in the reign of Ptolemy Philadelphus, the inhabitants of Mendes petitioned the king to have it examined by the priests of the House of Life. We know from the decree of Canopus that these scribes were interested in astronomy and the fact that they also engaged in politics is proved by two of them having joined the conspiracy against Ramesses III. This, together with other evidence, all goes to show that the House of

*The Theban necropolis.

Life was a group of scholars, theologians and savants, who preserved religious tradition, edited the annals of the kings and temples, recorded scientific discoveries and technical advances, and invented cryptography. In all probability it was in the House of Life that these discoveries and innovations first saw the light of day.

This all points to the fact that the temple must have been the focus of Egyptian life. Primarily it was the house of god where he was worshipped as befitted the blessings he bestowed. But it was also a centre of economic and intellectual activity, where the priesthood had created workshops and warehouses, schools and a library. There and only there could a man hope to emulate the good fortune of Plato and meet scholars and philosophers. And finally the temple was the setting for the birth and development of the plays whose legendary themes gave Egypt its drama and its comedy.

CHAPTER XII

THE RITES OF BURIAL

1. *Old Age*

THE maxims of the sage Ptahhotep and the tale of the adventures of Sinuhe make no attempt to sentimentalize over old age. It is a time of ugliness and of physical and moral weakness; of failing sight and hearing and memory, and of growing weariness, when food does the eater no good.[1] Nevertheless the Egyptians shared the universal desire of mankind not to quit this vale of tears before they must. The old man who by dint of infinite pains had managed to preserve the appearance of youth and to keep his faculties unimpaired was the object of universal admiration. The high priest Romeroy admits that he had been exceptionally blessed in reaching old age in the service of Amūn. 'My limbs are healthy, my sight is good and the food of his temple remains in my mouth.'[2] The court had once buzzed with talk of an old man aged 110 who thought nothing of eating 500 loaves and a shoulder of beef and of drinking 100 jars of beer 'up to this day': though we are not told whether this feat had taken him a day, a month, a season, or a year. Moreover, this ancient was a learned and potent magician, and Pharaoh accordingly resolved to summon him to his presence with a promise of feeding him on delicacies provided by the king and on provisions reserved for members of his suite, while he waited to join his forefathers in the necropolis. Pharaoh's own son conveyed the invitation in person, making the first stage of the journey by boat and the second in a chair carried by bearers, for chariots had not yet been invented. He found the object of his mission lying on a mat before his door, with one servant fanning his head, and another massaging his feet. To the prince's compliments he returned a gracious reply. 'Peace, peace be with you, Didifhor, beloved royal son of your father. May thy father, Cheops, whose voice is tuneful, praise thee and advance thee to such rank as befits a full-grown man. May thy *ka*-soul have power to thwart the designs of thy foes, and thy *ba*-soul know the secret way that leads to the Gate.' The prince stretched out his arm, raised the old man and led him by the hand to the water's edge. Travelling in three boats, they reached the king's residence and were immediately received. The king expressed his astonishment at not having previously made the acquaintance of his most venerable subject. With a noble simplicity and a perfect turn of flattery, the old man replied: 'A guest comes when he is bidden, my lord king. I have been called and lo! I am here.'[3]

A happy old age required something more than a mere absence of physical infirmity; it needed wealth, or at least a comfortable income. Anyone who had attained to the state of *amakhou* was not merely certain not to starve in old age but could rely on a first-class burial. When Sinuhe returned from exile he was given an estate and a house fit for a courtier. Many workmen were engaged on its construction and the wood used in it was new and not taken from a demolished building. 'I was brought food from the palace, three and four times each day, besides what the children of the royal household gave me in perpetuity.' Thereupon Sinuhe, who had been the recipient of the royal funerary offering, supervised the building of his house of eternity. He furnished it and made the most detailed arrangements for every aspect of the upkeep of his tomb and his funerary cult.[4] This was the kind of pleasure in which any elderly man might indulge, at least if he were a friend of the king, who could at his pleasure grant or withhold the coveted title of *amakhou*. But a monarch who, according to his panegyrists, was as good and as just as he was omnipotent and omniscient, could be relied on not to deny it to anyone who had done him good service.[5] Furthermore, every great man modelled his behaviour upon that of the king. Governors of towns and provinces, First Prophets and leading soldiers all had considerable staffs: and as his servants and dependants grew old a kindly master would see to it that they had a job within their failing powers and would guarantee them food and shelter while they awaited death. It was in order not to deprive Sinuhe of these essentials that Pharaoh, who had refused to pardon him for his flight while he was still in the prime of life, allowed him to return when he learned that he was getting old. Egypt took equal care of her old people and her children. I could not swear that on no occasion in this kindly land did an impatient heir ever curtail the span of an elderly relative who proclaimed too loudly his determination to live to the age of 110; some kings were, after all, deposed. But it is worth remembering that Amenemmes I, on handing over the effective control of affairs to his son after a reign of twenty years, lived peacefully for a further decade, during which he had leisure to compose some fairly cynical maxims: while Apries, though defeated and dethroned, could have saved his life had he not enraged public opinion by acts of senseless cruelty. Taking it by and large, Egypt was a good country for the elderly.

2. *The Weighing of Actions*

It would be a great mistake to imagine that the Egyptians regarded the prospect of dying with any pleasure. They knew that death would give ear to no complaint and could not be moved by prayer. It was vain to proclaim one's youth, for 'death seizes the child at his mother's breast as readily as the man that is grown old.'[6] Moreover, 'What are the years, be they never so many, that man passes on earth? The West is the land of dreams and deep shadows, the resting place of those that are there. They sleep in their swathing bandages and wake but to see their brothers. No more do they see their fathers nor mothers, and their heart remembers not their wife and their children. Fresh water, which is earth's gift for those that dwell on earth, is but stagnant water for me. The water comes near him that dwells upon earth, but the water that is by my side is stagnant.'[7]

An aspect of the other world which the pious found more attractive was that, there, one was done with one's rivals and enemies and could rest in peace at the last. There were even some cynics who remarked that 'No one returns from the grave to tell us how the dead behave or what they lack, in order to calm our spirits at the moment when we shall follow them where they are gone.' This particular sage added that all tombs fall into decay and that even the graves of the sages of old are as if they had never been.[8] Nevertheless he did not conclude that it was useless to devote so much thought to preparing one's tomb or to think of death so long before it came. Indeed even had he done so he would not have shaken the convictions of his contemporaries who, in the period covered by this book, as in the period when the pyramids were built, were accustomed to make the most elaborate preparations for their passage from this world to the next.

On entry to *Amentit*, the next world, all the dead had to undergo a formidable experience: the weighing of their actions.[9] The aged king who compiled his instructions for Merikarê warned his son against judges that oppress the poor, and this led him to speak of other judges. 'Do not believe that all will be forgotten in the day of judgement, and put not your trust in the length of years. They (the gods) regard life as but an hour. After death man continues to exist and all his deeds are piled up beside him. He that shall come without sin before the judges of the dead, he shall be there as a god, and will walk in freedom with the lords of eternity.'[9a] Setna, the son of Ramesses Ousirmarê, had the extraordinary good fortune to make his way into *Amentit* while yet alive, where he saw 'Osiris the great god seated on his throne of pure gold and crowned with the twin-plumed diadem: the great god Anubis on his left hand and the great god Thoth on his right: the gods of the council of the people of *Amentit* on his left hand and on his right the scales set up in full view among them all, where they weighed evil deeds against meritorious deeds, while the great god Thoth acted as the recorder and Anubis addressed them.' The accused were divided into three groups. Those whose evil deeds outweighed their good were thrown to the bitch-monster Amait. Those whose good deeds outweighed their evil were received among the council of the gods. The man whose good and evil deeds were of equal weight had to serve Sokar Osiris, covered with amulets.[10]

The Egyptians believed that only a very few sinless mortals would come before the supreme judge and it was accordingly necessary to win from the gods the boon that misdeeds should be cancelled and the sinner purified. This hope was very widely held and often finds expression in funerary literature: 'My sins are cleansed, my faults are swept away, my iniquities are destroyed.[11] Thou layest down thy sins at Nen-Nisou.'[12] 'The great enchantress purifies thee. Thou confessest thy sin which shall be destroyed for thee to make things according to all that thou hast said.[13] Homage to thee, O Osiris of Dedou, thou hearest men's words. Thou washest away his sins. Thou justifiest his voice (p. 306) against his foes and he is strong in his court of justice on earth.'[14]

'Thou standest firm and thy enemies fall. The evil that men say of thee doth not exist. Thou enterest the presence of the Ennead of the Gods and thou comest forth true of voice.'[15]

The whole of the one hundred and twenty-fifth chapter of the Book of the Dead was written in order to shrive the sinner of his sins. The Egyptians sometimes copied it on to a roll of papyrus which was then laid in the coffin between the mummy's legs. It reads like an eyewitness account of the last judgement—written in anticipation of the event—but this is a judgement where everything works out for the best. The room where it is held is, for some unexplained reason, called the room of the Two Truths. Osiris sits enthroned in a chapel with his two sisters, Isis and Nephthys, standing behind him. Below him in a line are fourteen assessors, while in the middle stands a large balance whose upright is decorated with the head of Truth, Anubis or Thoth. Near the scales a monster stands on guard. Thoth, Anubis and occasionally Horus and the Two Truths are busy in the middle of the room.

The dead man, wearing a linen robe, is led in by Anubis and greets his judge and all those who are present. 'Homage to thee, great god, Lord of the Two Truths. I am come into thy presence, having been brought hither. I have seen thy perfection. I know thee and I know thy name and the name of the forty-two gods who accompany thee in this hall of the Two Truths, who live as keepers of the wicked, who drink of their blood this day to pass judgement on the characters before the Good Being.' Then he repeats a long assertion of his innocence couched in negatives. 'I have not committed any sin against any man . . . I have not ill-treated my people . . . I have not made any man work beyond his strength . . . I have not slandered God. I have not bullied the poor man . . . I have not made any man hunger . . . I have not given short measure . . . I have not given short length . . . I have not falsified the measurements of the fields . . . I have not given short weight . . . I have not tampered with the needle of the balance . . . I have not taken milk from the mouths of little children . . . I have not dammed the water when it should flow . . . I have not stopped God when he went forth.'

After thirty-six denials of having done anything of which the devout would disapprove, the defendant would conclude that he was pure because he was the nose of the Lord of Breath who was

Weighing the heart

Plate XIV

the source of life for all who lived in Egypt. Therefore, as though he feared that he would not be believed, he began to protest his innocence all over again, addressing in turn the forty-two gods whom he had greeted on his first entry and who bore such terrifying names as Great Strider, Swallower of Shades, Breaker of Bones, Eater of Blood, Bawler, Announcer of Combat; after each salutation he would deny the commission of a sin. He added that he was not afraid to come beneath the knife of his judges, both because he had neither insulted god nor offended against the king and also because he had obeyed the laws of man and done those things that the gods approve. 'He has given god what he loves and has made him content. He has given bread to the hungry, water to the thirsty, clothes to the naked, and has lent his ferry boat to him that would cross the river. He is one to whom men cry "Welcome, welcome" when they see him.' He has performed many other pious and praiseworthy actions: for example he has listened to the dialogue between the donkey and the cat (most regrettably lost).

It only remained to bring this ordeal to its practical conclusion. On one side of the scales was placed the heart of the defendant, on the other a small statue of Truth. But supposing the heart were to speak and belie its owner? To guard against this danger the invocation contained in chapter thirty of the Book of the Dead was composed. 'Oh my heart, heart of my mother, heart of my forms! Set not thyself up to bear witness against me, speak not against me in the presence of the judges, cast not thy weight against me before the lord of the scales. Thou art my *ka* in my breast, the *Khnoum** which gives wholeness to my limbs. Let my name not stink, speak no falsehood against me in the presence of the god!' Thus adjured, the heart listened in silence to the two confessions. The result was unfailingly successful. Anubis stopped the trembling of the scales, declaring that the two sides were equally balanced and it only remained for Thoth to record the weighing, and to declare that the defendant had triumphed and that he was 'just of voice' (*maa kherou*). The realm of Osiris had gained yet another subject, while the monster who had hoped to devour the newcomer had waited in vain.

Did the Egyptians really believe that nothing was needed to erase their sins from the memory of gods and man, save to deny

*The creator god.

them in writing? Various recent works on Egyptian religion assert that chapter 125 of the Book of the Dead is a magical text.
The word 'magical' has many implications; but Egyptologists
should always remember that the treatise on how to restore an
old man to youth was also regarded as a magical text, until a more
careful examination revealed it as a specific for getting rid of
wrinkles, pimples, rashes and other unattractive attributes of old
age.[16] In my opinion when the author of the instructions to
Merikarê declared that no one could deceive the supreme judge,
he was only saying what everyone believed. It could be maintained that the very fact that an Egyptian insisted so strongly on
his purity and innocence showed that he had rid himself of the
burden of his sin during his lifetime, and that it was this conviction which released him from fear of the next world.

The essential aim was to be declared *maa kherou*, or 'just of
voice', a title which could only be gained as a result of having
pleaded one's case before the judges. From stelae, sarcophagi and
the walls of tombs we know the names of countless Egyptians
who are thus described and the theory has been advanced that it
represented a pious wish uttered by the living either on their own
behalf or on behalf of their parents or friends, but capable of fulfilment only in the next world; to such an extent that *maa kherou*
and 'dead' become virtually synonymous.[17] However, we know
of a number of Egyptians who claimed the title during their lifetimes, like Cheops, whom the Greeks accused of impiety* and
who was *maa kherou* when he was listening to his sons telling him
a succession of stories of magicians; like Pa Ramessu when commanded by Horonemheb to supervise the great works of the
temple of Opet, in the days before he became King Ramesses I;[18]
or like the Great Chieftain of the Mâ-people, Sheshanq, before
succeeding to the throne as Sheshanq I.[19] Bakenkhonsou the high
priest of Amūn was 'just of voice' when he secured from Ramesses
II the privilege of putting his statues in the temple where they
'joined the company of the Praised Ones'.[20] At this date he was
already ninety-one years old, but had several more years of life
before him. Similarly one of his successors, Ramessesnekht, is also
described as 'just of voice' in the inscription in the Wadi Hammamât which tells the story of the great expedition dispatched by
Ramesses IV to the mountain of *bekhen* stone (p. 135), in the third

*Herodotus II, 124.

year of his reign. We know that Ramessesnekht was still living in the fourth year of the reign of a king who can only have been either Ramesses IV or Ramesses V.[21]

I think that these examples will suffice to prove that the Egyptians could become *maa kherou* during their active lifetimes; but the question remains how they had succeeded in doing so. The first *maa kherou* had been Osiris who, after being restored to wholeness and life by the devotion of his wife, hounded his murderer Seth until he had brought him to the divine seat of judgement presided over by the god Rê and there had him condemned.[22] Isis had never wanted her struggles and the evidence of her devotion to be lost in oblivion and she had therefore instituted mysteries of the utmost sanctity to serve at once as a memorial of her labours and as a consolation to mankind. Whereas in Herodotus's day these mysteries still represented the sufferings of Osiris, at a far earlier date they had rehearsed the struggle of his supporters to release their lord's body and its triumphal return to the temple of Abydos. The next scene represented the mystery of judgement, and chapter eighteen of the Book of the Dead lists the towns which enjoyed the privilege of seeing this ceremony enacted, namely On, Didou, Imit, Khem, Pé and Dep, Rekhti in the Delta, Ro Setaou (a district of Memphis), Naref at the mouth of the Fayyum, and Abydos in Upper Egypt. All the evidence suggests that a pious Egyptian could ensure his salvation by imitating Osiris. The end of chapter 125 contains a rubric which must have been addressed to the living. 'To utter this chapter purely and correctly, wearing ceremonial garb, shod in white sandals, with eyes dusted with black powder, and anointed with the finest incense after making a full and complete offering of oxen and birds, terebinth, bread, beer and vegetables.' And the sacred text continues 'He who has done as much for himself, he shall be green (i.e. shall flourish) and his children shall be green. He will be looked on with favour by the king and the great ones. He shall want for nothing and shall at the last join the company of Osiris.'

We can now form a picture of this mystery of the judgement in which the Egyptians succeeded in gaining release from their sins. All those who felt that their days on earth were numbered, either from old age or sickness or because they had been visited by one of the secret warnings sometimes sent by Osiris to those who were destined soon to join his kingdom,[23] would hasten to throng one of the towns named in the previous paragraph and there take the stipulated precautions, being particularly careful to provide a full and complete offering.

A reading of chapter 125 suggests that there were two stages in the mystery of judgement. In the first it was Osiris who proved his own innocence, during which he addressed himself to the god Rê and proved by his thirty-six denials that throughout the whole year he had done no wrong. The faithful would repeat this declaration of innocence and draw strength and comfort from the judgement declaring the god guiltless. But this was not enough, and now, as it were, Osiris left the dock and took his seat upon the bench. The faithful repeated the second 'negative confession' and then in turn approached the scales. On one side was placed a heart of lapis lazuli engraved with their name, on the other the image of truth: and each could satisfy himself that the two sides were in equipoise. The petitioner was solemnly recorded and incribed as 'just of voice' and could return home in the certain knowledge that the gates of the next world would not be barred against him.

3. *The Preparation of the Tomb*

His mind thus at peace, every Egyptian could devote his whole attention to his 'house of eternity'.

The Pharaohs always gave this their attention in good time. The building of even quite a modest pyramid was a considerable undertaking and what were virtual expeditionary forces had to be dispatched to bring the blocks of granite or alabaster to the plains of Gizeh or Saqqara. By the beginning of the New Kingdom the royal necropolis had been moved to the Valley of the Kings, which lay to the west of Thebes. Though the descendants of Ramesses I had originally come from the Delta, they followed the practice of the dynasty whom they had supplanted and continued to cut their tombs into the mountain of Thebes. These subterranean vaults, or hypogea, might be as much as a hundred yards in length. Although the walls of their passages and chambers were covered with strange scenes, depicting the mighty voyage of Rê in the twelve regions of the underworld and his struggle against the enemies of light, there was nothing to recall what the king had done during his lifetime, nor anything designed for the eye of the visitor. In truth the royal tomb was not intended to be visited. It was an enclosed domain whose very entrance had to be kept secret.[24]

In this it differed completely from the tombs of private individuals, which usually consisted of two quite separate parts. A chamber hollowed from the rock at the bottom of a shaft was designed as the resting place of the dead. When he was laid there in his sarcophagus and the last rites had been performed, the entrance to the chamber was walled up, the shaft filled in and no one, in theory, should ever disturb his repose. But above the chamber there stood a substantial building, open to those who survived him. The façade stood at the far end of a courtyard in which stelae proclaimed to later generations the dead man's merits and services. Sometimes palm-trees and sycamores had been induced to grow near a pool of water[25] in the courtyard, which in turn gave access to an enchantingly decorated room, generally greater in width than in length. Even the ceiling was decorated with plant motifs or with brightly coloured geometrical patterns, and the pillars and walls were covered with paintings of the most characteristic moments in the dead man's life. A big landowner would be shown watching men at work in the fields, or hunting antelope in the desert or water birds with the boomerang or the hippopotamus with the harpoon, or fishing. We see him as superintendent of the workshops of Amūn, watching sculptors, jewellers and cabinet makers at work; as an official gathering in the royal revenues; as an officer drilling recruits. He might be portrayed being received in audience by the king, or introducing into the palace long lines of envoys from countries which knew not Egypt, who had come bowed with the weight of the gifts they bore to beg the breath of life. After making a circuit of this ante-room, the visitor would enter a wide passage. One wall carried a picture of the dead man voyaging by boat to Abydos, the other, scenes from the full burial ritual. This passage led into an inner chamber entirely devoted to displaying the dead man's piety and showing him worshipping the gods, pouring a libation of water in their honour, offering a lighted brazier and reciting hymns. The reward for his piety and forethought was to ensure an eternally renewed supply of food.[26]

Naturally the sarcophagus occupied the place of honour among the articles of funerary furniture. Neferhotep paid more than one visit during his lifetime to the workshop in which his own was being fashioned; there he saw his future resting place supported on two stools and the workmen, standing or sitting, busily engraving, polishing and painting it. He saw too the priest who was sprinkling it with holy water.[27] The king and the wealthy were not content with a single coffin. The mummy of King Psousennes not only wore a mask of gold but was enclosed in a silver sarcophagus shaped like a mummy, which in turn fitted tightly into another sarcophagus of black granite of similar shape. This was completely enclosed in a huge rectangular box decorated inside and out with figures of divinities keeping watch over the mummy. Along the upper surface of the curved lid lay the figure of the dead man with the attributes of Osiris, while on the under side hung Nout, the goddess of the sky, surrounded by the barques of the constellations. Her slender and graceful body lies a few inches above the black granite sarcophagus. With his eyes of stone the king could gaze with endless delight on the lovely goddess bestowing an eternal kiss on him. This fulfilled one of the wishes of every Egyptian for eternity, namely to dwell in heaven and wander among the stars that knew not rest and the planets that knew no destination. The sides of the sarcophagus were also carved both with eyes, with whose aid he could see as keenly as Rê and Osiris, and with doors through which he could leave or re-enter his palace at his pleasure.

The richness and diversity of the tomb furnishings naturally varied with the means of its occupant. Tutankhamūn's tomb, for example, baffles description with its ceremonial couches and beds, chariots and boats, coffers and chests, arm-chairs, plain chairs, stools, every kind of weapon, every variety of walking-stick then known, ornaments, games, metal and stone vessels and ritual objects. As a member of the kingdom of Osiris, the king would have to repeat the acts of piety which he had performed during his lifetime, while as head of a family and sovereign respectively he would have to continue to receive and entertain his children, relatives, friends and subjects. This accounts for the large quantity of dishes. Certain articles from the royal sideboard were put on one side to be laid in the tomb, and birds, meat, fruit, cereals, liquids and indeed every conceivable kind of food and drink were all prepared for consumption.

The complement to the sarcophagus was formed by a chest of wood or stone and four jars of the type wrongly known as

Canopic, intended to contain the organs removed from the body during the process of mummification and laid under the protection of four gods and four goddesses. The four gods were Amset, Hâpi, Douamoutef and Qebehsenouf, with the heads of man, dog, jackal and falcon respectively. Some people indulged in the further refinement of making miniature coffins of gold or silver, with separate bodies and lids, to hold little mummified packets of viscera. The coffins would then be enclosed in the alabaster jars.

The fields of Yalou, the realm of Osiris, resembled the garden of Candide—the most beautiful place on earth, but one which had to be ploughed, sown, weeded and harvested like an estate on earth. Not only must the irrigation canals be kept in repair but a number of operations whose utility escapes us had to be performed, such as moving the sand from one bank to the other. These operations, which a landowner would accept as pure routine, were on the contrary regarded as quite insupportable by those who had lived out their lives in idleness or had not followed an agricultural career. The Egyptians had a unique capacity for believing that the image of a thing or a person possessed to some degree the abilities and properties of the original, and the obvious way to deal with the problem was to make statuettes which could do the necessary work in the dead man's stead. These statuettes, of glazed faience or occasionally of bronze, were shaped like a mummy. The faces sometimes have sufficient character to make it probable that the artist intended a portrait. But even if no likeness was intended it did not matter, since an inscription gave at least the name and title of the person whose place it was to take, e.g. 'The Osiris, First Prophet of Amonrâsonter, Hornekhti.' Quite frequently a more extensive text defines the job which the statuette would be expected to perform. 'The Osiris N., he says: "O statuette (*oushebti*), if the Osiris N. is counted, called by name and summoned to do all the tasks which must be done there in the necropolis, as a man does them on his own behalf, to make the fields fertile, to make water flow through the channels, to carry the sand from east to west or from west to east, to pull up the weeds, like a man on his own behalf, you must say 'I will do it, here am I.' " '

Once this idea had caught on, there was no end to the manufacture of these statuettes which were designed to ensure permanent freedom from the dreadful threat of this forced labour.

Tools were carved in their hands, and bags on their backs. Statuettes not only of manual workers but also of scribes and overseers were manufactured, since close in the background of every gang of labourers lurked the inevitable official. Ultimately there developed a regular industry in the manufacture of a large range of miniature objects and tools in faience or bronze for the statuettes to use; yokes for the carriers of sand or water, large and small baskets, picks and mallets, each article inscribed with the name of the appropriate statuette to ensure that it was not stolen or used in defiance of its original's wishes.[28]

By an extension of the same idea, a number of statuettes of naked women were also made for the dead. Kings and princes had concubines and had no intention of doing without them in the next world. Examples were found in the antechamber of the tomb of Psousennes, some inscribed with the king's name, others with that of a woman. But he would deserve our sympathy if the concubines he enjoyed in his lifetime were anything like the puppets he chose for his tomb.[29]

Mummies loved adornment just as much as the living. Quite frequently indeed, a mummy was decked with the jewels which the dead man had worn in his lifetime, but it was more usual to make new ones. The following list shows what was essential for a king or a high dignitary:[30]

A mask, of gold for kings and princes of the blood, of papier mâché and painted plaster for private persons.

A collar formed of two stiff plaques of enamelled gold in the shape of a vulture with outspread wings.

One or more necklaces of gold, precious stones or faience beads, consisting of several rows of beads or pendants fastened with one or two clasps, occasionally fitted also with a pendant, usually of gold and precious stones graded in size, sometimes of faience.

One or more pectorals suspended on chains, the commonest device being a winged scarab with Isis and Nephthys as supporters, and the back engraved with the words of the famous invocation to the heart: 'Oh my heart, heart of my mother, heart of my forms, set not thyself up to bear witness against me, speak not against me in the presence of the judges, cast not thy weight against me before the lord of the scales. Thou art my *ka* in my breast, the *Khnoum* which gives wholeness to my limbs. Let not my name stink . . . speak no falsehood against me in the presence of the god!'

A number of other engraved scarabs with and without wings, but unmounted, and model hearts of lapis lazuli hung on a chain and engraved with the dead man's name.

Bracelets, flexible and rigid, hollow or solid, to be worn on wrists, arms, thighs and ankles.

Finger stalls for each finger and toe.

Sandals.

Amulets and statuettes of gods which would have been hung round the neck or attached to the pectoral.

Among the gods, Anubis and Thoth were specially responsible for watching over the dead man, on account of the part they played in the weighing of his deeds, but the choice was by no means confined to them. Their place might sometimes be taken by falcons or vultures with outspread wings or serpent heads (the serpent was the keeper of the bolt which barred the doors of the different sections of the next world), or by the fetishes of Osiris and Isis, or the magical eye-amulet, *oudja*.

Besides all these ornaments there were also a number of tiny reproductions of walking-sticks, sceptres, weapons, and attributes of royalty or divinity which it was always useful to have around.

To choose such an elaborate and expensive outfit, and to make sure that it was really well made, must have meant a great deal of work. For, whatever a few cynics might say, the future of the dead man largely depended upon the trouble he had taken over the preparation, furnishing and decoration of his 'house of eternity'. The next world was by no means a place of peace and quiet; it was full of traps into which it was all too easy to fall unless every conceivable precaution had been taken.

4. *The Priest of the Double and his Duties*

Our elderly Egyptian had now watched the construction of his future 'house of eternity', decorated it in accordance with his taste and means and commissioned a variety of tomb furnishings from the cabinet-maker and the joiner. From the goldsmith he had ordered a large quantity of ornaments, talismans and amulets —everything, he judged, that he could need in the next world. But he still had to ensure that his descendants should not fail in displaying due piety towards him, not merely by paying him their last respects and seeing that he was fittingly bestowed in his new dwelling, but throughout all generations to come. 'I made over my duties to my son while I was still alive,' says one Egyptian nobleman. 'I have bequeathed him more than my father left me. My house is firmly founded and my estates are in good order; all is stable and all my possessions are where they should be. It is my son that will make my heart to live on this stele; he has been an heir to me as a good son should.' The funerary texts often express the belief that a son would keep alive the name of his father, and even of his forefathers. Hâpidjefai, the governor of Siout, appointed his son as his *ka*-priest or 'priest of the Double'— practically equivalent to his executor. Goods inherited by the son in this capacity were privileged and were not shared with other children; and the son in turn would not divide them among his own children, but would bequeath them intact to the son appointed to be responsible for his grandfather's tomb and for supervising and participating in the ceremonies performed in his memory.[31] These ceremonies were generally held on New Year's Day and in connexion with the festival known as *Wâg*, which was held eighteen days later at the tomb, in the temples of Wepwawit, lord of Siout, and of Anubis, lord of the necropolis.

Five days before New Year's Day the priests of Wepwawit would go to the temple of Anubis and each deposit a loaf for the statue which stood there. On the last day of the old year an official of the temple would give the priest of the Double a candle which had already been used in the temple. The high priest of Anubis did likewise and gave a candle which had been used to help light the temple to an individual known as the chief of the staff of the necropolis. His duty was to make his way to the tomb with the keepers of the mountain, where they would meet the priest of the Double and give him this candle.

On New Year's Day each priest of Wepwawit had to present a loaf in' honour of the statue of Hâpidjefai after the illumination of the temple had ceased. They would then form up in a procession behind the priest of the Double and celebrate his memory: while for their part the chief of the necropolis and the keepers would offer bread and beer and conduct a similar celebration. In the evening of the same day the officials of the temple who had presented a candle on the previous evening would present another. So would the high priest of Anubis and, as on the previous evening, the statues of the dead man would be illuminated with candles already sanctified by their earlier use.

The same cycle of ceremonies with minor variations was due to be repeated for the *Wâg* festival. In the temple of Wepwawit each priest presented a white loaf in honour of the statue and formed a procession behind the priest of the Double in honour of Hâpidjefai, and a third candle would burn all night long before the statue. The priests of Anubis would go in procession, singing the god's praises as they went, as far as the monumental staircase leading to the tomb, and each would lay a loaf before the freshly illuminated statue that stood there.

After the officiating priest had performed the requisite ceremonies in the temple, he would offer loaves and beer in honour of this same statue. A second personage, namely the overseer of the desert hills, would also lay loaves and jugs of beer for the statue between the hands of the priest of the Double.

Hâpidjefai took good care not to be forgotten at the festivals held at the beginning of each season which, though less solemn than that on New Year's Day, were none the less of some significance. On these occasions the chief of the necropolis and the desert patrols would assemble near the garden of his tomb and carry to the temple of Anubis the statue that stood there. Now came his last and final behest. Since he was the head of the priesthood of Wepwawit, Hâpidjefai used to receive on every feast day —and we know how frequently they recurred—meat and beer. He gave orders that after his death these should be carried to his statue, under the supervision of the priest of the Double.

Attentions on this scale were bound to cost money, and to pay for them Hâpidjefai renounced some of the natural advantages which he enjoyed either as governor or as head of the priesthood of Wepwawit, mortgaging his offices for the purpose with a sublime egotism, and thus reducing the income they would yield, since his successor would be obliged to expend each year twenty-seven 'days of the temple'—i.e. twenty-seven three hundred and sixty-fifths, or nearly one fourteenth, of the temple's total annual revenue. No doubt the temple of Wepwawit was simply a provincial shrine, but its revenue was nevertheless considerable, and his heirs, obliged as they would be to forfeit something like $7\frac{1}{2}$ per cent of the temple staff's normal income, were likely to find their standard of living depressed, the more so because the capital sum itself had been further diminished by the devising of various estates. On this basis the upkeep of the tomb looked unpleasantly like being more expensive than its original cost and the whole of Egypt would gradually become crippled by a self-imposed burden. The indifference to this aspect of his wishes displayed by Hâpidjefai is emphasized by the fact that no princes in later generations would have the right to vary any arrangements made by a prince like himself with the priests of his own day. But in point of fact even the most elaborate funerary foundations usually failed after two or three generations—or rather their income was diverted to the benefit of those who had died more recently.[32] As we have seen, kings and private individuals alike regarded the restoration of funerary monuments and keeping their offering tables well supplied as a work of piety, but many of their foundations were permanently ruined during the War of the Unclean, the end of which found Egypt in a state of anarchy and, if not absolutely ruined, at any rate far too impoverished to be able to pay attention to those long since dead.

5. *Mummification*

Once an Egyptian, after due warning from Osiris, had had enough time to build and fit out his 'house of eternity', and had done everything that piety and respect for tradition required, there was nothing to keep him on earth. The day when he 'crossed to the other bank' (Egyptians disliked the word 'die' and this was the common euphemism) his relations went into mourning for at least seventy days, during which they did no active work and lived at home in silent grief. If they had to go out of doors, they smeared their faces with mud, like Anpou when he believed that his younger brother had been killed in his stead, and incessantly beat the top of their head with both hands.[33] But they still had to perform the urgent duty of handing over the body to the embalmers and of selecting the method to be employed, of which, according to Herodotus and Diodorus, there were three.[34] What might be called first-class embalming required much time and care, involving as it did the removal of the brains and all the internal organs except the heart; these were then treated separately and tied up in four separate packages to be put in the four Canopic jars. The body cavity was then cleaned out twice and filled up with aromatic spices. It was next pickled in natron, which was found in large quantities in the Wadi Natrûn, the salt plain north-west of Fayyum, as well as in the Nekheb area and was used for a wide variety of purposes, particularly for domestic cleaning. After seventy days the body was again washed and then wrapped in bandages which were cut from a roll of linen soaked in glue. As many as fifteen separate products were required for the complete operation: bees-wax to cover ears, eyes, nose, mouth and the incision made by the embalmer, cassia, cinnamon, cedar oil

Making Canopic jars and *oushebtiou*

(actually derived from the juniper-tree), gum, henna, juniper berries, onions, palm wine, various types of resin, sawdust, pitch, tar and, of course, the indispensable natron. Several of these items came from abroad, especially pitch and resin, which was extracted from the conifers of Lebanon, so that when the sea traffic to Byblos was interrupted, the embalmers and their wealthy clientele were in despair at the thought of being driven to find substitute materials.

After the whole process was finished the body was virtually a skeleton enclosed in a shrivelled skin, but the face was still recognizable despite its sunken cheeks and wizened lips. After thousands of years we can still gain an impression of the features and expression of the great King Sety I, and the same is true of many other mummies.

It was now time to dress and adorn the mummy. It was hung with necklaces, pectorals and amulets and decked with bracelets, finger stalls, rings and sandals. The incision through which the internal organs had been removed was covered with a thick gold sheet engraved or inlaid with the *oudja*, the sacred eye which had the power of healing wounds, and the four deities that protected the Canopic jars. Between the legs was laid a copy of the Book of the Dead, that indispensable guide to the underworld. Then body and limbs were completely wrapped in linen bands, and the mask was laid over the face. In the case of private people it was made of cloth and stucco: but for kings and a few high dignitaries it was of gold and in some cases attached by threads to a beaded garment.[35] The whole was then wrapped in an outer shroud which was secured by parallel strips. As a variant on this, the mummy of King Sheshanq, which was found at Tanis, in the antechamber of the tomb of the Pharaoh Psousennes, was protected by an outer covering of cartonnage on which leaves of gold and very thin panels of blue faience broadly reproduced the decoration engraved or embossed on the silver sarcophagus.[36] Provided that during the interval the cabinet-makers, joiners, armourers and all the various specialist craftsmen who had their part to play in making the funerary furniture had worked at full speed, it was possible to proceed two and a half months after the death to the actual closing of the coffin and the interment.

6. The Funeral. The Composition of the Cortège

An Egyptian funeral was a spectacle at once mournful and picturesque.[37] The members of the family would weep and gesticulate unashamedly throughout its progress. Both male and female mourners would have been hired for the occasion, no doubt from fear that too little grief might be manifested, and the women in particular were indefatigable. With faces smeared with mud, breasts bare and garments rent, they groaned and struck their heads incessantly. The more sober members of the procession were less abandoned in their gestures, but as they walked they would recall the virtues of the deceased. 'How fair is that which has happened to him . . . he has so filled the heart of Khonsou in Thebes that he has permitted him to reach the West accompanied by generation upon generation of his servants.'[38] Thereafter a funeral procession must have looked very like moving house.[39] The leading group of servants carried cakes and flowers, pottery and stone vases, and boxes slung on either end of a yoke, containing the figurines and their tools. A second and larger group bore such normal articles of furniture as seats, beds, chests

Plate XV   Contents of the tomb of Tutankhamūn as first discovered

and cupboards, not to mention the chariot. A third group was responsible for the personal effects—chests for the Canopic jars, sticks, sceptres, statues and sunshades. Jewels, necklaces, falcons or vultures with outspread wings, human-headed birds and other valuables were displayed on dishes or carried ostentatiously in open defiance of the crowds of idlers who watched the cortège pass. The sarcophagus itself was hidden beneath a catafalque drawn by a pair of cows and several men, and consisting of movable wooden panels or a framework hung with curtains of embroidered material or leather. It was mounted on a boat and flanked by statues of Isis and Nephthys, the boat itself being mounted on a sledge.

7.   *The Crossing of the Nile*

The procession made its way slowly to the banks of the Nile, where it was met by a number of boats.[40] The main vessel, whose prow and stern curved gracefully backwards and ended in papyrus umbels, was constructed with a very large cabin, the inside of which was hung with embroidered material and strips of leather. In this cabin the catafalque was laid, together with the statues of Nephthys and Isis. A priest with a panther's skin draped round his shoulders burned incense while the female mourners bowed their heads. The crew consisted of a single sailor who took soundings with a long pole, since the boat bearing the catafalque was to be towed by another vessel with a large crew under the command of a captain who stood in the bows with a steersman in charge of the rudder posted at the stern. This latter vessel also had a large cabin, on the roof of which the female mourners, with bare breasts, continued to cry and gesticulate in the direction of the catafalque. One of their dirges ran as follows: 'Let him go swiftly to the west, to the land of truth. The women of the Byblite boat weep sorely, sorely. In peace, in peace, O praised one, fare westwards in peace. If it please the god, when the day changes to eternity, we shall see thee that goest now to the land where all men are one.' We may well wonder what the Byblite boat (*kebenit*), designed for the open sea, is doing here, when the boat with the catafalque was designed simply to make the crossing of the Nile. They had something in common, for when Isis in Byblos had succeeded in regaining the sacred tree which contained the body of

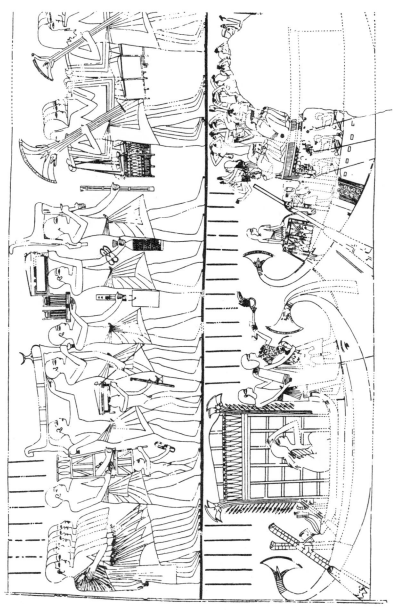

Funeral procession

her husband Osiris, she carried it on to a boat that was on the point of leaving for Egypt in which she held it in her arms and bedewed it with her tears. In the same way the women of the family wept bitterly while their boat crossed the Nile.

Those who wanted to accompany the dead man to his journey's end, together with the funerary furniture, were embarked on four other boats. Others, who wished to go no farther, remained on the bank and uttered a last wish to their friend. 'Mayest thou fare to the west of Thebes in peace' or 'To the West, to the West, the land of the just. The place thou didst love groans and laments.' This was the moment when the widow's sorrowful voice was heard: 'Oh my brother, oh my husband, oh my friend! Stay, rest in thy place, leave not the place where thou dost abide. Alas, thou goest hence to cross the Nile. Oh, ye sailors, hasten not, let him be: ye shall return to your houses, but he is going to the land of Eternity.'

8. *The Ascent to the Tomb*

Preparations had already been made to meet the convoy on the farther bank.[41] A group of people had gathered and a number of little stalls had been put up, plentifully stocked with devotional objects for the use of those who might have failed to bring a sufficient supply from the city. Someone grasped the bow of the leading boat and the catafalque, passengers and all the furniture were soon put ashore. The procession formed up again, perhaps slightly reduced in number by comparison with its size on leaving the house of embalming, but in approximately the same order. A boat of archaic design, mounted on a sledge, was hauled by a pair of cows. Isis and Nephthys were back in their place. The man with the roll (p. 278) walked beside the drivers, who carried whips. The women of the family, children and female mourners sorted themselves out as best they could. Here and there a woman was shaking crotals. The dead man's colleagues, their deportment as grave as ever, walked soberly, stick in hand, followed by the porters and talking as they went of their friend and his tastes, interspersing their remarks with observations on the blows of fate, and the uncertainty and brevity of human life. The route led past lightly constructed booths, near which stood men waving lighted braziers; and so the procession crossed the boundary of the cultivated land, and arrived at the foot of the Libyan plateau. Here the road began to climb and the surface grew rough. The cows were unharnessed and the catafalque was hauled and, if necessary, carried by men, led by a priest who ceaselessly sprinkled water from a ewer and held a lighted censer pointed towards the catafalque. At this point the goddess Hathor, in the shape of a cow, emerged from the mountain to welcome the newcomers, pushing aside a clump of papyrus which had miraculously sprung from the barren rocks.

9. *Farewell to the Mummy*

At last the procession completed its laborious journey and stood before the tomb.[42] Here too there were little stalls at which men were preparing braziers with handles and putting water in large jars to keep cool. Near the stele the invisible presence of the goddess of the West was symbolized by a falcon on its perch. The sarcophagus was removed from the catafalque and set upright against the tomb stele, and a woman knelt beside it and clasped it in her arms.[42a] On its head a man placed a scented cone similar to

Women mourners

those placed on the heads of guests at a party. The weeping and head-beating of the relations, children and female mourners were intensified. But the priests had an important task to perform. They had already laid on the table not merely the ingredients of a meal—bread and jugs of beer—but a number of strange implements: an adze, a curved knife shaped like an ostrich feather, an imitation leg of beef, a palette ending in two scrolls. Their object was to empower the priest to counteract the effects of the embalming and to restore to the dead man the use of his limbs and his missing organs, so that he might once more be able to see, to open his mouth and speak, to eat and to move his arms and legs.

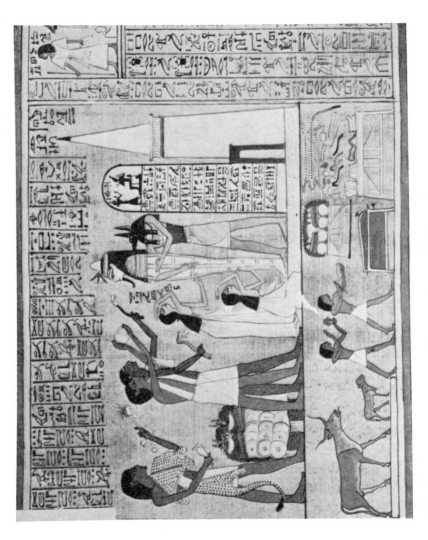

Plate XVI   The last rites before the tomb

The moment of parting had nearly been reached. The cries of grief rose to a climax. The wife cried: 'Oh my lord, it is thy wife, Meryt-Rê, that speaks. Leave me not! Dost thou wish that I should be parted from thee? If I depart thou wilt be alone, and none will be left to follow thee. Though thou wast wont to be merry with me, now thou art silent and speakest not.' Her women echoed her cries: 'Woe, woe, thrice I say, mourn without respite! The good shepherd is departed to the land of eternity. The crowd of people departs from thee, and now thou art in the land which loves solitude. Thou who didst love to walk freely, now thou art held fast, a prisoner swathed in thy bands. Thou who hadst a great store of fine stuffs now sleepest in the linen of yesterday.'

It only remained to descend into the tomb and there bestow the sarcophagus and all the funerary furniture.[43] The catafalque was left empty, and the priests, who had hired it out for the ceremony, took it back to the town, where it had already been booked by a fresh set of clients. The mummiform coffin was laid in its square stone receptable which had long before been cut, carved and lowered into its place. Various objects—sticks, weapons and possibly some amulets—were placed around it, and then the heavy stone lid was manoeuvred into position. Near the sarcophagus were laid the chest with the Canopic jars, the boxes of *oushebtiou* (p. 311) and all the rest of the furniture. It was especially important not to forget what would be most useful of all after death— food for the dead man and what we call the sprouting Osiris figures, i.e. wooden frames in the shape of a mummified Osiris, with a base of coarse material and filled with a mixture of barley and sand. They were watered regularly for several days, whereupon the barley germinated and grew thickly. When it had reached a height of about two or three feet it was allowed to dry off and was finally wrapped in a linen cloth. The hope was thereby to encourage the dead man's resurrection, since Osiris himself had sprouted in the same way at the moment when he had been resurrected. In earlier times the same result had been secured by laying in the tomb jars made in two separate pieces, the lower containing water, and the upper, which had a pierced bottom, containing a lotus-rhizome, whose roots grew through the holes into the water. Meanwhile the plant was also producing shoots through the one or three holes in the neck, and these came to flower. This practice was extremely common under the Middle Kingdom, but was

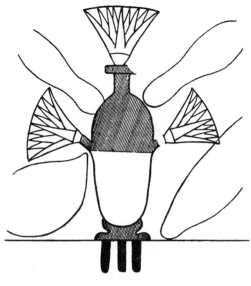

Lotus jar

abandoned when the sprouting-corn Osirises came into fashion. The lotus was the plant of Rê and the change represented a fresh victory of the Osiris religion over the ancient sun worship.[44]

10. *The Funeral Feast*

When the vault had been duly arranged, the priest and his assistants were free to withdraw and the mason walled up the doorway. The relations and friends, however, who had accompanied the dead man to his 'house of eternity' had no intention of separating and returning home forthwith. Their emotional orgy had sharpened their appetites, and the porters, besides the considerable load they had carried for the dead man's benefit, had had the foresight to include some food for the sustenance of the living. The company would gather either in the tomb or in the courtyard immediately in front of it or occasionally a little way off among the temporary stalls.[45]

A harpist then entered from the direction in which the mummy lay. He opened his performance by recalling that, thanks to everything that had been done for him, the dead man was faring excellently well. 'Thou makest thy call to Rê: Kheper hears thee and Atum answers thee. The lord of all things brings to pass that which pleaseth thee . . . the west wind blows straight on thee into thy nostrils. For thy pleasure the south wind changes and blows from the north. Thy mouth is laid against the udder of the cow Hesat. Thou becomest pure in order to gaze upon the sun, thou cleansest thyself in the divine pool . . . all thy limbs are perfect and whole, thou are justified in the presence of Rê, thou endurest in the sight of Osiris. Thou receivest well-prepared offerings. Thou takest food as thou didst upon the earth. Thy heart is at ease in the necropolis. Thou comest to thy long home in peace. The gods of the *Douat* say to thee "Come to thy *ka* in all quietness." All the dwellers of the other world wait to do thy pleasure. Thou art called upon to make their complaints known to the Great One. Thou makest the law, O Osiris Tjanefer, the justified.'[46]

Another harpist performed in more melancholy strain, in honour of the divine father Neferhotep. Be it remembered that the dead man is indeed highly favoured. Countless tombs lie in ruin, their offerings long but a memory, their loaves thick with dust: but 'the walls of thy tomb are strongly built, thou hast planted trees round thy pool. Thy *ba*-soul rests beneath them and drinks of their water.' The occasion seemed particularly appropriate for indulgence in a little moralizing. 'Men's bodies have gone to the grave since the beginning of time and a new generation taketh their place. As long as Rê shall rise in the morning and Atum shall set in the west, man shall beget and woman conceive and breath shall be in men's nostrils. Yet each that is born returns at the last to his appointed place.' Therefore life must be enjoyed. Curiously enough all this was addressed to the dead man in his tomb, but the company present took it to heart. They would do full justice to the food and drink and make their way back to the town with even more noise, and in a far more cheerful mood, than when they had left.

This is a description of the funeral of a wealthy Egyptian. Needless to say, those of the poor were far less elaborate affairs. The embalmer did not bother to open up the body and remove the internal organs but simply injected a fatty liquid, derived from the juniper, through the rectum and pickled the body in natron. In the case of the very poor, the juniper oil was replaced by an even simpler disinfectant.[47] After these preparations the mummy was put in a coffin and carried to a disused tomb, stacked with coffins to the roof, which had been turned into a communal burying place. But even in these cases the mummy was not entirely deprived of all that it would need in the next world: and the coffin would contain tools, sandals of woven papyrus, several bronze or faience rings, bracelets, amulets, scarabs, *oudjas*, and miniature figures of gods, also of faience. There were some folk who were even poorer still: they were destined for the common burial pit. A paupers' burial place lay in the middle of the rich cemetery district of Assassif in Thebes. Into this the mummies, wrapped in a coarse cloth, were thrown, covered with a thin layer of sand and another body quickly thrown on top.[48] Fortunate indeed were those among the poor that were named or depicted on the walls of a tomb of a vizier or a Viceroy of Kush, for they would continue to serve their master in the next world as they had done on earth, and since all work earned payment, they could live on the proceeds. To some extent they could enjoy in perpetuity the advantages promised to the favourites of fortune who were also men of justice.

11.   *The Relationship of the Living and the Dead*

Anyone who thought of *Amentit* as a place of peace and quietness was in danger of disillusionment. The dead were suspicious and vindictive, fearful alike of robbers attracted by the gold and silver deposited in the tomb, and of the malice or even the indifference of the countless sightseers that ventured to wander among the vast necropolis city of the west, and mistrustful of the officials responsible for its upkeep. They threatened the direst punishment on those who might neglect their duties in this respect. 'He will give them over to the fire of the king in the day of wrath . . . they will capsize in the sea which will engulf their bodies. They shall not receive the honours which are owed to men of virtue. They shall be unable to consume the offerings of the dead. No man shall pour for them libations of water from the flowing river. They shall have no son to succeed them. Their wives shall be raped before their eyes . . . they shall not hear the words of the king when he is joyful. . . .' But if, on the contrary, they keep good guard over the funerary foundation . . . 'may they enjoy all possible good. Amon-Rê, king of the gods, shall favour you with length of days. . . . The king that shall reign in those days shall reward you as he alone can do. Office shall be added to office for you, which you shall receive from son to son and heir to heir . . . they shall be interred in the necropolis after reaching the age of one hundred and ten, and offerings shall be multiplied for them.'[49]

Others among the dead were ill-disposed, some perhaps because they had been abandoned by their descendants, and others for no better reason than a love of malice. The gods ought to have prevented them from doing any harm, but they had managed to evade their watchful eyes and left their tombs to make the lives of the living a misery.[50] They might belong to either sex and most illnesses were ascribed to them. The mother feared that they might harm her child: 'If thou art come to take this child in thy arms, I will not let thee take him. If thou art come to put him to rest, I will not let thee put him to rest. If thou art come to take him away I will not let thee take him.'[51]

Whether inspired by fear or piety, the Egyptians paid frequent visits to the houses of eternity. Parents, children and the widowed alike would scale the hill, bringing with them a few provisions and a little water to be laid on an offering table which stood in front of the stele or between the palm trees which overshadowed the entrance court, while to satisfy the wishes of the dead they would repeat the following rubric: 'Thousands of loaves of bread and jugs of beer, oxen and birds, oil and incense, linen and ropes, all things pure and good which the Nile brings, which the earth creates and on which the god lives, for the *ka* of (so and so), justified.'

Occasionally one who prayed over the tomb of a loved one was racked with anxieties. Earlier (p. 53) we have quoted the protestations of a faultless husband and inconsolable widower. We know of his great merits only because the poor man was so sorely tried. After his wife's death nothing went right for him, and this led him to write her the long letter which we still possess. When he came to sum up the whole story and to recall everything that he had done for the dead woman both before and after her death, he could not help expressing his resentment at being so hardly done by: 'What wicked thing have I done to thee that I should have come to this evil pass? What have I done against thee that thy hand should be so heavy on me, when I have done thee no wrong? I make my appeal to the gods of the West by the words of my mouth and judgement shall be given between thee and this that I have written.'[52]

The writer of this letter, who lived during the period of the early Ramessids, was following an ancient custom. We possess examples of earlier date, which is clear evidence that men continued to believe in its efficacy. During the Middle Kingdom the letter to the dead man was generally written on the package containing the food offered to him, to ensure that it was not overlooked. For example, we find a grandfather being informed of the existence of a plot to cheat his grandson of his inheritance. The dead man was assumed to be anxious to thwart such manoeuvres and was therefore expected to summon the members of his family and his friends to the victim's aid, since in setting up house a son established the household of his forefathers and so endowed their name with life, and his ruin involved his ancestors no less than his descendants.

But however great the piety of the Egyptians towards their dead might be, it could not suffice for the upkeep of all those who lay in the necropolis. Whatever an individual might resolve to do in honour of his parents or his grandparents, no threats or curses could make him decide to do the same for his more distant forebears. One day what the harpist foresaw and the seer of old had foretold, would come to pass. 'Those that have builded there in granite, those who have fashioned a chamber within a pyramid . . . their offering tables are as bare as the tables of them that die in misery on the open field with none to survive them.'[53] Accordingly the necropolis tended to become the meeting place of the curious who walked past the tombs and idly read their inscriptions. Some of them inevitably felt the itch of the modern tourist to leave some evidence of their visit, though they would record that their motives were pious: for example, 'Scribes A and B have come to visit this the tomb of Antefoker; and many, many are the prayers that they have uttered.' Others were content to report that the tomb was well kept: 'They found it like the sky in its inner chambers.'

A certain Amenemhat modestly records that a nimble-fingered scribe, yea, a scribe without a peer in the whole of Memphis, has visited the funerary monument of the ancient King Zoser, where he was astonished to see writing of inferior quality and full of mistakes, whose author must be a weak woman rather than a scribe writing under the inspiration of Thoth. We ought to add that he was not complaining about the original inscriptions, which were admirable examples of the work of highly skilled artists, but about the crude scribbles of his own day made by some ignorant or hurried visitor. In the reign of Ramesses II, Hadnakhti the scribe of the Treasury made a trip in search of amusement to the west of Memphis with Panekhti, his brother, a scribe of the vizier. 'Oh all ye gods of the west of Memphis and all ye gods who reign over the sacred land, Isis, Osiris and the great spirits who are to the west of Ankh Tawi, grant me a goodly span of life to serve your *ka*s. May I live to a happy old age and be buried in a beauteous tomb whence I may gaze upon the west of Memphis as befits a much honoured scribe and as ye do yourselves.' Nenoferkaptah, the hero of a story which was probably a late composition, though he himself is believed to have lived in the time of the Ramesside monarchs, appeared to have 'no other object in life than to wander about the Memphite necropolis reading aloud the inscriptions on the tombs of the Pharaohs and the stelae of the scribes of the House of Life, as well as the inscriptions carved in the necropolis; inscriptions were his hobby'.[54] Nenoferkaptah had a rival no less learned or interested in antiquities than himself— namely Prince Setnakhamwas, son of Ousirmarê (Ramesses II) who had found underneath a mummy's head the magic formulae contained in papyrus 3248 of the Louvre collections.[55] Again, from an inscription recently·discovered on the southern face of the pyramid of Unas at Saqqara, we learn that Ramesses II had charged the royal son Khamwasit, the high priest of On, with responsibility for restoring the name of Unas, King of Upper and Lower Egypt, which had disappeared from the pyramid: for Khamwasit was very fond of restoring the monuments of the kings of the south and the north, which despite their solid construction were threatened with decay.[56]

We may wonder whether it ever crossed the mind of this scholarly precursor of Mariette and the experts of the Egyptian Antiquities Service that, after centuries of oblivion, the descendants of the barbarians 'who knew not Egypt at all' would follow in his footsteps as they explored the necropolis of south and north, seeking to bring to life again the names of his ancestors and contemporaries and to learn to understand them. We hope that the reader with patience enough to persevere to the end of the book will have formed a generally favourable impression of the Egyptian way of life. We can no longer accept Renan's picture of a horde of slaves impotent before the whims of a merciless Pharaoh and a bigoted and rapacious priesthood. We must admit that in our period many lost their inheritance, and that the stick was too commonly used. Yet often enough Pharaoh and his officials show themselves humane masters, while religion had its consolations to offer. I believe that for the ordinary man the good moments of life outnumbered the bad.

GLOSSARY

of words and expressions which recur in the text of this book

akh: the human spirit or 'shining one', in the form of a crested ibis.

akhit: the first season of the year, the season of the Nile flood (see p. 32).

amakh or *amakhou:* lit. 'venerable, revered': an honour entitling the holder to burial at the king's expense.

Amentit: the realm of the gods of the dead.

aroura: measure of area: 100 sq. cubits, about two-thirds of an acre.

ba: the soul in its form as the bird jabiru (*mycteria aphipporhyncus*).

Book of the Dead: a collection of magical spells intended to help the dead man in his passage through the netherworld.

Canopics, Canopic jars: four containers in which the viscera of the mummy were buried (see p. 317).

cavetto cornice: an architectural ornament with concave profile surmounting pylon or gateway.

Coffin Texts: a collection of magical formulae painted or inscribed on coffins.

corvée: forced labour on public works.

crotals: a form of castanets.

cubit: a measure of length, the span of the forearm from elbow to knuckle: about 18 inches.

cynocephalus: the dog-headed baboon, sacred to Thoth, the god of wisdom.

deben: a measure of weight: see table below.

demotic: a cursive script much used in the late period.

Douat: the Underworld.

Ennead: the nine cosmic gods of the Heliopolitan cult.

Great Green: the sea.

hieratic: (the 'priestly' script) an earlier cursive writing, with reed pen on sherd or papyrus, of the monumental hieroglyphics.

hieroglyphics: the picture writing of the ancient Egyptians.

House of Life: scribal centre or scriptorium attached to a temple (see p. 297ff).

ka: the soul or "double"; sometimes the personality or fortune of a man.

ka-servant: priest who maintained the funerary cult of a dead nobleman in return for revenues from a mortuary endowment (see p. 313ff).

maa kherou: 'true of voice' . . . (see p. 306).

migdol: (Hebrew, 'tower') a fortress or fortified tower of Syrian type.

naos: (Greek) a shrine.

necropolis: city of the dead, cemetery-town; often on the west of the river, as at Memphis, Thebes.

nilometer: device for measuring the annual rise of the River Nile.

Nine Bows: the traditional personification of the nations of mankind.

nome: (Greek νομός) administrative district, province.

nomarch: governor of nome.

obelisk: a tall shaft surmounted by a pyramidion, set up in temples as a sun symbol.

Opening of the Mouth: a ceremony performed on the mummy by a priest at the tomb, to enable the dead to breathe and eat (see p. 322).

On: Heliopolis, north of modern Cairo (see map).

Opet: Thebes (Karnak and Luxor).

ostrakon: potsherd or flake of stone used as a vehicle for writing or drawing.

oudjat: the Eye of Horus, a powerful amulet.

oushebti or *shawabti:* lit. 'answerer'; a figurine placed in the tomb as a substitute labourer (see p. 311).

palmette, palmetto: decoration in the form of stylized fronds of palm.

papyrus: writing material made from the compressed stem fibres of the papyrus plant.

perit: winter, the season of 'emergence' (from the Nile flood) and of sowing.

pylon: tall sloping walls flanking a temple gateway.

pyramid: tomb with stepped or sloping sides on a square base.

pyramidion: pyramid-shaped top of an obelisk, symbol of Rê; the sloping surfaces reflected the sun's rays.

qite: a measure of weight: see table below.

shawabti: see *oushebti.*

shemou: summer, the third season of the year, harvest-time.

sistrum: ceremonial rattle, especially associated with the worship of the goddess Hathor.

sphinx: symbolical figure, lion-bodied and usually human-headed, an emblem of royal might.

stele, stela: slab of stone, generally with a rounded top, inscribed with a votive, commemorative or funerary text.

temenos: the sacred precinct of temple.

Todjeser: the necropolis.

Tomery: the Beloved Land, i.e. Egypt.

Tonoutir: the Divine Land—Punt, or sometimes the Lebanon.

Two Lands: Upper and Lower Egypt, the united kingdom.

vizier: the highest administrative official under the king.

wâb: 'pure one', a member of the lowest grade of priesthood.

Measures of weight

10 *qite*	=	1 *deben*
10 *deben* of copper	=	1 *qite* of silver (in the time of Ramesses II).
6 *deben* of copper	=	1 *qite* of silver (in the late Ramesside period).

Measures of length

4 fingers = 1 palm

7 palms = 1 cubit (18 inches).

(For the *iter* or *atour* see note p. 210).

ABBREVIATIONS

A.E.M.: A. Lucas, *Ancient Egyptian Materials and Industries,* 3rd edn., London, 1948.

A.E.P.: Nina M. Davies, *Ancient Egyptian Paintings,* 2 vols., Chicago, 1936.

Aldred: C. Aldred, *New Kingdom Art in Ancient Egypt,* London, 1951.

Ani: The so-called Boulak Moral Papyrus, or Maxims of Ani. F. Chabas, *Les Maximes du Scribe Ani,* Paris, 1876.

A.R.: J. H. Breasted, *Ancient Records of Egypt,* 5 vols., 1906–7.

A.S.A.E.: Annales du Service des Antiquités de l'Egypte, Cairo, 1900–.

A.Z.: Zeitschrift für aegyptische Sprache und Altertumskunde, Leipzig, 1863–.

Bibl. aeg.: *Bibliotheca aegyptiaca:* Fondation Reine Elisabeth, Brussels, 1930–, comprising:—
  I. Alan H. Gardiner, Late-Egyptian Stories, 1932.
  II. A. M. Blackman, Middle-Egyptian Stories I, 1932.
  III. R. O. Faulkner, The Papyrus Bremner-Rhind, 1933.
  IV. C. F. Sander-Hansen, Historische Inschriften der 19. Dynastie I, 1933.
  V. W. Erichsen, Papyrus Harris I, 1933.
  VII. A. H. Gardiner, Late-Egyptian Miscellanies, 1937.

B.I.F.A.O.: Bulletin de l'Institut français d'archéologie orientale du Caire, Cairo, 1901–.

Br. Hist.: J. H. Breasted, *A History of Egypt,* 2nd edn., London, 1941.

Br. Mus.: British Museum.

Bull. M.M.A.: Bulletin of the Metropolitan Museum of Fine Art, New York.

Cat. gén.: Catalogue général des antiquités égyptiennes du musée du Caire.

Davies, El Amarna: N. de G. Davies, *The Rock Tombs of El Amarna,* Egypt Exploration Society, 6 vols., London, 1903–8.

E.E.F.(E.E.S.): Egypt Exploration Fund, later Egypt Exploration Society.

E.Lit.: A. Erman, *The Literature of the Ancient Egyptians,* trans. A. M. Blackman, London, 1927.

Erman, Life: A. Erman, *Life in Ancient Egypt,* trans. H. M. Tirard, London, 1894.

Grands prêtres: G. Lefebvre, *Histoire des grands prêtres d'Amon de Karnak,* Paris, 1929.

Griffith, H. P. M.: F. Ll. Griffith, *Stories of the High Priests of Memphis,* Oxford, 1900.

Griff. Stud.: *Studies presented to F. Ll. Griffith,* Egypt Exploration Society, London, 1932.

Hamm.: J. Couyat and P. Montet, *Les inscriptions hiéroglyphiques et hiératiques du Ouâdi Hammâmât,* Cairo, 1912.

Hist. Tech.: Charles Singer, E. J. Holmyard, and H. R. Hall. *A History of Technology,* vol. 1, Oxford, 1954.

J.E.A.: *Journal of Egyptian Archaeology,* Egypt Exploration Society, London, 1914–.

J.N.E.S.: *Journal of Near Eastern Studies,* Chicago, 1942–.

Kêmi: Kêmi, Revue de philologie et d'archéologie égyptiennes et coptes, 1928–54.
Klebs, Reliefs: L. Klebs, *Die Reliefs u. Malereien des neuen Reiches,* I. *Szenen aus dem Leben des Volkes,* Heidelberg, 1934.
L.D.: R. Lepsius, *Denkmäler aus Aegypten und Aethiopien,* 5 vols, Leipzig, 1897–1913.
Leg.: The Legacy of Egypt, ed. S. R. K. Glanville, London, 1940.
L.E.M.: R. Caminos, *Late Egyptian Miscellanies,* Oxford, 1954 (a translation of, and commentary on, *Bibl. aeg.* VII).
Med. Habu: Medinet Habu, Epigraphic survey by the Oriental Institute of Chicago:—
    I. Earlier Historical Records of Rameses III.
    II. Later Historical Records of Rameses III.
    III. The Calendar, the Slaughterhouse and Minor Records of Rameses III.
Mém. miss. fr.: Mémoires publiés par les membres de la mission archéologique français au Caire, 1884–, esp. Vol. V (tomb of Rekhmarâ) and Vol. XVIII (tomb of Anna).
Mem. Tyt.: Robb de Peyster Tytus Memorial series, New York, 1917–, comprising the following vols, by N. de G. Davies:—
    I. *The Tomb of Nakht at Thebes,* 1917.
    II, III. *The Tomb of Puyemrê at Thebes,* 2 vols., 1922–3.
    IV. *The Tomb of Two Sculptors at Thebes,* 1927.
    V. *Two Ramesside Tombs at Thebes,* 1927.
M.I.F.A.O.: Mémoires publiés par les membres de l'Institut français d'archéologie orientale, Cairo, 1884–.
M.M.A.: Metropolitan Museum of Art, New York: Egyptian Expedition:—
    1. A. C. Mace and H. E. Winlock, *The Tomb of Senebtisi at Lisht,* 1916.
    5. N. de G. Davies, *The Tomb of Ken-Amun at Thebes,* 2 vols, 1930.
    9. N. de G. Davies, *The Tomb of Nefer-hotep at Thebes,* 2 vols., 1933.
    11. N. de G. Davies, *The Tomb of Rekh-mi-Ré at Thebes,* 2 vols., 1943.
    18. H. E. Winlock, *Models of Daily Life in Ancient Egypt from the Tomb of Meket-Rê at Thebes,* 1955.
Mon. Piot: Fondation Eugène Piot, Monuments et Mémoires, publiés par l'Académie des Inscriptions et Belles-Lettres, Paris, 1882–.
Montet, Vie privée: P. Montet, *Scènes de la vie privée dans les tombeaux égyptiens de l'Ancien Empire,* Strasbourg, 1925.
O.I.C.: The Oriental Institute of Chicago.
Ounamon: The Story of Wen-amun, see *Bibl. aeg.* I, pp. 61–76.
Paheri: J. J. Tylor and F. Ll. Griffith, *The Tomb of Paheri at El Kab,* Egypt Exploration Fund, 11th memoir, London, 1894.
Pap. Chester Beatty, I. A. H. Gardiner, *The Library of A. Chester Beatty: The Chester Beatty Papyri, No. 1,* London, 1931.
    III. A. H. Gardiner, *Hieratic Papyri in the British Museum (Chester Beatty Gift),* 1935.
Pap. Ebers: B. Ebbell, *The Papyrus Ebers,* Copenhagen, 1937.
Pap. Harris I: The Great Papyrus Harris I. See *Bibl. aeg.* V for text, *A.R.* IV, pp. 87–206 for translation.
Pap. Harris 500: British Museum, Dept. of Egyptian and Assyrian Antiquities, *Facsimiles of Egyptian hieratic papyri,* London, 1923, Ser. II, pls. 41–6 (pap. 10060).
Peet, Tomb Robberies: T. E. Peet, *The Great Tomb Robberies of the Twentieth Egyptian Dynasty,* 2 vols., Oxford, 1930.
Petosiris: G. Lefebvre, *Le Tombeau de Petosiris,* Service des Antiquités de l'Egypte, 1923–4.

Rec. trav.: *Recueil de travaux relatifs à la philologie et l'archéologie égyptiennes et assyriennes,* Paris, 1870–1921.

Scepter: W. M. Hayes, *The Scepter of Egypt,* New York, 1953.

Siut: F. Ll. Griffith, *The Inscriptions of Siut and Dêr Rîfeh,* London, 1889.

Th. T. S.: The *Theban Tomb Series,* edited by N. de G. Davies and Alan H. Gardiner, 5 vols., *E.E.S.,* London, 1915–, comprises:—

    I. The Tomb of Amenemhet (No. 82), 1915.

    II. The Tomb of Antefoker, vizier of Sesostris I, 1920.

    III. The Tombs of Two Officials of Thutmosis IV (Nos. 75 and 90), 1923.

    IV. The Tomb of Huy, viceroy of Nubia in the reign of Tutankhamūn (No. 40), 1926.

    V. The Tomb of Menkheperrasonb, Amenmose and another (Nos. 86, 112, 42 and 226:, 1932.

Top. Bibliog.: B. Porter and R. Moss, *A Topographical Bibliography of Ancient Egyptian hieroglyphic texts, reliefs and paintings,* 7 vols., Oxford, 1927–51.

Urk.: Urkunden des aegyptischen Altertums, in Verbindung mit K. Sethe und H. Schäfer herausgegeben von G. Steindorff, Leipzig, 1906–:—

    I. Urkunden des alten Reiches (4 vols.).

    II. Hieroglyphische Urkunden der griechisch-römischen Zeit (3 vols.).

    III. Urkunden der älteren Aethiopenkönige (2 vols.).

    IV. Urkunden der 18, Dynastie (4 vols.), continued by W. Helck, 1955–.

Wb.: A. Erman and H. Grapow, *Wörterbuch der aegyptischen Sprache,* Leipzig, 1926–.

Wr. Atl.: W. Wreszinski, *Atlas zur altaegyptische Kulturgeschichte,* 2 parts, Leipzig, 1913–35.

NOTES

INTRODUCTION

[1] e.g. Juvenal, *Satire* XV; Herod. II, 35.

[2] Montet, *Vie privée*; Klebs, *Reliefs*.

[3] P. E. Newberry, *Beni-Hasan*, I (London, 1893), pl. 28, 30, 31, 38.

[4] F. Ll. Griffith and P. E. Newberry, *El Bersheh*, I (London, 1894), pl. 13, 17.

[5] H. Carter, *The Tomb of Tut-Ankh-Amun*, 3 vols, London, 1923–33; Penelope Fox, *Tutankhamun's Treasure*, London, 1951; Pierre Montet, *Tanis*, Paris, 1942, chapter VII.

[6] G. Steindorff and Keith Seele, *When Egypt ruled the East*, Chicago, 1957.

[7] On this period see P. Montet, *Le drame d'Avaris*, Paris, 1941, chapters III and IV.

CHAPTER I

[1] Plan in W. M. F. Petrie, *Illahun, Kahun and Gurob,* pl. 14.

[2] General description of the city and principal buildings in J. D. S. Pendlebury, *Tell el Amarna*, London, 1936; photograph and plan of the central city in J. D. S. Pendlebury and others, *The City of Akhenaton*, III, London, E.E.S., 1951, pl. 1, 2, 24.

[3] General plan of Karnak in *Top. bibliog.* II, 2, 98.

[4] *Wr. Atl.* II, 30, 31.

[5] *Top bibliog.* II, 112.

[6] O.I.C. communications, no. 15, 1, 28; no. 18, frontispiece.

[7] See *Med. Habu* IV, pl. 193–249, *Wr. Atl.* II, 184–90, and W. Wolf, *Das schöne Fest von Opet*, Leipzig, 1931, pl. I, II, for processions depicted in the temples of Medinet Habu, Abydos and Luxor respectively.

[8] P. Montet, *Le drame d'Avaris*, Paris, 1941, chapters. II and IV.

[9] P. Montet, *Tanis*, Paris, 1942, pp. 9, 23, 107, 128.

[10] *Pap. Harris I*, 78, 8; *A.R.* IV, §410.

[11] *Pap. Harris I*, 8, 2–6; *A.R.* IV, §215–16.

[12] *Pap. Harris I*, 27–29; *A.R.* IV, §271–2.

[13] E. Chassinat, *Le Temple de Dendara*, 1935, pl. 15; J. Robichon and A. Varille, *Le temple du scribe royal Amenhotep, fils de Hapou*, Cairo, 1936, p. 35.

[14] J. D. S. Pendlebury, *Tell el Amarna*, London, 1936, pp. 87, 112.

[15] L. Fougerosse, *Le grand puits de Tanis,* in *Kêmi* V (1935), pp. 71–103.

[16] G. Posener, *La première domination perse en Egypte*, Cairo, 1936, pp. 15–16.

[17] *A.S.A.E.* XVIII (1918), p. 145.

[18]*Kemi* VIII (1946), pp. 50 ff.

[19]*A.S.A.E.* XXX (1930), pp. 40, 41.

[20]*Bibl. aeg.* VII, 12=*L.E.M.*, p. 37; cf. P. Montet, *Le drame d'Avaris*, Paris, 1941, pp. 135–6.

[21]*O.I.C.* Communications 7, pp. 1–23; cf. W. C. Hayes, *Glazed tiles from a palace of Ramesses II*, M.M.A. Papers 3, New York, 1937.

[22]*A.S.A.E.* XI (1911), pp. 49–63.

[23]*Pap. Harris I*, 29, 8; T. H. Lewis in *Transactions of the Society of Biblical Archaeology* VII, 1882, op. 177–92; H. Wallis, *The Egyptian ceramic art*, London, 1898.

[24]W. M. F. Petrie, *Tell el Amarna*, London, 1894, pls. 2, 3 and 4; N. de G. Davies in *J.E.A.* VII, pl. 1 and 2; H. Frankfort, *The Mural Paintings of 'El Amarneh*, London, E.E.S., 1929; see also note 37.

[25]*Mem. Tyt.* V, 28–29. For the house of Tbouboui see *Griffith, H. P. M.*, pp. 34–35.

[26]*M.M.A.* 9, pl. 14.

[27]J. D. S. Pendlebury, *op. cit.*, pp. 105–7.

[28]ibid., pp. 118–19.

[29]*Wr. Atl.* I, 60; *Mem. miss. fr.* XVIII, 1.

[30]*M.M.A.* 11, pl. 110.

[31]*Wr. Atl.* I, 66, 222; *M.M.A.* 5, 47; fresco in *B.M.*; *Wr. Atl.* I, 92.

[32]See E. Mackay in *Ancient Egypt*, 1916, pp. 170–1, and N. de G. Davies, *The town house in ancient Egypt*, M.M.A. Studies I, May, 1929, pp. 233–55.

[32a]Davies, *El Amarna*, IV, pl. 24.

[33]*Kêmi* VIII (1946), pl. IX and pp. 190–1.

[34]Davies, op. cit., pp. 242, 243, 246, 247.

[35]*Pap. Ebers*, pl. 97–98.

[36]Fine specimens of chairs, in a remarkable state of preservation, were found in the tomb of Yuya and Touïou (H. Carter, *The Tomb of Iouiya and Touiyou*, pl. 23–26) and in the tomb of Tutankhamūn (P. Fox, *Tutankhamun's Treasure*, pl. 9–11, 60). Representations of handsomely carved chairs are to be found on the walls of temples and tombs, e.g. *Mem. Tyt.* V. pl. 5, 9, 25; ibid. IV, pl. 7; *Th. T.S.* I, pl. 15–16; ibid. V, pl. 41, 43.

[37]Fresco from the king's palace at Akhetaton, now in the Ashmolean Museum; see N. de G. Davies, 'Mural Paintings in the city of Akhetaten,' *J.E.A.* VII (1921), pls. 1, 2; and J. D. S. Pendlebury, *Tell el Amarna*, pl. VII(c).

[38]An amazing number of these stone vases, found in the underground chambers of the Step Pyramid, can be seen at Saqqara: E. Drioton and J.-P. Lauer, *Sakkarah, the Monuments of Zoser*, Cairo, 1939, pl. 60, 61.

[39]P. Montet, *Vases sacrés et profanes du tombeau de Psousennès*, Mon. Piot XXXVIII (1941), pp. 17–39; C. C. Edgar, *The Treasure of Tell Basta*, Musée égyptien, II, pp. 93, 108; J. Vernier, *Cat. gén.*, Bijoux et orfèvreries, 104, 106.

[40]*Med. Habu* II, pl. 55.

[40a]P. Montet, *Vases sacrés . . .* loc. cit.

[41]*M.M.A.* 5, pl. 13, 20.

E.L.E.—Z

[42]Montet, *Vie privée*, pl. 13 and p. 145; J. Černý, *Papyrus and books in ancient Egypt*, University College, London, 1952.

CHAPTER II

[1]G. Maspero, *Hymne au Nil*, Bibliothèque d'étude de l'Institut français d'archéologie orientale, vol. V, Cairo, 1912.

[2]*Pap. Harris I*, 37b, 1; 41b, 6; 54a, 2; 56a, 12.

[3]A. Moret, *La mise à mort du dieu en Egypte*, Paris, 1927, pp. 10, 13.

[4]Decree of Canopus *Urk.* II, 138; see A. H. Gardiner, 'The House of Life', *J.E.A.* XXIV (1938), p. 170 ff.

[5]*Med. Habu* III, pl. 152.

[6]*Pap. Chester Beatty* I, verso C1, p. 30.

[7]*Pap. Anastasy* IV, 10, 1, 3.

[8]Hymn to Sesostris III: F. Ll. Griffith, *The Petrie Papyri: Hieratic Papyri from Kahun and Gurob*, London, 1898, p. 1 ff.

[9]Inscription of Horourrê, *Kêmi* I (1928), pp. 111–12.

[10]*Pap. Ebers*, 18, 2; 61, 4–5; 61, 65; Berlin Medical Papyrus (Pap. Berlin 3038), 11, 12; *Pap. Hearst*, 2, 17; 10, 11. For bibliography, see C. D. Leake, *The Old Egyptian Medical Papyri*, Univ. of Kansas, 1952.

[11]Strabo, XVII, 46.

[11a]*Hist. Tech.*, pp. 793–801.

[12]*Siut*, pl. 6, line 278 (second contract).

[13]*M.M.A.* 5, pl. 38–39.

[14]*A.S.A.E.* XXXIX (1939), pp. 219, 399.

[15]*Pap. Sallier* IV, see E. Chabas, *Le calendrier des jours fastes et néfastes de l'année égyptienne*, Paris and Chalons, 1870; E. A. T. W. Budge, *Facsimiles of Egyptian Hieratic Papyri in the British Museum*, I (1910), pp. 41ff and pl. 31–32; II, pl. 88 ff.; F. Ll. Griffith, *The Petrie Papyri*, p. 62 and pl. 25.

[16]On Seth (Ares) at Papremis, see Herodotus II, 59 and 63.

[17]The hours of the day: E. Chassinat, *Edfou*, III, pp. 214, 229. The hours of the night: Bucher, *Les textes des tombes de Thoutmosis III et de' Amenophis II*, pp. 8–77.

[18]*Urk.* I, 106=*A*.R. I, §320.

[19]*Urk.* I, 130=*A*.R. I, §353.

[20]A. Erman and H. Ranke, *Aegypten u. aegyptisches Leben im Altertum*, pp. 399, 402; R. W. Sloley, *Primitive methods of measuring time*, J.E.A. XVII (1931), 166–78.

[21]R. W. Sloley, loc. cit., pls. 19, 22.

[22]ibid., pp. 170–4.

[23]G. Maspero, *Etudes égyptiennes*, I, Paris, 1879, pp. 185–6.

[24]*Urk.* IV, 655=*A*.R. II, §428.

[24a]*Urk.* IV, 6=*A*.R. II, §430.

[25]Sinuhe, B., 10, 12, 20: *Bibl. aeg.* II, pp. 9–12; *Bibl. aeg.* VII, 30=*L.E.M.*, p. 105; the 'Bulletin' of Kadesh, line 5; Ch. Kuentz, *La bataille de Qadech*, M.I.F.A.O. 55, 1928, p. 329.

[26]Diodorus, I, 70.

[27]*Pap. Harris* 500; *Bibl. aeg.* I; *J.E.A.* XI (1925), p. 227 ff.

[28]J. Vandier d'Abbadie, *Les ostraca figurés de Deir el Medineh*, nos. 2337, 2339, 2342, 2344, 2347.

[28a]Mme. E. Brunner-Traut, *Die Wochenlaube*, Mitteilungen des Instituts für Orientforschung, III, Heft 1, 1955; Weindler, *Geburts u. Wochenbettdarstellungen auf altaegyptischen Tempelreliefs*, Munich, 1915.

[29]*A.R.* II, §§810–15.

[30]G. Maspero. *The Struggle of the Nations*, London, 1898, p. 434; but see *A.R.* III, §582, note *b*.

[31]*Urk.* III, 61, 62 = *A.R.* IV, §922.

[32]*Pap. Chester Beatty* III; A. H. Gardiner, *Hieratic Papyri in the British Museum*, 3rd series, London 1935, no. 3: 'If a man sees himself in a dream.'

[33]ibid., pp. 20, 21.

[34]Herodotus, II, 83. C. Sourdille, *Hérodote et la religion de l'Egypte*, Paris, 1910, ch. VI.

CHAPTER III

[1]The Instruction of Ptahhotep, maxim 21: *Erman Lit.*, p. 61.

[2]*Urk.* IV, 2–3 = *A.R.* II, §7.

[3]*Urk.* IV, 30, 31.

[4]Louvre, C. 100; G. Maspero, *Etudes égyptiennes*, I, Paris, 1879, pp. 257–8.

[5]*Pap. Harris* 500, obverse: B.M. *Facsimiles of Egyptian hieratic papyri*, London, 1931, pl. 41–46.

[6]*Pap. Chester Beatty* I, verso c.4, 6–c.5, 2, p. 34.

[7]ibid., verso c.1, 8, p. 31.

[8]ibid., verso c.1, 9–c.2, 1, p. 31.

[9]ibid., verso c.2, 3–4, p. 31.

[10]ibid., verso c.3, 5–7, p. 33.

[11]ibid., verso c.3, 10–c.4, 4, p. 33.

[12]*Pap. Harris* 500, recto, IV, 2, V, 3.

[13]See *Griffith, H. P. M.*, first tale.

[14]The story of the Doomed Prince (*Pap. Harris* 500, verso), *Bibl. aeg.* I, pp. 1–9a; *Erman Lit.*, p. 161 ff.

[15]*M.M.A.* 9, pl. 36, 37; *Mem. Tyt.* IV, p. 5; V, pp. 5–7. It must be remembered that words denoting relationship, besides being used in their exact meaning, have in Egyptian a wider connotation: *iôt*, 'father', often means 'ancestor', while *sen* and *senet*, literally 'brother' and 'sister', frequently denote members of a group; the verb *sensen* means 'to be in association'.

[16]G. Maspero, *Contes populaires*, 4th edn., Paris, 1905, p. 129, note 1; A. Moret, *Le Nil et la civilisation égyptienne*, Paris, 1926, pp. 110, 318–19.

[17]Herodotus, III, 31.

[17a]J. Černý, 'Consanguineous Marriages in Pharaonic Egypt', *J.E.A.* XL (1954), pp. 23–29.

[18]*Th.T.S.* I, p. 4; *A.Z.* XLVIII (1911), p. 50.

[19]*Griffith, H. P. M.*

[20]J. Černý, 'La constitution d'un avoir conjugal en Egypte', *B.I.F.A.O.* XXXVII (1937), p. 41 ff.

[21]J. de Linage, 'L'acte d'établissement . . . d'un esclave', *B.I.F.A.O.* XXXVIII (1939), pp. 217–34.

[22]For instance, *Mem. Tyt.* IV, pl. 1.

[23]The Instruction of Ptahhotep, maxim 18: *Erman Lit.*, p. 60.

[24]From the Tale of King Cheops and the Magicians (pap. Westcar): *Erman Lit.*, pp. 36–47.

[25]The Tale of the Two Brothers (Pap. d'Orbiney, in the British Museum, no. 10183): *Bibl. aeg*, I, pp. 9–30=*Erman Lit.*, pp. 150–61.

[26]See note 24.

[27]do.

[28]*Griffith*, H. P. M., p. 36.

[29]*Bibl. aeg.* II, pp. 32–33 (*Pap. Chester Beatty* II, recto 4–5).

[30]*B.M.* 1027; G. Maspero, *Études égyptiennes*, I, pp. 185–6.

[31]*Pap. Leiden*, 37: A. H. Gardiner and K. Sethe, *Egyptian letters to the Dead*, London, E.E.S., 1928.

[32]Two Brothers (note 25), 8, 7–8: *Bibl. aeg.* I, p. 18.

[33]Two Brothers, 9, 8–9: *Bibl. aeg.* I, p. 19.

[34]See note 24.

[35]From the Maxims of Ani, *Ani* II, 13, 17; *Erman Lit.*, pp. 234–42. The same threat is found in the Instruction of Ptahhotep, maxim 18.

[36]A. de Buck, *The Egyptian Coffin Texts*, vol. II, ch. 146, p. 180 ff.

[37]*B.M.* 10052, XV, 4. Peet, *Tomb Robberies*, I, p. 156. Another tomb-robber also had more than one wife. (Peet, *The Mayer Papyri A and B*, London, E.E.S., 1920, 13E, 6–7, p. 18.)

[38]*B.I.F.A.O.* XXXVII (1937), pp. 41, 599.

[39]The Story of the Shipwrecked Sailor, *Bibl. aeg.* II, pp. 41–48; *Erman Lit.*, pp. 29–35.

[40]*B.I.F.A.O.* XLI (1942), p. 31.

[41]Strabo, XVII, 2, 5.

[42]Diodorus, I, 80, 5–6.

[43]For example, the admonitions of Hapidjefai to his son, in the introductory portion of his 'contract' inscription, *Siut* I, 269, 272.

[44]*Pap. d'Orbiney*, IX, 8–9.

[45]*Pap. Harris* 500, verso IV, 3–4.

[46]Herodotus, II, 82.

[47]*Pap. Sallier*, IV: Bibliothèque égyptologique, XII, pp. 153–4, 160–1.

[48]*Pap. Ebers.* 97; 13, 14 (recipes).

[48a]H. Ranke, *Die aegyptischen Personennamen*, Hamburg, 1932–52.

[49]*Griffith*, H. P. M., pp. 42–45.

[50]ibid., p. 19.

[50a]A. H. Gardiner, 'The House of Life', in *J.E.A.* XXIV (1938), pp. 157–79.

[51]Relief in Berlin, no. 14506, *Wr. Atl.* I, 387.

[52]The maxims of Ani, *Erman Lit.*, p. 239.

[53]*M.M.A.* 5, pl. 51 and p. 9.

[54]*Paheri*, pl. 4.

[55]*Urk.* IV, 34=*A.R.* II, §344.

[56]*M.M.A.* 5, pl. 35: a group of servants behind their master's chair.

[56a]A. Bakr, *Slavery in Pharaonic Egypt*, Cairo, 1952.

[57]*Bibl. aeg.* VII, 3=*L.E.M.*, p. 12.

[58]ibid., 66, 67=*L.E.M.*, pp. 254–8.

[59]*M.M.A.* 9, pl. 43. For laws relating to runaway slaves see W. C. Hayes, *The Brooklyn Papyrus*, New York, 1956.

[60]*Urk.* IV, 11=*A.R.* II, §§12, 13, 16, 39.

[61]A. H. Gardiner, 'Four papyri of the 18th dynasty from Kahun', *A.Z.* XLIII (1906), 278–99.

[62]Peet, *Tomb Robberies,* p. 152; another of the accused women says that she had bought her slaves with revenue from her estate (ibid.).

[63]A. H. Gardiner, 'Lawsuit arising from the purchase of slaves', *J.E.A.* XXI (1935), pp. 140–6.

[64]*Urk.* I, 75=*A.R.* I, §279.

[65]N. de G. Davies, *Five Theban Tombs,* E.E.F., Archaeological Survey, 21, 1913, pl. 25–28.

[66]*Mem. Tyt.* V., pl. 34.

[66a]For Egyptian breeds of domestic dog, see *Illustrated London News,* June 23, 1956, p. 782.

[67]N. de G. Davies, loc. cit. pl. 4.

[68]*Mém. miss. fr.* V, p. 547.

[69]J. Vandier d'Abbadie, *Catalogue des ostraca figurés de Deir el Medineh,* nos. 2035, 2037–8, 2040.

[70]ibid., nos. 2003–4.

[71]*Wr. Atl.* I, 123B.

[72]P. E. Newberry, *Beni-Hasan,* IV, pl. 5.

[73]B.M. 37977 in *Wr. Atl.* I, 423.

[74]*Mem. Tyt.* V, pl. 25.

[75]*Mem. miss. fr.* V, p. 552; on Berlin ostrakon 21443 a cat is drawn playing with a monkey.

[76]Ch. Kuentz, 'L'oie du Nil', in *Archives du Museum d'Historie naturelle de Lyon,* XIV, p. 21; tomb 217 at Thebes.

[77]J. Vandier d'Abbadie, op, cit., no. 2201.

[78]*Mem. Tyt.* I, pl. 10.

[79]*Mem. Tyt.* V, pl. 30.

[80]Kuentz, op. cit., pp. 1–64.

[81]*Bibl. aeg.* VII, 102=*L.E.M.*, p. 381 and note, p. 382.

CHAPTER IV

[1]Herodotus, II, 37. Laundrymen are sometimes shown: *Wr. Atl.* I, 57=*Mem. Tyt.* V, 28; Davies, *El Amarna,* III, 8.

[2]Sinuhe B. 291–2; *Bibl. aeg.* II, p. 39=*Erman Lit.*, p. 28.

[3]ibid., 293–5; P. Montet, *Byblos et l'Egypte,* Paris, 1928, p. 610.

[4]G. Jéquier, 'Les frises d'objets des sarcophages du Moyen Empire', *M.I.F.A.O.* 47, Cairo, 1921.

[5]e.g. the vizier Ptah-mosé, stele 88 in Lyons Museum, published by A. Varille in 'Mélanges présentés a M. V. Loret', *B.I.F.A.O.* XXX (1930), p. 497.

⁶J. Quibell, *The Tomb of Hesy*, Cairo, 1913, pl. 21; for razors and other toilet articles see W. M. F. Petrie, *Tools and Weapons*, British School of Archaeology in Egypt, 1917, pl. LVIII–LXIV; Bénédite, 'Objets de toilette', *Cat. gén.*, 1911.

⁷*A.E.M.*, pp. 99–104, 114; *Hist. Tech.*, pp. 293–4; *Pap. Ebers*, 65, 10–11; 66, 7–9; 79–84.

^{7a}*Hist. Tech.*, pp. 287–92.

⁸*Pap. Hearst*, 10, 4–11; *Pap. Ebers*, 86, 4; 87; 67, 3; *Pap. Hearst*, 10, 15; 15, 1.

⁹V. Loret, 'Pour transformer un vieillard en jeune homme', *Mélanges Maspero*, I, pp. 853–77.

¹⁰*Wr. Atl.* I, 44.

¹¹Sarcophagus of the Princess Kawit in the Cairo Museum (No. 623): see *The Art of Egypt through the Ages*, ed. Sir Denison Ross, London, 1931, p. 142.

¹²*Pap. d'Orbiney*, 2, 9; 3, 2. *Erman Lit.*, p. 152.

¹³N. de G. Davies, *Five Theban Tombs*, E.E.F. Memoirs, 21, 1913, pl. 4, 26; *Th.T.S.* V, pl. 9, 10; IV, pl. 17; *Mem. Tyt.* I, pl. 12, 18; IV, pl. 7, 8, 11; V. pl. 30.

¹⁴*Urk.* I, 102 = *A.R.* I, §312.

¹⁵Two pairs of golden sandals were found in the tomb of Psousennes: P. Montet, *Tanis*, 156. Sandals of leather and papyrus can be seen in the British Museum. See also W. M. F. Petrie, *Objects of Daily Use*, British School of Archaeology in Egypt, Research Account, London, 1927, pl. LIV.

¹⁶*Pap. Ebers*, 78, 4 ff.; *Pa* = *p. Hearst*, 12, 8.

¹⁷Davies, *El Amarna,* IV, 26; *Med. Habu*, pl. 75, 112.

^{17a}For ancient Egyptian costume see *Erman, Life*, ch. 10.

¹⁸*M.M.A.* 9, pl. 36, 37, 41, 50; *Th.T.S.* IV, pl. 6; *Mem. Tyt.* IV, pl. 1, 5; V, pl. 1, 9, 25.

¹⁹*M.M.A.* 9, pl. 15, 36–37, 50, 52; *Mem. Tyt.* IV, pls. 1, 5; V, pls. 1, 7, 9, 25.

²⁰*Pap. B.M.* 10052, XI, 7–8; cf. J. Vandier, *La famine dans l'Egypte ancienne*, Cairo, 1931.

²¹Sinuhe B. 86–88; *Bibl. aeg.* II, pp. 23–24 = *Erman Lit.*, p. 20.

²²Shipwrecked Sailor, 47–52; *Bibl. aeg.* II, p. 43 = *Erman Lit.*, p. 31.

²³*Wr. Atl.* II 185–8; *Med. Habu*, 173. For the various types of cattle see P. Montet, 'Les boeufs égyptiens', in *Kêmi* XIII (1951), p. 43 ff.

²⁴*Pap. Harris* I, 13, 7–8, 20a, 3–11; 35b, 8–14; 51a, 13. A team of Syrian oxen pulling a block of stone is shown in the quarry at Ma'sara, see G. Daressy in *A.S.A.E.* XI (1911), p. 263 ff.

²⁵*Pap. Harris* I, 20a, 13–15; 71b, 9–10.

²⁶For the Old Kingdom see *Montet, Vie privée*, chapter V, and for the New, *Wr. Atl.* I, 188; *Med. Habu*, 173. Butchers at work: *Wr. Atl.* I, 48, 101, 107, 252, 255.

^{26a}But for evidence of the domestic fowl in the Middle Kingdom and New Kingdom, see R. Cotevieille-Giraudet, *Les fouilles de Medamoud*, Cairo, 1931, pp. 41–43, and p. 74.

²⁷*Med. Habu*, 148, 152, 160; *Pap. Harris* I, 20b, 53b. Fowlers with their birds: *Wr. Atl.* I, 395, 157.

[28]*Urk.* III, 54=*A.R.* IV, §882.

[28a]Statue from Tanis in the Cairo Museum, *Encyclopédie photographique de l'art,* ed. 'Tel', Le Musée du Caire, pl. 63.

[29]*Pap. Harris I,* 20b, 12–21a, 1; 65c, 7–8.

[29a]*Wr. Atl.* I, 413. P. Montet, 'Les poissons employés dans l'écriture hiéroglyphique', *B.I.F.A.O.* XI (1913), pp. 39–48. C. Gaillard, 'Recherches sur les poissons représentés . . .' in *M.I.F.A.O.*, vol. 51, Cairo, 1923.

[30]*Pap. Harris* I, 19a, 13–14; V. Loret, 'L'ail chez les anciens Egyptiens', *Sphinx,* 1905, pp. 135–47.

[31]*Numbers,* XI, 5.

[32]Herodotus, II, 38; Diodorus, 1, 89, 4.

[33]V. Loret, *La flore pharaonique,* nos. 128–9, 152, 157.

[34]*Pap. Chester Beatty* I, verso 11, 9–12; L. Keimer, *Die Gartenpflanzen im alten Aegypten,* pp. 1–6.

[35]Diodorus, I, 34.

[36]Both honey and carob-beans came under the control of the vizier: see *M.M.A.* 11 (Rekhmirē), pl. XLVIII, XLIX, and pp. 44–45; *Urk.* IV, 1040–41. Cf. *Med. Habu,* 146, 281, 286; *Pap. Harris* I, 28, 46, 48.

[37]G. Steindorff and W. Wolf, *Die thebanische Gräberwelt.* Leipzig, 1932, p. 18.

[38]Scenes of cooking: *M.M.A.* 5, pl. 88–89; *Wr. Atl.* I, 255, 286, 325–6, 356.

[38a]Cooking utensils, etc. in W. M. F. Petrie, *Objects of Daily Use* . . .

[38b]*Wr. Atl.* I, 220. See *Hist. Tech.,* pp. 271–5 .

[39]*Pap. Ebers,* 6, 14; 10, 12–13; 13, 20; 20. *Pap. Hearst,* 2, 12; 3, 12, 34.

[39a]*M.M.A.* 11, pl. 49 and p. 44.

[40]Herodotus, II, 77.

[41]*Wr. Atl.* I, 84; *Mem. Tyt.* I, 22. L. Keimer, 'La boutargue dans l'Egypte ancienne', in *B.I.F.A.O.* XXI (1939), pp. 215–43.

[41a]*Pap. Harris* I, 20b, 12; 73, 4.

[42]ibid., 16a, 20b, 36a, 65c; *Mem. Tyt.* I, 26; *Wr. Atl.* I, 16, 22; *Mem. Tyt.* V, 30, 37. For salting see *Hist. Tech.* pp. 258–9, 263–6.

[42a]But see Professor J. Percival, 'Cereals of Ancient Egypt and Mesopotamia', in *Man,* Aug. 15, 1936.

[43]*Wr. Atl.* I, 87, 109, 180, 398; Montet, *Vie privée,* pp. 231–6; Davies, *Five Theban Tombs,* pl. XXXVIII.

[43a]Bakers: e.g. *Wr. Atl.* I, 87; *M.M.A.* 11, 38, 41 and pp. 38–9, 44; *Wr. Atl.* I, 221, 301, 374.

[44]*Th.T.S.* II, pl. 11.

[45]J. D. S. Pendlebury, *Tell el Amarna,* London, 1936, p. 111. W. Wreszinski in *A.Z.* 61 (1926), pp. 1–15.

[46]Brewing: Montet, *Vie privée,* pp. 242–54; *M.M.A.* 5, pl. 58; *Th.T.S.* II, 8–10; *Wr. Atl.* I, 301; *Leg.,* pp. 156–8; *Huist. Tech.,* pp. 276–81.

[47]*Bibl. aeg.* VII, 41–2.

[48]*A.Z.* LVIII (1923), 25. Jar-sealings from E. Amarna bore the name of the vineyard, or often the label, 'good wine', 'very good wine', or even 'very, very good wine': J. D. S. Pendlebury, etc., *City of Akhenaten,* III, London, 1951, pp. 147–50 and pl. 81–83.

[49]P. E. Newberry, *Beni-Hasan,* II, pl. 6; *B.I.F.A.O.* IX, pp. 8–9.

[50]G. Farina, *La pittura egiziana,* Milan, 1929, 17.

[51]Davies, *El Amarna*, III, pl. 4–6.

[52]*Th.T.S.* III, pl. 6; *Wr. Atl.* 86b; 245.

[52a]*Bibl. aeg.* I, pp. 13–14; *Erman Lit.*, p. 153.

[53]A. Erman and H. Ranke, *Aegypten* . . ., Tübingen, 1923, p. 218.

[54]P. Montet in *Kêmi* VIII (1946), p. 173 and pl. III.

[55]*Siut*, contracts V, VII and IX.

[56]N. de G. Davies, 'A peculiar form of New Kingdom lamp, *J.E.A.* X (1924), pp. 9–14; cf. *Urk.* IV, 17: 'May the lamp burn for thee during the night, until the sun appears once more!' See also *Hist. Tech.*, p. 232 and fig. 149.

[57]*A.R.* I, 474; A. de Buck in *Mélanges Maspero*, pp. 847–52.

[58]*Bibl. aeg.* VII, 37, 38=*L.E.M.*, pp. 255–8.

[59]*Bibl. aeg.* VII, 5–6=*L.E.M.*, p. 18.

[60]*Bibl. aeg.* VII, 7=*L.E.M.*, pp. 22–23.

[61]Banqueting scenes are frequent in Theban tombs, e.g. *Paheri*, p. 1. 6–7; *M.M.A.* 9, pl. 18; *Th.T.S.* I, pl. 6, 15; III, pl. 4–6, 21; *Mem. Tyt.* I, 15; IV, 5; *Wr. Atl.* I, 7, 39, 76, 91, 122, 245. But see note 45 on chapter XII.

[62]The Instruction of Ptahhotep, maxim 18: *Erman Lit.*, p. 60.

[62a]To the references in note 61 add: *Wr. Atl.* I, 145; Davies, *El Amarna*, V, 5; V. Loret, 'Note sur les instruments de la musique de l'Egypte ancienne', *L'Encyclopédie de la musique,* Paris, 1913, pp. 1–34; H. Hickmann, 'Instruments de musique', *Cat. gen.,* Cairo, 1948; Curt Sachs, *Die Musikinstrumente des alten Aegyptens*, Berlin, 1921; H. G. Farmer, *The Music of Ancient Egypt*, in the Oxford History of Music, Vol I, ed. Egon Wellesz, London, 1957.

[62b]P. E. Newberry, *Beni-Hasan*, E.E.F., London, 1893, vol. I, pl. 31.

[62c]I. Lexova, *Ancient Egyptian Dances*, Prague, 1935; E. Brunner-Traut, *Der Tanz im alten Aegypten*, Glückstadt, 1938.

[63]e.g. *Wr. Alt.* I, 179; G. Maspero, *Etudes égyptiennes*, I, pp. 172–7.

[63a]M. Lichtheim, 'The Songs of the Harpers', *J.N.E.S.* IV (1945), pp. 178–212.

[64]ibid., p. 195.

[65]ibid., pp. 192–3.

[66]Herodotus, II, 78; Plutarch, *Isis and Osiris*, 17; Lucian, *De Luctu*, 21; Petronius, *Satyricon*, 34.

[67]*Paheri*, pl. 7.

[67a]Plutarch, *Isis and Osiris*, 17.

[68]*M.M.A.* 9, pl. 18; *Wr. Atl.* I, 392 (Brussels E2877), 179.

[68a]For this and other games see W. M. F. Petrie, *Objects of Daily Use*, London, 1927, chapter XIV; *Scepter*, pp. 249–51.

[69]*Wr. Atl.* I, 49, 418; *B.I.F.A.O.* XXVII, pl. 7 (Tomb 219 at Deir el Medineh); *Petosiris*, 50.

[70]Montet, *Vie privée*, pp. 372–6; H. Junker, *Giza*, IV, Mastaba des Kai-em-anch, 1940, p. 37.

[70a]e.g. W. B. Emery, *The Tomb of Hemaka*, Cairo, Service des Antiquités, 1938, p. 40 and pl. 19.

[71]*Griffith, H. P. M.*, p. 31.

[72]Montet, *Vie privée*, pp. 368, 372; E. S. Eaton in *Bulletin of the Boston Museum of Fine Arts*, 35 (1937), p. 54 ff. A different explanation of this game is given by Zaki Saad, drawing upon memories of his childhood; see 'Khasa Lawiza', in *A.S.A.E.* XXXVII (1937), p. 212 ff.

[73]Davies, *El Amarna*, VII, pl. 18.

CHAPTER V

[1]*Bibl. aeg.* VII, 104 (*Pap. Lansing* 5, 7–7, 4); 83 (*Pap. Sallier I*, 5, 11–6, 9) =*L.E.M.*, pp. 389–90, 315–16.

[2]Herodotus, II, 14; Diodorus, I, 36.

[2a]From the Tale of the Eloquent Peasant, *Erman Lit.*, p. 116 ff.

[3]Montet, *Vie privée*, pp. 258–60.

[4]*M.M.A.* 9, pl. 46–47 and commentary, p. 70; *Mem. Tyt.* V, pl. 28–29; *Hist. Tech.*, pp. 522–3.

[5]Most of these names will be found in W. Spiegelberg, 'Bemerkungen zu den hieratischen Amphorinschriften des Ramesseums', in *A.Z.* LVIII, 25; cf. P. Montet, *Le drame d'Avaris*, Paris, 1941, pp. 153–4, and *Mem. Tyt.* V, pl. 19. In the Roads of Horus, in the eastern Delta, there were also vineyards.

[6]*Pap. Harris* I, 7, 10–12.

[7]Frequently depicted, e.g. in *Paheri*, pl. 4; *Wr. Atl.* I, 265, 282, 338, 355; *Th.T.S.* III, 30; *M.M.A.* 9, pl. 48; *Mem. Tyt.* I, 22; V, 30, 68, 230; *Petosiris*, pl. 12.

[8]Montet, *Vie privée*, p. 267.

[9]This scene is well painted in the tomb of Pouyemrê, *Mem. Tyt.* II, pl. 12. For wine-making in general see *Hist. Tech.*, pp. 282–5.

[10]*Petosiris*, texts 43 and 44.

[10a]Klebs, *Reliefs*, pp. 15–16; *Wr. Atl.* I, 48, 83, 143, etc.; *Mem. Tyt.* I, 20; V, 30.

[11]e.g. *Mem. Tyt*, I, pl. 18 (tomb of Nakht); V, 30 (Apouy); *Th.T.S.* III, 9; *Wr. Atl.* I, 424 (*B.M.*37982); 231–4 (Menna); 9, 51, 193–5 (Khâemhat); 83, 385, 422; *Paheri*, pl. 3.

[12]Pap. d'Orbiney, II, 2=*Erman Lit.*, p. 152.

[13]For Old Kingdom reliefs showing the same operation see Montet, *Vie privée*, p. 183 ff.

[14]*Wr. Atl.* I, 112 (tomb of Panehsy).

[15]*Paheri*, pl. 3.

[16]*Petosiris*, pl. 13.

[17]*Bibl. aeg.* VII, 104 (*Pap. Lansing*)=*L.E.M.*, p. 390.

[18]*Paheri*, pl. 3.

[19]Herodotus, II, 14; *Wr. Atl.* I, 57b; *Paheri*, pl. 3 and 4; L. Keimer in *Bulletin de l'Institut de l'Egypte*, XIX (1937), pp. 147–56.

[20]Plutarch, *De Iside et Osiride*, 70.

[21]Montet, *Vie privée*, p. 191; A. Moret, *La mise à mort du dieu en Egypte*, Paris, 1927, pp. 33–35.

[22]Deuteronomy, XI, 10–11.

[23]Surveying the fields: *Th.T.S.* III, 10; *Wr. Atl.* I, 11, 191, 232; cf. S. Berger, 'Some scenes of land measurement', *J.E.A.* XX, p. 54 and pl. 10.

[23a]*Wr. Atl*, I, 232.

[24]*Bibl. aeg.* IV, no. 4, and *J.E.A.* XIII (1927), p. 193 ff.

[24a]Reaping scenes in, e.g., *Wr. Atl.* I, 142, 177, 189, 231–3, 385, 422; *L.D.* III, 162, 212; *Paheri*, pl. 3; *Mem. Tyt.* II, 28.

[25]*Wr. Atl.* I, 14, 19.

[25a]*Wr. Atl.* I, 233.

[26]*Petosiris*, inscr. 52.

[27]Montet, *Vie privée*, p. 207.

[27a]*Paheri*, pl. 3.

[28]*Petosiris*, inscrs. 51–52.

[29]Tomb relief in Leiden, catalogue no. 50 = *Wr. Atl.* I, 422. Memphite reliefs of Old Kingdom date show the harvested grain already stowed on donkey-back (Montet, *Vie privée*, p. 206).

[30]e.g. in the tomb of Panehsy, *Wr. Atl.* I, 61.

[31]*Paheri*, pl. 3.

[32]*Wr. Atl.* I, 193, 231, 346.

[33]Winnowing scenes: *Mem. Tyt.* I, 120; V, 30; and the refs. in note 32 above.

[34]Psalm 126, verse 5.

[35]*Mem. Tyt.* 1, pl. 64, and Winifred S. Blackman, 'Some occurrences of the corn-'*arūseh*', *J.E.A.* VIII (1922), p. 235 ff.

[36]H. Gauthier, *Les fêtes du dieu Min*, Cairo, 1931, p. 225.

[37]*Mem. Tyt.* V, pl. 30: *Wr. Atl.* I, 19, 193, 346, 422. Pulling flax is also represented in Middle Kingdom tombs at Beni-Hasan, Meir and El Bersheh; cf. *Petosiris*, pl. 13.

[37a]*Wr. Atl.* I, 193, 231; *Ancient Egypt*, II, 1914, p. 1 ff.

[38]*E.Lit.*, p. 46.

[39]C. Gaillard, 'Sur deux oiseux figurés dans les tombeaux de Beni-Hasan', *Kemi* II, pp. 19–40.

[40]Montet, *Vie privée*, pp. 260–5.

[41]*Wr. Atl.* I, 33 (Berlin Museum no. 18540).

[42]*Pap. Harris* I, 20b, 8.

[43]C. Gaillard, 'Les tâtonnements des Egyptiens de l'Ancien Empire à la recherche des animaux à domestiquer,' *Revue d'ethnographie et de sociologie*, 1912; F. E. Zeuner in *Hist. Tech.* I, pp. 327–52, esp. pp. 340–3.

[44]*Bibl. aeg.* VII, p. 102 (*Pap. Lansing*)=*L.E.M.*, pp. 381–2.

[45]Renny, nomarch of El Kab, enumerates 122 oxen, 100 sheep, 1,200 goats and 1,500 pigs (*Urk.* IV, p. 75).

[45a]But see note 26[a] on chapter IV.

[46]Ramesses III made efforts to increase the country's livestock: 'I have made for thee (i.e. Amūn) flocks in the south and in the north, with oxen and fowls, and small cattle by the hundred thousand, with overseers of cattle, scribes, herdsmen of horned cattle, watchmen and numerous shepherds behind them' (*Pap. Harris* I, 7, 9). The oryx was at all times an offering acceptable to the gods; Ramesses III sent huntsmen to the desert to catch them (*Pap. Harris* I, 28).

[47]*Th.T.S.* IV, pl. 8.

⁴⁸Ostracon from Deir el Medineh (J. Vandier d'Abbadie), *Les ostraca figurés de Deir el Medineh*, Cairo, 1936, pl. 19, no. 2159; rider from the tomb of Horonemheb, now in the Bologna Museum, *Aldred*, pl. 141.

⁴⁸ᵃFattened oxen: Davies, *El Amarna*, V, pl. 21.

⁴⁹A. M. Blackman, *Rock Tombs of Meir*, II, E.E.F. 1915, pl. XXX(1).

⁵⁰Montet, *Vie privée*, chapter III.

⁵¹P. E. Newberry, *El Bersheh*, I, E.E.F., London, n.d., pl. 18.

⁵²*Petosiris*, text 46 and 48.

⁵³*Mem. Tyt.* II, pl. 12 (Pouyemrê); *Wr. Atl.* I, 264 (Anna).

⁵⁴*Th.T.S.* III, 31; *Wr. Atl.* I, 187 (Ousirhat), 289.

⁵⁵*Mem. Tyt.* V, pl. 30 and 34.

⁵⁶*Wr. Atl.* I, 395. Pelicans appear among the water-birds in *Wr. Atl.* I, 249.

⁵⁷Montet, *Vie privée*, chapter I. For New Kingdom scenes of marsh life see, e.g., *Wr. Atl.* I, 2 (Menna); 423 (*B.M.*37977); 117 (Baki); 343 (Senemiâh); *Mem. Tyt.* I, 24; II, 9.

⁵⁷ᵃ*Wr. Atl.* I, 30; *Mem. Tyt.* I, 15-19.

⁵⁸Montet, *Vie privée,* 73; *Mem. Tyt.* II, pl. 15, 18, 19.

⁵⁹*Wr. Atl.* I, 250.

⁵⁹ᵃKlebs, *Reliefs*, pp. 86-87; Montet, *Vie privée*, pp. 20-66; W. Radcliffe, *Fishing from the Earliest Times*, London, 1926.

⁶⁰*Wr. Atl.* I, 250; *Mem. Tyt.* II, pl. 65; V, 30 and 35; Montet, *Vie privée*, pp. 23-41.

⁶¹e.g. *Wr. Atl.* I, 2, 40, 70, 77, 117, 183, 294, 343, 354; *Mem. Tyt.* I, pl. 26; *M.M.A.* 5, pl. 51; Davies, *Five Theban Tombs*, pl. 39.

⁶²Montet, *Vie privée*, pp. 21-22; *Th.T.S.* I, pl. 1 and 28; *Wr. Atl.* I, 271.

⁶²ᵃ*Mem. Tyt.* V., 30.

⁶³*A.E.P.*, pl. LXV.

⁶⁴Montet, *Vie privée*, p. 42; *Mem. Tyt.* V, pl. 30; *Wr. Atl.* I, 24, 184, 344; *Mem. Tyt.* I, 22-23; II, 15; *Wr. Atl.* I, 249.

⁶⁵Montet, *Vie privée*, pp. 6-8, 66. In the temple of Edfou, the goddess Sekhet is depicted announcing to the king, 'I give thee all birds in their marshes' (Chassinat, *Edfu*, II, pl. 164).

⁶⁶*Th.T.S.* V, pl. 9.

⁶⁷See note 46 above.

⁶⁸*Th.T.S.* II, 6-7; I, 9; *Wr. Atl.* I, 53; *Mem. Tyt.* II, 7; Davies, *Five Theban Tombs*, pl. 12, 22, 40.

⁶⁹*M.M.A.* 5, pl. 48.

⁷⁰Davies, *Five Theban Tombs*, pl. 12.

⁷¹ibid., pl. 23-24; *Wr. Atl.* I, 32, 53.

⁷²*Wr. Atl.* I, 26.

CHAPTER VI

¹K. Sethe, *Die Bau- und Denkmalsteine der alten Aegypter und ihre Namen*, Berlin, 1933; *A.E.M.* Chaps V, XVI and XVII.

¹ᵃ*A.S.A.E.* XIII (1914), pp. 43-47; stele of the year VIII found at Heliopolis, *A.S.A.E.* XXXVIII (1938), p. 219.

²R. Engelbach, 'The quarries of the western Nubian desert and the ancient road to Tushka', *A.S.A.E.* XXXVIII (1938), p. 369 ff.

[3]J. Couyat and P. Montet, *Les inscriptions hieroglyphiques et hiératiques du ouadi Hammâmat,* Cairo, 1912. (*Hamm.*)

[3a]*Hamm,* inscr. 12; see L. Christophe in *B.I.F.A.O.* XLVIII (1948), pp. 29–38, and *A.R.* IV, §461 ff. For *bekhen* stone see also *A.S.A.E.* XXXVIII (1938), p. 151 ff. and XLI (1942), p. 189 ff.

[3b]*Hamm.* inscr. 222, 240.

[3c]*A.R.* I, §448; *Hamm.* inscr. 113.

[4]*Hamm.* inscr. 87, line 10.

[4a]Somers Clarke and R. Engelbach, *Ancient Egyptian Masonry,* London, 1930.

[5]*Hamm.* inscr. 19, cf. p. 24.

[6]*Hamm.* inscr. 110; *A.R.* I, §436.

[7]*Hamm.* inscr. 191.

[8]*Hamm.* inscr. 192.

[9]*A.E.M.* pp. 64–93; *Hist. Tech.* I, pp. 569–70; Clarke and Engelbach, op. cit., chapters 2 and 3.

[10]*Th.T.S.* IV, 4; P. E. Newberry, *Beni-Hasan, E.E.F.,* 1893, vol. I, pl. 8; *Pap. Harris* I, 12a, 7. The map of the gold-mining region is in the Turin Museum; see *Hist. Tech.* I, p. 580, fig. 385, and *Leg.,* pl. 33.

[11]Redesiyeh inscriptions: *Bibl. aeg.* IV, no. 5 = *A.R.* III, §162 ff.

[12]Stele of Ramesses II found at Kouban, 68 miles south of Aswan, now in the Grenoble Museum: see P. Tresson, *La stèle de Kouban,* Cairo, 1922; *Bibl. aeg.* IV, no. 6; *A.R.* III, §§282–93.

[13]Diodorus, III, 11–13.

[14]The statuettes found in the sarcophagus of Hornekht at Tanis (*Kêmi* IX (1942), nos. 94–102, pp. 31–32) are obviously made of very much adulterated gold.

[15]*A.E.M.,* p. 231; V. Loret, 'La turquoise chez les anciens Egyptiens', *Kêmi* I, pp. 99–114.

[16]*A.E.M.,* p. 232; P. E. Newberry, 'Shesmet, Malachite', in *Studies presented to F. Ll. Griffith,* London, 1932, p. 320 ff. For copper-mining see C. N. Bromehead in *Hist. Tech.* I, pp. 513–16.

[17]V. Loret, op. cit. (in *Kemi*), pp. 111–13.

[18]*L.D.* III, 26, 1; cf. *Wr. Atl.* I, 64, 341, 342.

[19]*M.M.A.* 11, pl. LX and pp. 58–59.

[20]P. E. Newberry, *El. Bersheh,* I, pls. XIV, XV, and pp. 17–26.

[21]*M.M.A.* 5, 38–40.

[22]*Mem. Tyt.* II, 23.

[23]*Th.T.S.* V, 11; III, 8.

[23a]Q. Weigall, 'Weights and balances', *Cat. gén.* vol. 42, 1910; *Wr. Atl.* I, 41, 50, 74, 78, 164, 395, etc.

[24]E. Vernier, 'La bijouterie et la joaillerie égyptiennes', *M.I.F.A.O.* II (1907), 2nd part. For metalworking in general see R. J. Forbes in *Hist. Tech.* I, pp. 572–9.

[25]*Wr. Atl.* I, 316–17; *M.M.A.* 11, pl. 52 and p. 53. Subsequent processes in the jewellers' workshops are shown in *Th.T.S.* III, 8; V, 11–12; *Mem. Tytl* II, 23; IV, 11; *Wr. Atl.* I, 50, 59, 229, 263. See also *Hist. Tech.* I, pp. 657–62.

[26]Montet, *Vie privée,* pp. 298–311; *Wr. Atl.* I, 314–15, 384, 420; *Mem. Tyt.*

IV, 11; C. Aldred in *Hist. Tech.* I, pp. 684–703. For bow drill see *Hist. Tech.* I, pp. 189–92.

27*Mem. Tyt.* V, 37.

28*Th.T.S.* III, 10; V, 11–12; *Mem. Tyt.* II, 23; *Wr. Atl.* I, 227, 307. Chariot-makers: *Wr. Atl.* I, 17a; *Th.T.S.* V, 11, 12.

29*Th.T.S.* V, 12.

30Montet, *Vie privée*, pp. 311–14.

31'Les antiquités égyptiennes du Louvre', *Encyclopédie photographique de l'art* (ed. Tel), 74–77.

31ªPenelope Fox, *Tutankhamun's Treasure*, London, 1951, pl. 14. 23,

31ᵇCairo, 1787: Montet, *Vie privée*, pp. 315–18.

32*Wr. Atl.* I, 312, 313; *M.M.A.* 11, pl. 37 and p. 50.

33*M.M.A.* 5, pl. 13–24.

34*Wr. Atl.* II, 25; *Urk.* IV, 626–42.

35*Mem. Tyt.* II, 37–38.

36*Urk.* IV, 1154=*A.R.* II, 759; *M.M.A.* 11, pl. 58 and p. 57.

37*A.S.A.E.* XXXVIII (1938), p. 219 ff.

38*Pap. Sallier* II, 3, 9; *Pap. Anastasy* VII, 1, 1.

39Louvre, C 14; see H. Sottas in *Rec. Trav.* XXXVI (1914), p. 153 ff.

40*Th.T.S.* I, 8.

41*Urk.* I, 23.

42*Rec. Trav.* XXIV, pp. 185–7.

43Tomb 359 at Thebes: *A.Z.* XLII, pp. 128–31.

44Ostracon 21447 in the Berlin Museum, published in *A.Z.* LIV, p. 78; cf. J. Robichon and A. Varille, *Le temple du scribe royal Amenhotep fils de Hapou*, Cairo, 1936, p. 9, where it is argued that the titles 'prince' and 'scribe' refer to a professional artist.

45*Exodus*, I, 11–16; cf. A. Mallon, *Les Hébreux en Egypte,* Rome, 1921, pp. 134–8. Brickmaking and brickbuilding scenes: *Wr. Atl.* I, 319–21; *M.M.A.* 11, pl. 58, 59, and *Paintings from the Tomb of Rekhmirē*, pl. 16, 17.

45ªSeton Lloyd in *Hist. Tech.* I, pp. 473–5.

46*Wb.* I, 94, and II, 385. A. H. Gardiner, *Ancient Egyptian Onomastica* I, Oxford, 1947, 72.*

47For potters at work see *M.M.A.* 5, 59; *Wr. Atl.* I, 301, 404; *Hist. Tech.* I, pp. 388–97, for pottery techniques.

48*Th.T.S.* III, 1; *Mem. Tyt.* V, 25 and 34.

49*Wr. Atl.* I, 44.

49ªFor razors see note 6 on chapter IV.

50P. Montet in *Kemi* IV, 178–89.

51*Grands prêtres*, pp. 151–2.

52ibid. 128.

53In the so-called 'Negative Confession' of the Book of the Dead, chapter 125 A, phrase 6, the deceased declares, 'I have not compelled people, day by day, to work harder than they were able.'

54Wm. F. Edgerton, 'The strike in Ramesses III's 29th year', *J.N.E.S.* X (1951), pp. 137–45.

54ªFor the story of the Eloquent Peasant see E. Wallis Budge, *The Literature of the Ancient Egyptians*, London, 1914, pp. 169–84.

[55] *Wr. Atl.* I, 200.
[56] N. de G. Davies and R. O. Faulkner, 'A Syrian Trading Venture to Egypt', *J.E.A.* XXXIII (1947), p. 40.
[57] *Urk.* I, 157; H. Sottas, *Etude critique sur un acte de vente immobilière au temps des pyramides*, Paris, 1913.
[58] A. H. Gardiner, 'Four papyri of the 18th dynasty from Kahun', *A.Z.* XLIII (1906), pp. 27–48.
[59] A. H. Gardiner, *The Chester Beatty Papyri*, no. 1, London, 1931, pp. 43–44.
[60] *Br. Mus. Pap.* 10052, pl. 11, 14–30; *Pap.* 10053, verso, pl. 111, 6–16.
[61] *Pap. Chester Beatty* I, verso D and p. 43.
[62] *Pap. Cairo* 65739; A. H. Gardiner, 'A lawsuit arising from the purchase of two slaves', *J.E.A.* XXI (1935), pp. 140–6.
[63] *Ounamon*, II, 39–41; *Bibl. aeg.* I, p. 71; *E. Lit.*, pp. 181–2.
[63a] See note 55 above.

CHAPTER VII

[1] A. de Buck, *The Egyptian Coffin Texts*, I, Chicago, 1935, Spell 3, p. 10.
[2] *Pap. d'Orbiney*, 13, 1; *Bibl. aeg.* I, p. 22.
[3] *Urk.* I, 98 ff. = *A.R.* I, §312.
[4] *Siut.*, pl. 11 (Tomb III), lines 10–11.
[5] G. Maspero, *The Struggle of the Nations*, ed. A. H. Sayce, London, 1896, p. 123.
[6] Strabo, XVII, 44. Swimmers are depicted in the tomb of Mereruka (*The Mastaba of Mereruka*, II, pl. 130.)
[7] *Br. Mus. Pap.* 10052, p. xiii, lines 1–15.
[8] *Bibl. aeg.* I, p. 43; *Pap. Chester Beatty* I, verso 5.
[9] Montet, *Vie privée*, pp. 379–80.
[10] *Bibl. aeg.* VII, p. 37 = *L.E.M.*, pp. 137–8 (*Pap. Anast.* IV, 3, 4–6).
[11] *Th.T.S.* III. 6.
[12] *Th.T.S.* I, 12; *Mem. miss. fr.* V, pp. 517, 582; *Wr. Atl.* I, 308.
[12a] A. Erman, *Die Märchen des Papyrus Westcar*, Berlin, 1890; see *E. Lit.*, pp. 43–44.
[13] *Th.T.S.* IV, 11–12.
[14] ibid., 32–33; *Wr. Atl.* I, 199, 323; Davies, *El Armarna*, I, 29; *M.M.A.* 11, pl. 61 and p. 57.
[15] *Wr. Atl.* I, 129.
[16] *Paheri*, pl. 3.
[17] *Hamm.* inscr. 192.
[18] *Wr. Atl.* I, 21; *Mém. miss. fr.* V, p. 277 and pl. 5.
[19] P. E. Newberry, *Beni-Hasan*, I, pl. 30; II, pl. 4, 13.
[20] ibid., I, pl. 45; *Wr. Atl.* II, 6.
[21] *A.S.A.E.* XXXIX (1939), p. 57.
[22] *Hamm.* inscr. 199.
[23] *Hamm.* inscr. 1.
[24] Reproduced in *Bibliothèque égyptologique*, X, pp. 183–230; cf. A. H. Gardiner in *The Cairo Scientific Journal*, VIII, p. 41.

²⁵*Pap. Harris* I, 77, 7–8.

²⁵ᵃV. Loret, 'Le résine de térébinthe, *sonter*, chez les anciens Egyptiens', *Recherches de l'Institut français d'archéologie orientale*, vol. 19, Cairo, 1949.

²⁶*Bibl. aeg.* II, p. 46.

²⁷*Pap. Harris* I, pl. 28, 3–4; pl. 48, 2.

²⁸P. Montet, *Le drame d'Avaris*, pp. 19–28, 35–43.

²⁹P. Montet, *Byblos et l'Egypte*, Paris, 1928, pp. 236–7, 295–305; M. Dunand, *Byblia Grammata*, Beirut, 1945; D. Diringer, *The Alphabet*, London, 1947; G. R. Driver, *Semitic Writing*, British Academy, London, 1948.

³⁰*Bibl. aeg.* I, pp. 61–76; *E.Lit.*, pp. 174–85.

³¹*Pap. Harris* I, 7, 8.

³²P. Montet, *Le drame d'Avaris*, pp. 26–28.

³³For voyages to Punt see T. Säve-Söderbergh, *The Navy of the Eighteenth Egyptian Dynasty*, Uppsala, 1946, chapter 2. The most important series of texts and illustrations are those in the temple of Hatshepsut at Deir al Bahari. For later voyages down the Red Sea, see *Pap. Harris* I, 77–78.

³⁴Montet, *Le drame d'Avaris*, pp. 131–3.

³⁵T. Säve-Söderbergh, loc. cit.

³⁵ᵃFor Egyptian boat-construction see *Hist. Tech.*, pp. 732–6.

³⁵ᵇE. Naville, *The Temple of Deir el Bahari*, E.E.F., 1894–1906, vol. III, pl. 69–86.

³⁵ᶜ*Urk.* IV, pp. 315–55.

³⁶*Hamm.* no. 114.

³⁷Strabo, XVI, 22.

³⁸This expression, *mou qedy*, is found only in *Pap. Harris* I and on a stele of Tuthmosis I (H. Gauthier, *Dictionnaire des noms géographiques contenus dans les textes hiéroglyphiques*, Cairo, Institut français, 1925–31, III, p. 33). The usual translation, 'inverted water', assumes that the Egyptians had noticed that the Euphrates flowed approximately from north to south, in the opposite direction to their own River Nile. In fact, the Egyptian scribes, who loved puns and rebuses, here wrote the name of the land Qedy as the participle of the verb *qdy*, 'to be upside down'.

³⁹G. A. Reisner in *A.Z.* LXIX (1933), pp. 24–39.

³⁹ᵃ*Pap. Harris* I, 77 8–78, 1; *A.R.* IV, §407.

³⁹ᵇ*Bibl. aeg.* II, p. 42.

⁴⁰*A.E.M.*, pp. 455–6; T. Pinches and P. E. Newberry in *J.E.A.* VII, 1921, p. 196.

⁴¹Lapis lazuli from Tefrer is mentioned as early as the Middle Kingdom, in the inscription of a traveller named Khety (*J.E.A.* IV, pl. IX) and in a list of precious stones (E. Chassinat and C. Palanque, *Fouilles d'Assiout*, pp. 108, 212). It is also mentioned in an inscription of Ramesses II (Piehl, *Inscriptions hiéroglyphiques*, I, 145*d*). I found in the tomb of Psousennes a necklace of large gold-mounted lapis lazuli beads, one of which bore a cuneiform inscription read by M. Dhorme; it contained the name of a country near Elam, a king and a princess. See E. Dhorme, 'L'inscription cunéiforme du collier de Psusennès', *Mon. Piot*, vol. 41, Paris, 1946, pp. 23–28 and pl. IV; and for a different interpretation, P. Montet, *La nécropole royale de Tanis*, II, Paris, 1951, pp. 139–43.

[42]For a translation of the story of the prince of Bakhtan see the article by P. Tresson in *Revue biblique* 42 (1933), pp. 57–78.

[43]e.g. Oudjahorresne, the Saïte doctor whom Cambyses summoned to him (G. Posener, *La première domination perse en Egypte*. Bibliothèque d'études, no. 11 of the French Institute in Cairo, 1936, pp. 1–2).

[44]Arrian, *Indike*, V, 5; Diodorus, I, 55; Strabo, XVI, 4, 4.

CHAPTER VIII

[1]*Pap. Harris* I, 57, 3 ff.

[2]C. Kuentz, *Deux stèles d'Amenophis II*, Bibliothèque d'études, X, Cairo, 1925, p. 12 ff.

[3]H. Gauthier, 'La grande inscription dédicatoire d'Abydos', *A.Z.* XLVIII (1911), pp. 52–66.

[4]*Urk.* IV, 765–7.

[5]A. Moret, *Du charactère religieux de la royauté pharaonique*, Paris, 1903.

[6]*Urk.* III, 14 (Piankhi stele).

[7]ibid., 27–28.

[8]ibid., 38–40.

[9]P. Montet, *Le drame d'Avaris*, pp. 108–10.

[10]*Grands prêtres*, p. 117 ff.

[11]Stele 88 at Lyons; see A. Varille in *B.I.F.A.O.* XXX (1931), pp. 497–507.

[12]Reliefs showing the king in ceremonial dress can be found in all temples, especially at Karnak, Luxor, Abydos and Medinet Habu. See in particular *Med. Habu*, 123–4.

[13]The mummies of Tutankhamūn at Thebes, and of Sheshanq and Psousennes found at Tanis, were richly decked with royal regalia; see Penelope Fox, *Tutankhamun's Treasure*, London, 1951, pl. 31, 34, 35–37; P. Montet, *La nécropole royale de Tanis*, II, Paris, 1951, *passim*.

[14]Diodorus, I, 70–71.

[15]*Kêmi*, VIII (1946), p. 39 and pl. 3; S. Sauneron and Y. Yoyotte in *B.I.F.A.O.* L (1951), and in *Revue d'Egyptologie* VIII (1951).

[16]Inscription A in the temple of Redesiyeh, *Bibl. aeg.* IV.

[17]*Hamm.* nos. 240 and 12. Sir Alan Gardiner, on the other hand, thinks it very improbable that the king would have gone in person to the Wadi Hammamat (*J.E.A.* XXIV (1938), pp. 162–3).

[18]This is the Kubban stele, now in the Grenoble Museum; see Tresson, *La stèle de Kouban*, Bibliothèque d'études, IX, Cairo, 1922.

[19]Nebounnef tells us this himself in the inscription in his tomb at Thebes; see K. Sethe in *A.Z.* XLIV (1907), pp. 30–35; *Grands prêtres*, p. 117 ff.

[19a]Sinuhe B, 254: *Bibl. aeg.* II, p. 37; *J.E.A.* XX (1934), p. 49.

[20]*Erman Lit.*, pp. 14–29; *Bibl. aeg.* III, pp. 1–41.

[21]*Mém. miss. fr.* V, p. 496.

[22]Davies, *El Amarna*, VI, pl. 29–30.

[23]Similar scenes of the rewarding of high officials are frequently found in New Kingdom tombs, cf. Davies, *El Amarna*, I, 6, 30; III, 16–17; IV, 6; VI, 4–6, 17–20; *M.M.A.* 9, 9–13; Louvre C 213; *Mém. miss. fr.* V, p. 496; Tomb 106 at Thebes (*Top. Bibliog.* I, pp. 134–5).

[24]*M.M.A.* 9, 14–18.

[25]These reliefs from the tomb of Horonemheb at Memphis are now in Leiden; see Cyril Aldred, *New Kingom Art in Egypt*, pl. 139–43.

[26]*Grands prêtres*, pp. 194–5; G. Lefebvre, *Inscriptions concernant les grands prêtres d'Amon Romé-Roy et Amenhotep*, pl. 11.

[27]These scenes are discussed in detail by Montet in *Les reliques de l'art syrien dans l'Egypt du Nouvel Empire*, Paris, 1937, chapter 1.

[28]Diodorus, I, 53, 3–4.

[29]Stele found in the temple of Mōnth at Hermonthis (Armant), see Sir R. Mond and O. H. Myers, *Temples of Armant*, I, pp. 182–4 and pl. 103.

[30]Great stele found at Gizeh in 1936 and published by A. Varille, *B.I.F.A.O.* XLI (1942), p. 31 ff. and plate.

[31]C. Kuentz, op. cit., pp. 6–7. For other texts praising the physical prowess of Amenophis II see B. van de Walle, 'Les rois sportifs de l'ancienne Egypte', *Chronique d'Egypte* 13, Brussels, 1938, pp. 234–57.

[31a]Varille, op. cit. pp. 34–35.

[31b]ibid.

[32]*Urk.* III, pp. 21–22.

[33]*Med. Habu*, 109–10.

[33a]Varille, op. cit. pp. 36–37.

[34]The so-called Dream Stele of Tuthmosis IV, erected between the paws of the great sphinx at Gizeh: *Urk.* IV, 1539a–1544 = *A.R.* II, §§810–15.

[35]See G. Reisner, 'Inscribed Monuments from Gebel Barkal', *A.Z.* LXIX, pp. 24–39; inscription of Amonemheb, *Urk.* IV, 890.

[36]*Med. Habu*, 35, 116, 117.

[37]C. Kuentz, *La bataille de Qadech*, Cairo, 3 vols., 1928–34, pp. 338–9.

[38]Davies, *El Amarna*, III, 30–34, also, 4, 6, 13, 18; IV, 15.

[39]*Urk.* IV, 27–28.

[40]Montet, *Le drame d'Avaris*, 116–29.

[41]Marriage stele of Ramesses II: *A.S.A.E.* XXV (1925), pp. 181–238, and *Bibl. aeg.* VII, 12; cf. Montet, op. cit. pp. 134–5.

[42]Harem conspiracy: Devéria, 'Le papyrus judiciaire de Turin et les papyrus Lee et Rollin', *Bibliothèque égyptologique* V, Paris, 1897, pp. 97–251; *A.R.* IV, §§416–56; A. de Buck in *J.E.A.* XXIII (1937), pp. 152–64.

[43]*A.R.* IV, §418.

[44]ibid. §455.

[45]ibid. §421.

[46]ibid. §424.

[47]ibid. §451.

[47a]See note 20, chapter X.

[48]G. Maspero, 'Les Momies royales de Deir el Bahari', *M.I.F.A.O.* I, 4, Cairo, 1889, p. 782; idem, *The Struggle of the Nations*, p. 79.

[49]A. Scharff, *Der historische Abschnitt der Lehre für König Merikaré*, Munich, 1936; G. Maspero, *Les enseignements d'Amenemhait 1er à son fils Sanouasrit 1er*, Cairo, 1914; A. de Buck in *Mélanges . . . Maspero* I, Cairo, 1935–8, pp. 847–52; B. Gunn in *J.E.A.* XXVII (1941), pp. 2–6; A. Volten, *Zwei altägyptische politische Schriften*, Copenhagen, 1945.

E.L.E.—AA

⁵⁰*Pap. Harris* I, see the convenient publication of it in *Bibl. aeg.* V.

⁵¹*Pap. Harris* I, 78, 13–79, 5.

⁵²ibid., 22, 3–23, 6.

CHAPTER IX

¹*Bib . aeg.* VII, 26=*L.E.M.*, pp. 91–95.

²*Bibl. aeg.* VII, 27=*L.E.M.*, pp. 95–99.

³*Urk.* IV, 999=*A.*R. II, §1 ff.

³ᵃE. Vernier, *La bijouterie et la joaillerie égyptiennes*, *M.I.F.A.O.* 2 (1907), pl. 20.

⁴*Urk.* IV, 995.

⁵*Urk.* IV, 997.

⁶The career of Nebamun is described by the texts and pictures in his tomb at Thebes (no. 90): *Th.T.S.* III, esp. pl. 24–29.

⁷*Urk.* IV, 911; *Wr. Atl.* I, 186, 280.

⁸*Th.T.S.* III, pl. 21, 31–33.

⁹Ch. Kuentz, *La bataille de Qadech*, Cairo, 3 vols., 1928–34, pp. 172–85; *Erman Lit.*, p. 265.

¹⁰*Pap. Harris* I, 78, 9–12; *Bibl. aeg.* V, pp. 95–96.

¹¹Herodotus, II, 164–8; Diodorus, I, 73.

¹²*Wr. Atl.* I, 236.

¹³Davies, *El Amarna*, III, pl. 31, 39; *Wr. Atl.* II, 13.

¹³ᵃR. O. Faulkner, 'Egyptian Military Organisation', *J.E.A.* XXXIX (1953), p. 45.

¹⁴Reliefs from the temple of Ramesses II at Abydos: see Kuentz, op. cit., pl. 22.

¹⁵*Pap. Harris* I, 76; *Med. Habu, passim*.

¹⁶See *Med. Habu* 112 for this scene.

¹⁷E. Cavaignac, *Subbiluliuma et son temps*, Paris, 1932, pp. 70–72; O. Gurney, *The Hittites*, Pelican Books, Harmondsworth, 1951, p. 31.

¹⁸The Carnarvon Tablet; see *J.E.A.* III (1916), pp. 95–110.

¹⁹Stele of Sety I from Beisan: see *B.I.F.A.O.* XXX (1931), pp. 751–63; Alan Rowe, *The Topography and History of Beth-Shan*, London, 1930.

²⁰*Med. Habu.*, pl. 29.

²¹P. Montet, *Les reliques de l'art syrien dans l'Egypte du Nouvel Empire*, Strasburg, 1937, pp. 32–33; *Kêmi* IV, pp. 200–10.

²²Montet, op. cit., pp. 34–36; R. Maxwell-Hyslop in *Iraq* VIII (1946), London, p. 31 ff.

²³*Wr. Atl.* II, 1. For arms and armour generally see H. Bonnet. *Die Waffen der Völker des alten Orients*, Leipzig, 1926; W. Wolf, *Die Bewaffnung des altaegyptischen Heeres*, Leipzig, 1926; *Scepter*, pp. 277–84.

²⁴Montet, op. cit., pp. 37–38.

²⁵*Med. Habu*, 16, 31, 62.

²⁵ᵃibid., 25; *Wr. Atl.* II, 18. For the Egyptian war-chariot in general see F. Schachermeyer in *Anthropos*, XLVI (1951), p. 705 ff.

[26]*Med. Habu,* 17–31.

[27]*Wr. Atl.* II, 34, 40, 43, 44.

[28]*Urk.* III, 8.

[29]e.g. *J.E.A.* XXI (1935), pp. 219–23.

[30]Montaigne, *Essays,* ed. Firmin-Didot, I, p. 20 (I owe this reference to M. Jean Yoyotte). For similar declarations see P. Montet, *Le drame d'Avaris,* Paris, 1948, p. 29.

[31]*Book of the Dead,* chapter 125B, phrase 25 : 'O announcer of battle (*sr hrw*) who cometh forth from Ounes.' Ounes was a city of Seth.

[32]*Urk.* IV, 649 ff.; H. Nelson, *The Battle of Megiddo,* Chicago, 1913; S. Yeivin, in *J.N.E.S.* IX (1950), p. 102 ff.

[33]A. Scharff, *Der historische Abschnitt der Lehre für König Merikaré,* Munich, 1936.

[34]See C. Kuentz, *La bataille de Qadech,* Cairo, 1928, for the events described on pp. 236–245; illustrations in *Wr. Atl.* II.

[35]Camp scene from the tomb of Horonemheb, see J. Capart in *J.E.A.* VII (1921), p. 33 and pl. VI; *Wr. Atl.* I, 386.

[36]*Urk,* III, 14–17; *A.R.* IV, §841.

[37]C. Kuentz, op. cit., pp. 310–19.

[38]ibid., pp. 320–2.

[39]*Med. Habu,* 18–20.

[40]ibid., 72.

[41]ibid., 32, 37.

[42]ibid., 42.

[43]*Aldred,* pl. 142.

[44]*Med. Habu,* 95.

[45]ibid., 94.

[45a]For woods used in Egypt see *A.E.M.,* chapter XVIII.

[46]Montet, *Reliques* . . ., pp. 10–11.

[47]*Wr. Atl.* II, 34–35.

[48]*Med. Habu,* 9; *Wr. Atl.* II, 165–6; A. J. Arkell, *A History of the Sudan,* London, 1955, chapter V.

[49]e.g. *Med. Habu,* 10–11, 24; *Wr. Atl.* II, 25, 34.

[50]*Wr. Atl.* II, 39.

[51]*Urk.* IV, 1297=*A.R.* II, §797.

[52]*Med. Habu,* 85–86 (poem on the second Libyan war, lines 26–34); ibid., 75.

[53]*Pap. Harris* I, 77.

[54]Montet, *Reliques* . . ., pp. 22–26.

CHAPTER X

[1]G. Maspero, *Etudes égyptiennes,* II, 1–66; cf. A. H. Gardiner, *Ancient Egyptian Onomastica,* Oxford, 1952.

[2]*Grands prêtres,* chapter 2.

[3]H. Gauthier, *Le personnel du dieu Min,* Cairo, 1931.

[4]See the Stele of the Year 400, *Kêmi* IV, pp. 210–13.

[5]*Urk.* IV, 1020–1.

[6]Nauri decree, *Bibl. aeg.* IV, 4, pp. 13–24 (see note 21).

[7]*Grands prêtres*, p. 131.

[8]*Ani* maxim VII=*E.Lit.*, p. 239.

[9]*Pap. Chester Beatty* II, 5: *Bibl. aeg.* I, p. 32.

[10]G. Maspero, *Hymne au Nil*, pl. XIII and p. 19; for Instructions of Amenemhet see note 49 on chapter VIII. For a good example of a Ramesside school exercise faultily written see J. Barns, *The Ashmolean ostrakon of Sinuhe*, Griffith Institute of Oxford, 1952.

[10a]See *Scepter*, pp. 292–6, for a scribe's equipment.

[11]*Pap. Anastasy* I, 13, 5 ff. in A. H. Gardiner, *Egyptian hieratic texts*, Leipzig, 1911, pp. 16–34.

[12]*Bibl. aeg.* VII, 23–24; sim. ibid., 36=*L.E.M.*, pp. 83–85, 131 ff.

[13]ibid., VII, 47=*L.E.M.*, pp. 182–8.

[14] *Ani*, 3–6, 11.

[15]ibid.

[16]*B.I.F.A.O.* XXX (1931), p. 497.

[17]*M.M.A.* 11, pp. 79–83.

[18]*Grands prêtres*, p. 127 ff.

[19]*A.S.A.E.* XL (1940), p. 605.

[20]K. Pflüger, 'The Edict of King Haremhab', *J.N.E.S.* V (1946), pp. 260–76.

[21]Nauri decree, *Bibl. aeg.* IV, 4; see W. F. Edgerton in *J.N.E.S.* VI (1947), pp. 219–30, and A. H. Gardiner in *J.E.A.* XXXVIII (1952), pp. 24–33.

[22]*Bibl. aeg.* VII, 5–6=*L.E.M.*, pp. 18–20.

[22a]The story of the Eloquent Peasant, *E.Lit.*, pp. 116–31.

[23]*Urk.* I, 23.

[24]*Siut* I, 223–9; the tomb of Pouyemrê at Thebes contains a similar declaration, *Kêmi*, III, 46–48.

[25]Inscription in the Redesiyeh temple, *Bibl. aeg.* IV, 5, pp. 25–29.

[26]*Grands prêtres*, p. 213.

[27]Stele 138 in Br. Mus. See C. Robichon and A. Varille, *Le temple du scribe royal Amenhotep, fils de Hapou, Fouilles de l'Institut français en Egypte*, no. 11, Cairo, 1936, pp. 3–4.

[28]The account of the legal proceedings that follows is largely based upon the following hieratic documents: the Abbott, the Amherst and the Leopold papyri, as well as several papyri in the British Museum. See *Peet, Tomb Robberies*, and J. Capart and A. H. Gardiner. *Le papyrus Léopold II aux Musées royaux de Bruxelles et le papyrus Amherst à la Pierpont Morgan Library de New York*, Brussels, 1939.

[29]e.g. P. Duell, *The Mastaba of Mereruka*, O.I.C. Publications, vols. 39–40, 1938, pl. 37.

[30]*Peet, Tomb Robberies*, pp. 146–7.

[31]Montet, *Reliques* . . .; J. Vercoutter, *Egyptiens et Préhelleènes* (*L'Orient ancien illustré*, VI), Paris, 1954.

[32]*Th.T.S.* IV, 23–30; cf. *Wr. Atl.* I, 35, 56, 224.

[33]G. Reisner in *J.E.A.* VI (1920), pp. 28–55, 73–88; H. Gauthier in *Rec. Trav.* XXXIX (1921), pp. 179–238; T. Säve-Söderbergh, *Aegypten u. Nubien*, Lund, 1941, pp. 175–230.

CHAPTER XI

[1]Herodotus, II, 37.

[2]Josephus, *Contra Apionem*, I, 232 and 254–5.

[3]*Kêmi* IX (1942), pp. 40–42.

[4]The priest, for instance, who offered to show Nenoferka-Ptah a book written by Thoth himself (story of Setna Khaemwese, *Griffith, H. P. M.,* pp. 16–20).

[4a]*Pap. Harris* I, 3, 9–10.

[5]*Bibl. aeg.* VII, 16, 17=*L.E.M.,* pp. 56–59.

[6]*Bibl. aeg.* VII, 60=*L.E.M.,* pp. 232–4.

[7]C. Kuentz in *B.I.F.A.O.* XXVIII, pp. 113–72 and pl. 11.

[8]Herodotus, III, 28–29; Strabo, XVII, 1, 31; Plutarch, *De Iside et Osiride,* 43; Ammianus Marcellinus, XXII, 14.

[9]Herodotus, II, 67. The Ibis necropolis was discovered in 1936, in the desert opposite Shmoun, near the tomb of Petosiris. See *Illustrated London News,* June 12, 1937, pp. 1088–9; May 13, 1939, pp. 838–40. There are many ibis mummies in the British Museum.

[10]P. Montet, *Le drame d'Avaris,* pp. 140–1 and pl. VI.

[11]A. H. Gardiner, 'The Astarte papyrus' in *Studies presented to F. Ll. Griffith,* Oxford, 1932, p. 83 ff.; S. A. B. Mercer in *Egyptian Religion,* III (1935), pp. 192–203.

[12]Montet, op. cit., p. 134.

[13]ibid., pp. 142–3.

[14]*Bibl. aeg.* VII, pp. 88–91=*L.E.M.,* pp. 333–49.

[14a]A. Moret, *Le rituel du culte journalier en Egypte,* Paris, 1902 (Annales du Musée Guimet, Bibliothèque d'études, 14).

[14b]A. M. Blackman, 'On the position of Women in the Ancient Egyptian Hierarchy', *J.E.A.* VII (1921), p. 8 ff.

[15]W. Peyte and F. Rossi, *Les papyrus hiératiques de Turin,* Leiden, 1869–76.

[16]Hapi-djefai, nomarch of Siut, addressing the members of the temple staff at Siut, says 'I am the son of a priest, like every one of you.' (*Siut* I, 288).

[17]*Bibl. aeg.* VII, pp. 5–6=*L.E.M.,* pp. 17–20.

[18]Minmosé, in the time of Ramesses II, was 'chief of the secrets of heaven, of earth and of the underworld' (Louvre C 218).

[19]S. A. B. Mercer, *The Religion of Ancient Egypt,* London, 1949, pp. 336 ff. A. Moret, op. cit.

[20]The ritual is known to us from three papyri in the Berlin Museum and from the reliefs of Sety I in the temple of Abydos. See A. Moret, op. cit.

[20a]C. J. Gadd, *Ideas of divine rule in the Ancient East,* Schweich Lectures of the British Academy for 1945, London, 1948, lecture II; H. Frankfort, *Kingship and the gods,* Chicago, 1948.

[21]H. P. Blok, 'Remarques sur quelques stèles dites 'à oreilles',' *Kemi* I (1928), pp. 123–5.

[22]P. Lacau, *Les statues 'guérisseuses' dans l'ancienne Egypte,* Mon. Piot XXV (1922), pp. 189–209; A. Erman, *La religion des Egyptiens,* p. 355; G. Lefebvre in *B.I.F.A.O.* XXX (1931), p. 89 ff.

[23]Stele Brit. Mus. 589 and stele 102 in Turin: see A. Erman, *Denksteine aus der thebanischen Gräberstadt,* Berlin 1911, p. 1100.

[24]Stele 23077 in the Berlin Museum: see Erman, op. cit., pp. 1088–97.

[25]J. Černý, 'Le culte d'Amenophis I[er]chez les ouvriers de la nécropole thébaine', *B.I.F.A.O.* XXVII (1927), p. 159 ff.

[26]E. Naville, *Inscription historique de Pinodjem III*, 1883.

[27]*Urk.* III, 94–95 (Coronation Stela, lines 18–19).

[28]C. Boreux, *Catalgoue guide aux antiquités égyptiennes,* Paris, Musée du Louvre, 1932, pp. 534–5. Cf. G. Loukianoff, 'Une statue parlante ou oracle du dieu Ré-Harmakhis', *A.S.A.E.* XXXVI (1936), p. 187–93.

[29]J. Černý, 'Questions adressées aux oracles', *B.I.F.A.O.* XXXV (1935), p. 41 ff.; cf. *J.E.A.* XI, pp. 249–55; XII, pp. 176–85.

[30]Herodotus, II, 59–60.

[31]From reliefs in the temples at Medinet Habu and Karnak, see H. Gauthier, *Les fêtes du dieu Min*, Cairo, 1931.

[32]Gauthier, op. cit., pp. 230–1, 239–40. Lefebvre, Moret and Gauthier all assumed that the bull was sacrified, but no sacrifice is anywhere represented. The part actually played by the bull was recognized by H. Jacobsohn, *Die dogmatische Stellung des Königs in der Theologier der alten Aegypter*, Glückstadt, 1939.

[32a]W. Wolf, *Das schöne Fest von Opet*, Veröffentlichungen der E. von Siegelin-Expedition in Aegypten, Bd. 5, Leipzig, 1931.

[33]G. Daressy in *Rec. trav.* XVIII (1896), p. 181 ff.

[34]*Wr. Atl.* II, 189–202. The same festival is represented in the temple of Ramesses III at Karnak.

[35]G. Foucart, 'La belle fête de la vallée', *B.I.F.A.O.* XXIV (1924), pp. 1–209.

[36]ibid., p. 48 ff. and pl. 14; *Wr. Atl.* I, 118–19.

[37]H. Schaefer, *Die Mysterien des Osiris in Abydos*, Leipzig, 1904; scene in the tomb of Kherouef in Thebes, in A. Moret, *Mystères égyptiens*, Paris, 1912, p. 11; stelae of Ramesses IV, in A. Mariette, *Abydos*, II, pp. 54–55.

[38]Herodotus, II, 63.

[39]Juvenal, XV.

[40]Near Denderah there was a 'place of slaughter of Seth, opposite this goddess (i.e. Hathor)': H. Gauthier, *Dictionnaire des noms géographiques*, V, 84–85.

[41]The Pharaoh Menkheper-Rê Siamon, in the story of Setna Khaemwese: *Griffith, H. P. M.*, p. 55–57.

[42]*Bibl. aeg.* I, 4, 'The Contendings of Horus and Seth'.

[43]G. Goyon, 'Les travaux de Chou et les tribulations de Geb', *Kemi* VI, pp. 1–42.

[44]E. Drioton, *Le théâtre égyptien*, Paris, 1942.

[45]Stele of Neferhotep, year 2: A. Mariette, *Abydos*, II, pp. 28–30.

[46]A. H. Gardiner, 'The House of Life', *J.E.A.* XXIV (1938), pp. 157–79, has collected a large number of references to the House of Life.

CHAPTER XII

[1]The Instruction of Ptahhotep, Introduction: *Erman Lit.*, pp. 54–55; Sinuhe B, 168–70, in *Bibl. aeg.* II, p. 30.

[2]*Grands prêtres*, p. 148.

[3]*Pap. Westcar*: *Erman Lit.*, pp. 41–42.

[4]Sinuhe B, 295–310, in *Bibl. aeg.* II, pp. 39–40.

[5]Ch. Kuentz, 'Deux versions d'un panégyrique royal', in *Studies presented to F. Ll. Griffith*, Oxford, 1932, pp. 39–110; A. H. Gardiner in *J.E.A.* XLI (1955), p. 30 ff. and XLII (1956), p. 8 ff.

[6]*Ani*, III, 16: *Erman Lit.*, p. 237.

[7]*Br. Mus.* stele no. 1027, see G. Maspero, *Etudes égyptiennes*, I, pp. 187–8; A. H. Gardiner, *The Attitude of the Ancient Egyptians towards Death and the Dead*, Cambridge, 1935.

[8]M. Lichtheim, 'The Songs of the Harpers', *J.N.E.S.* IV (1945), pp. 192–3.

[9]J. Speigel, *Die Idee vom Totengericht in der aegyptischen Religion*, Glückstadt and Hamburg [1935].

[9a]See note 49 in chapter VIII for bibliography of the Instructions of Merikaré

[10]*Griffith, H. P. M.*, p. 45 ff.

[11]*A.Z.* XLVII, p. 165.

[12]A. de Buck, *The Egyptian Coffin Texts*, Chicago, 1935–8, spells 1 and 13.

[13]ibid., I, 146, chapter 37.

[14]ibid., I, 151, chapter 37.

[15]*Bibl. aeg.* VII, 38=L.E.M. p. 138.

[16]V. Loret in *Mélanges Maspero*, p. 853 ff.

[17]J. H. Breasted, *Development of Religion and Thought in Ancient Egypt*, London, n.d., p. 256.

[18]See the two statues of Pa-Ramessu found by Legrain at Karnak, *A.S.A.E.* XIV (1914), pp. 29–40.

[19]H. Gauthier, *Le Livre des rois de l'Egypte*, III, p. 318.

[20]*Grands prêtres*, pp. 133–4.

[21]*Hamm.* no. 12; *Grands prêtres*, p. 264.

[22]J. Černý, *Ancient Egyptian Religion*, London, 1952, p. 88.

[23]*Pap. Chester Beatty* I, 15; *Bibl. aeg.* I, p. 58 (letter of Osiris to Rê).

[24]Anna, or Ineni, who lived under the first three Tuthmoses, tells us that he directed the construction of the royal tomb (of Tuthmosis I) in solitude, 'none seeing, none hearing' (*Urk.* IV, p. 57; *A.R.* II, §106).

[25]For the technique of tomb-painting see R. J. Forbes in *Hist. Tech.*, pp. 238–45.

[26]For a detailed description see *Th.T.S.* I, Introduction.

[27]*M.M.A.*, 9, 27; *Wr. Atl.* I, 124.

[28]L. Speleers, *Les figurines funéraires égyptiennes*, Brussels, 1931; *Kêmi* IX (1942), pp. 82–83.

[29]*Kêmi* IX (1942), pp. 78–79.

[30]My conclusions are drawn from the contents of the tomb of Psousennes: P. Montet, *La nécropole royale de Tanis*, Paris, 1951, chapter IX.

[31]For the contracts made by Hapi-djefai of Siut with his *ka*-priest see *Siut*, pl. 4–9; *Kêmi* III (1930), pp. 52–69; see too F. Ll. Griffith, 'Tomb endowment in Ancient Egypt', *A.Z.* LX (1925), pp. 79–98.

[32]For the history of a funerary temple see J. Robichon and A. Varille, *Le temple du scribe royal Amenhotep fils de Hapou*, Cairo, 1936, pp. 31–43.

[33]See the commentary by V. Loret on *Pap. d'Orbiney*, VIII, 6–7, in *Kêmi* IX (1942), pp. 105–6; cf. Diodorus, I, 72.

[34]Herodotus, II, 86; Diodorus, I, 91. For a detailed scientific description of the methods used see *A.E.M.* chapter XII; also G. Elliot Smith and W. R. Dawson, *Egyptian Mummies*, 1924; and H. E. Winlock, *Materials used at the Embalming of King Tutankhamūn*, *M.M.A.* Papers, no. 10, New York, 1941.

[35]Mask of Tutankhamūn: P. Fox, *Tutankhamūn's Treasure*, London, 1951, pl. 32–33; in colour, K. Lange and M. Hirmer, *Egypt*, Phaidon Press, 1956, pl. 185. Mask of Sheshonq: P. Montet, op. cit., pl. 22; Mask of Psousennes, ibid., pl. 104.

[36]P. Montet, op. cit., pp. 38–40, and pl. 21.

[37]G. Maspero, 'Etude sur quelques peintures et sur quelques textes relatifs aux funérailles', *Etudes égyptiennes*, I, pp. 81–194.

[38]Maspero, op. cit., o. 134.

[39]*Wr. Atl.* I, 388–421.

[40]*M.M.A.*, 9, 22–23; *Mem. Tyt.* IV, 19, 24, 25,

[41]*M.M.A.*, 9, 20–21; *Mem. Tyt.* IV, 22.

[42]*M.M.A.*, 9, 24; *Mem. Tyt.* IV, 19, 21; *Wr. Atl.* I, 131, 166, 217.

[42a]*Aldred*, 65.

[43]*M.M.A.*, 9, 25–26.

[44]J. G. Frazer, 'Adonis, Attis, Osiris', *The Golden Bough*, 2nd edn., London, 1907; P. Montet, 'Les vases à fleurs', *Kêmi* IV (1931), pp. 161–8.

[45]Banqueting scenes are frequent in the tombs at Thebes, but a distinction must be drawn between those which depict the feast served at a funeral and those which represent a domestic celebration. On this see A. H. Gardiner's discussion in *Th.T.S.* I, pp. 36–41.

[46]A. Varille, 'Trois nouveaux chants de harpistes', *B.I.F.A.O.* XXXV (1935), pp. 155–7; Miriam Lichtheim, 'The Songs of the Harpers', *J.N.E.S.* IV (1945), pp. 178–212.

[47]*A.E.M.*, pp. 307–77.

[48]Herodotus, II, 87–88; G. Maspero, *The Struggle of the Nations*, London, 1896, pp. 525–6.

[49]Robichon and Varille, op. cit., pp. 4–7.

[50]Fear of the anger of the dead is voiced in the Old Kingdom (Pyramid texts, 63), and its expression continues in the New Kingdom (*Book of the Dead*, chapter 92). See A. H. Gardiner, *The Attitude of the Ancient Egyptians to Death and the Dead*, Cambridge, 1935, p. 16 ff.

[51]A. Erman, 'Zaubersprüche für Mutter und Kind', in *Abhandlungen der kön. Preuss. Akademie der Wissenschaften*, I, 9, 2, 6. A similar formula in II, 7, 12, 3.

[52]A. H. Gardiner and K. Sethe, *Egyptian letters to the dead*, London, *E.E.S.*, 1928.

[53]A. Erman, *Gespräch eines Lebensmüden mit seiner Seele*, p. 60 ff.; cf. R. O. Faulkner, 'The man who was tired of life', *J.E.A.* XLII (1956), p. 21 ff.

[54]A. H. Gardiner, 'The House of Life', *J.E.A.* XXIV (1938), p. 175.

[55]*Griffith*, H. P. M., first tale.

[56]E. Drioton and J. P. Lauer in *A.S.A.E.* XXXVII (1937), p. 201 ff.

A SHORT LIST OF GENERAL WORKS

BREASTED, J. H. *A History of Egypt from the earliest times to the Persian conquest.* 2nd edition. London, 1925.
Ancient Records of Egypt. 5 vols. Chicago, 1906–7.
The Dawn of Conscience. London and New York, 1935.

BUDGE, E. A. T. W. *The Dwellers on the Nile: chapters on the Life, History, Religion and Literature of the Ancient Egyptians.* London, 1926.

CERNÝ, J. *Ancient Egyptian Religion.* London, 1952.

DAVIES, N. DE G. *Ancient Egyptian Paintings.* 2 vols. Chicago, 1936.

ERMAN, A. *The Literature of the Ancient Egyptians.* Trans. A. M. Blackman. London, 1927.

ERMAN, A. and RANKE, H. *Aegypten und aegyptisches Leben im Altertum.* Tübingen, 1923.

FRANKFORT, H. *Ancient Egyptian Religion: an interpretation.* New York, 1948.
Kingship and the Gods. Chicago, 1948.

GARDINER, A. H. *Egyptian Grammar, being an introduction to the study of the Hieroglyphs.* 3rd edition. Oxford, 1957.

GLANVILLE, S. R. K. and others. *The Legacy of Egypt.* Oxford, 1947.

LUCAS, A. *Ancient Egyptian Materials and Industries,* 3rd edition. London, 1948.

MONTET, P. *Scènes de la vie privée dans les tombeaux égyptiens de l'Ancien Empire.* Paris and Strasbourg, 1925.
Le drame d'Avaris. Essai sur la pénétration des Sémites en Egypte. Paris, 1941.
Tanis. Duex années de fouilles dans une capitale oubliée du Delta égyptien. Paris, 1942.

PETRIE, W. M. F. *Social Life in Ancient Egypt.* London, 1924.
Arts and Crafts in Ancient Egypt. London, 1909.

SHORTER, A. *Everyday life in Ancient Egypt.* London, 1932.

WILSON, J. A. *The Burden of Egypt: an interpretation of ancient Egyptian culture.* Chicago, (1951).

SELECT INDEX
(to be used with table of contents)

362